Test of Professional Competence in Management Accounting

Paper T4 (Part B – Case Study Examination)

Skills Development Text

CIMA PUBLISHING

WORKING TOGETHER FOR YOU

ELSEVIER

KAPLAN PUBLISHING

CIMA Publishing is an imprint of Elsevier
The Boulevard, Langford Lane, Kidlington, Oxford, OX5 1GB, UK
225 Wyman Street, Waltham, MA 02451, USA
Kaplan Publishing UK, Unit 2 The Business Centre, Molly Millars Lane, Wokingham, Berkshire RG41 2QZ

Notice

No responsibility is assumed by the publisher for any injury and/or damage to persons or property as a matter of products liability, negligence or otherwise, or from any use or operation of any methods, products, instructions or ideas contained in the material herein.

British Library Cataloguing in Publication Data
A catalogue record for this book is available from the British Library

ISBN 978-0-85732-586-0

Printed and bound in Great Britain

12 13 14 10 9 8 7 6 5 4 3 2 1

Contents

Jot Toy Case

Paper Introduction

Overview

The Test of Professional Competence in Management Accounting comprises two component parts that must both be achieved in order to complete the test. Credits are used to ensure success, rather than marks. To pass the Test of Professional Competence in Management Accounting, students must achieve an aggregated minimum of 75 credits – comprising a minimum of 50 credits for Part A (maximum 50 credits) and a minimum of 25 credits for Part B (maximum 50 credits).

Students are advised to undertake Part A and Part B concurrently, although either can be taken in any order once all strategic level examinations have been completed. The overall result for the Test of Professional Competence in Management Accounting can only be given when both component parts have been completed.

T4 Part A – Initial professional development – Work based practical experience

Overview

Students must gain a minimum of three years' relevant work based practical experience. Experience may be drawn from any of the following three areas, but a minimum of 18 months must be gained within the 'Core' area.

Area 1 – Basic experience	Area 2 – Core experience	Area 3 – Supplementary experience
1a. Preparing and maintaining accounting records	2a. Preparation of management accounts	3a. Financial strategy
1b. Statutory and regulatory reporting	2b. Planning, budgeting and forecasting	3b. Corporate finance
1c. IT desktop skills	2c. Management reporting for decision making	3c. Treasury management
1d. Systems and procedure development	2d. Product and service costing	3d. Taxation
	2e. Information management	3e. Business evaluation and appraisal
	2f. Project appraisal	3f. Business strategy
	2g. Project management	3g. External relationships
	2h. Working capital control	
	2i. Risk management and business assurance	

Note: Some or all of the required experience may have been gained before registering as a CIMA student.

Practical experience must be recorded by students within a Career Profile and submitted to CIMA for assessment. An approved Career Profile is awarded 50 credits – the amount needed to meet the requirements for Part A of the Test of Professional Competence in Management Accounting.

Full details of the practical experience requirements and how to complete the CIMA Career Profile can be found on the CIMA website and within a separate publication entitled 'Practical Experience Requirements'. Employers and their students are advised to refer to these documents.

T4 Part B – Case Study Examination

Overview

The examination is based upon a case study that is set within a simulated business context relating to one or more fictitious organisations. However, the context described in the case material is based on a real business or industry.

The examination comprises a three hour assessment of competence, completed within a supervised examination environment. It provides an integrated test of syllabus content that is mainly included within the three strategic level papers – E3, F3 and P3. However, it will also draw upon content covered within the management and operational level papers. The Case Study Examination therefore has no specific syllabus content of its own.

The Case Study Examination primarily involves the application of strategic management accounting techniques to analyse, recommend and support decisions. Students will be required to deal with material in a less structured situation than those encountered in previous strategic level papers, and to integrate a variety of skills to arrive at a recommended solution. It is unlikely that there will be a single right answer to such a complex business problem, and students will be expected to recognise the possible alternatives in dealing with a problem.

The emphasis will be on assessing the student's capabilities and competence in the application of appropriate, relevant knowledge, the ability to demonstrate the higher level skills of synthesis, analysis and evaluation, and skill in effectively presenting and communicating information to users.

Assessment aims

The purpose of the Case Study Examination is to test the capabilities and competence of students, to ensure that they:

A   have a sound technical knowledge of the specific subjects within the curriculum;

B   can apply technical knowledge in an analytical and practical manner;

C   can extract, from various subjects, the knowledge required to solve many-sided or complex problems;

D   can solve a particular problem by distinguishing the relevant information from the irrelevant, in a given body of data;

E   can, in multi-problem situations, identify the problems and prioritise them in the order in which they need to be addressed;

F   appreciate that there can be alternative solutions and understand the role of judgement in dealing with them;

G   can integrate diverse areas of knowledge and skills;

H   can communicate effectively with users, by formulating realistic recommendations in a concise and logical fashion;

I   can identify, advise on and/or resolve ethical dilemmas.

Assessment strategy

There will be a written examination paper of three hours, plus 20 minutes of pre-examination question paper reading time. The paper will have 2 requirements:

- Requirement 1(a) will require the production of a report (and will be worth 90 marks)

- Requirement 1(b) will be a further communication document (and will be worth 10 marks)

 The questions will be based upon:

(a) a case study (pre-seen material), which will be published on the CIMA website, at least six weeks in advance of the examination. This will provide an opportunity, before the examination, to undertake preparatory analysis based upon the pre-seen material. The volume of pre-seen material is likely to be between 10 and 20 sides of A4;

(b) further information regarding the case (unseen material), which will be added as part of the examination paper. This will allow further developments to be explained and additional issues to be raised. The volume of unseen material is likely to be between three and six sides of A4 paper.

Questions will test the students' capabilities and competence in the application of appropriate knowledge, and the processes undertaken in dealing with the problems identified in the examination, together with the ability to present and communicate information in a variety of formats. The pre-seen material will also contain details of the Assessment Criteria showing the scoring system to be used when assessing the capabilities and competence of candidates.

To successfully pass Part B of the Test of Professional Competence in Management Accounting – Case Study Examination, students must score a minimum of 25 credits (out of a possible maximum of 50 credits).

Learning outcomes

Students will be required to go through the following stages to prepare for, and to answer, the requirements of the Case Study Examination:

A – Preparatory to the exam

- analyse the context within which the case is set;
- analyse the current position of the organisation;
- identify and analyse the issues facing the organisation.

Note: These activities will be undertaken using the published 'pre-seen' case study material.

B – During the exam

- analyse the current position of the organisation;
- identify, analyse and prioritise the issues facing the organisation;
- identify, evaluate and discuss possible feasible options / courses of action available;
- recommend and justify a course of action;
- prepare and present information in a report format and to a standard suitable for presentation to senior management as specified in the question requirement;
- prepare and present a further communication document in a format as specified in the question requirement.

Note: These activities will be undertaken using the 'pre-seen' and 'unseen' case study materials.

How to Use the Materials

These Official CIMA learning materials brought to you by Elsevier/CIMA Publishing and Kaplan Publishing have been carefully designed to make your learning experience as easy as possible and to give you the best chances of success in your *T4 Part B Case Study Examination*.

This Study Text has been designed with the needs of home-study and distance-learning candidates in mind. Such students require the facility to undertake extensive question practice. However, the Study Text is also ideal for fully taught courses.

The aim of this text book is to walk you through the stages to prepare for, and to answer, the requirements of the Case Study Examination. This will include:

- identifying the knowledge required,
- demonstrating the most efficient techniques and
- developing the skills you will require to be successful at the Case Study Examination.

To give you an accurate picture of what to expect, this text uses two recent T4 Case Study Examinations, CeeCee Retail Fashion (May 2010) and V & Y Productions (November 2010). Using the pre-seen material for these exams, we show the key preparatory stages and then, using the unseen material, we demonstrate the stages that must be covered during the exam itself.

Practical hints and realistic tips are given throughout the book making it easy for you to apply what you've learnt in this text to your actual Case Study Exam.

Where sample solutions are provided, they must be viewed as just one interpretation of the case. One key aspect, which you must appreciate early in your studies, is that there is no single 'correct' solution. Your own answer might reach different conclusions, and give greater emphasis to some issues and less emphasis to others, but score equally as well if it demonstrates the required skills.

Further Case Study Examinations, including the CeeCee exam set in March 2010, and the V & Y productions exam set in September 2010, can be downloaded from your MyCIMA area of the CIMAglobal website (www.cimaglobal.com).

In addition to this T4 Case Study text, which will help you to learn the techniques and practice using past T4 case studies, CIMA Publishing also produce a Case Analysis Workbook (CAW) relevant to each Case Study Examination. It is strongly recommended that you also purchase the CAW relating to the specific Case Study Examination you will be sitting in order to help familiarise yourself with the pre-seen information after you have worked through the past two cases in this book.

If you work conscientiously through the official CIMA Study Text according to the guidelines above, as well as the Case Analysis Workbook relevant to your case study, you will be giving yourself an excellent chance of success in your examination. Good luck with your studies!

Icon Explanations

Focus - details about the exam which you must understand.

Key Skills - identifies skills that are key to success.

Test Your Understanding - exercises which give the opportunity to test your application of knowledge or skills. Suggested solutions can be found at the back of each chapter.

Illustration - examples to help develop an understanding of topics.

Warning - pay attention to anything written next to this symbol as it will be crucial to your ability to pass this exam.

Footsteps - helpful tutor tips.

Study technique - Passing exams is partly a matter of intellectual ability, but however accomplished you are in that respect you can improve your chances significantly by the use of appropriate study and revision techniques. In this section we briefly outline some tips for effective study during the earlier stages of your approach to the subject. Later in the text we mention some techniques that you will find useful at the revision stage.

Planning

To begin with, formal planning is essential to get the best return from the time you spend studying. Estimate how much time in total you are going to need for each subject you are studying for the Case Study Examination. You may find it helpful to read "Pass First Time!" second edition by David R. Harris ISBN 978-1-85617-798-6. This book will provide you with proven study techniques. Chapter by chapter it covers the building blocks of successful learning and examination techniques. This is the ultimate guide to passing your CIMA exams, written by a past CIMA examiner and shows you how to earn all the marks you deserve, and explains how to avoid the most common pitfalls. You may also find "A Student's Guide to Writing Business Reports" by Zoe Robinson and Stuart Pedley-Smith ISBN 978-0-85732-207-4 helpful. Both Zoe and Stuart are senior Case Study lecturers at Kaplan Financial with a track record of successful students including many worldwide prizewinners. This book provides clear guidance on the whole process of preparing a report with an emphasis on commercial thinking that will help to ensure a successful outcome. It is an easy-to-use guide that delivers step-by-step advice to help you focus on your reader, plan effectively, structure your report, develop commercial arguments, write clearly and concisely and present convincing recommendations. Each part of the report writing process is demonstrated before detailed exercises allow you to practise the techniques and develop your skills.

With your study material before you, decide which chapters you are going to study in each week, which weeks you will devote to practicing past exams, and which weeks you will spend becoming familiar with your case study pre-seen material.

Prepare a written schedule summarising the above and stick to it!

Students are advised to refer to articles published regularly in CIMA's magazine (Financial Management), the students e-newsletter (Velocity) and on the CIMA website, to ensure they are up-to-date.

Tips for effective studying

(1) Aim to find a quiet and undisturbed location for your study, and plan as far as possible to use the same period of time each day. Getting into a routine helps to avoid wasting time. Make sure that you have all the materials you need before you begin so as to minimise interruptions.

(2) Store all your materials in one place, so that you do not waste time searching for items around your accommodation. If you have to pack everything away after each study period, keep them in a box, or even a suitcase, which will not be disturbed until the next time.

(3) Limit distractions. To make the most effective use of your study periods you should be able to apply total concentration, so turn off all entertainment equipment, set your phones to message mode, and put up your 'do not disturb' sign.

(4) Your timetable will tell you which area to study. However, before diving in and becoming engrossed in the finer points, make sure you have an overall picture of all the areas that need to be covered by the end of that session. After an hour, allow yourself a short break and move away from your Study Text. With experience, you will learn to assess the pace you need to work at.

(5) Work carefully through a chapter, making notes as you go. When you have covered a suitable amount of material, vary the pattern by attempting a practice question. When you have finished your attempt, make notes of any mistakes you made, or any areas that you failed to cover or covered more briefly.

(6) Make notes as you study, and discover the techniques that work best for you. Your notes may be in the form of lists, bullet points, diagrams, summaries, 'mind maps', or the written word, but remember that you will need to refer back to them at a later date, so they must be intelligible. If you are on a taught course, make sure you highlight any issues you would like to follow up with your lecturer.

(7) Organise your notes. Make sure that all your notes, calculations etc can be effectively filed and easily retrieved later.

Introduction to the Case Study Examination

Chapter learning objectives

Upon completion of this chapter you will be able to:

- Appreciate the skills being assessed in the T4 Case Study Examination.

- Understand how the Case Study Examination works including what you will have to produce and how you will be assessed.

- Be aware of what you will be expected to use the pre-seen material for.

- Understand the purpose of the unseen material and appreciate how you will use it on the exam day.

- Know more about the requirements in the case study exam.

- Appreciate the time pressured nature of the exam and the importance of planning both the content of your report and how to spend your time in the exam.

- Know about the key problems students often experience.

- Explain the Case Study Assessment Criteria.

- See how the criteria relate to the three stage planning model.

- Explain how to gain marks under each of the criteria.

1 Why a Case Study Examination?

The Case Study Examination is an attempt to simulate workplace problem solving, and allows examiners to move one step closer to the assessment of competence than is possible with essay-style questions. It is a test of your professional competence.

The syllabus states candidates will be required to apply mainly strategic management accounting techniques to make and support decisions within a case study (a simulated business context). CIMA wishes to assess:

* your possession of the higher skills of synthesis, analysis and evaluation, in addition to;

* your technical knowledge of management accounting, and

* your skill in presenting and communicating information to users.

Since the examination tests your higher level skills, preparing for this examination needs to be different from studying for a 'traditional' examination paper. The purpose of this text is to suggest how you might prepare for the examination by developing and practising your skills.

2 How the Case Study Examination works

The Case Study Examination is a written exam paper of three hours (with an additional 20 minutes of reading time). Candidates cannot take the examination until they have successfully completed all the 'strategic' level subjects: E3, F3 and P3.

The exam is based on:

* pre-seen material issued in advance of the exam day, supplemented by

* additional, previously unseen material given to you in the exam room.

 There will be two requirements, to prepare:

(a) A report that prioritises, analyses and evaluates the issues facing the organisation and makes appropriate recommendations. This will be worth 90% of your final mark.

(b) An additional communication document (either a short slide presentation, an e-mail, a letter, a chart or a graph) worth 10% of your mark. The aim of this requirement is to test your ability to communicate effectively.

The pre-seen material is an extended scenario consisting of 10 to 20 pages of information about a business organisation. You will be taking on the role of a management accountant who works for the organisation, and your report will usually be addressed to your superior.

The pre-seen material is published on the CIMA website at least six weeks before the examination, and gives you the opportunity for familiarisation and analysis. You therefore have at least six weeks to study the material: taking notes, analysing the information, doing background reading and research, and revising any technical topics that you think might be relevant.

You cannot take your copy of the pre-seen material, nor any notes or calculations that you have made relating to the pre-seen material into the examination. Similarly, you will not be allowed to take in any textbook. Normal 'closed book' examination conditions will apply.

In the examination room you will be supplied with a fresh booklet containing the pre-seen material and the unseen material. The unseen material will be up to six pages in length and will give you a more up to date picture of the issues facing the organisation. Discount tables and a formulae sheet will be provided.

Typically, the question in the examination will require you to demonstrate your ability to assess and evaluate the operational, financial and strategic position of the organisation in the case study, and to recommend suitable courses of action to deal with the issues involved. In the position of a management accountant working for the company, many of the issues presented will focus on practical management accounting issues whilst still having sensitivity to wider strategic and management issues.

You must be prepared for anything to come up in the context of being a management accountant.

There will not be a 'correct' or 'incorrect' answer, but you will be expected to identify the key issues from the unseen material provided, and to use your judgement to analyse the impact of the issues, evaluate alternative solutions and make commercially sensible recommendations, with suitable justifications. Your ability to communicate your findings effectively will also be key.

Your script will be marked against nine specific Assessment Criteria, the core elements of which are technical / application, judgement and logic. All of the assessment criteria are outlined in detail later in this chapter.

3 The pre-seen approach

CIMA releases the pre-seen material at least six weeks before the examination. This is posted on the student area of the CIMA website (www.cimaglobal.com) and it is your responsibility to download it and to print off a copy. Candidates without access to download and printing facilities can ask CIMA to post them a copy.

The pre-seen material is an introductory scenario to set the scene for the case study, together with accounting and financial information. Much of the financial information will probably be in the form of appendices to the main text, but the main text of the pre-seen might include some figures too.

The purpose of giving you access to this information in advance of the exam is to enable you to prepare notes, analyse and become very familiar with the organisation(s) and industry described. Remember, you have the role of a management accountant within this organisation and so you should use the pre-seen material to get a similar background knowledge as would be expected from someone in this situation.

 The best approach to this can be summarised by the following steps:

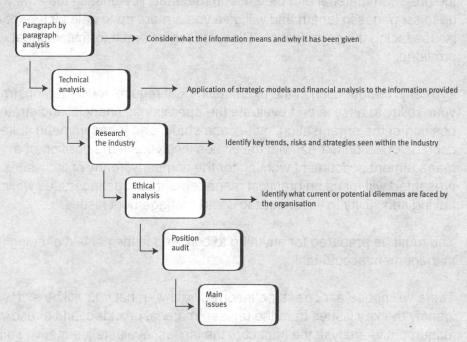

(1) *Detailed paragraph-by-paragraph analysis*

As you review each paragraph ask yourself questions about what each piece of information means and what the implications of it might be for the organisation. Try to consider why the examiner might have provided this information.

(2) *Technical analysis*

Now it's time to apply many of the models you covered at strategic level to help you understand the organisation and the industry in which it operates in more depth. As a minimum you should perform:

– Ratio analysis of financial statements and financial plans.

– Business strategy analysis, including generation of strategic options.

    –   Financial strategy analysis, including how the business is financed, how future finance could be raised and valuation techniques.

    –   Identification of key risk areas, and an evaluation of the presence and suitability of management controls and performance measures (where applicable).

(3) *Researching the industry involved*

To ensure you have a good understanding of the context of the case, you should carry out some wider reading including researching the industry in which the organisation operates. You should look at some of the real life key players and see what strategies they are adopting. Look for key trends within the industry and the risks that have to be addressed. Be sure to consider what impact the economic climate or broader business influences (such as the political or regulatory environments) may be having on the industry.

(4) *Ethical analysis*

An analysis of the ethical issues facing the organisation now and a consideration of those which could arise in the unseen material.

(5) *Overall position analysis, incorporating a SWOT*

Once you have complete all of the above, you should be able to stand back and see the bigger picture of the organisation within the case material. You should complete a position audit, including a SWOT analysis so you have a clear understanding of where the organisation is and where it might want to go.

(6) *Identification of key issues*

Out of your SWOT analysis, you should now be able to identify a short list of key issues facing the organisation. An appreciation of these will assist you when prioritising the new issues introduced in the unseen material in the exam.

Each of these steps will be reviewed in more detail in Chapter 3 of this text book.

4 The unseen approach

In the examination room, you will be provided with:

•   a clean copy of the pre-seen material as well as the further pages of the unseen material

- the question, broken down into two specific requirements (a report for 90 marks and a further document communicating your findings on a specific matter for 10 marks)

- two blank answer booklets (for those sitting the written exam) or one blank Word file and one blank Excel file (for those sitting the computer examination).

The unseen material will be a continuation of the pre-seen and will usually bring the scenario up to date. In many cases there is a 'twist' in the unseen i.e. a development that students might not have anticipated from the pre-seen. The unseen may focus on a number of issues that appeared in the unseen or it may just focus on one or two; either way it will provide the basis for the content of your answer.

In order to answer the requirements, you will need to complete the familiarisation process again, but this time you'll need to be much quicker. You must:

- Update your SWOT analysis for the new information.

- Consider the implications of the information in order to assess the impact and implications.

- Identify and evaluate the alternative courses of action open to the organisation.

- Present detailed and justified recommendations that are both practical and commercial.

 A common mistake made by weaker students is that they place too much emphasis on their analysis of the pre-seen material and do not develop the information in the unseen material adequately. The decision on the key issues to be discussed in your answer should be driven by the new information in the unseen material.

In order to address both of the requirements in the time available, you must continually think about the Assessment Criteria against which you'll be marked and manage your time effectively to ensure you deliver in all areas.

5 A detailed look at the requirements
Requirement 1(a)

 Over most recent exams the first requirement (often referred to as question 1(a)) has been of the following form:

'Prepare a report that prioritises, analyses and evaluates the issues facing [the company's name], and makes appropriate recommendations'.

Although your requirement is likely to be of a similar form, it is vital that you review it in detail to check that it is as you expect it to be. For example, you could be asked to report to a particular individual (as opposed to the whole Board of Directors) or you could be asked to ensure a particular area is covered (for example, in the September 2008 exam a specific note was added to the requirement asking the student to address cultural change issues).

Examining this requirement in more depth, you need to:

- *Prioritise the issues*

  This means that you must consider the issues detailed in the unseen and present them in order of importance to the company and its stakeholders.

  Typically you will be looking to prioritise issues based on the impact they have on the company, the likelihood of the events happening and the urgency of those issues. In Chapter 8, you will learn some specific techniques to assist with prioritisation.

  In your report, you should include a section showing the priorities of your issues, along with your justification of those priorities. As a general guide it is the top 4 issues which will form the basis for both this and later sections of your report.

- *Analyse the issues*

  The official CIMA definition of analyse is to 'Examine in detail in order to discover meaning or essential features'. To achieve this aim, for each of the key issues you should:

  - outline the key stakeholders who will be affected and what the impact for them is or could be;
  - examine the financial implications of the issue, including financial or numerical analysis of the numbers presented to you;
  - relate the issue to the company's current market position and strategy.

  A common error is to focus too narrowly in the analysis, considering just the financial implications or the impact on one key stakeholder. Breadth, as well as depth of analysis is important here.

  In your report, you should include a section showing your analysis of this situation.

– *Evaluate the issues*

The next step is to examine a range of possible courses of action. For some issues the examining team will outline the actions that the company are considering. For others, you will be expected to generate actions of your own. In both cases you will need to evaluate each alternative, as a way to work towards the solution you will recommend later in your report.

Evaluation of possible courses of action, should include financial evaluation, where you are given financial information, often done in appendices, or can be carried out by doing an analysis of Advantages and Disadvantages or through use of a formal model such as the Johnson, Scholes and Whittington's, Suitability, Acceptability, Feasibility model that you learnt in the E3 Enterprise Strategy paper.

It is vital that financial analysis is undertaken on any issue where financial information is presented to you in the unseen. Remember that you are studying for an accountancy qualification, and so preparing financial analysis is a core skill you must demonstrate that you have.

– *Make appropriate recommendations*

On many occasions, the examining team have stated that the most important part of your answer is the recommendations. If you have undertaken a good quality analysis and evaluation, then this should be easy, since these recommendations should follow on naturally from that evaluation.

You must make clear recommendations on **what** actions should be taken along with the justification of **why** you have selected this course of action. You should complete your recommendations by detailing **how** they should be undertaken and the specific actions required to implement them effectively.

– *Prepare a report*

All of the elements of the requirement must be brought together in a stand-alone report which reads well, covers all of the key issues, makes well-reasoned and justified recommendations and is supported by appropriate calculations. It should be the sort of report a non-financial manager or director could clearly understand and act upon.

In summary, the suggested report format, which is not compulsory, but is recommended by the examination team, is summarised below:

- Contents page
- Introduction
  - A brief background on the company of around 8–10 lines.
- Terms of reference
  - A brief 4–6 lines to set the scene of who you are – e.g. a management accountant, and to state who the report was commissioned by, and who it is aimed at.
- Prioritisation section
  - Identify and prioritise the main issues facing the company, showing the top four issues in priority order together with justification for the ranking of these issues.

  - Issues analysis
    – This is the main body of your report and should be divided up into sections which should include an analysis of each of the issues that you have prioritised.
    – For each issue facing the company, you should discuss the impact this issue has on the company and its stakeholders and evaluate a range of alternative actions to overcome these issues.
    – Your discussion of each issue should be supported by analysis, including technical theories (see Chapter 4), supporting calculations showing an evaluation of the impact and alternative solutions (which should be shown in appendices), and relevant examples from the real world.

- Ethical issues
  - Ideally you should cover two ethical issues, explaining the issue, justifying why you consider it to be ethical and offering clear recommendations on how the issue should be handled.

- Recommendations
  - This is the most important part of the report and should pick up on each of the issues discussed earlier; you should provide guidance on **what** must be done, **why** and **how**.

  - Each recommendation should be clear and well justified as to why you are recommending a particular course of action.

  - As a general rule, be decisive and try to avoid recommending that more information needs to be collected before a recommendation can be made.

  - Recommendations should also include what actions need to be taken in order to implement the recommendation you are making.

- Conclusion
  - A brief 5–8 lines for closing comments.
  - Appendices
    - These should include some strategic models, such as a SWOT analysis, as well as detailed calculations
    - The appendices must be referred to within your report.
    - Your answer to part b of the requirement is usually included as an appendix to your report (see below).

Note that an executive summary is NOT required. In Chapter 6, there is a more detailed analysis of this report format, along with an explanation of how you should prepare and structure your answer.

Requirement 1(b)

The purpose of the second requirement (usually referred to as question 1 (b)) is to assess the candidate's effective communication skills relating to one or more particular issues which will have been analysed and considered in question 1(a) of the Case Study Examination. It should be noted that the issues dealt with in question 1(b) may, or may not, be what the examiners suggested answer to requirement 1(a) subsequently identifies as the most important issue(s).

Question 1(b) will require candidates to go beyond a re-statement of what has been produced within their answer to the relevant issue in question 1(a). Question 1(b) will be a requirement of all T4 Part B Case Study Examinations. It will always be worth 10 marks.

The format of the communication is limited to either:

- a summary for use in a presentation in bullet point format;

- an e-mail containing short phrases or sentences;

- a draft letter;

- a graph or a chart (sometimes as an attachment to another document such as an e-mail or presentation).

It is important to note that the format, or layout of your answer, whilst being important, will not be the most important aspect in gaining marks for this requirement. Of far greater significance is the content of what you've written. Communicating effectively requires the author to focus on the user and the overall purpose of the document. You may be required to adopt a different tone, depending on who you are writing to or the purpose of the communication; for example you may need to be persuasive, or conciliatory.

A common mis-conception about the second requirement is that you are just repeating information from either the unseen or from what you wrote in your answer to the first requirement. Such an approach will score poorly.

A further common error is not leaving enough time to complete this second requirement, not including financial information or not providing clear recommendations.

6 A time pressured exam

The case study exam is a very time pressured exam and what adds to this pressure is the general nature of the requirements. Unlike previous exams you've sat, you aren't given a detailed breakdown of the allocation of marks associated with individual elements of the requirements, so you aren't able to neatly divide your time across the elements you have to produce.

 Success in the case study exam is often driven as much by your ability to effectively manage your time as it is by your ability to comment sensibly on the matters in hand. To ensure you address all of the areas in the time available, and to ensure your report has a logical flow, you must break down the 3 hours and 20 minutes into slots for specific tasks, and one of those tasks must involve planning your answer.

More advice on time management is provided in Chapter 7.

7 Lessons from the examiner's Post Exam Guidance

At the end of each exam the Examiner produces a Post Exam Guidance (PEG) report. This provides an analysis of the exam, and guidance on what candidates did well and less well. Two recent PEG reports are included in this book in Chapters 12 and 18.

Over a range of sittings, a range of common problems are highlighted in these PEGs, and by understanding these and ensuring that you do not repeat the same errors that many other students have in the past, you can improve your chances of passing the exam. With this in mind, here is a list of key problems often highlighted in the PEGs.

Students have:

- based their answer primarily on the pre-seen material rather than on the requirement set and the new material presented on the day;

- not carried out the required financial analysis / calculations or made indefensible errors within these;

- not explained or commented upon their calculations;

- not demonstrated real world awareness in their answer meaning commercial implications have not been thought through;

- not provided and evaluated a range of solutions to each issue;

- not prepared clear and well-reasoned recommendations;

- stated that they are unable to make recommendations without further material – you must make clear recommendations, even if you state that these are subject to satisfying the Board on outstanding matters where more information is wanted;

- not stated why they consider an issue to have an ethical side to it, or clearly explained what that ethical issue is;

- not made clear recommendations for each ethical issue presented;

- not adhered to the guidance given regarding format of the second requirement;

- not completed the second requirement;

- not finished the paper (most likely due to poor time management).

In addition to the PEGs included in this text book (Chapters 12 and 18) you should also consider reviewing other PEGs, available on the CIMA website, to improve your awareness of the common problems faced by students in the exam.

8 Computer v written

Written exam

You will be required to present your answers in the main answer booklet, and you may use the supplementary booklet for any appendices or workings, if you wish. If you use the supplementary answer booklet for presenting appendices, you should make sure that they are clearly labelled and neatly presented.

Computer exam

When you arrive in your exam room, your computer will have one word file and one excel file open. There is no hard and fast rule about which sections of your report should go in which file (for example, you don't have to put all of your appendices in the excel file). As a general rule, you'll probably find it easier and quicker to carry out any calculations within the excel file.

You do **not** need to copy any of your work carried out in excel into your word document. However, you must ensure that your appendices within excel are clearly labelled.

9 The Case Study Assessment Criteria

Recap of the strategic planning process

From your studies in E3 – Enterprise Strategy you will recall the three stage planning model of Johnson, Scholes and Whittington (JSW):

Strategic analysis
- External analysis to identify opportunities and threats
- Internal analysis to identify strengths and weaknesses
- Stakeholder analysis to identify key objectives and to assess power and interest of different groups
- Gap analysis to identify the difference between desired and expected performance.

↓

Strategic choice
- Strategies are required to 'close the gap'
- Competitive strategy – for each business unit
- Directions for growth – which markets/products should be invested in
- Whether expansion should be achieved by organic growth, acquisition or some form of joint arrangement.

↓

Strategic implementation
- Formulation of detailed plans and budgets
- Target setting for KPIs
- Monitoring and control.

This is a useful model for understanding the case study exam and the marking process and assessment criteria.

What CIMA expect from you in the exam

CIMA have given the following guidance on passing the case study exam:

In order to succeed in the case study exam, you need to:

(1) Use analytical techniques to help you analyse the issues in the unseen with relevant reference to the pre-seen material and the industry setting as well as real life parallels of the issues; you will also need to apply your technical knowledge.

(2) Prioritise the issues and discuss the impact these issues may have on the organisation; you will then need to suggest a range of alternative actions that the organisation could undertake to address the issues. You will need to discuss the impact these issues may have on the organisation. In doing this, you also need to recognise any relevant ethical implications of the issues.

(3) Make recommendations on your choice of action for each issue from the alternative actions discussed earlier.

(4) Communicate your findings in a professional way and in the formats specified in both requirements 1(a) and (b).

Assessment criteria

Marks are awarded for fulfilling each of the three stages according to the criteria shown below.

Analysis of issues (25 marks)

- Technical (5)
- Application (15)
- Diversity (5)

Strategic choices (35 marks)

- Focus (5)
- Prioritisation (5)
- Judgement (20)
- Ethics (5)

Recommendations (40 marks)

- Logic (30) (20 marks relating to requirement 1(a) and 10 relating to 1(b))
- Ethics (5)
- Integration (5)

These are discussed in more detail below.

10 Technical

The aim of this part of the assessment is to test whether you 'have a sound technical knowledge of the specific subjects of the curriculum'.

CIMA Guidance

Use different relevant technical theories and frameworks to help you analyse the case material, especially the issues raised in the unseen material.

How to score the marks

The way to score highly for technical skills is to include five different techniques or models in your answer.

A typical report should contain the following:

- a SWOT analysis, summarising the strategic position of the firm
- the analysis of an opportunity using JSW's framework of suitability, feasibility, acceptability
- up to three other techniques, specially selected for their relevance to the case (common models would include Porter's Generic Strategies, Mendelow's, Ansoff's and motivation theories – see Chapter 4 on technical models for a quick refresher).

One approach to scoring technical marks is to put your detailed models in the appendices of your report. However, if doing this, you must be careful to still *use* the model to aid your analysis and not to spend too much time on your appendices at the expense of analysing your issues in full and giving detailed recommendations. In practice you may not feel that it is appropriate to show a Porter's Five Forces analysis, say, explicitly and would rather put just the key issues identified through such a model into your analysis within your report. This is acceptable although you must ensure you *'use'* the model and don't just name drop.

Assuming a total of 5 marks for technical skills in the matrix, you could expect to score a mark per technique for appropriate (i.e. relevant) use.

A common error in the technical criterion is to 'shoe-horn' in a predetermined list of technical theories rather than using the models as appropriate. The key word in that last sentence was 'use'. Technical models should not be regarded as a tick-list to be worked through regardless of the scenario; they are actually useful tools that can be used to help assess the impact of an issue or to help generate ideas for actions to be taken.

So, instead of walking into the exam hall with a list of technical models that you're going to fit to the issues, no matter what comes up, try reversing it; try to take a more skilful approach. For every issue you're presented with, ask yourself "which technical model can I use to help me understand the impact of this issue or to help me identify alternative courses of action?"

11 Application

The aim here is to test whether you have the ability to 'apply technical knowledge in an analytical and practical manner including financial analysis'.

Marks will be awarded for the way in which technical knowledge is used in application to the case study and the requirements of the question(s).

 ### CIMA Guidance

> Using technical knowledge in the context of the case and preparing a small range (usually two or three sets) of relevant calculations.

How to score the marks

To some degree, the marks you earn here will be dictated by how many techniques and models you have used. If you have only used two techniques, say, then you are limited to only two techniques' worth of application marks.

 To ensure you capture the application marks, you must ensure you apply the models correctly, given the case material. It is important that rather than just regurgitating the model or framework, you present it in such a way that it conveys information which is relevant to the case. For example, you should interpret any ratios calculated rather than just leaving them as figures in an appendix. A good way to check whether you have 'used' the model correctly is to put yourself in the position of the reader of your report. If after mentioning a technical model, the reader would be left asking 'so what?' you probably haven't applied it properly.

More marks will be available for some models. So, for example, the application of Mendelow's Matrix might only be worth 1 application mark, yet a SWOT analysis might attract up to three marks in Application.

Aside from the technical models, approximately 10 of the 15 application marks available will be for performing calculations. These are an essential part of your report and should not be neglected; after all, this is your final test of professional competence before becoming a qualified accountant. The types of calculations will vary, but they could include assessing the financial viability of alternative proposals or preparing forecast data.

Imagine that preparing your report is like constructing a house; the walls are represented by your judgement on the impact of the issues and alternative courses of action, the roof represents your recommendations. In this context, your technical models and calculations, perhaps better referred to as strategic and financial analysis, should be regarded as the foundations. Without a sound application of strategic models and without preparing accurate calculations, your judgement and recommendations will not hold up.

12 Diversity

The aim here is to test whether you can bring in real-world commercial considerations into your discussion.

You will be awarded marks for the breadth of knowledge you demonstrate in your answer.

 CIMA Guidance

Use a range of relevant real-life examples to illustrate the points you are making throughout your report.

How to score the marks

As well as including different technical areas, you can earn extra diversity marks by incorporating two aspects in your answer:

- Incorporate facts you have researched regarding the industry concerned. These could include the activities and strategies of real-life firms, recent trends and critical success factors.

- If the unseen material suggests a possible strategy, then bring in pre-learned details of the practicalities of such strategies. For example, if a joint venture is put forward as a possible strategy for the firm, then you could suggest something along the lines of: 'In situations such as this, the key areas of negotiation are normally the sharing out of risks and rewards,…'

Examples to illustrate the point you are making could be from relevant companies in the industry setting but could also be about other real life companies in other industries as long as it is relevant to the point you are making.

Like your application marks, any real world comment included in your script must 'add value' if it is to score. You should never leave your reader asking "so what?" after reading your comment.

13 Focus

The aim of focus is to test whether you have the ability to 'solve a particular problem by distinguishing the relevant information from the irrelevant in a given body of knowledge'.

You will be rewarded for your ability to focus on the issues in the question, and use what is relevant but ignore what is not relevant.

CIMA Guidance

Select the issues that are regarded as the most important and make sure that you properly address these issues in the report you produce.

How to score the marks

This is not a section of the report as such. Marks are awarded based on the issues which are contained and discussed within the report.

This criterion looks at your ability to sift through the mass of pre-seen and unseen data provided, and pick out only those facts that should be used in order to formulate a valid argument. Focusing on the unseen, dealing with the main issues, using the data to analyse into information as input to a model, calculation or support an argument and ignoring relatively minor issues will enable you to meet this criterion.

Focus marks are commonly confused with prioritisation marks (see next section).

14 Prioritisation

The aim of prioritisation is to test whether you have the ability to 'in multi-problem situations, rank the issues in the order in which they need to be addressed'.

CIMA Guidance

Rank the issues raised in the unseen material, stating clearly and concisely your justification for your ranking. Issues should be given high priority because of their impact on the organisation in the case. Their urgency may also be a factor.

How to score the marks

Higher marks are gained for placing the most crucial issues among your top two or three priorities. You do not have to arrive at the same priority order as the examiner in order to gain top marks. A good approach is to:

- Start by identifying your top four issues. This should be based on a mixture of criteria including impact, likelihood and urgency on the strategic goals of the organisation;

- With issue number one describe it as your 'top priority' and justify why it is the most important. Repeat with the rest of your top issues;

- Ensure you clearly explain the issue, usually by linking back to key stakeholders within the organisation, to competitive strategies or to financial performance;

- Ensure that the order of sections within your report reflects your prioritisation.

15 Judgement

The aim of this criterion is to test whether you have the ability to think through the impact of an issue, appreciate that there can be alternative solutions and understand the role of judgement in dealing with them. 'Judgement' might be defined as 'informed common sense'.

CIMA Guidance

Exercise commercial and professional judgement to discuss the key issues. Discuss the impact the priority issues have on the organisation. Discuss alternative courses of action, with reasons, that the organisation could take to resolve these issues. Your analysis should include relevant supporting analysis drawn from the 'application' criterion.

How to score the marks

Your discussion of each of the issues in the unseen material will make up most of the body of your report, so this is an important area. For each prioritised issue your analysis should incorporate the following:

- The impact of the issue.

- At least two alternative courses of action available to the organisation.

- Arguments justifying why each one might be an appropriate course of action. This should include analysing the financial implications of the issue or proposal and weighing the relative merits or demerits of the options against each other.

When doing this, you should incorporate a discussion of any supporting calculations together with real-life business awareness points as well as points extracted from the material.

It is acceptable for students to present "straw men" when detailing an alternative solution (a first proposal for a solution to a problem, which is offered more as a place to start looking for a solution than as a serious solution for a final action), and then to explain why this would not be appropriate or realistic.

16 Ethics

To all business issues there is an ethical dimension. Business is about compromise and, necessarily, someone must benefit at the expense of another. This criterion rewards you for recognising the ethical issues and, if appropriate, recommending action. Ethics is a broad topic, and you should consider whether the following different aspects are relevant to the case:

- Personal and professional ethics, as you will be acting the role of a newly qualified Chartered Management Accountant.

- Business ethics, as you will be acting as part of an organisation.

- Social responsibility, as strategic decisions often impact on the world outside the organisation's boundary.

Although the Ethics criterion is shown under both the 'Strategic Choices' and 'Recommendations' section, it is not necessary for your discussion of ethical issues to be split in this way within your report. If you choose to do so, it is quite acceptable for the ethical issues contained in the case to be discussed within a single section of your report. You should take into account when you discuss ethical issues that some of them may impact on your discussion under the Judgement and Logic criteria.

CIMA Guidance

Five marks are available for using your judgement to highlight and analyse the ethical issues in the case and state why you consider these issues to have ethical implications. Discuss alternative courses of action that the organisation could take to resolve the issues.

A further five marks are available for making clear, well justified recommendations for two or three ethical issues and ensuring the reasoning for the recommended courses of action is clearly stated. The recommendations should follow on logically from the weight of the arguments you make in your report.

How to score the marks

Some students make the mistake of only discussing ethics if it is considered to be a key issue in the case. Rather ethical issues should be included for **all** cases.

To score high marks for ethics you should do the following:

- Identify at least two ethical issues using the types mentioned above – personal and professional ethics, business ethics corporate and social responsibility.

- For each issue, explain why it has an ethical dimension. This could include highlighting the conflicts of interest involved.

- For each issue, recommend what should be done to resolve it.

17 Logic in requirement 1(a)

The aim of this is to test whether you have the ability to 'communicate effectively with users by formulating realistic recommendations in a concise and logical fashion'.

The ability to think logically is a prime quality in a management accountant, and you will be awarded marks for your ability to demonstrate logical thinking and a logical approach.

CIMA Guidance

Make clear recommendations on each of the prioritised issues, justify your choice of action for each issue and explain what steps need to be taken to implement your recommendations. The recommendations should follow on logically from the weight of the arguments and choices of actions given earlier in the report.

Throughout your report, the content should be structured in such a way that the arguments you put forward lead logically to your conclusions and recommendations. Failure to provide recommendations really makes your answer a waste of time, and would not gain much credit in this criterion.

How to score the marks

Marks are awarded not just for the recommendations themselves but also, crucially, for the rationale and strength of argument supporting them. There are three key elements to scoring high logic marks on your first requirement:

- State clearly **what** you are recommending for each key issue.

- Give clear justifications for **why** this course of action is preferable to others (referring to financial viability where relevant).

- Consider **how** your recommendations should be implemented (resource requirements, time scale etc).

In order to earn marks in Logic your recommendations must be commercially realistic. You are also encouraged to communicate in a 'concise' manner. The marker will not give you credit for writing at unnecessary length.

18 Integration

This is not a section of the report, but a holistic view of its entirety.

This criterion will assess whether your report is fit for purpose. A low mark will apply in integration if analysis is not sufficiently carried out or if there is insufficient reasoning behind recommendations.

 ### CIMA Guidance

> Produce a cohesive, comprehensive report that reaches well-justified recommendations on each of the issues discussed. Include commercially viable comments that would help the management team to decide what to do about the issues facing it.
>
> These marks are awarded holistically according to the overall quality and functionality of your report.

Note that the skills of judgement, integration and logic are very much linked and are essentially marks for your ability to reach a professional judgement and communicate your views in a realistic and logical manner.

How to score the marks

Many students struggle to understand what integration is really looking for. The marker will be looking at the report as a whole, rather than at just one section and will be concerned that:

- The report is complete. All key issues identified must be discussed in sufficient detail and should result in recommendations being made. For example, some students identify four key issues but only make clear recommendations on two of them. This is usually due to poor time allocation. It is better to discuss issues in less depth if it results in a better balanced report that is 'finished'.

- The report flows well.

- That the numerical analysis is strong and is used effectively to guide further analysis and recommendations.

- The recommendations given are commercial and realistic.

The higher-skills aspect of integration is to look at each of the key issues and consider the overall balance and fit of the strategies concerned. For example, three strategies may be proposed, each of which has sufficient merit to recommend accepting them. However, the firm may be experiencing capital rationing and so could only undertake one. Identifying this problem and discussing how to proceed would score highly on integration.

This criterion is often the last on which marks are awarded when scripts are marked. Markers will often use this criterion to assess whether a borderline script should pass or fail the exam based on whether they feel the report is of a high enough quality.

19 Logic in requirement 1(b)

This tests your communication skills in relation to one or more specific issues in the unseen material.

This is the only criterion where the secondary task earns marks, reflecting that the secondary requirement will always focus on your ability to communicate your findings and recommendations effectively after having consideration for the user of the document.

CIMA Guidance

Communicate, in a competent professional way, your analysis, findings and financial implications relating to a particular issue contained in the unseen material.

You must carefully consider the purpose of the communication, for whom it is intended, and the salient points that you wish to communicate. Thought also needs to go into the effectiveness of the communication which means that it should have clarity, be to the point and not ambiguous.

How to score the marks

Marks are awarded based on the strength of the communication provided. There are marks available for commentary on the strategic importance of an issue and the inclusion of relevant financial or numerical information, the benefits and disadvantages of a particular course of action and a recommendation.

There are six key elements to scoring high logic marks on your second requirement:

- Follow the guidance given regarding the format of the communication (if it says 10 short sentences then deliver 10 short sentences).

- Consider the user and purpose of the document and adjust the tone accordingly. For example, your document may need to be persuasive or conciliatory.

- Include relevant financial analysis.

- Include your recommendation on the issue(s).

- Go over-and-above what you have already written in the your answer to question 1(a). This requirement is about more than simply re-gurgitating analysis you have already written.

- Ensure you devote sufficient time to this requirement. At 10 marks you should expect to spend approximately 18 minutes completing this task.

20 Checklist for the assessment criteria

The above comments can be summarised into the following checklist for the assessment criteria.

Criterion (marks)	What you need to do
Technical (5)	Prepare appendices or use key techniques.
	A SWOT should be the starting point, and should include all of your prioritised issues and the impact they have on the company.
	Other examples: ratios, Ansoff, PEST, Porter's Five Forces, Porter's Generic Strategies, BCG, Product lifecycle, balanced scorecard, motivation theories, suitability/feasibility/acceptability, etc.
Application (15)	Use/apply the above techniques / technical knowledge.
	Prepare relevant accurate calculations presented in the appendices.
Diversity (5)	Show real-world awareness for both the industry dealt with in the scenario and situations and events that impact a business in general (e.g. franchising, acquisitions, etc) throughout your report to illustrate the points you are making.
Focus (5)	Select the issues that are regarded as the most important.

Prioritisation (5)	Using your SWOT, identify four key issues from the unseen material. Following the approach:
	• Clearly identify the issue.
	• Justify the prioritisation of the issue.
	You must ensure it is CLEAR why you have prioritised. Good phrases include:
	'The following key issues identified from the SWOT analysis identified in Appendix x have been prioritised in the following order.'
	'The most important priority is……'
	'The second most important issue is... It ranks behind the first issue because...'
Judgement (20)	Discussion of the four key issues in greater detail.
	Assess the significance (impact) of each of the issues.
	Discuss your financial analysis.
	Evaluate any options and consider alternative courses of action.
Ethics (5 + 5)	Identify two ethical issues.
	Explain/justify the issues.
	Give practical, justified recommendations.
Logic (30)	20 marks for your report (question 1(a)) – Clear, well justified recommendations should be given for the four key issues first and then any other areas discussed in the report.
	Avoid recommendations without prior discussion.
	10 marks for question 1(b) – Identify the key areas of advice / opinions and convey succinctly. Include financial implications and your recommendation.
Integration (5)	Does the report cover the main issues and flow from identification to recommendation?
	Prioritised Discussed Evaluated Recommendations
	Is your report complete?

CeeCee: Pre-seen material

Chapter learning objectives

By the end of this chapter you will:

- Appreciate the benefits of working through more than one case in order to learn about the T4 case study exam and to hone your techniques.

- Have been introduced to the first of your practice case studies.

1 The benefits of practice case studies

The T4 Case Study Examination is like no other CIMA exam; there is no syllabus to review or formulae to learn. The best way to be successful at this level is to practise using past case study exams and mock exams based on your real live case study. By reviewing previous case studies alongside your current case you will improve your commercial thought processes and will be more aware of what the examiner expects. By sitting mock exams, under timed conditions you can hone your exam techniques and, in particular, your time management skills.

This text book is therefore based on this principle. It presents two previous case studies and uses these to demonstrate the skills and techniques that you must master to be successful.

The first case, CeeCee Retail Fashion, will be used to walk-through the processes and approach. The second case, V & Y Productions, an independent TV production company, has been presented as a case for you to work through in order to practise the techniques. This can be found in Chapters 13 onwards.

The remainder of this chapter contains the CeeCee pre-seen material; this exam was originally sat in March and May 2010. We would advise that you skim read this now before moving on to Chapter 3 where you will be provided with more guidance on how to familiarise yourself with the pre-seen material.

2 The CeeCee Retail Fashion pre-seen material

Industry overview

Over the last decade, the European clothing market has grown by almost 20% (as measured by sales revenue). However this headline sales figure hides many of the underlying tensions involved when competing in this market sector. The clothing market has suffered from strong deflationary pressures due to the influx of "value" retailers and intense competition. "Value" retailers are defined as low price retailers which import low cost clothing manufactured principally in Asia. These "value" retailers include some High Street chains as well as supermarket chains that sell clothing.

Generally it is accepted that there are 3 tiers of clothing retailers, which are:

- Couture houses and top designer labels
- High Street retailers of fashion clothing
- "Value" retailers (as defined above) which retail at the inexpensive end of the market.

There are a wide variety of retailers which compete in the High Street and in shopping centres all over Europe (and some globally) whose prices, quality and branding varies greatly.

Historically, clothing-only retailers dominated the market, taking nearly two thirds of all sales, with large department stores coming second. More recently large supermarket retailers, known principally for their grocery lines, have gained market share with a major push into non-food sales. Furthermore, in an increasingly competitive market, "value" retailers are also growing quickly. The major force for change in the clothing retail market came from the "value" retailers which began to offer clothing at extremely low prices. This sector caused traditional retailers to question all aspects of their business models. The sometimes breathtakingly low prices offered by the "value" retailers changed shoppers' attitudes.

Branding and differentiation were considered to be critical for retailers operating outside the "value" sector. To achieve effective differentiation, greater focus was required in the areas of quality of design and customer service.

A further opportunity, and challenge, was the introduction of online shopping. The key for shop-based retailers is to integrate the online shop with the wider brand proposition, while building the social and product experience at each shop.

In European surveys of "consumer's clothing wants", four key trends in consumer behaviour were identified. These impact on the development of clothing retailers' future strategies and are:

- Customers increasingly demand a wider range of sizes and fittings. This creates challenges for larger shops, as well as online operators.

- Improvements within each shop such as better stock availability, quicker service and improvements to changing rooms.

- Half of all clothing shoppers look at the price tag first when looking at clothes. About a third believed that cheap cannot be consistent with quality. This indicates that there is clearly more to selling clothing than simply price.

- Shoppers are increasingly turning to online shopping, but this has not yet had a significant impact on sales in shops, as research has shown that half of all shoppers think it is necessary to touch or try clothes on before buying. Therefore, making the product accessible is a key weapon for retailers fighting against an online threat.

Another factor in the traditional clothing industry is that the design and production processes often result in long lead times to getting clothing to the shops. Often up to six months is required between the initial design of a garment and its delivery to shops. This model effectively limits manufacturers and distributors to just two or three collections per year. Predicting consumer tastes ahead of time presents inherent difficulties. Therefore clothing retailers face the constant risk of being left with unsold inventory that has to be marked down considerably and sold off. This can often result in over 20% of inventories being sold off in end of season sales at write down prices, often only barely covering the cost of the production.

CeeCee overview and history

Carla Celli founded CeeCee in 1989 and is currently the Chief Executive Officer (CEO). She is a designer by trade and built up her experience of the industry working for other fashion retailers. When Carla Celli opened her first shop, she used a new business model which is known as "fast fashion". Fast fashion essentially replicates the principles of the manufacturing technique of "Just In Time" (JIT). For details on the fast fashion business model, refer to the paragraph "Business model and supply chain".

Carla Celli opened her first shop in 1989 in her home country with the aim of focussing on up to the minute fashion styles for women at affordable prices. This first shop featured reasonably priced "look alike" clothing ranges which were very similar to higher-end clothing fashion shops. The shop proved to be a success, particularly with young professional women who wanted to wear stylish clothing but who had limited budgets.

While her initial inspiration was driven by her keen following of fashion trends, she realised that if she wanted to scale up her business model to cover more cities she would have to become much more business minded and try to think "outside the box". Following meetings in early 1990 with Paulo Badeo, who had been working as a logistics IT consultant, she decided to implement her ideas for the fast fashion model for a greater number of retail shops. Within six months of their initial meeting Carla Celli had convinced Paulo Badeo to join the Board of CeeCee. The company was able to open 5 shops during 1991 and this was the start of CeeCee as a European-wide retailer.

CeeCee's personnel are detailed in **Appendix 1**.

From the outset some traditionalist logistics professionals argued that the fast fashion model would inevitably fail because the costs of constantly changing and shipping new fashions could not be recouped by high enough margins. They argued that the last twenty years of "mass" fashion industry experience showed that the way to go was long production runs and the outsourcing of production to low cost producers in Asia. In order to try and address these concerns Carla Celli had recruited a set of experienced professionals in the design, finance and logistics areas to help implement effective cost management, while at the same time allowing the fast fashion model to develop.

By the late 1990s CeeCee was a favourite with European "young professional" shoppers. At this stage, CeeCee was retailing only women's clothing but Carla Celli had plans to expand into menswear, children's clothing and some home furnishings.

In 2000 CeeCee was listed on a major European stock exchange. The cash raised at the time of the listing enabled a faster rollout of shops across Europe. The listing also gave CeeCee access to less expensive debt finance. At the end of 2000 there were 280 CeeCee shops across Europe.

With cash generated from operations and from the listing, CeeCee has opened around 40 shops each year. At the end of 2008, CeeCee had 610 shops across 18 European countries. Due to the weak economic climate during 2009, CeeCee only opened 20 new shops, bringing the total number of shops to 630 by the end of 2009. All shops are rented under short term rental agreements. CeeCee operates and manages all of its shops. CeeCee now sells men's clothing, children's clothing and a range of home furnishings at selected medium and larger size shops. At the end of 2009, around 500 out of the 630 shops sold men's clothing and around 300 sold children's clothes and home furnishings. However, CeeCee is still considered to be mainly a ladies fashion clothes shop.

CeeCee achieved an overall gross margin of 60.1% during the year ended December 2008.

The gross margin is defined as selling price, net of sales tax, less the purchase cost of the product. Neither delivery costs nor any direct sales staff costs have been charged in arriving at the gross margin. All costs, except the purchase cost of the product sold, are included in overhead costs.

The range of home furnishings that CeeCee now sells includes textiles, such as bed, table and bathroom linen, as well as tableware items including cutlery, glassware and decorative home items such as mirrors and picture frames. The home furnishing ranges are constantly being updated and new designs launched, which are proving very popular with CeeCee's target customers of young professionals, as they set up their own homes. The home furnishings range, which represents only 4% of total sales revenue, generates a higher gross margin than average at 72%.

Another product range that generates high gross margins is clothing accessories, such as handbags, hats, shoes, men's ties and jewellery. All CeeCee shops stock limited ranges of accessories, whereas in large sized CeeCee shops, the full range of accessories is on display throughout the shop to encourage shoppers to purchase, for example, new shoes together with a new dress. The gross margin achieved on accessories averages 75%, but some products generate an even higher gross margin. Accessories are a product range which Juliette Lespere, the Sales and Marketing Director, would like to expand.

A summary of CeeCee's shops and relevant key statistics is shown in **Appendix 2**.

The success of CeeCee's shops is attributed to several key factors, including its innovative business model, as detailed below. However, the 5 key factors are considered to be:

(1) Prime locations for all of its shops, and in some city centres CeeCee has seized the opportunity to use historic buildings in key shopping areas.

(2) Spacious shops which use sophisticated architectural details and designs to make shops appealing to customers to browse and to provide a comfortable environment in which to shop.

(3) Carefully designed shop window displays which are changed at least once each week, allowing the latest clothing designs to be "show cased" to prospective customers.

(4) Careful and visually appealing layout of clothing displays, so as to attract customers to choose coordinating clothes and accessories and to maximise sales revenue.

(5) Excellent customer care. CeeCee carefully recruits and trains all of its employees to ensure that the customer is put first. This philosophy is behind all aspects of the work in all of CeeCee's shops. The emphasis is put on providing an uncrowded, pleasant shopping experience where the customer is not approached by shop staff unless asked, but shop staff are constantly available if required. All shop managers encourage team work and the building of long term working relationships to improve the standard of customer care.

Business model and supply chain

The traditional method of high inventories and long lines of products to prevent "stock-outs" where demand exceeds supply has been ignored. In traditional retail sales, a "stock-out" is considered to be the worst scenario. However, CeeCee's business model aims to generate sales in an entirely different way.

CeeCee targets its customers by making its clothes appear to be exclusive by having short production runs of many designs. Indeed in 2009, CeeCee had over 250,000 product lines each year (each size or colour of the same clothing item represents a different product line).

Each shop stocks limited numbers of each design and there is an air of exclusivity, since only a few products of each range are on display. This has resulted in customers making quick decisions to buy what they see, as they know that there is a chance that if they do not buy when they first see the item, they may lose the chance if it is sold out or not available in the size or colour that they would like.

This fast fashion concept relies on 4 key factors:

- Sophisticated IT systems that feedback sales data to Head Office daily
- Close contact, via IT systems, with all of CeeCee's manufacturers
- Fast creation and supply to shops of small numbers of new products
- Swift sale of new inventory items, shortening the product life cycle

CeeCee employs over 180 designers, all of whom are young (with an average age of 27) who create approximately 15,000 new designs each year. CeeCee uses a range of clothing manufacturers, both in Europe and in Asia, who are contracted to work exclusively for CeeCee. They work closely with CeeCee's designers and are linked into CeeCee's IT inventory control systems and have daily updates on what items to produce and what products to discontinue.

CeeCee manages to produce very fast turnarounds for its fashion designs. CeeCee's designers have the systems in place to ensure that the time taken from final design to the product being in the shops has reduced. Currently, with CeeCee's IT support systems, it is able to get some new product designs into its shops within just 10 to 15 days.

This fast fashion system depends on a constant exchange of information throughout every part of CeeCee's supply chain, which includes shop managers, designers, production staff, buyers and external clothing manufacturers. The supply chain also includes complex logistics to enable the correct level of inventory to be delivered to shops at the right time.

CeeCee's logistics run well and are very reliant on good outsourced distributors and its own sophisticated IT systems.

CeeCee's fast fashion model results in its retail stock being constantly changed with new designs. Instead of having 2 or 3 "seasons" of clothes each year, CeeCee has a rolling production of new designs with new clothing designs appearing in shops every 3 weeks on average. This encourages customers to return often to its shops, with the average number of visits to a CeeCee shop being around 17 times each year rather than 4 times a year for traditional fashion retailers. CeeCee's customers know that clothing items will only be available for a short time and this encourages them to make their purchases more quickly, as they know that if they returned a day or two later, the CeeCee shop might no longer have the item in stock.

CeeCee also prices its clothing in a different way from traditional retailers. Instead of using the cost plus principle, CeeCee prices its clothes in a competitive way in each of the countries in which it competes. The price tag on each product displays the price in Euros as well as the local currencies of the countries in which CeeCee operates, where the Euro is not the national currency. However, the price shown in local currencies may not equal the price in Euros based on recent exchange rates, as the prices in local currencies take account of the pricing levels that can be achieved in each country. CeeCee's Sales and Marketing Director, Juliette Lespere, is aware that if the clothes are priced too cheaply, they will "appear" as if the quality is low. Therefore each product is priced based on an element of exclusivity which ensures that the price is competitive but at a premium to that of lower quality competitors.

When CeeCee first launched its fashion range in its first shops in the 1990s, CeeCee used a network of small "sewing cooperatives" in rural areas of Carla Celli's home country. As the number of shops grew and the range of products expanded, the company appointed a range of manufacturing companies to produce its clothing. CeeCee still uses the original sewing co-operatives for some of the quality stitching on its top-of-the-range products.

CeeCee's Operations Director, Paulo Badeo, has set out a number of specific criteria to its potential suppliers. These have ensured that long-term working relationships, that are beneficial to both parties, are being achieved. Obviously CeeCee has chosen its suppliers well, as it has had very few major problems with any of its suppliers and almost all of them are still supplying clothes and furnishings to CeeCee. Furthermore, the clothes are selling well and sales revenue is at an all time high.

The criteria CeeCee uses in the selection of its suppliers are:

- Quality of production
- Ethical workplace practices including safety issues and minimum age for workers
- Agreed code of conduct
- Ability to be flexible to meet the changing needs of CeeCee's customers
- Meets CeeCee's purchase price targets
- Operates in a country that recognises the legal protection of intellectual property rights (IPR's)

CeeCee also audits all of its suppliers on a regular basis to monitor a variety of key production aspects. CeeCee has established a close relationship with all of its suppliers, all of which are sharing in CeeCee's growth and success. At the end of 2009 CeeCee had over 350 suppliers.

The locality of supply has changed over the last decade, due to the low cost of production in Asia and also some Eastern European countries. Initially 100% of CeeCee's production was sourced in Europe. In 2001, CeeCee started sourcing some of its standard products (including woollens and cotton T-shirts) from Asia. By the end of 2009 over 30% of products were manufactured in Asia. The remaining 70% are manufactured in a number of European countries. Around a third of the clothing manufactured in Asia is air freighted to Europe, rather than being shipped by sea, to speed up the time taken from design board to shops.

CeeCee has a large distribution centre in Northern Europe, close to a shipping port, which enables it to move all products, with the minimum of handling, to meet the inventory requirement for each of its shops.

CeeCee's Head Designer, Laura Russo, is keen that all of CeeCee's designs are innovative and at the leading edge of the current trends, without making the clothing too dramatic. The designers all follow the fashion shows of leading fashion designers and use the current trends for their designs. The designers are not allowed to copy another designer's idea, due to intellectual property rights owned by the original fashion house. However, they can change aspects of the garment to make it slightly different, but still appear to be a High Street copy of a "designer label" clothing item. It is a fine line, but Laura Russo always wants CeeCee's designs to have a style of their own rather than a copy of other designers. Indeed, several other High Street retailers have in the past launched their own version of CeeCee's designs.

Inventory analysis

As stated above, CeeCee does not concern itself with "stock-outs" and has a continuing stream of new products arriving at its shops throughout the year. If a product is selling well, then further manufacturing runs may be agreed, depending on what other new replacement products are due at the shops.

CeeCee carries a reasonable level of inventory at each of its shops and also its central distribution centre carries some inventory for its vast numbers of product lines. There are often peaks and troughs in inventory levels due to different factors that affect inventory, such as:

- Seasonal factors – larger numbers of "party" clothes are stocked in the period up to Christmas

- More sales are made in the middle and end of each month, coinciding with the dates that monthly paid customers get paid and have cash available for purchases

- Large deliveries of new clothes arriving at the distribution centre in Europe

The average number of days for inventory was 97 in 2008, a small increase from 90 days in 2007. The latest forecast for 2009, is a decrease to 94 days.

CeeCee has a policy that slow moving product lines are withdrawn from the shop floor within 21 days. These products are rarely put in "end of season" sales. They are sold in bulk at very low prices, sometimes below the cost of production, to distributors who will sell them through other sales channels. These alternative sales channels include selling at market stalls or through smaller clothes shops that sell only "end of lines" from a variety of other High Street clothing retailers.

CeeCee is fortunate that as a result of its short production runs and its ability to closely monitor sales, only about 10% of its volume of purchases is sold off in this way. Many other retailers experience wastage or unsold items of over 20% of their volume of purchases.

CeeCee's integrated inventory system (see below) has enabled management to develop and closely monitor its flexible supply chain and this allows the company to maintain greater control over its inventory. Due to the detailed inventory control system, inventory of slow moving items are written down (or written off) on a regular weekly basis, so that inventory is correctly valued at the lower of cost or realisable value.

IT systems

CeeCee has invested in its IT systems to enable the fast fashion model to work. CeeCee employs its own IT staff but it also outsources some specialised design and update work to a leading global IT solutions specialist company. This enables CeeCee to take advantage of continuing enhancements in retail and inventory management systems.

Its integrated inventory, production and logistics system, known as CCIPL, has had to be continuously improved and enhanced to meet the changing number of shops, suppliers and numbers of product lines. It had recently undergone a large upgrade at a cost of over €40 million to enable all shop managers to be able to review sales data and amend orders using a handheld PDA (Personal Digital Assistant).

At the end of 2009, CeeCee invested over €10 million in the launch of its website to offer online shopping to its customers. The newly launched website is clear and easy for customers to use and allows customers to view inventory levels. It also enables customers to zoom in closely on all angles of each product, thereby allowing them to get as "close" to the product as online shopping allows.

CeeCee's finance systems, CCF, interface directly with the CCIPL system. The CCIPL system feeds sales data, cost of sales data, inventory and many other costs directly into the CCF system enabling the production of monthly management accounts and annual statutory accounts. The system also has the ability to generate weekly and daily sales revenue and margin information for management to monitor actual against plans.

The management team and all executive Directors have access to an executive information system, called CCIS, which highlights key variances from agreed budgets and plans. This system identifies where sales revenue differs (either higher or lower) from plans and generates exception reports on margins or fast-selling production lines. The CCIS allows the management team to drill down to identify what is happening at each shop, or by country or product line or product category. This enables the management team and the designers to closely monitor sales data within 1 working day and to compare data to plans and to take action where a new product appears to be successful, or unsuccessful, in the shops.

CeeCee's competitors

CeeCee is operating in a very competitive market. Furthermore, in the current economic environment, CeeCee is trying hard to retain its customers, some of which are now making purchases from "value" retailers who are not direct competitors.

CeeCee has shops in key locations in High Streets and shopping centres in cities across 18 countries in Europe. All fashion retailers have had to react to increased competition and the effect the economic situation has had on customers' spending.

A summary of key statistics for CeeCee and for some of its many competitors is shown below:

All figures for year ending 2008	CeeCee	Competitor 1	Competitor 2	Competitor 3
Sales revenue €m				
(excluding sales tax)	2,700	9,400	3,700	2,500
Gross margin %	60.1	56.2	59.0	55.7
Number of shops (end year)	610	3,850	900	600
Number of countries	18	75	35	20
Sales area – end year				
(square metres)	632,000	2,140,000	850,000	650,000

[handwritten left margin: €4m per shop.]

[handwritten: €4 per m²]

Financial results and business plan

CeeCee is a highly profitable business with an operating profit margin, before finance costs and tax, of 22.8% for the year ended 31 December 2008 (based on operating profit of €616 million).

As noted above, all sales revenue figures exclude any sales tax (such as VAT) and gross margins are stated after the purchase cost of the manufactured products only.

Extracts from CeeCee's Statement of Comprehensive Income, Statement of Financial Position and Statement of Changes in Equity are shown in **Appendix 3**.

CeeCee's Finance Director, Diane Innes, is pleased that the latest full year forecast for 2009 is not as bad as was first feared, although it was lower than originally planned. The full year forecast for the year ended 31 December 2009 generated an operating profit (before finance costs and tax) of €634 million.

The accounts for the year ended 31 December 2009 have not been finalised, or audited, yet. However, Dianne Innes is confident that the actual accounts will reflect the results shown in this latest full year forecast for 2009.

[handwritten: Op. Profit | Dec 2008 €616 m   Dec 2009 €634m]

The latest 5 year plan has been prepared and was approved by the CeeCee Board at the end of November 2009. It includes sales from online shopping as well as the roll out of new shop openings, with 800 CeeCee shops in operation by the end of 2014. These new shop openings include expansion outside of Europe. Sales revenue is planned to rise from current levels of nearly €3 billion to over €5.1 billion by 2014.

CeeCee currently has 2 loans, totalling €300 million, with a total of €32 million payable in finance costs each year on these loans. One of the loans is for €200 million, at 12% interest per year, and it is repayable in October 2014. It is planned that a new loan will be taken out in 2014 to cover the repayment of this loan and to generate funds required to meet the agreed expansion plans. The second loan is for €100 million, at 8% interest per year, is due for repayment in July 2016.

Extracts for CeeCee's 5 year plan, together with the latest forecast for 2009, is shown in **Appendix 4**. All financial figures shown in the plan are based on 2009 prices.

Trading conditions in the last 12 months

CeeCee, as well as many other retailers, experienced exceptionally difficult trading conditions at the end of 2008 and during 2009 due to the world recession. The start of 2009 was particularly difficult with low numbers of customers at all of its shops across Europe. Some countries fared better than others, although the number of people going shopping and making purchases fell considerably. Some shopping centre statistics stated that the footfall (defined as the number of people visiting a shopping centre) was down over 40% from previous comparable periods.

CeeCee's like for like sales (based on same selling space) during 2009 were down 2%. Some other clothing retailers ceased trading, whilst others experienced sales revenue falling by 20% or more. Overall, Carla Celli considered that CeeCee had survived this particularly difficult trading period rather well. CeeCee only opened 20 new shops during 2009, compared to the original plan of 40, and the additional shops added 5.1% to the total sales area for all CeeCee shops at the end of 2009, to a new high of 664,000 square metres.

2009 was an unusual year for sales of different product lines. Sales of suits and white shirts, for men and ladies, increased substantially. These products replaced previously high sales volumes of "party" clothing, as more young professionals purchased smart clothes for work rather than for social occasions. However, there was a large inventory write down for clothing ranges that had not sold as expected and most of these clothes were sold at below cost price. Children's clothing stayed more or less at the same volume as 2008, and home furnishings were down by 10%. However, as the home furnishings products have a longer "selling life" (as they do not go "out of fashion" as quickly), there were fewer inventory write downs on the home furnishings products. Overall, despite inventory write downs, the forecast operating profit margin remained at 22.8%.

CeeCee reduced the number of employees at some shops in the early part of 2009, with fewer part-time employees. CeeCee, as a responsible employer, did not make any full-time employees redundant at all, but there were some full-time positions that were not filled when an employee left the company.

At the end of 2009, CeeCee had just over 44,000 employees. However, the majority of these employees work part-time, with an average of only 12 hours worked each week. The number of full-time equivalent (FTE) posts was 12,880 at the end of December 2009.

Marketing

Juliette Lespere is CeeCee's Director of Sales and Marketing and she joined the company in 2008. She has been trying to introduce a number of changes to the way in which CeeCee markets itself and has been fighting for a larger marketing budget. So far she has been unsuccessful as Carla Celli considers that the CeeCee designs and the shops are the group's greatest assets and that money spent on marketing is not necessary.

With the difficult trading conditions in 2009, Juliette Lespere was under pressure to deliver sales revenue as close to the original planned level as possible. A number of new marketing initiatives were trialled, and some were more successful than others. She considered that the company did well with sales only down 2% from 2008 on a like for like basis.

CeeCee has a marketing budget of 0.5% of sales revenue, which in 2009 was around €14 million. Many other High Street retailers have marketing budgets of 6 or 7 times this amount at approximately 3 to 4% of sales revenue.

Instead of advertising on TV and in fashion magazines, the CeeCee fast fashion business model is based on the shops being the main medium for advertising. By selecting prime locations for its shops and having its new clothing displayed in limited quantities in its shop windows, this entices customers into its shops. Furthermore, market research has shown that CeeCee customers visit its shops more frequently than they might other clothing retailers. In a recent survey, retail customers were asked how many times each year they went shopping for clothes. In respect of the usual High Street retailers, the answer averaged only 4 times per year compared with 17 times each year for CeeCee's customers.

Juliette Lespere wants to have a larger marketing budget so that she can allocate funds to shop managers to run local events to attract customers into their shops and boost sales revenue. She also considers that e-marketing is a tool not used as effectively as it could be. She is working with Roberta Downs, the IT Director, to get automated links to customers who make online purchases, so that this data can be used to ask the customer to complete a short feedback survey and to reward them with discount vouchers against further purchases.

Juliette Lespere is also concerned that a small number of shops (fewer than 10) are not in the best location for those cities. When they were opened, some over 15 years ago, they had a prime site, but now newer shopping centres have opened, and she wants the CeeCee shops moved to a better location. She is working closely with Ruth Giddens, the Head of Property Management, to secure better locations. The other Board members agree that whilst Juliette Lespere has been impatient for change, she has brought a fresh outlook to the company and has an eye for detail that could make CeeCee shops even more successful.

Capital expenditure and shop opening plan

At the end of December 2009, CeeCee had 630 shops open. A summary of shops and relevant key statistics is shown in **Appendix 2**.

In order to maintain flexibility and to grow the chain of CeeCee shops as quickly as possible, all shops are rented. The only premises that CeeCee owns are:

- Head Office building which accommodates all departments, including designers, administration, IT and purchasing.

- Distribution centre – all products that have been procured from Asia arrive at this centre, together with the majority (but not all) of products manufactured in Europe. Where possible, goods are delivered direct to shops rather than moving into, and then out of, the distribution centre.

At the end of 2009, CeeCee's gross value of non-current assets was €2,472 million. This represents the costs of the shop fittings at all 630 shops, the Head Office, the distribution centre, IT equipment and owned vehicles (not delivery lorries as delivery is outsourced). The accumulated depreciation provision at 31 December 2009 was €985 million; resulting in net non-current assets of €1,487 million (at 31 December 2008 net non-current assets were €1,438 million).

CeeCee's policy is to completely refurbish all shops about every 7 years, and sometimes more quickly. Shop fittings are depreciated over 7 years. IT equipment installed in shops (to capture inventory and sales details by product line) as well as all Head Office IT equipment is depreciated over a 4 year life. The fixtures and fittings at CeeCee's owned premises (Head Office and distribution centre) are depreciated over an 8 year life, and the value of the buildings is depreciated over a 50 year life.

The capital expenditure on new shop openings currently runs at around €100 million each year. A further €70 million was spent on shop refurbishments during 2009. As the number of shops increases over the next 5 years, the cost of the rolling refurbishment programme increases to over €162 million during 2014.

The properties are well managed by Ruth Giddens, the Head of Property Management. When a city is selected for CeeCee's expansion, she works hard to find and secure a competitive rental agreement on a suitable shop. She is proud to state that the expansion programme has never been held up by a delay in finding a suitable location for the next CeeCee shop. Furthermore, Ruth Giddens is working closely with other CeeCee Board members to secure better locations in some cities that have opened new shopping centres, to ensure that CeeCee shops are always sited in a position to attract its target customers.

CeeCee's shareholders and relevant financial statistics

CeeCee became a listed company almost 10 years ago and the company has seen strong growth in sales, number of shops and earnings per share (EPS). The company has 100 million shares in issue and the majority are held by institutional shareholders.

The company made a profit (after finance costs and tax) of €416 million in 2008, resulting in EPS of €4.16 per share. The profit for the year ended 31 December 2009 is expected to be €424 million, which is in accordance with the forecast. This equals EPS of €4.24, a growth of only 1.9%. Investors were generally pleased with the forecast performance in 2009, particularly in a difficult trading period.

The Board has indicated that dividends will remain at the same payout rate per share as paid in 2008 and 2009.

CeeCee's share price at 31 December 2009 was €33.70 per share with a market capitalisation of €3.37 billion. Prior to the recession, CeeCee's shares were trading at over €45.00 per share.

Corporate Social Responsibility (CSR)

As would be expected of a listed company such as CeeCee with over 44,000 employees and operating in 18 European countries, it takes its CSR responsibilities seriously.

Jeroen de Joost, CeeCee's Head of Environmental Impact is responsible for all aspects of CeeCee's CSR reporting. This involves developing initiatives, getting proposals approved, data capture and monitoring and regular reporting on CeeCee's CSR aims.

An extract from the draft CSR report for the year ended 31 December 2009 is included in **Appendix 5**.

CeeCee's corporate aims

The Board of CeeCee is focused on the following priorities, particularly in the current economic environment:

(1) Consistently delivering products that align with our target customers

(2) Improving customer experience and continuing to invest in shops to achieve an improvement in return on invested capital

(3) Managing inventory to protect operating profit margins

(4) Monitoring and improving gross and operating profit margins by improving operational efficiency.

Appendix 1

CeeCee personnel

Non-executive Chairman – Frank Bartoli
Frank Bartoli, aged 48, joined the CeeCee Board just before the company became listed in 2000. He brings a wealth of commercial experience having been in senior positions for a leading global fashion brand for many years. He has enjoyed the challenges of CeeCee's fast growth and has aspirations for expansion of the group outside of Europe.

Chief Executive Officer (CEO) – Carla Celli
Carla Celli is 52 years old. After starting her career as a designer, she moved on to managing retail fashion shops before she launched CeeCee. Her idea for CeeCee was to employ young designers, often recent graduates of Italian fashion schools, to "re-interpret" current catwalk fashions. CeeCee's shops soon became favourites with young professional women who wanted to look fashionable but at a reasonable cost.

Operations Director – Paulo Badeo

Paulo Badeo, who is 53, is an old school friend of Carla Celli's and they had kept in touch while he studied for an engineering degree at a prestigious Italian University and then a masters degree in operations research at a leading US graduate school. Paulo Badeo had worked for around 10 years in the USA for a leading IT company and then subsequently for a specialist IT logistics consultancy company. Paulo Badeo joined CeeCee in 1990 and was instrumental in the roll out of the CeeCee brand across Europe. He also manages all supplier purchases, helped enormously by a very competent procurement manager.

Finance Director – Diane Innes

Diane Innes is 42 years old. Instead of the more 'traditional' career path of working for years in a large Italian conglomerate or audit partnership, Diane Innes had studied economics and accounting in the UK at undergraduate level before qualifying as an accountant for an internationally recognised accounting body. She had been employed in a middle management finance role for 10 years and had established a good reputation for managing change. She joined CeeCee in 1999, just before CeeCee was listed, and has driven through some tough changes and cost management techniques throughout the company.

Head Designer – Laura Russo

Laura Russo is 39 years old and a graduate of a prestigious postgraduate school of fashion based in Italy. After leaving fashion school, she started her own design studio and also opened a shop in Italy. Although her designs had repeatedly received plaudits in the Italian fashion press, she found the administration concerned with managing a shop distracted her from her passion of designing. She joined CeeCee as a designer in 1995, and worked her way up to the role of Head Designer in 2003. She actively recruits talented young designers to ensure that there is a pool of designers who can achieve the vast number of new designs that are required each year to maintain CeeCee as a leader of fashion clothes for both men and women.

Head of Logistics – Jim Bold

Jim Bold is a 52 year old engineering graduate but has worked in logistics roles all over the world. He joined CeeCee in 2002 and has been instrumental in improving the time taken to get new designs from the design board to the finished clothing item in over 600 shops across Europe.

Human Resources Director – Alan Howard

Alan Howard is 48 years old and has held a senior position at a leading HR consultancy company. He wanted a challenge, and after working closely with CeeCee in a consultancy role, joined the company around 10 years ago. He has seen the number of employees rise from 2,000 to the current level of over 40,000. Many shop based employees work part-time, and in total, including Head Office, there were over 44,000 employees, equivalent to 12,880 full-time equivalent (FTE) posts at the end of 2009.

IT Director – Roberta Downs

Roberta Downs is 38 years old with considerable experience working for major IT consultancy firms. She is a very accomplished manager and had a reputation for meeting both deadlines and clients' expectations. Her friends were surprised when she left the "big IT league" to join CeeCee. She argued that she needed the challenge of something new rather than working on huge IT projects, and wanted to become part of a new wave of IT professionals working at the cutting edge of the fashion industry, although she did mention in confidence to a close friend that she only intended to stay at CeeCee for a maximum of 5 years to gain experience, before setting up her own specialist fashion IT consultancy.

Sales and Marketing Director – Juliette Lespere

Juliette Lespere is a 35 year old graduate with an MBA from a world class USA based business school. During her MBA studies, she discovered a passion for marketing and then she worked briefly as a marketing manager for two USA based Internet start up companies. Then she worked for a fashion house in the USA, which sparked her interest in the challenges of fast fashion. She joined CeeCee in 2008 after the Sales and Marketing Director left for a rival retailing company.

Head of Property Management – Ruth Giddens

Ruth Giddens is 58 years old. She has worked in property management all of her career, latterly for an international property developer. She wanted a more challenging role and brought a wealth of experience to CeeCee when she joined in 2005.

Head of Environmental Impact – Jeroen de Joost

Jeroen de Joost is 48 years old and worked for a global oil company for the last 22 years. He had progressed through the ranks of the organisation moving between jobs in general management before finally settling in the corporate social responsibility (CSR) department as a junior manager. After more than 22 years with the company, a sustained period of low commodity oil prices resulted in a number of redundancies in middle management and he was made redundant. He was pleased to join CeeCee which takes its CSR responsibilities seriously.

Non-executive directors

CeeCee has 6 non-executive directors on the Board.

Appendix 2 – Summary of CeeCee's shops and relevant key statistics

	Y/E 31 December 2007 Actual	Y/E 31 December 2008 Actual	Y/E 31 December 2009 Latest full year forecast
Number of shops:			
Start of year			
Large	60	80	100
Medium	164	190	210
Small	300	300	300
Total	524	570	610
New shop openings			
Large	20	20	10
Medium	26	20	10
Small	0	0	0
Total	46	40	20
End of year			
Large	80	100	110
Medium	190	210	220
Small	300	300	300
Total	570	610	630
Average for the year			
Large	70	90	105
Medium	177	200	215
Small	300	300	300
Total	547	590	620
Total sales area (all shops) (square metres)			
– end year	568,000	632,000	664,000
– average for the year	532,400	600,000	648,000
Average sales area (square metres)	973	1,017	1,045
Average sales revenue per square metre €	4,429	4,500	4,292

Average gross margin %	59.8%	60.1%	59.1%
Operating profit €m (before finance costs and tax)	534	616	634
Average operating profit %	22.6%	22.8%	22.8%

Appendix 3 – Extracts from CeeCee's accounts:

Statement of Comprehensive Income	Year ended 31 December 2008	Year ended 31 December 2007
	€ million	€ million
Sales revenue	2,700	2,358
Operating costs	2,084	1,824
Operating profit	616	534
Finance costs (net)	22	26
Tax expenses (effective tax rate is 30%)	178	152
Profit for the period	416	356

Statement of Financial Position	Year ended 31 December 2008		Year ended 31 December 2007	
	€ million	€ million	€ million	€ million
Non-current assets (net)				
Current assets		1,438		1,363
Trade receivables	24		20	
Inventory	286		234	
Cash and cash equivalents	313		174	
		623		428
Total assets		2,061		1,791
Equity and liabilities				
Equity				
Share capital		50		50
Share premium		40		40
Retained earnings		1,038		830
		1,128		920
Non-current liabilities		300		300

Current liabilities

Trade payables	455	419
Tax payable	178	152
	633	571
Total equity and liabilities	**2,061**	**1,791**

Note: Paid in share capital represents 100 million shares of €0.50 each at 31 December 2008.

Statement of Changes in Equity	Share capital	Share premium	Retained earnings	Total
	€ million	€ million	€ million	€ million
Balance at 31 December 2007	50	40	830	920
Profit for the period	–	–	416	416
Dividends paid	–	–	208	208
Balance at 31 December 2008	**50**	**40**	**1,038**	**1,128**

Appendix 4 – 2009 Full year forecast and extracts from 5 year plan

	Latest Full year forecast	Extracts from 5 year plan *Note: All figures shown in the financial data below are based on 2009 prices*				
	2009	2010	2011	2012	2013	2014
Number of shops:						
End year	630	650	672	702	750	800
Average for year	620	640	661	687	726	775
Sales area for all shops (square metres)						
Average for year	648,000	680,000	713,200	752,400	808,800	879,600
	€ million	€ million	€ million	€ million	€ million	€ million
Sales revenue *	2,781	2,985	3,319	3,781	4,390	5,156
Operating profit	634	690	780	896	1,045	1,237

* Sales revenue for 2010 to 2014 includes sales revenue generated by shops and online trading.

Appendix 5 – Extracts from CeeCee's Corporate Social Responsibility (CSR) report for the year ended 31 December 2009

Product Suppliers

In 2009 the company audited and pre-qualified all new suppliers for compliance with the existing Code of Conduct for suppliers, which states that our goods must be produced lawfully, without exploiting the people who made them, in decent working conditions and without damaging the environment.

Actions for 2010: the company will publish a new Guidebook to the Code of Conduct. The number of supplier audits will increase to ensure that all suppliers are visited at least once each year.

Product Quality

In 2009 the system of independent product testing, to ensure that no substances are used that are recognised to pose a threat to human or environmental health, was expanded to ensure that all products are tested annually.

Actions for 2010: the system of independent product testing will be further expanded to test all new products before they are sold.

The range of Fair trade products and organic cotton products will be expanded.

Suppliers' employees

In 2009 a number of studies and pilot projects explored the extent to which suppliers paid workers a "living wage." These showed that the suppliers concerned paid more than "neighbouring" companies supplying other customers and appeared to pay more than any legal minimum wage in force locally. These studies considered all payments made, including overtime.

Actions for 2010: studies are planned to enable CeeCee to assess further what a "living wage" is. Studies are also planned to understand some of the potential problems CeeCee's suppliers have, in respect of the suppliers' employment of migrant workers.

Energy efficiency

In 2009 a decision was taken that every major shop refurbishment would include re-wiring work to isolate essential and non-essential lighting during non-trading hours. Changing from high energy lighting to energy efficient alternatives has continued during the year.

Actions for 2010: it is planned to finish the installation of energy efficient lighting at all shops and at Head Office. A new project will commence to install smart meters to minimise waste of electricity.

Transport

In 2009 our road transport partners delivering clothing and home furnishing products to shops continued to reduce emissions per delivery. They achieved this by using more efficient scheduling of deliveries and by replacing vehicles on a three year cycle to keep up to date with the latest fuel efficiency technology.

Actions for 2010: a new vehicle tracking system will be introduced to monitor mileage and to reduce "miles per product".

Packaging, recycling and waste

In 2009 all shops made great efforts to recycle waste. Some 85% of waste in shops is polythene and cardboard, and virtually 100% of this is collected and recycled.

Actions for 2010: a number of schemes will be initiated to recycle clothes hangers.

The decision has been taken to reduce the size and weight of plastic carrier bags. The new bags will be phased in as existing contracts for the supply of the current carrier bag come up for renewal.

A CeeCee branded organic cotton carrier bag will be launched at a low price, so that all customers can re-use the bag that they purchased CeeCee clothing in.

Product packaging standards were reviewed in 2009 and it is planned to further reduce the amount of packaging by eliminating the use of tissue paper and also to use thinner polythene.

Health and Safety

In 2009 new procedures were introduced for training new staff in safe working procedures.

Actions for 2010: these procedures will be reviewed and rolled out to all shops.

All staff will be offered first aid courses.

Workplace diversity

In 2009 the company reviewed and reworded a policy statement that demonstrated that the company is fully committed to the elimination of unlawful and unfair discrimination in recruitment and employment.

Actions for 2010: independent auditors will conduct a review of practices in a range of shops and the extent to which practice is consistent with group policy.

SWOT Analysis

Strengths

Weaknesses

Opps

Threats

How to analyse the pre-seen material and prepare for the exam

Chapter learning objectives

By the end of this chapter you will:

- Understand the importance of the familiarisation process and how you will use your familiarisation in the exam.

- Be aware of an approach to assist with the familiarisation process.

- Appreciate the key role that technical models have in helping you analyse the pre-seen information.

- Understand the importance of real-world awareness and industry research.

- Have considered how ethics may impact on your pre-seen analysis.

- Understand the need to identify the factors that will influence the prioritisation of issues in the exam.

1 The importance of familiarisation

The pre-seen material is released at least six weeks before you sit the exam and one of your first tasks will be to analyse the context within which the case is set. Although the issues you'll report on in the exam will be driven by the unseen material, you will only be able to assess the impact of each event on the organisation if you have a sufficient depth of knowledge and awareness on both the organisation and the industry in which it operates.

The purpose of the pre-seen material is to allow you to gain that knowledge and awareness. Remember, you will be acting in the position of a management accountant who works for the organisation. It will therefore be expected that you will have the same level of familiarisation as someone fulfilling that role.

It is extremely important that you study the pre-seen material thoroughly before you go into the examination. There are two main reasons for this:

- It will save time in the examination itself if you are already familiar with the pre-seen material.

- It enables you to develop a view of the situation facing the organisation in the case study, and in particular its strategic and financial position and prospects.

 You will not be able to answer the examination question itself from the pre-seen material alone; the unseen material given to you in the examination will present significant new information that will alter the situation substantially. Even so, a major step towards success in the examination is a careful study, exploration and understanding of the pre-seen material.

Each pre-seen material is different but as a general rule, you can expect the following:

- Industry background
- History of the business
- Key personnel
- Current business / industry issues
- Financial Statements

Each of these areas will need reviewing in detail. You should question what each piece of information tells you, and why the examiner may have given you it. You will also need to gain some real world awareness by studying the industry in which the case is set. Only after doing all of this will you have fully analysed the context within which the case is set.

2 The pre-seen approach

In Chapter 1 we introduced the pre-seen approach; a series of steps which, if followed, will familiarise you with the pre-seen material and the industry in which the organisation operates.

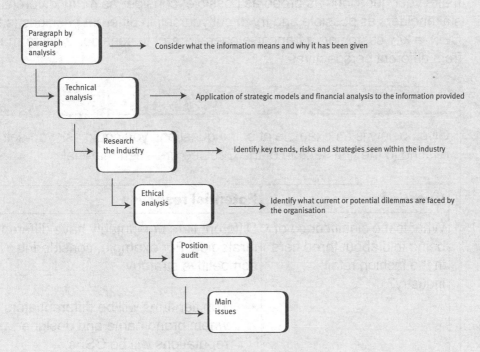

Whilst it is important that you have an organised approach to the analysis, it would be wrong to suggest that there is a unique method or technique to performing such analysis. What works for one person might not work for another. Part of the time you're investing now, learning about the case study exam and what makes it different from all other exams, should be spent finding a way that works for you. The rest of this chapter will focus on the different stages of the pre-seen approach. We'll look specifically at the objective of each stage and consider some of the techniques you can use to achieve that objective.

3 Stage 1 – Paragraph-by-paragraph analysis

The purpose of this initial stage is to lay a foundation for further analysis. It's more about asking questions than finding solutions.

Before you do anything else, you should **read the pre-seen material from beginning to end without making any notes,** simply to familiarise yourself with the scenario.

Read the material again, as many times as you think necessary, without making notes. You can do this over a period of several days, if you wish. When you think you are reasonably familiar with the situation described by the material, you should start to make notes.

By making notes, you will become more familiar with the detail of the scenario. Try to make notes on each paragraph (or each group of short paragraphs) in the pre-seen material. Think about what the paragraph is telling you, and consider why this information might be of interest or relevance. Ask yourself "why might the examiner have told me this?". Try to make your questions as broad as possible; consider as many different stakeholders as possible and try to put yourself in different positions (say the CEO, a key customer, a franchise operator etc) to consider the information from different perspectives.

Illustration 1 – Fashion retail: an industry overview

Given below is an example of some questions you could ask yourself relating to the first section of the CeeCee pre-seen material.

Question	Potential response
What is the significance of being told about three tiers in the fashion retail industry?	Different tiers presumably have different strategies. For example, considering competitive strategy: • Top tier firms will be differentiators for whom brand name and designer reputations will be CSFs. • Value retailers will be cost-leaders for whom cost is critical. • Middle tier operators will be in danger of becoming "stuck in the middle" and so must ensure they have a sustainable competitive advantage. One aspect of the case may involve considering **which** tier CeeCee will be competing against. Finally you may need to evaluate CeeCee moving into a different tier.

What have been the main reasons why supermarkets, such as Asda and Tesco in the UK, have successfully entered the clothing market?	Supermarkets have been able to bypass barriers to entry due to having the following: • Established distribution and retail chain. • Purchasing power. • Brand strength – value for money. • Huge number of existing customers. • Customer convenience.
List the factors customers consider when choosing whether to buy a garment.	• Price – half of shoppers look first at the price. • Brand name / designer's name / reputation. • How fashionable the garment is. • Quality – fabrics, finish, design, ease of care, other features such as waterproofness for a coat. • The shopping "social and product experience" – displays, changing rooms, attentiveness of staff, etc. • After sales service e.g. being able to take it back.

Evaluate online fashion retailing.	Pros
	• Should have lower overheads which could be reflected in lower prices.
	• Makes comparisons easier for customers.
	• Easier for customers to shop from home.
	• Can have more stock than can be held in a typical store, thus offering greater choice.
	• May actually be targeting different customers – half of customers do **not** feel it is essential to try garments on.
	• Unlike selling via catalogue, you don't need to maintain levels of stock for all product lines for the whole season. When stock runs out, you just update the website and change the product lines.
	Cons
	• Customers cannot try garments on to check sizing and how they look / feel - half of customers feel this is necessary.
	• Customers miss out on the fun of the shopping experience.
	• Postage costs.
	• Extra hassle returning garments.
	In summary the most successful online retailers may be those firms who already have a high street presence, or those who sell only branded goods.

What are the advantages and disadvantages of having a shorter lead time?	Pros • Can be more responsive to market trends, thus reducing the risk of "fashion miss". This should result in less stock that has to be sold off at large discounts. • Can change lines more frequently encouraging customers to keep coming back to see what is new. Cons • May result in smaller production runs and hence a loss of economies of scale. • If competitors have correctly anticipated customer wants, then they will get a strong foothold in the market before the short lead time operator can respond.

Techniques for more effective note taking

 When you're making notes, try to be as creative as possible. Psychologists tell us that using conventional linear notes on their own use only a small part of our mental capacity. They are hard to remember and prevent us from drawing connections between topics. This is because they seek to classify things under hierarchical headings.

Here are some techniques that candidates find useful. See which ones work for you as you practise on the past cases in this text.

Spider diagrams

Spider diagrams (or clustering diagrams) are a quick graphic way of summarising connections between subjects.

Illustration 2 – Spider diagrams

Towards the end of the section on CeeCee's overview and history, you are told about the 5 key factors in CeeCee's success. An example of a spider diagram where you've explored each of these in more detail is given below.

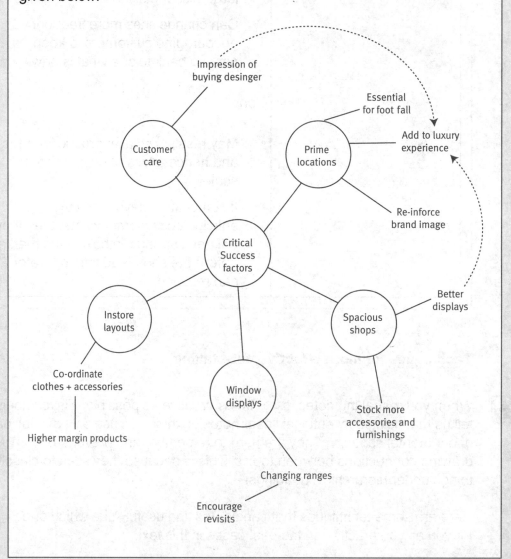

You cannot put much detail into a spider diagram, just a few key words. However, it does help you to 'visualise' the information in the case material.

Note also the attempt to connect across the different legs of the diagram, in this case between the customer care and the spacious shops back to customers having a 'luxury' experience.

You must expect to update your spider diagram as you go along and to redraft it when it starts to get too messy. It is all part of the learning process.

Candidates usually draw several of these diagrams exploring different aspects of the case. Each one can be drawn on a single piece of A4 paper.

Timelines

Timelines are valuable to make sense of the sequence of events in the pre-seen and to understand where the company in the case study presently stands.

The T4 case study exam takes place in real time, so you need to be clear how long is likely to elapse between the data in the pre-seen and the actual exam. This is the time period during which the issues facing the company or strategic alternatives can be incorporated in to the unseen material. The case writer is not trying to trick you or spring something entirely unexpected on you, but you need to be aware of the timeframe and the changes that have already occurred in the company's history, so that you can offer realistic advice for the company's future.

Given below is an illustration of a timeline for the CeeCee case study.

Illustration 3 – Timelines

Key Dates – time line

1989 - Carla Celli founded CeeCee
1990 - (say January) - Met Paulo Badeo
1990 - (say June) - Paulo Badeo joins the board
1991 - 5 shops opened
1998/9 - CeeCee was a favourite with European "young professional" shoppers.
2000 - CeeCee was listed on a major European stock exchange
2000 - CeeCee had 280 shops across Europe
2001 - CeeCee started sourcing from Asia
2008 - CeeCee had 610 shops across 18 European countries
2008 - Juliette Lespere is CeeCee's Director of Sales and Marketing joins
2009 - (say December) CeeCee had 630 shops
2009 - had over 250,000 product lines each year
2009 - (say December) CeeCee had over 350 suppliers
2009 - (say December) Over 30% of products were manufactured in Asia
2009 - (say December) CeeCee invested over €10 million in the launch of its website
2014 - October, €200 million loan repayable
2016 - July, €100 million loan repayable

Organisation charts

Preparing an organisation chart will familiarise you with the roles and the overlaps, and also help you to identify gaps or ambiguities in roles, as well as helping you to remember the names and roles of the key people in the case. In some cases this will be provided for you; where it isn't, you may want to draw one out.

Post-it-notes

Post-it-notes can be used to stick onto each page of the pre-seen material and to jot key points on. Additionally, you may want to keep a post-it-note for each person, and as you work through the pre-seen material.

 You could even stick the notes on your desk, a notice board or wall so that you can keep glancing at them to remember who's who in the case and what issues and problems have been identified.

You could also jot down your ideas for alternative strategies that the company could take, to prepare you for exam day.

Colours

 Colours help you remember things you may want to draw upon in the exam room. You could write down all your financial calculations and observations in green whilst having red for organisational and blue for strategic. Some candidates use different colour highlighter pens to emphasise different aspects of the pre-seen material perhaps using the same colour coding suggestion.

Additionally, sometimes making notes in different colours helps you to remember key facts and some of the preparation that you have done using the pre-seen material.

Use whatever colours work for you – but it does help to make notes on both the pre-seen material and the research you do. DO NOT just read the material – you must take notes (in whatever format) and if colours help you to understand and link your research together then use colours.

4 Stage 2 – Technical analysis

Now you're reasonably familiar with the material it's time to carry out some technical analysis to help you identify and understand the issues facing the company.

A starting point

A good starting point is to **revise any 'technical' topics that might be relevant.** The pre-seen material might make a reference to a particular 'technical' issue, such as the balanced scorecard approach, corporate governance requirements, internal controls, the use of derivative instruments, company valuations, and so on. If you have forgotten about any topic that might be relevant, go back to your previous study materials and revise it.

Chapter 4 of this text goes over some of the more commonly used technical models, all of which were covered within your strategic level studies.

Consider the strategic planning process

You'll recall from your Enterprise Strategy studies, the strategic planning process as outlined below.

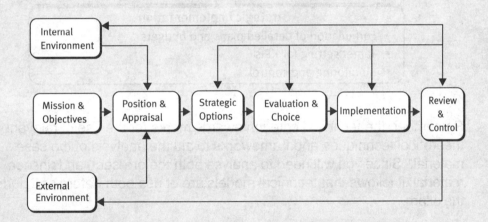

Johnson, Scholes and Whittington took the above stages and grouped them into three main areas (as we saw in Chapter 1):

> **Strategic analysis**
> - External analysis to identify opportunities and threats
> - Internal analysis to identify strengths and weaknesses
> - Stakeholder analysis to identify key objectives and to assess power and interest of different groups
> - Gap analysis to identify the difference between desired and expected performance.

> **Strategic choice**
> - Strategies are required to 'close the gap'
> - Competitive strategy – for each business unit
> - Directions for growth – which markets/products should be invested in
> - Whether expansion should be achieved by organic growth, acquisition or some form of joint arrangement.

> **Strategic implementation**
> - Formulation of detailed plans and budgets
> - Target setting for KPIs
> - Monitoring and control.

Remember, the technical criterion awards marks for the use of relevant theoretical techniques and frameworks to aid the analysis of the case material. Since you will need to analyse both the pre-seen and unseen material, it follows that technical models are of use both before and during the exam.

When analysing the pre-seen material, you need to work through the different technical models, with an emphasis on strategic analysis. To a lesser extent, you may consider strategic choice and implementation, although given you don't know the requirements yet, much of this will be hypothetical. However, when you are in the exam, the technical models you choose to use will be a mixture of those focusing on analysis and those focusing on choice and implementation.

 Before the exam, you should look to cover a wide range of technical models (any that seem relevant) to help familiarise yourself with the material and to allow you to analyse the current strategic and financial position and prospects of the organisation. You can use any techniques for analysis with which you are familiar.

As a minimum you should work through the following models:

- PEST(EL) analysis
- Porter's Five Forces model analysis
- SWOT analysis (see step 5 of the pre-seen approach below)
- Mendelow's Matrix
- Identifying critical success factors (together with key performance indicators where appropriate)
- Identifying, assessing and managing risks

Chapter 4 will give you an opportunity to refresh your memory on these key models and to apply them to the CeeCee pre-seen material.

Do some financial analysis

You will almost certainly be given some figures in the pre-seen material. These might relate to the company's profits or losses, or product profitability. There might be income statements and financial position statements for previous years, future business plans, cash flow statements, capital expenditure plans, EPS and share price information and so on.

A key part of stage 2 will be to perform some simple financial analysis, such as financial ratio calculations or a cash flow analysis. These might give you a picture of changes in profitability, liquidity, working capital management, returns on capital, financial structure or cash flows over time, and will help ensure you have a rounded picture of the organisation's current position.

Exercise 1 – Basic financial analysis

Complete the following table and then comment on your findings.

Ratio:	2008	2007
Revenue growth		
Growth in operating profit		
Operating margin		
Net margin		
Capital employed (€m)		
ROCE		
Current ratio		
Quick ratio		
Receivables days		
Cost of sales		
Payables days		

Inventory days		
Length of operating cycle		
Gearing using book values (debt/equity)		
Dividend payout ratio		

If a cash flow statement is not provided, it is always worth preparing a summary of cash flows. You may have to make some assumptions if the detailed information isn't provided but even with these, these is great value in appreciating where the money has come from, and where it is being spent.

Exercise 2 – Cash flows

Prepare a cash flow statement for CeeCee by completing the following table. (**Note:** You will need to make some assumptions in relation to depreciation and expenditure on non-current assets). Comment on your results.

	€m
Operating profit	**616**
Add: depreciation	
Less: increase in inventories	
Less: increase in receivables	
Add: increase in trade payables	
Net cash flow from operations	
Net finance costs paid	
Tax paid	
Purchase of tangible non-current assets	
Dividends paid	
Cash inflow / (outflow) before financing	
Equity raised	
Long-term debt raised	
Loans repaid	
Increase (decrease) in cash and cash equivalents	

In some cases you may be presented with additional numerical information that can be analysed in order to reveal further insights. An example in the CeeCee case is the information given in appendix 4. Given your role as a management accountant, such information is likely to be crucial to the issues you are dealing with.

Exercise 3 – Additional numerical analysis

Complete the following table and comment on your results.

	2009	2010	2011	2012	2013	2014
Average revenue per sq. metre (€)						
Operating margin						
Average revenue per shop (€000)						
Average sales area per shop (sqm)						
Average operating profit per sq. metre (€)						

---

5 Stage 3 – Research the industry

Why you need to conduct industry research

Diversity marks are awarded for the display of knowledge of relevant real life situations within the same or similar context as that in which the case is set, or for the display of knowledge of real life commercial or organisation issues relevant to the situation in the case.

However, it is a mistake to think that any work you perform researching the industry will only gain you diversity marks within the exam. Remember, part of your preparatory work is to analyse the context within which the case is set. A full analysis is not possible without an understanding of the industry.

From this analysis, you will be better able to prioritise the key issues, identify realistic alternative solutions and present recommendations that are both commercial and practical.

An understanding of the industry in which the case is set is therefore crucial to success in this exam.

The pre-seen material usually contains a good summary of relevant information about the industry. This can be relied on as accurate at the time it is published.

You should further research the industry setting for the case you are working on so that you can demonstrate a sound understanding of the problems (and opportunities) facing companies in this industry. It will also help you to understand the pre-seen material and any industry-specific information given in the case. Hopefully, it will also stop you from making unrealistic comments in your answer on the day of the exam.

Finally, there will be a strong linkage between your research of the industry and the technical analysis you will be carrying out. Industry research will allow you to add further comments in terms of:

- identifying industry lifecycle stage and the factors driving it;

- identifying whether any of the five forces are strong or strengthening and the factors causing this;

- considering the competitive strategies being followed by companies operating in the real world and how they are achieved (e.g. special technologies, use of brands) and whether they could be adopted by the company in the pre-seen;

- identifying real-world issues against the PEST framework (this may involve some basic research into the laws and technologies of the industry);

- considering the impact of globalisation on the future of the industry and on the firm in the pre-seen.

But don't think that your preparation should stop at just looking at the industry. A wider understanding of the way business is conducted and the influence of the economic and political environments on business is just as important. For example, an additional factor to consider is the state of the investment markets, which will affect costs of capital and share prices.

 One of the best ways to achieve this wider appreciation is to regularly read the business pages of a good national newspaper.

How to conduct industry research

One of the big problems with conducting industry research is knowing where to stop. In today's technology driven society, a wealth of information is available at your fingertips so perhaps the most important aspect when performing research is to focus on reliable sources.

In order to help direct your research, think about the following sources of information:

Personal networks

Some candidates have been lucky enough to find themselves facing a set of pre-seen material describing the industry they work in. In this situation, they have plenty of colleagues they can talk to about.

Alternatively, and depending on the industry in the Case Study, it is possible that you know someone in the business from whom you can get information. Likely contacts include:

- people who work in the industry or who have worked in it;

- family members or their friends;

- contacts at work who have dealings with the industry in the case;

- other people sitting the case study exam, either via your tuition provider or using online forums, such as CIMAsphere.

Discussing the case and your analysis of the situation of the business with an expert will help you to test out your understanding of what is important. Some tuition providers engage an expert on the industry to deliver presentations to their students followed by organised question and answer sessions to enable a better understanding to be obtained.

Visiting similar firms

Again, this depends on the accessibility of the industry. For example, when studying for the CeeCee Fashion Retail case it was possible for students in many parts of the world to visit a range of high street fashion retailers, see how they operate and see the level of customer service provided, an excellent way in which to gain an idea of what they are doing right and what areas could be improved for you as a customer.

In other situations, this might not be possible. Few of us will have had the pleasure of a visit to the set of a TV production, although what better excuse to convince someone to give you a tour around for a day!

Trade media and news media

A journalist is a paid professional who searches out and presents information about an industry. If you can find a trade journal for the industry in the case, it will save you a lot of searching for yourself. It is also easier than a web page or conversation to cite as a source in your final report.

Trade journals can be located in four ways:

- Visit a good newsagent. The difficulty here is that only very large industries such as accounting, financial advising, computing, music and construction provide enough customers for a newsagent to consider stocking the magazine.

- Visit a business library. Most universities and better colleges will permit you a reader's ticket to consult their journals on a read-only basis. However, such libraries will not let you borrow journals and may place restrictions on photocopying them. Good librarians will be able to locate relevant journals for you too.

- Ask someone who works in the industry for the name of the journals for the industry.

- Use the Internet. Many trade journals now have websites and, in many cases, the journals can be downloaded as PDFs. Naturally there will be restrictions on logging in if you have not paid, but there is a surprising amount of free media available. The best approach is to go to a search engine and type in a search inquiry such as: 'trade magazine for [name of industry} industry' or 'articles on {name of industry or real-world firm]'. Again, some tuition providers actually arrange for their students to have access to a leading trade website as part of the resources they offer to students.

News media is more general although some quality business newspapers may carry special supplements on particular industries from time to time.

 It is also very important to spend time reading the financial pages of any good newspaper, not necessarily the Financial Times. It is relevant to understand what is happening in the real world with acquisitions, mergers, downsizing, boardroom conflicts, etc. The more widely that you read the financial press, the more it will help you to understand and fully appreciate all of the many complex factors that affect companies and the selection and implementation of their strategies.

It is also recommended that you should keep yourself updated with latest information on exchange rates, interest rates, government policies, the state of the economy, and particularly what is happening in the business sectors concerning mergers and acquisitions. The acquisition of a competitor, or a hostile takeover bid is a very important strategic move. Acquisitions happen everyday in the real world and you can familiarise yourself with how these work by reading the business press.

Obviously, news media is available in hard copy from shops but also most good newspapers have websites that give you the day's stories and also have searchable archives on past stories about the industry or specific firms within it.

Using the Internet

This is the most convenient and commonly used method of researching the industry, but as noted above, try to target the information you're looking for in order to avoid wasting time.

 Generally, you will be looking for the following sorts of information:

- Websites of firms similar to the one(s) in the pre-seen material. This can help you learn about the sorts of products and competitive strategies they follow and may also yield financial information that can be compared with the data in the pre-seen material.

- Trade journals of the industry in the pre-seen. This will provide information on real-world environmental issues facing the business.

- Articles on the industry in journals and newspapers. These will keep you up to date on developments.

- Stock market information on the real firms.

- Financial statements of real firms (often these can be downloaded from companies' websites free of charge).

- Industry reports produced by organisations such as the DTI and the large accountancy firms, which are surprisingly common, and often available for free on the Internet, if you search well.

You should review the accounts and establish:

- typical industry working capital ratios,

- typical ratios of non-current assets to sales,

- margins,

- growth rates.

You should then compare the accounts with the current share price and compare the market capitalisation with the asset value, and review all the normal investment ratios.

You may provide yourself with some 'normal' industry figures as a basis for any comparisons you may wish to make of the unseen material in due course. You should also review all the non-financial information provided, looking in particular for:

- new technological developments, new products;

- the competitive situation.

 If companies can be identified that are in the same or similar industries to the industry in the case, indicating that they are simple companies, not conglomerates, it is possible to gain much information from these websites. It is not helpful, as some candidates and tutors have done, to concentrate on any one single company, however similar you believe that is to the case. The examination team have made it clear that no past T4 case has ever been based exclusively on just one real-world company and hence data will differ from any sets of accounts that you may consider the case is based on. In addition, your answer needs to demonstrate a wide industry awareness, and use of examples from a variety of companies is important to show this.

Company websites of public companies in similar industries can provide the annual report and accounts, any press releases, publicity material and product descriptions, and detailed documentation on such matters as rights issues and share option schemes. Often they contain specially commissioned pieces of market research that you can download. However, it's worth remembering that this research is there to encourage investors to anticipate higher returns in the future and will tend to put an optimistic gloss on events.

 One very efficient way to use the internet for research is to set up Google alerts for the topics you're interested in. This will provide you with daily e-mails containing links to new information on your specified areas.

Professionally produced industry analysis

Those of you attending courses with tuition providers will probably find that your tutorial college produce some information for you on the industry. These can be real time savers and can help give you a good initial background to the industry. However, they should only be taken as a starting point for the research that you do. One common trend is for students to pick up on a particular example used by these colleges, either in their study material or their mock exam solutions, and believe that since the college has used that example, that must be a good one for students to use too. While that might be the case, from the marker's perspective, seeing the same introduction (as an example) as they've seen many other students produce does not give a good first impression, and impressions are important in this exam, since you are aiming to produce a high quality report that demonstrates your overall ability.

6 Stage 4 – Ethical analysis

Ethics and the Case Study Examination

One criterion on which you will be assessed in the Case Study Examination is your ability to advise on or resolve ethical dilemmas. 10 marks in total will relate to ethics, 5 for highlighting and analysing ethical issues, including clearly stating why an issue has an ethical implication, and 5 for giving justified recommendations for the action that should be taken.

Ethical issues could relate to any of the following areas:

*   corporate social responsibility;
*   personal ethical behaviour of individuals in the case;
*   business ethics.

Before the exam, you should take some time to remind yourself of CIMA's Guidelines on ethical conduct. You can download a copy of the Ethical Guidelines from CIMA's website, if you want to read the full text.

The Ethical Guidelines are also included in the syllabus for Paper P3 *Performance Strategy.*

Although these are useful, you must remember that the ethical issues in the exam are not necessarily ethical issues facing the management accountant, but more issues facing the business as a whole. An awareness of general 'corporate ethics' and 'corporate and social responsibility' will therefore be beneficial. More fundamentally, the ethical issues which appear in the unseen will focus on 'doing the right thing' and so the industry research you perform will also help brief you for common issues and they way in which they are typically resolved.

Application to the case study pre-seen

Although you will be presented with new ethical issues to deal with in the unseen information, an understanding of those given in the pre-seen, together with those affecting real life companies in the industry will help to prepare you for the issues that may arise in the exam.

Remember, to score highly in your ethics section you must explain the ethical dimension to the issue as well as provide clear recommendations for the Board.

The illustration below shows the sort of questions you should try to answer at this stage of your preparation.

Illustration 4 – Identification of ethical issues

Question	Potential response
Comment on CeeCee's approach to CSR.	Board has identified CSR aims and a Head of Environmental Impact is in position. However, the CSR report lacks detail and appears to have gaps – e.g. use of child labour, environmental impact of using Asian suppliers for European stores.
Are there any areas of dubious business or personal ethics that can be identified from the pre-seen?	None so far but there may well be in the unseen!

What ethical issues face fashion retailers in the real world?	**Allegations aimed at manufacturing** • Use of child labour. • Excessively long hours. • Underpaid staff. • Sexual and other discrimination. • Choice of fabrics e.g. animal fur. **Allegations re retailing** • Copying designs. • Encouraging waste as customers throw away old clothes to get the latest designs. **Allegations re the fashion industry in general** • Use of size zero models can make customers feel more body conscious and contribute towards anorexia / bulimia, particularly among young girls.

7 Stage 5 – Position audit

Once you've analysed all of the above you're ready to carry out a position audit.

 CIMA defines a position audit as:

Part of the planning process which examines the current state of the entity in respect of:

- resources of tangible and intangible assets and finance,
- products brands and markets,
- operating systems such as production and distribution,
- internal organisation,
- current results,
- returns to stockholders.

What you should be attempting to do is stand-back so you can appreciate the bigger picture of the organisation. Within your SWOT analysis you should look for:

- Threat homing in upon weakness – the potential extinction event.

- Threat on a strength – should be able to defend against it but remember competencies slip.

- Opportunity on a strength – areas they should be able to exploit.

- Opportunity on a weakness - areas where they could exploit in the future if they can change.

In addition to preparing a SWOT analysis, it is useful to prepare a two - three page summary of your analysis. Try not to simply repeat information from the pre-seen but add value by including your thoughts on the analysis you've performed. See Chapter 5 for a summary of the CeeCee exam.

8 Stage 6 – Identifying the main issues

Once you've prepared your summary you are finally able to consider the key issues facing the organisation.

The purpose of this is not to create a ranked list of the issues they need to address; remember the issues you must deal with in the exam could be very different. Your conclusion on the main issues arising from the pre-seen will more be to direct your focus and aid your prioritisation of issues in the exam.

Make sure you are clear about what will drive your prioritisation; what sort of factors should you be on the look out for to help you decide whether an issue is key or not (see Chapter 5 for some thoughts on the CeeCee case).

Once you've got a list of the main issues, give yourself more time to think. Spend some time thinking about the case study, as much as you can. You don't have to be sitting at a desk or table to do this. You can think about the case study when you travel to work or in any spare time that you have for thinking.

- When new ideas come to you, jot them down.

- If you think of a new approach to financial analysis, carry out any calculations you think might be useful.

Remember, all of the above preparatory work enables you to feel as if you really are a management accountant working for this organisation. Without the prep, you're unlikely to be convincing in this role.

Test your understanding answers

Exercise 1 – Basic financial analysis

Ratio	2008	2008 working	2007	2007 Working
Revenue growth	14.5%	2,700/2,358	-	N/A
Growth in operating profit	15.4%	616/534	-	N/A
Operating margin	22.8%	616/2,700	22.6%	534/2,358
Net margin	15.4%	416/2,700	15.1%	356/2,358
Capital employed (€m)	1,428	300+1,128	1,220	300+920
ROCE	43.1%	616/1,428	43.8%	534/1,220
Current ratio	0.98	623/633	0.75	428/571
Quick ratio	0.53	(623 - 286)/633	0.34	(428 - 234)/571
Receivables days	3	365 × 24/2,700	3	365 × 20/2,358
Cost of sales	1,077	2,700 × (100 - 60.1)%	948	2,358 × (100 - 59.8)%
Payables days	154	365 × 455/1,077	161	365 × 419/948
Inventory days	97	365 × 286/1,077	90	365 × 234/948
Length of operating cycle	(54)	3+97-154	(68)	3+90-161
Gearing using book values (debt/equity)	0.27	300/1,128	0.33	300/920
Dividend payout ratio	2	416/208	-	N/A

Comments

Profitability

- The overall performance from 2007 to 2008 is very impressive, especially given the economic downturn at the end of 2008. CeeCee saw revenue growth of 14.5% and operating profit growth of 15.4%.

- Furthermore margins also improved.

- On the other hand, ROCE is down. Given capital employed increased, this is probably due to the time lag between stores opening and the resulting extra revenues and profits materialising.

Liquidity

- At first glance the current and quick ratios appear problematic as they are less than one.

- However, on closer look CeeCee has significant cash reserves and has a negative cash operating cycle – i.e. cash is received before payment needs to be made. This is typical for high street retailers.

- Provided capital investment is financed, there should be few worries over liquidity.

Gearing

- Book gearing is very low. Given the share price is of the order of €33 – €45 and the nominal value is €0.50, gearing measured using market values will be much lower still.

- However, it could be argued that the gearing on the statement of financial position is somewhat misleading, given all shops are held under rental (operating lease) arrangements.

Exercise 2 – Cash flows

	Working	€m
Operating profit		**616**
Add: depreciation (Note 1)	(1438-1363) - 100 - 70	95
Less: increase in inventories	286-234	(52)
Less: increase in receivables	24-20	(4)
Add: increase in trade payables	455-419	36
Net cash flow from operations		**691**
Net finance costs paid (Note 2)		(22)
Tax paid	2007 tax	(152)
Purchase of tangible non-current assets (Note 1)		(170)
Dividends paid		(208)
Cash inflow / (outflow) before financing		**139**
Equity raised		0
Long-term debt raised		0
Loans repaid		0
Increase (decrease) in cash and cash equivalents	313-174	**139**

Note 1

- We are not told the details for disposals of non-current assets, so will assume these to be zero.

- We are told that typical expenditure on new shop openings is €100m p.a.

- We are not given the refurbishments figure for 2008 so have used the 2009 figure of €70m and assumed that the level of expenditure is consistent from year to year.

Note 2

- You could separate this figure out as €32m paid less €10m received (balancing figure to give the €22m in the Income statement).

Comments

- Net cash flow from operating activities is very strong.

- Investment in new non-current assets is a key figure – high growth may be difficult to resource without further financing – see comments on business plan below.

- Net cash flow before dividends = 621-22-152-170= €277m, giving a cash-based dividend cover figure of 277/208 = 1.33. This is less than 2, indicating a higher risk attached to future dividends than the income statement (dividend cover 2) would suggest.

Exercise 3 – Additional numerical analysis

	2009	2010	2011	2012	2013	2014
Average revenue per sq. metre (€)	4,292	4,390	4,654	5,025	5,428	5,862
Operating margin	22.8%	23.1%	23.5%	23.7%	23.8%	24.0%
Average revenue per shop (€000)	4,485	4,664	5,021	5,504	6,047	6,653
Average sales area per shop (sqm)	1,045	1,063	1,079	1,095	1,114	1,135
Average operating profit per sq. metre (€)	978	1,015	1,094	1,191	1,292	1,406

Comments:

- Apart from investment in new shops and the inclusion of online trading in the figures, there is no explanation given as to why it would appear that everything is going to be bigger and better in the future!

- It is difficult to assess predicted store performance with the internet figures included.

- Significant online sales could explain why revenue per square metre is improving as additional sales are made without increases in area being needed. We are told later in the pre-seen that sales in 2009 were down 2% compared to 2008 on a "like for like" basis. Beyond 2010 some of the increase in revenue per square metre could be due to this figure reversing as economic conditions improve.

- Operating margins would also be boosted by online sales as overheads will be lower. An alternative explanation is perhaps CeeCee expects to sell a larger proportion of higher margin products such as accessories.

- The increase in the average area per shop reflects the fact that CeeCee is looking at larger premises to show the full range of products. For example, the average shop size in 2009 was 1,045 sqm but the extra 20 shops add 32,000 sqm in area so must be 1,600 sqm on average. Larger shops may also explain some of the increase in operating margins due to economies of scale.

Application of technical models

Chapter learning objectives

By the end of this chapter you will:

- Be aware of the more commonly used technical models within the case study exam.

- Have revised these models from your previous studies.

- Know how to identify relevant technical models and apply them in the exam to gain marks.

- Have applied some of these models to the CeeCee pre-seen material.

1 A reminder of key models

The aim of this chapter is to provide a detailed review of the most common technical models that can be used and applied within the case study. For each we:

- Provide a reminder of the model / framework.
- Comment on how it is best used to support the analysis of the issues (from both the pre-seen and unseen) and recommended actions in the exam itself.

2 PEST

PEST analysis involves the analysis of environmental influences on a company or an industry, within the four categories: political, economic, social, technological. These are regarded as four categories of environmental influence that might be significant.

Factor	Examples to look for
Political	Government policy affecting the industry or firm
	Stability of government in firm's main countries of operations
	Potential trade wars
	Change of government and possibility of change in taxation or attitudes to industry and the economy
Economic	Whether the economy is wealthy or poor
	Whether the industry is producing goods which are price elastic or inelastic
	Growth rate of the economy and potential for recession
	Level and trends in interest rates and effects of firm's markets and costs of borrowing
	Exchange rates and the risk of a rise or fall in key exchange rates
Social	Trends in buying behaviour
	Demographic changes (location, age of customers)
	Distribution of income between social groups
	Lifestyle changes

Technological	Changes in the technologies of consumption (e.g. buying methods)
	Changes in the technology of production
	Changes in the technology of organisations (e.g. applications of IT to improve efficiency and effectiveness)
	Replacement technologies which could impact on demand for current products

The analysis can be extended if relevant into a PESTEL, adding two further categories of ecological/ethical and legal.

Factor	Examples to look for
Ecological/ethical	Impact of the industry on natural environment: pollution, waste, sustainability issues
	Impact of the firm's activities on the community
Legal	Competition policy
	Regulation of wages and prices
	Regulation of employment (e.g. rules on discrimination)
	Regulatory or government policy on pricing

How to use before the exam

A PEST analysis will be a key tool to help you understand the environment in which the organisation operates and so should definitely be used when familiarising yourself with the pre-seen information. You should start by populating your PEST analysis based on the information in the pre-seen. You can then add to this when you start performing research on the industry.

Exercise 1 – PEST

Using the above headings prepare a PEST analysis for CeeCee based on the pre-seen material.

How to use during the exam

 To score marks for using the PEST model you **_don't_** have to produce the whole model in an appendix. This will waste valuable time and result in you writing information that is not relevant to the point you're making. Instead you should consider doing an extract from the model, just highlighting the forces you're referring to. Better still, you could just refer to the model in the body of your report, explaining the impact on revenue growth or margins. This way you cut down the risk of spending time on an appendix that you later forget to refer to.

Only in the situation of investing in a new country or industry might a full PEST be worth considering.

3 Porter's Five Forces model

Porter has argued that the long-term profitability of companies within an industry is reduced by the presence of one or more strong competitive forces. The profitability and survival of any company in the industry will depend on countering these five forces.

Force	This force is strong if:
Buyer power This is the power of buyers in the industry – the organisation's customers. Strong buyer power: • forces down prices • exerts pressure for expensive quality improvements and service improvements.	The industry or company depends on a small number of buyers/customers. The company's product is unbranded or undifferentiated, so that buyers have no particular reason to select the company for its supplies. The company has excess capacity or the industry is in recession. There are no costs or few costs involved for buyers in switching from one source of supply to another. The buyers have information on prices of alternative producers in the industry.

Supplier power	The product/service provided by the supplier is unique or differentiated, and buyers have no alternative choice of supply.
This is the power of suppliers to firms in the industry. Strong supplier power:	
	There are few suppliers in the industry, and possibly a monopoly supplier.
• reduces profits by raising prices	
• reduces the pressure on suppliers to provide a high quality product and service	
• increases the risk of unreliability in supply.	The cost of switching from the current supplier to a new supplier would be high.
Threat of entry	The industry has good long-run market potential, giving new entrants opportunities to enter and gain a competitive position.
This is the threat that new competitors will enter the market and increase the competition. When the threat from new entrants is strong:	
	There are low set-up costs. New entrants can enter the industry without incurring high costs.
• long-run profitability in the industry will be low	
• companies in the industry may reduce prices to deter entry by new competitors, forcing down short-term profitability.	A company in the industry has a good market share but poor financial position, making it a potential takeover target for a more powerful new entrant.
Substitutes	The substitute product can perform the same function just as well or even better.
When there are substitute products, customers in the industry have the option of switching from buying one product to buying the substitute/alternative. The existence of a substitute:	
	The substitute is reasonably priced.
• reduces demand for the product,	It is easy for customers to transfer to the substitute and the costs of transferring would be low.
• forces manufacturers of the product to keep their prices low.	

Competitive rivalry	Competitive forces can be particularly strong when:
The strength of rival firms in the industry is clearly a major competitive force. Strong competition: • forces down prices, • forces firms to make costly quality improvements to be competitive, • creates a risk of takeovers in the industry.	• the rate of growth in the industry is slowing down, • customers are prepared to change to a lower price supplier, • companies in the industry have high fixed costs that must be absorbed and covered by sales income.

How to use before the exam

Again, this is another useful tool to help you analyse the pre-seen information. For the purpose of analysing the pre-seen material, you can assess the apparent strength of any of these five factors and whether they might be relevant to the future strategic direction that the organisation should be taking.

An understanding of the key forces within an industry will be particularly important when it comes to prioritising issues in the exam itself.

Exercise 2 – Porter's Five Forces

Using the information in the pre-seen material, together with any background industry knowledge, assess the industry using the Porter's Five Forces model.

How to use during the exam

Similar to PEST, preparing a full appendix containing analysis of all of the five forces can waste valuable time, especially if you only apply the model briefly in your report. A better approach is to prepare an extract, highlighting the forces that are relevant or even just refer to the model in the body of your report, explaining the impact of the force on the organisation's margins.

4 Strategic position analysis: SWOT analysis

One of the most important technical models that you'll use in the exam is a SWOT analysis; for this reason it has been presented first within this chapter.

A SWOT analysis of an organisation is simply a listing of the following:

- The STRENGTHS of the organisation. These are internal factors that give the organisation a distinct advantage.

- The WEAKNESSES of the organisation. These are internal factors that affect performance adversely, and so might put the organisation at a disadvantage.

- The OPPORTUNITIES available. These are circumstances or developments in the environment that the organisation might be in a position to exploit to its advantage.

- The THREATS or potential threats. These are factors in the environment that present risks or potential risks to the organisation and its competitive position.

Strengths and weaknesses are internal to the organisation, whereas opportunities and threats are external factors.

A SWOT analysis can be presented simply as a list of strengths, followed by weaknesses, then opportunities and finally threats. It would be useful to indicate within each category which factors seem more significant than others, perhaps by listing them in descending order of priority.

Alternatively a SWOT analysis, if it is not too long and excludes minor factors, can be presented in the form of a 2 x 2 table, as follows:

Strengths	Weaknesses
Opportunities	Threats

With this method of presentation, the positive factors (strengths and opportunities) are listed on the left and the negative factors (weaknesses and threats) are on the right.

The analysis is improved if:

- the factors within each category are listed in descending order of priority, and

- minor factors are excluded entirely.

 You should not forget that you will be assessed on your ability to prioritise the problems and issues facing the organisation in the case study, and preparing a SWOT analysis will help you to organise your thoughts.

How to use before the exam

By preparing a SWOT analysis before the exam, you not only improve your understanding of the issues facing the organisation, but you lay a foundation for your prioritisation process on the day.

When analysing the pre-seen, many of the techniques of assessment described throughout this chapter should give you ideas about the future problems and potential of the firm in the case study. The preparation of a SWOT analysis may therefore be regarded as one of the final steps in your pre-seen process, that pulls many of these points together in one place.

Exercise 3 – SWOT analysis

Prepare a SWOT analysis for CeeCee based on your analysis of the pre-seen material.

How to use during the exam

 Your SWOT analysis should drive your prioritisations in the exam, and as such, it is a key model. You should always have a SWOT analysis as the first appendix of your report. You must make sure that it contains all of the issues that appear in the unseen. It is also good if you include a couple of issues from the pre-seen. The examiner is very critical if students don't fully update their SWOT analysis for the new information presented on the day.

Don't go over the top. You haven't got time to give lots of background information on each of the points you make. Neither have you got time to list 10 strengths, weaknesses etc. Try to aim for 3 or 4 points under each heading (although be prepared to be flexible where necessary).

If you're in doubt as to whether an issue is a Weakness or a Threat – put it in both! Furthermore, some Opportunities could also be a Threat so try to ensure you think through the implications of the issues and clearly explain what the threat is and what the opportunity is.

Finally, after investing all the hard work preparing the appendix, you must remember to refer to it in the body of your report. The easiest place to do this is in your prioritisation section. As an opening sentence you can say:

"The following issues have been prioritised based on the SWOT analysis contained in appendix A".

Another excellent place to refer to your SWOT analysis is in your recommendations section. A sign of a good candidate is one who is able to link the four quadrants as part of their recommendations. For example, you may suggest a company could utilise a strength to take advantage of an opportunity or to overcome a weakness.

5 Porter's Value Chain

Porter's Value Chain

This is a means by which the activities within and around the organisation are identified and then related to the assessment of competitive strength. It can also be a useful model to help identify ways in which the organisation can reduce its production costs.

Resources are of no value unless they are deployed into activities that are organised into routines and systems. These should then ensure that products are produced which are valued by customers and consumers. Porter argued that an understanding of strategic capability must start with an identification of the separate value-adding activities.

Primary activities

These activities are involved in the physical creation of the product, its transfer to the buyer and any after-sales service. Porter divided them into five categories:

(1) **Inbound logistics** are activities concerned with receiving, storing and distributing the inputs to the product. They include materials handling, stock control, transport.

(2) **Operations** transform these various inputs into the final product - machining, packing, assembling, testing and control equipment.

(3) **Outbound logistics** relate to collecting, storing and distributing the product to buyers.

(4) **Marketing and sales** provide the means whereby consumers and customers are made aware of the product and transfer is facilitated. This would include sales administration, advertising, selling and so on.

(5) **Service** relates to those activities which enhance or maintain the value of a product such as installation, repair, training and after-sales service.

Support activities

Each of the primary activities are linked to support activities and these can be divided into four areas:

(1) **Procurement** refers to the processes for acquiring the various resource inputs to the primary activities – not the resources themselves. As such it occurs throughout the organisation.

(2) **Technology development** - All value activities have a technological content, even if it is just 'know how'. IT can affect product design or process and the way that materials and labour are dealt with.

(3) **Human resource management** which involves all areas of the business and is involved in recruiting, managing, training, developing and rewarding people within the organisation.

(4) **Infrastructure** refers to the systems of planning, finance, quality control, information management etc. All are crucially important to an organisation's performance in primary activities. It also consists of the structures and routines that sustain the culture of the organisation.

How to use before the exam

This model will only be of relevance to some cases and so should not be something you complete as a matter of course. Only attempt this if you have sufficient information within the pre-seen to assess the activities.

How to use during the exam

Performing a full value chain analysis will take up far too much time. A better approach is to prepare an extract, highlighting the value and cost drivers that are relevant or even just refer to the model in the body of your report, explaining the impact on the organisation's competitive strategy.

6 Porter's Diamond

Porter's Diamond is a specialist tool that looks at how and whether a company's geographical location can add to its global competitive advantage.

Porter's study suggests reasons why some nations are more competitive than others and why some industries within nations are more competitive than others.

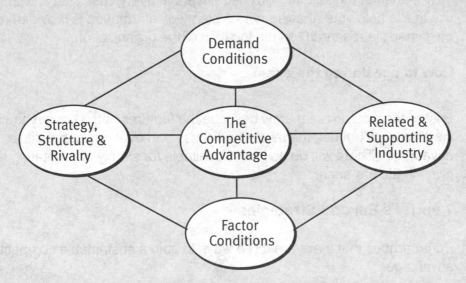

Factor conditions – supply side

A supply of production factors that convey advantage. Basic factors are unsustainable as they are easily copied (unskilled labour) whilst advanced factors can convey the advantage as they are less easy to emulate (scientific expertise).

Demand conditions – demand side

Sophisticated home demand can lead to the company developing significant advantages in the global marketplace. Fussy consumers set high standards for products whilst past experience of the product's progress through the life cycle in the home market can provide valuable input to new strategic initiatives.

Related and supporting industry – the value chain and system

Advantage conveyed by the availability of superior supplier industries, e.g. Italy has a substantial leatherwear industry which is supported by leather working plants and top fashion and design companies.

Strategy, structure and rivalry – the competition element

Different nations have different approaches to business in terms of structure and the intensity of rivalry that can take place. If a company is used to dealing with strong competition then it will have experience of rivals' attacks and so will be better able to fight them off.

How to use before the exam

This is another model that won't be relevant to every case study. You should use this to help your analysis where plenty of information is provided (or can be gained via research) on the location of the organisation.

How to use during the exam

Ensure that you do not merely describe the features of the country under consideration but use the model to discuss and evaluate competitive advantage. There will be no marks available for simply regurgitating facts given in the pre-seen.

7 Porter's Generic Strategies

Porter argues that there are three ways to gain a sustainable competitive advantage.

Overall cost leadership

- Based on achieving the position of lowest cost producer in the industry for **standard** products and services – not necessarily inferior ones.

- The company can operate in even the most marginal segments of the market and undercut rival's prices at any time. (Price usually becomes the main weapon in competing.)

- Cost advantages come from economies of scale, large production runs, automation, learning effects, etc – use the value chain if you need more detail.

Differentiation

- Based on offering a **better** quality product than competitors (or one that is perceived to be better quality).

- Customers are willing to pay extra for this differentiation.

- The difference must be valued by customers and may be real or created via advertising.

Focus/niche

- A company may find it difficult to gain a cost or quality advantage across the whole industry but can do so by focusing on a particular buyer group, market segment or a section of the product range.

'Stuck in the middle?'

- Porter argues that firms must choose between cost leadership and differentiation. Any attempt to do both will result in the firm achieving neither – a recipe for disaster.

How to use before the exam

Porter's Generic Strategies can be used in a number of ways. Before the exam it is most useful when performing a position analysis; competitive advantage is a key part of a SWOT analysis e.g. being stuck in the middle is a major weakness.

How to use during the exam

During the exam, it can be used to help with:

- Prioritisation – maintaining a competitive advantage in a competitive marketplace would be considered important in most scenario.

- Strategy evaluation – competitive advantage is a useful issue to include when assessing potential strategies.

The easiest way to utilise Porter's Generic Strategies in the exam is to refer to the model within the body of your report (rather than via an appendix). However, care must be taken to ensure you go into sufficient depth to earn both the technical and the application marks.

It is not good enough merely to state that the company operates a cost leadership or differentiation strategy. You must explain how they achieve that and the things that might threaten their ability to maintain this (in which case this will lead to them becoming "stuck in the middle").

8 Financial analysis

In Chapter 3 we provided some guidance on the ratios you should calculate for CeeCee. However, on future cases you may need to think more independently about what ratios will be relevant to the scenario.

Here is a brief checklist of ratios and other calculations you might find useful. You should be familiar with all of them.

Analysing trends and magnitudes

Financial indicator	Things to look for
Sales turnover • Absolute figure shows the size of the company • % change per annum shows growth rate	• The company's stage in the product or industry life cycle. • Healthy companies have annual growth rate in sales in excess of the rate of inflation. • If the company is unprofitable, or profits are falling, then the case study is probably about a profitability crisis and finding a turnaround strategy. • A high % increase in profit in comparison to % increase in sales turnover indicates a high fixed cost base. Look for increases in sales turnover that do not generate a large increase in profit. Does this indicate a problem?
Group operating profit • Absolute figure shows the amount of profits • Annual growth in annual profit shows rate of increase	• If the company is unprofitable, or profits are falling, then the case study is probably about a profitability crisis and finding a turnaround strategy. • A high % increase in profit in comparison to % increase in sales turnover indicates a high fixed cost base. Look for increases in sales turnover that do not generate a large increase in profit. Does this indicate a problem?
Divisional sales revenue and operating profit • Absolute figure for divisional profit • % change per annum in divisional profit	• Assess the relative size and importance of the divisions. • Loss-making divisions need to be dealt with urgently. • Compare growth rates of each division to assess where strategic investment should perhaps take place.
Borrowings (loans and overdraft)	• High or rising borrowings might suggest high financial risk. • Consider why finance is debt and not equity.

Share price	• An upward trend in share price is healthy.
• The change in price through time • P/E ratio compared to rival companies	• A low or falling share price shows loss of investor confidence.

Ratios

Profitability ratios

You might find useful information from an analysis of profit/sales ratios, for:

- the company as a whole
- each division, or
- each product or service.

Profit margins can be measured as a net profit percentage and as a gross profit percentage. You can then look at trends in the ratios over time, or consider whether the margins are good or disappointing.

Analysing the ratio of certain expenses to sales might also be useful, such as the ratio of administration costs to sales, sales and marketing costs to sales or R&D costs to sales. Have there been any noticeable changes in these ratios over time and, if so, is it clear why the changes have happened?

Liquidity ratios

The two main measures of liquidity are:

- the current ratio (= ratio of current assets: current liabilities)
- the quick ratio or acid test ratio (= ratio of current assets excluding inventory: current liabilities).

The purpose of a liquidity ratio is to assess whether the organisation is likely to be able to pay its liabilities, when they fall due for payment, out of its operational cash flows.

The current ratio is probably more useful when inventory is fairly liquid and inventory turnover is fast. The quick ratio or acid test ratio is a better measure of liquidity when inventory turnover is slow.

Check these ratios for any significant change over time, or for the possibility of poor liquidity. As a very rough guide, a current ratio below 2:1 and a quick ratio below 1:1 might be low. However, the liquidity ratios are only likely to be of significance for the case study when the ratios get very low, or the deterioration in the ratios is very large. For example, if a company has current liabilities in excess of its current assets, a liquidity problem would seem likely.

Working capital ratios

Working capital ratios can be calculated to assess the efficiency of working capital management (= management of inventory, trade receivables and trade payables). They can also be useful for assessing liquidity, because excessive investment in working capital ties up cash and slows the receipt of cash.

The main working capital ratios are:

*   average turnover period for inventory: slow turnover might indicate poor inventory management

*   'receivables days' or the average time that customers take to pay: the industry average might be 30 or 60 days

*   average time to pay suppliers: again, the industry average might be 30 or 60 days.

You should be familiar with these ratios and how to calculate the length of the cash cycle or operating cycle.

Financial structure ratios

You might be required to consider methods of funding in your case study examination. If a company plans to expand in the future, where will the funds come from?

*   Additional debt finance might only be possible if the current debt levels are not high, and financial gearing is fairly low. (The interest cover ratio is also a useful measure of debt capacity. It is the ratio of profit before interest and tax to interest costs. When the ratio is low, possibly less than 3, this could indicate that the company already has as much debt capital as it can safely afford.)

*   If a company will need additional equity finding, will internally generated profits be a sufficient source of funds or will a new share issue be necessary?

You should be able to accurately prepare gearing ratios, which is debt: debt + equity.

Cash flow analysis or funding analysis

If the main objective of a company is to maximise the wealth of its shareholders, the most important financial issues will be profitability and returns to shareholders. However, other significant issues in financial strategy are often:

- cash flows and liquidity, and
- funding.

If the pre-seen material gives you enough data, you might be able to carry out a rough assessment of the company's cash flows, by constructing a cash flow statement. The purpose of such an analysis should be to get an idea of where the company has been getting its cash, and how it has been using the cash. A possible cash flow problem occurs whenever the cash flows from operations do not appear to be sufficient to cover all the non-operational cash payments that the company has to make, such as spending on capital expenditure items.

An analysis of future funding can be carried out by looking at the history of changes in the statement of financial position. It is a relatively simple task to look at the growth in the company's assets over time, and at how the asset growth has been funded – by equity, long-term debt or shorter-term liabilities. If equity has funded much of the growth in assets, it might be possible to see how much of the new equity as been provided by retained profits, and how much has come from new issues of shares (indicated by an increase in the allotted share capital and share premium reserve).

 It is crucial that you are able to accurately calculate and interpret the key ratios such as margins, ROCE, P/E ratios and gearing.

How to use before the exam

Financial ratio analysis is a very useful approach to finding out about the financial position of an organisation, and its financial strengths and weaknesses. Depending on the information provided in the pre-seen material, you might be able to carry out some simple ratio analyses on historical data or on the data in a financial plan or business plan.

How to use during the exam

 To answer the questions in the case study examination, you will have to do much more than calculate and analyse some commonly used financial ratios. However, if further financial information is presented, you should update some of the key ratios, especially those that may have an impact on some of the recommendations you make (for example, gearing).

When analysing any issue and making recommendations, it is important that you address the impact on cash. This may mean that the organisation needs to access further cash, in which case you would be expected to assess how much cash is required and to think about likely sources.

Don't neglect the opposite problem that can arise. If the organisation has too much cash, it would be important to consider what they should do with it. One option may be to invest in a new project (perhaps an acquisition or some other form of investment) but don't neglect the potential for paying higher dividends or even a share buy-back.

9 Mendelow's power/interest matrix

Stakeholders are groups or individuals who have a stake in, or an expectation of, an organisation's performance.

It is important to understand the needs of each stakeholder and the power and influence they have within / over the organisation.

Mendelow proposed the diagram below to help analyse stakeholders.

Stakeholder Mapping: The Power Interest Matrix

This matrix can be used to track changes in stakeholder influence over time and to assess the impact of various groups on strategy.

Power = the means by which stakeholders can influence objectives.

Interest = the consideration of two factors; where their interest rests (e.g. dividends, higher wages etc) and how interested they are.

- **Minimal effort**

    Their lack of interest and power makes these stakeholders open to influence. They are more likely than others to accept what they are told and follow instructions. The best strategy for dealing with these stakeholders is direction – simply tell them what to do.

- **Keep informed**

  These stakeholders are interested in the strategy but lack the power to do anything. Management needs to convince opponents to the strategy that the plans are justified; otherwise they will try to gain power by joining with parties with high power but low interest. These stakeholders need educating and should be consulted with to prevent them joining forces with stakeholders with higher power.

- **Keep satisfied**

  The key here is to keep these stakeholders satisfied to avoid them gaining interest and moving to the "key players" box. This could involve reassuring them of the outcomes of the strategy well in advance. These stakeholders need reassurance to prevent their interest building, changing them into key players.

- **Key players**

  These stakeholders are the major drivers of change and could stop management plans if not satisfied. Management, therefore, needs to communicate plans to them and then discuss implementation issues. Participation is the key to dealing with these stakeholders. Consultation is vital since these stakeholders can force change.

How to use before the exam

Mendelows Matrix is best applied to a specific issue or strategy and so it can be difficult to use at this stage. Having said this, you can identify all the stakeholders in the business, and attempt to classify them based on a 'neutral' state (i.e assuming no problems). This will then help you consider how the position of a stakeholder may change when an issue arises in the exam.

Exercise 4 – Mendelow's Matrix

Assess CeeCee's stakeholder relationships using Mendelow's Matrix.

How to use during the exam

It is not good enough to merely state that unions are a key player or that the institutional shareholders have high power but low interest. You must ensure you expand your comment to cover the implications of your categorisation.

10 Critical success factors

Critical success factors (CSFs) are the factors that will determine whether a firm will be a success in its industry. CSFs vary from industry to industry.

CSFs can often be identified by answering four questions:

- What factors drive costs in the industry?
- What factors influence the revenues the firm can generate?
- What drives asset investment?
- What poses risks for the firm?

The following table expands on these by indicating what to look for.

Critical success factor	Things to look for
What factors drive costs in the industry?	- If fixed costs are high, this means that gaining sales volume is critical. - If product complexity is being used to gain orders (e.g. special customisation of products or width of product range), this will increase costs. Firms must understand and allow for this. - If economies of scale (volume) or economies of scope (breadth of product range) are available, this makes relative size and market share a critical success factor. - If a firm must incur high spending on advertising, research and development or asset refurbishment in order to compete, the firm must be able to afford it. - Where costs can be reduced by merger/acquisition, the firm needs to gain size and look for a merger partner or a takeover target. - If costs are affected by exchange rates or the availability of cheaper supplies from abroad, the firm might need cross-border supply chains.

What factors influence the revenues the firm can generate?	• If the firm's product commands a premium price, this means that sales promotion, brand image, meeting customer needs and technical quality are critical. • If the product competes by low prices it is critical that this market segment continues to include a substantial number of buyers willing to buy on price. • If revenue growth has been gained by accessing new customers and wider locations, the marketing and logistic skills of the firm are critical. • If revenue growth has been accomplished by new products and exploiting the early stages of product life cycles, it means that innovation and launch marketing are critical. • Competitors and new entrants will put pressure on revenues and so it is critical that competitive advantages are sustained and enforced.
What drives asset investment?	The CSFs in industries subject to high ongoing asset investment are: • ability to afford the costs of investment. • ability to project manage and implement investment swiftly and successfully. Ensure that the firm's management (and you) appreciate that asset investment includes intangibles such as human resources and brands. • In consumer industries their rising expectations will necessitate continuous improvement and updating of premises, customer service and facilities. • In technological industries there will be need for continuous investment in R&D and production technology. • Sales growth drives asset investment if it needs extra production or distribution capacity. • Industries utilising IT strategically will need to ensure systems are kept up to date. The progress of IT applications is swift and continuous.

What poses risks for the firm?	These are events that could close the business down or severely restrict its space to operate and its earnings. **Asset risk:** factors that could result in loss of productive assets or their earning power (e.g. theft, destruction, legal challenges to their use). **Commercial risk:** reduction of earnings below forecast due to loss of customers, failure of new products, successful competition by rivals. **Operational risk:** breakdown in ability to provide the product or service, leading to loss of earnings and potential costs of legal claims by customer, suppliers and staff. **Financial risk:** loss of value of investments due to volatility of markets, adverse foreign exchange movements or adverse interest rate movements.

How to use before the exam

An awareness of the critical success factors (CSFs) will be crucial to your ability to prioritise the issues in the exam as well as analyse potential solutions. It is therefore essential groundwork to perform before the exam.

> **Exercise 5 – Critical success factors**
>
> Using the CeeCee pre-seen material identify that factors that are critical to success and comment on how well CeeCee performs in these areas.

How to use during the exam

Whenever you refer to a CSF you must clearly explain why it is a CSF and the nature of any potential threat to it (or indeed how a CSF may be strengthened by an opportunity).

11 KPIs and a balanced scorecard

Each of the CSFs identified above should be measured by a number of key performance indicators (KPIs). If not, there is the risk that the issue concerned will not be monitored and controlled sufficiently.

A useful way of incorporating these is to use the balanced scorecard, which looks at a range of issues / factors relevant to different stakeholders:

Financial perspective	**How do we look to shareholders?**
Customer perspective	**How do customers see us?**
Innovation and learning	**Can we continue to improve and create value?**
Internal business processes	**What must we excel at and what business processes should be improved to enhance efficiency?**

How to use before the exam

By considering suitable KPIs for each of the CSFs you have identified, you can equip yourself to handle the new information that will arrive in the unseen. To the extent that any KPIs are quoted in the pre-seen, you can try to benchmark these against real life competitors in order to better appreciate how the organisation is performing.

How to use during the exam

More often than not, the balanced scorecard will be part of the recommendations you are giving to the Board. As such, an appendix giving example KPIs for each of the four perspectives is generally the easiest way to convey the benefits of such an approach. Be careful not to spend too much time on the appendix though. One or two examples under each perspective is more than enough.

12 Identifying risks

How to use before the exam

Identifying the risks facing the organisation will help to reveal potential issues that could crop up in the unseen information, thereby allowing you to feel better prepared.

In addition, it will provide a greater awareness of the pressures facing the Board and will ensure you fully consider the implications of recommendations that you make.

It is therefore a useful background model but is not one you would normally have to reproduce in the exam.

Exercise 6 – Identifying risks

Using the CeeCee pre-seen material, identify the risks facing the company under the following headings:

• Business risks

• Financial risks

• Political and legal risks

• Technology risk

• Economic risk

• Reputation risk

13 Motivation theories

Maslow's hierarchy of needs

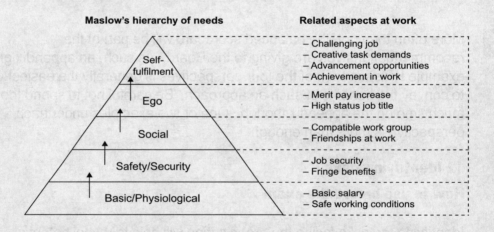

Each individual has a set of needs which can be arranged in a hierarchy (as above). The lowest needs must be satisfied first. Only then do the next become available for management to use in motivating staff.

Herzberg

Frederick Herzberg's two factor theory of motivation describes motivational and hygiene factors.

• Hygiene factors – are based on a need to avoid unpleasantness. They do not provide any long-term motivating power. A lack of satisfaction of hygiene factors will demotivate staff.

• Motivator factors – satisfy a need for personal growth. Satisfaction of motivator factors can encourage staff to work harder.

Herzberg believed that only motivators can move employees to action: the hygiene factors cannot. They can only prevent dissatisfaction.

In order to motivate the workforce management must avoid dissatisfaction and put in place motivators to encourage the staff.

Hygiene factors

To avoid dissatisfaction there should be:

- Policies and procedures for staff treatment.
- Suitable level and quality of supervision.
- Pleasant physical and working conditions.
- Appropriate level of salary and status for the job.
- Team working.

Motivator factors

In order to motivate staff managers should provide:

- Sense of accomplishment (achievement) through setting targets.
- Recognition of good work.
- Increasing levels of responsibility.
- Career advancement.
- Attraction of the job.

How to use before the exam

Your ability to utilise these models before the exam will depend on the depth of the information presented. Often, the information provided at this stage is too superficial to enable any in-depth analysis.

How to use during the exam

To score marks for using a motivation model you *don't* have to produce the whole model in an appendix. This will waste valuable time and result in you writing information that is not relevant to the point you're making. Instead you should consider doing an extract from the model, just highlighting the aspects you're referring to. Better still, you could just refer to the model in the body of your report, explaining the impact on staff or whichever stakeholder is suffering from motivational issues. Provided you explain the theory and don't just name drop, you'll pick up the marks and cut down the risk of spending time on an appendix that you later forget to refer to.

14 Business valuations

The main approaches to business valuations are:

- Market capitalisation (assuming the organisation is a quoted company).
- Dividend valuation model (DVM) – based on the return paid to a shareholder.
- Income/earnings based – based on the returns earned by the company.
- Asset based – based on the tangible assets owned by the company.

Market capitalisation

A firm's market capitalisation is found by multiplying its current share price by the number of shares in issue.

NB1 The share prices of companies on stock exchanges move constantly in response to supply and demand, and as they move, so do market capitalisations.

NB2 The values calculated in this way do not necessarily reflect the actual market value of companies, as is shown when one company launches a takeover bid for another and (as frequently happens) pays a premium over the pre-bid price.

The DVM approach

The value of the company/share is the present value (PV) of the expected future dividends discounted at the shareholders' required rate of return.

$$P_o = \frac{D}{r_e}$$

or

$$P_o = \frac{D_o(1 + g)}{r_e - g}$$

Assuming: a constant dividend **or** constant growth in dividends

r_e = shareholders' required return, expressed as a decimal

g = annual growth rate

P_o = value of company, when D = Total dividend.

This method of valuation is the least likely to come up within the case study examination.

Income / earnings based method

The most common method of valuation involves using P/E ratios. P/E ratios are quoted for all listed companies and are calculated as:

Price per share / Earnings per share (EPS)

This can then be used to value shares in unquoted companies as:

Value of company = Total earnings × P/E ratio

NB: Earnings = profit after tax after finance costs.

Value per share = EPS × P/E ratio

using an adjusted P/E multiple from a similar quoted company (or industry average).

Note: It may be necessary to make an adjustment(s) to the P/E ratio of the similar company to make it more suitable, e.g. if the company being valued:

- is a private company as its shares may be less liquid

- is a more risky company – fewer controls, management knowledge etc.

- has a higher projected growth level.

Another method involves discounting future expected cash flows although this is not common within the case study examination.

Asset-based measures

Measure	Strengths	Weaknesses
Book values	• None	• Historic cost value
NRV – assumes a break-up basis (NRV less liabilities)	• Minimum acceptable to owners • Asset stripping	• Valuation problems especially if quick sale • Ignores goodwill
Measure	**Strengths**	**Weaknesses**
Replacement cost – going concern	• Maximum to be paid for assets by buyer	• Valuation problems – similar assets for comparison? • Ignores goodwill

How to use before the exam

This will depend on the information provided. However, you may wish to look up P/E ratios of real life competitors and consider the implications on the value of the business in the case.

How to use during the exam

 An appreciation of the different methods of valuing an organisation could prove useful if the unseen material reveals a potential sale or acquisition of all or part of a business.

The key is to keep your calculations simple on the day and clearly state any assumptions made.

15 Ansoff's matrix

Ansoff's matrix analyses current and proposed strategies into four classifications:

	Existing products	**New products**
Existing markets	*Market penetration* • Price cuts? • Spend more on advertising? • Small improvements to products? • Buy rivals? • Competitive strategy?	*Product development* • R&D could be critical • Acquire rights to make other firms' products • Buy in products and re-badge • Joint developments • Can use existing distribution channels
New markets	*Market development* • New customer segments • Industrial v consumer markets • New regions of the country • Foreign markets • Barriers to entry?	*Diversification* • Related diversification (e.g. vertical integration) • Unrelated diversification (conglomerate diversification)

How to use before the exam

Ansoff's matrix is very easy to use; as well as classifying current strategies it is particularly useful at identifying possible directions for growth.

This can be helpful before the exam as it allows you to consider potential strategies that may be presented in the unseen and evaluate them in advance.

How to use during the exam

The problem often experienced when using Ansoff's within the case study exam is ensuring you do *apply* the model rather than just making statements like "this would be classified as product development" which leave the reader asking the question "so what?!"

To apply Ansoff's to your issue you need to focus your argument on risk and the key factors to ensure the success of that strategy. So for example you could comment that:

- A product development strategy (or market development strategy) would result in additional risk for the company over and above a market penetration strategy

- A market development strategy will be more successful the closer the characteristics of the new markets are to existing markets

- When following a product development strategy success will only be achieved if the new product satisfies the critical success factors required in existing markets.

16 Strategic choice

The suitability/acceptability/feasibility model developed by Johnson, Scholes and Whittington is an excellent model for evaluating proposed strategies and is much better than simply discussing the advantages and disadvantages. Whilst you're unlikely to use it much in your pre-seen analysis, you should expect to be able to apply it in the majority of case study exams:

Suitability – is the strategy consistent, both externally and internally?

- Does it give the firm a better fit with the environment?
- Portfolio analysis – how do new products fit with existing ones?
- Are their synergies with other parts of the business?
- Resource deployment analysis – how does the strategy match against strengths and weaknesses?

Feasibility – is the strategy within the resources and capability of the organisation?

- Is the time-scale achievable?
- Do we have the critical success factors necessary to implement the strategy?

Acceptability – look at risk and return.

- Is the risk acceptable?
- Does the strategy meet the criteria for 'success' for different stakeholder groups?
- Techniques could include NPV, IRR, expected present value.
- Problems dealing with multiple objectives and non-quantifiable objectives.
- Could involve sensitivity analysis to assess risks.

How to use before the exam

There will not always be scope to use this model before the exam. If a strategy is presented in the pre-seen, you could evaluate it using SFA but always be mindful of whether the strategy is proposed or underway.

How to use during the exam

You should expect to use this model in every exam:

- You will usually be required to evaluate a strategy somewhere
- It qualifies as a strategic model
- If gives you an answer structure for your report
- It prompts areas to consider in your discussion

Don't make the mistake of thinking that a good heading (e.g. 'suitability') negates the need for argument and justification within your discussion. Also try to ensure your points are under the right heading!

17 Net Present Value (NPV)

Discounted cash flows (especially NPV) allow you to assess the impact of future plans on shareholder value. This is particularly useful if

- Evaluating a strategic proposal
- Business valuation
- Determining a tender price for a contract

To appraise the overall impact of a project using discounted cash flow techniques involves discounting all the relevant cash flows associated with the project back to their present value (PV).

If we treat outflows of the project as negative and inflows as positive, the NPV of the project is the sum of the PVs of all flows that arise as a result of doing the project.

The NPV represents the surplus funds (after funding the investment) earned on the project, therefore:

- if the NPV is positive – the project is financially viable
- if the NPV is zero – the project breaks even
- if the NPV is negative – the project is not financially viable
- if the company has two or more mutually exclusive projects under consideration, the profitability index should be calculated (NPV / investment required) as this takes account of the size of the capital investment. Alternatively, the NPV result could be viewed alongside a discounted payback calculation to consider the speed of payback.
- the NPV gives the impact of the project on shareholder wealth.

Assumptions used in discounting

Unless the examiner tells you otherwise, the following assumptions are made about cash flows when calculating the net present value:

- all cash flows occur at the start or end of a year
- initial investments occur T_0
- other cash flows start one year after that (T_1).

 You should never include interest payments within an NPV calculation as these are taken account of by the cost of capital.

Neither should you include any non-cash flows such as depreciation. Only the relevant cash-flows (those that are in the future and are incremental to the decision) should be included in the calculation.

How to use before the exam

There are unlikely to be opportunities to calculate an NPV based on information provided in the pre-seen material. However, you should revise this model carefully and aim to have completed at least one calculation in the context of the case material (either as part of a mock exam or by mocking up a scenario yourself).

How to use during the exam

Most students are happy setting out their workings in an appendix but to capture all the marks it is imperative that you

- State any assumptions you have made regarding figures used – e.g. growth forecasts, choice of discount rate used.

- Refer to the answer in your report, cross referencing.

- Use the figure as part of your analysis, arguments or recommendations. You need to "make the numbers talk". For example, if a NPV is positive then this can be incorporated into a discussion of "acceptability" when assessing a strategy.

- Ensure the numbers are balanced by non-financial considerations as well. Just because the NPV is positive doesn't mean the project should definitely go ahead.

Test your understanding answers

Exercise 1 – PEST	
Political	• Restrictions on imports from Asian countries (e.g. there were EU quotas restricting imported clothing from China up until 2008) • Some countries insist on local ownership of firms. Should CeeCee wish to open shops in such countries, then it may have to consider an alternative business model, such as franchising. • Changes in legislation relating to safety issues.
Economic	• Half of all customers look at the price first. Thus any economic downturn will have a big impact on pricing • Economic development in supplier countries also has an impact – e.g. rising standards of living and, in particular, rising wages, in India (say) may undermine any cost advantage gained from using such suppliers. • Exchange rate risk between Euro and supplier countries' currencies
Social	• Customers want a wider range of sizes and fittings, possibly due to increasing obesity • Increasing consumer awareness of ethical supply chains • Increasing customer concerns over the environment could lead to problems with garments flown in from Asia • Ageing population could present an opportunity to target older customers. • Most clothing is bought by women – even men's clothing!
Technological	• While some shoppers are turning to online purchasing, this opportunity / threat is not as high as with some products (e.g. CDs) as half of all customers still like to try clothes before buying • Automated production lines

Exercise 2 – Porter's Five Forces

Force	Your response
Competitive rivalry	Intense rivalry • Large number of rivals • Low switching costs for customers other than brand loyalty and design strength • Designs can be copied – this is the basis of CeeCee's strategy but its very short lead times give it an edge over rivals • Difficult economic conditions forcing retailers to cut prices to gain customers
Threat of entry	Threat is low for physical stores since barriers to entry are high. This is less so for internet. Barriers to entry include the following: • Brand name, although some stores sell branded goods, which will get round this • Capital investment required to obtain stores, although rental agreements reduce this • Design skills (unless selling branded goods), although these are only scarce in the top tier of the market • Establishing relationships with suppliers, although there are numerous suppliers available (**Note:** CeeCee's exclusivity arrangements enhance barriers here) • Establishing a distribution network • Setting up websites and online marketing

Supplier power	Low
	• Given that CeeCee has over 350 suppliers under exclusivity arrangements, the suppliers are more dependent on CeeCee than vice versa.
	• Switching costs are low – while there will be learning curves and working relationships to be managed, it should be fairly straightforward for CeeCee to get a different supplier to make garments if necessary.
	• On the other hand suppliers can cause short term problems for CeeCee if there are supply problems.
Customer power	Low
	• Individually customers have little power due to a lack of overall purchasing power.
Threat of substitutes	Medium
	• Under substitutes we shall consider online shopping as a substitute for stores – clearly there are few substitutes for clothing!
	• We are told that half of customers still feel the need to try garments on and feel before buying so prefer to shop in stores. However, this means that half are willing to shop online giving a significant opportunity or threat.
Summary	• Competitive rivalry most significant force, so need to have a sustainable competitive strategy.
	• In the longer term need to incorporate online retail.

Exercise 3 – SWOT analysis

SWOT

Strengths	Weaknesses
• Impressive financial performance (operating profit margins high at around 23%) despite difficult economic conditions. Positive cash generating company.	• Sales always difficult to forecast
• Listed company with a market presence in 18 countries	• Difficult to increase margins due to fast fashion model
• Efficient supply chain, giving very quick lead times (fast fashion)	• Dependent on suppliers for quality
• Strong brand names and a clear competitive advantage via differentiation	• Some shops no longer in prime locations
• Low risk of fashion miss so less inventory to sell off cheaply (10% v 20% for some competitors)	• Over-reliance on Carla Celli?
• 630 shops, most in prime locations	• CSR reporting lacks detail
• IT/IS enabling next day reporting and response	
• Exclusive arrangements with suppliers	

Opportunities	Threats
• As economies move out of recession there will be opportunities for growth • Moving some stores to better locations • Online sales • Increase the mix of higher margin goods – e.g. accessories • Further product development – e.g. perfume, furniture,... • Further market development – e.g. open stores in new countries. • Vertical integration – e.g. buying a key supplier	• Increasing competition from value retailers – customers may be unwilling to pay the premium for CeeCee goods • Brand loyalty is difficult to maintain • Increased threat from online retailers • Litigation re copying of designs • Damage to reputation – e.g. if some suppliers are found to be using child labour • Recession deepens? • Any threat to the supply chain is potentially major (e.g. fire at central distribution centre) as speed to market is essential in fast fashion. • Competitor products – direct competitors may launch a better summer range for example.

Exercise 4 – Mendelow's Matrix

Key stakeholders

	Low Interest	High Interest
Low Power	• Part-time staff may well have less interest since they may not rely on CeeCee for their main source of household income. They also have little power. • National media will have little interest in or power over CeeCee unless there is a good story – e.g. if it turns out that one of CeeCee's suppliers is using child labour, then the media would pick up on this and could seriously damage the CeeCee brand. At this point their classification would change to one of the other quadrants depending on the scenario.	• Most suppliers are dependent upon CeeCee due to exclusivity arrangements so interest will therefore be high. Furthermore CeeCee has over 350 suppliers so switching would presumably be straightforward should a particular supplier become "awkward". This means power would be regarded as low.
High Power	• Institutional shareholders with the potential that an issue where they are unhappy could increase their interest. • Non-Executive Directors again, with scope to change classification if an issue arises.	• Board Executive Directors. • Full time staff have high interest due to job security but may also have high power if unionised. We are not told if this is the case. If not, then they would be low power.

• Customers have a low interest in CeeCee as a company; they are simply interested in being able to buy up to the minute fashions. However, CeeCee must put the customer first in all decision making if it is to be successful to ensure they remain satisfied.	

In summary key relationships that need to be managed are:

- Unions, if they exist.

- Institutional shareholders - issues must be handled so as to prevent their interest rising.

Exercise 5 – Critical success factors

Critical success factors

CSF	Organisation
Quality	• Low % of goods that need to be sold at a discount indicates that CeeCee is designing and making garments that customers want.
Brand	CeeCee has a strong brand as shown by: • its success despite an economic downturn, • the high number of times customers visit the shop.
Retail outlet location	Outlets are in prime locations.
Lead times / speed to market	Very short lead times.
Cost	Margins are very strong, due partly to perceived quality pricing but (presumably) also to good cost control.

Exercise 6 – Identifying risks

Key risks

Risk category	Source
Business risks	• Intense competitive rivalry, so essential to have a sustainable competitive strategy. • Retaining and motivating CeeCee's design team.
Financial risks	• Many suppliers are based in Asia whereas most sales are in Europe, giving rise to foreign exchange risk. If the Euro weakens then the cost of imported goods will rise.
Political and legal risks	• Quotas on imported clothing - not a problem at present. • Health and safety legislation, consumer protection legislation.
Technology risk	• Growth in internet sales. • IT/IS failure would cause major inventory problems and a collapse of the supply chain.
Economic risk	• Current economic downturn, although CeeCee has coped well to date.
Reputation risk	• Customers very aware of ethical aspects of supply chain so any bad publicity (e.g. use of child labour by suppliers) could have a significant impact.

5

CeeCee: Summary of the pre-seen material

Chapter learning objectives

By the end of this chapter you will:

- Understand the key issues facing the organisation.

- Have considered the big picture perspective of the case.

Introduction and background

CeeCee is a fashion retailer based in Europe. It prides itself on being a differentiator providing up to the minute fashion styles through a business model known as "Fast Fashion".

Founded in 1989 by Carla Celli, the company began by selling "look alike" clothing ranges which were popular with young professional women. The company expanded rapidly, and opened 5 more shops in 1991. In 2000 CeeCee was listed on a major European Stock Exchange, with the cash raised at the time enabling a faster rollout of shops across Europe. At the end of 2000 there were 280 CeeCee shops across Europe and with growth averaging 40 shops per year, this grew to 610 shops across 18 European countries by the end of 2008. Due to economic conditions only 20 shops were opened in 2009 resulting in 630 shops in total by the end of that year. CeeCee operates and manages all of its shops.

The six key factors in CeeCee's success are considered to be:

- Prime locations for all shops.

- Spacious shops with sophisticated architectural details.

- Carefully designed shop window displays which are changed at least once a week to show-case latest designs.

- Appealing layout of clothing displays to include co-ordinating accessories.

- Excellent customer care

- Speed of new designs to stores.

CeeCee products

As well as expanding the number of shops, the product range was also extended to include accessories, menswear, children's wear and home furnishings, as well as the traditional women's clothing. At the end of 2009, around 500 out of the 630 shops sold men's clothing and around 300 sold children's clothes and home furnishings. One the key drivers behind the range of products stocked is the size of each shop. At the end of 2009, 110 of the 620 shops were classified as 'large', 220 as 'medium' and 300 as 'small'. In the three years ending Dec 2009, 106 shops were opened, 50 of which were large and 56 medium. This pattern reflects the trend towards larger, 'out-of-town' stores that enable a broader product range to be stocked.

CeeCee achieved an overall gross margin of 60.1% during the year ended December 2008. However, the different product ranges do experience very different margin levels, with the highest being accessories at an average of 75% and home furnishings at an average of 72%. It is therefore unsurprising that these are areas in which the Board would like to expand. In larger stores, a full range of accessories is on display to encourage shoppers to purchase, for example, new shoes together with a new dress.

CeeCee targets customers by making its clothes appear to be exclusive by having short production runs of many designs. Fashion designs are turned around quickly with some product designs getting into shops within just 10 to 15 days. Speed to market is clearly important to CeeCee's success.

The Industry

Fashion retail can be split into three tiers:

- Couture houses and top designer labels
- High Street retailers of fashion clothing
- "Value" retailers, including supermarkets.

Key trends are as follows:

- Customers increasingly demand a wider range of sizes and fittings.
- Improvements in shops such as better stock availability, quicker service and improvements to changing rooms.
- Half of all clothing shoppers look at the price tag first when looking at clothes.
- Growth in online shopping, although half of all shoppers think it is necessary to touch or try clothes on before buying.

In this intensely competitive industry having a sustainable competitive advantage is critical. One way in which high street retailers achieve this is by partnering with well known fashion designers to create 'capsule collections'. For example, H&M collaborated significantly with the likes of Karl Lagerfeld and Stella McCartney. These collections are often showcased at one of the high profile 'fashion weeks' that take place in many major capital cities around the world. Celebrities being seen wearing your labels is also another key way in which demand can be boosted.

Perhaps the biggest threat to the traditional high street 'fast fashion' retailers is the rise of the 'value' retailers such as Primark. As a result of recessionary pressures Primark were one of the few high street retailers to grow like-for-like sales (growth of 7% was seen) in 2009. As the value retailers grow, they are able to realise further economies of scale, allowing them to reduce the lead times to a point where customers are willing to wait just those few extra days in order to significantly reduce the price they pay.

Another key issue within the industry is the fine line between following the trends established by leading designers and copying designs. The original fashion house owns the intellectual property rights (IPRs) to all of their designs and care must be taken to ensure these rights are not breached.

Ethical aspects within the industry

With the rise of the 'value' retailer has come an increased focus on the ethical aspects of the industry. Key issues include:

- Environmental issues (including waste and recycling, chemical, energy and water usage, and environmental damage caused by transportation).

- Labour conditions in the supply chain (including the use of under-age workers, the health and safety of workers and the more general provision of good working conditions).

- Community support and charitable donations.

- Intellectual property rights (as noted above).

Supply chain

Central to the delivery of fast fashion is a secure supply chain. IT systems play a vital role in communicating with suppliers to ensure the right products arrive at the right time. CeeCee has invested in its own integrated inventory, production and logistics system known as CCIPL.

CeeCee has one large distribution centre located in Northern Europe, close to a shipping port, which enables it to move all products, with the minimum of handling, to meet the inventory requirement for each of its shops.

The relationship with suppliers must also be good. In order to reduce costs, many suppliers will be located overseas, most commonly in Asia and Eastern Europe; by the end of 2009 CeeCee manufactured around one third of garments in Asia. Although the price per garment is much lower, additional costs are incurred in transportation. Although air freight is the quicker method of transportation, it is much more expensive and gives rise to ethical concerns re carbon footprint. In order to speed up the time taken from design board to shops, CeeCee air freights around one third of the clothing manufactured in Asia to Europe.

CeeCee selects its suppliers based on set criteria. These are:

- Quality of production.
- Ethical workplace practices
- Agreed code of conduct
- Ability to be flexible

- Meeting purchase price targets

- Operating in a country that recognises the legal protection of IPRs

CeeCee audits all of its approx 350 suppliers on a regular basis.

At the end of the supply chain lies the branches, and in particular the branch managers who fulfil a key role in ensuring the right amount of stock of the right lines is held in branches as well as improving the standard of customer care.

Headline Financials

For the year ended 31 December 2009, the latest forecast revenue was €2,781m to generate an operating profit of €634m

Positives:

- Growth in revenue of 14.5% from 2007 to 2008 and expected 3% from 2008 to 2009, despite the economic downturn

- Gross margin of 60.1% in 2008 (although this is forecast to fall to 59.1% in 2009)

- Operating margin constant at 22.8% in both 2008 and 2009 (expected)

- Cash operating cycle is such that CeeCee typical receives cash from customers 54 days before it has to pay suppliers.

Negatives:

- ROCE has fallen, but probably due to the time lag between new investment and profitability.

Existing and future strategy

CeeCee's current strategy is as follows

- CeeCee bases its designs on what customers want now rather than in 6 month's time – e.g. copying major designer's clothing, looking at what celebrities are wearing, etc

- It then uses a very efficient supply chain to produce and deliver these designs to its stores in around 10 –15 days – the "fast fashion" model. This compares to lead times of up to 6 months for traditional fashion retailers.

- Suppliers are carefully selected and offered exclusive deals.

- Garments are typically held in stores for just 3 weeks. This encourages customers to buy items straight away as they may be gone later and to keep returning to stores (typically a customer visits the store 17× a year v industry average of 4×)

- If items are not selling well, then they will be removed from the shelves at this point and sold at a discount elsewhere. This affects 10% of items (compared to industry 20%)

- CeeCee tries to ensure a quality shopping experience by renting architecturally interesting buildings in prime locations, training staff to be attentive but give customers space to shop and careful design of window and in-store displays.

CeeCee's future strategy is based on opening more stores, with the five year plan targeting 800 shops by the end of 2014. These will be either medium or large to allow greater stocking of accessories and furnishings. Expansion outside of Europe is also planned within the next 5 years. Planned revenue in 2014 is €5,156m, generating an operating profit of €1,237m.

Summary of key issues facing the organisation at present

- Increasing competition, especially from the 'value' sector in the current economic climate – maintaining competitive advantage is vital (quality, speed, design).

- Achieving growth targets to meet institutional shareholder expectations.

- Managing growth effectively.

- Protecting and building on its supply chain.

- Maintaining the speed of new designs to its stores.

Recommended format of your answer

Chapter learning objectives

By the end of this chapter you will:

- Know how best to structure your answer to requirement 1(a).

- Be aware of what to include within each section.

- Appreciate what constitutes as a good writing style for the case study exam.

- Be aware of the aim of requirement 1(b).

- Understand what is meant by a communication document.

- Understand the importance of content as well as format and the need to consider the user and purpose of the document.

- Know the potential scope of requirement 1(b).

- Be aware of how to layout your answer.

1 Requirement 1(a) – Report contents

Requirement 1(a) (which carries 90 marks) usually asks you to prepare a report that:

- prioritises, and
- discusses the issues facing the company, and
- makes appropriate recommendations.

It is thus vital that your report is structured to clearly separate these three steps. While many different report formats are used in practice, we recommend that you use the following format unless you have strong reasons to do otherwise.

Front sheet

All reports have a front sheet. Yours should contain the following information:

- The word 'report' large and clear on it somewhere
- The recipient of the report e.g. 'To the Directors of X'
- The producer of the report (don't write your own name here – your script must be anonymous)
- Date
- The title of the report
- The status of the report e.g. 'draft', 'confidential'.

Contents page

A contents page shows the marker how you have structured your report and should help towards integration marks.

A typical report could have the following contents:

1.0	Introduction
2.0	Terms of reference
3.0	Prioritisation of key issues
4.0 – 7.0	Analysis of issues
8.0	Ethical considerations
9.0	Recommendations
10.0	Conclusion

Appendices 1, 2, … 5

Note: Your answer to requirement 1(b) can be presented as an appendix to your report.

Introduction

The introduction sets the scene for the report and, to some degree, reveals why the report has been requested. A good introduction will give a good first impression but it is important that you don't spend too long writing this as there is perhaps only 1 specific mark available (under integration) for your introduction. However, it is possible to gain some extra marks under the technical or diversity criteria if you can use some technical models or real world observations within this section of your report. To do this, your introduction should ideally be constructed using three short paragraphs covering the following:

- Current position, possibly incorporating some key ratios (Financial analysis) or commenting on effectiveness of competitive strategy (Porter's Generic Strategies)

- A real world observation linked with your first paragraph (e.g. market or competitor data to act as a benchmark). However, don't go overboard. You should not stuff lots of real life introductions into your introduction; instead you should use your examples throughout your report where they are relevant to illustrate the point you are discussing.

- Key challenges and future prospects facing the firm, focused on the unseen. (**Note:** This will provide evidence of prioritisation from the beginning of your report).

Terms of reference (TOR)

The terms of reference section usually answers the 'who, what, why?' of report writing:

- **Who** has asked for the report and who are we?
- **What** have we been asked to do?
- **Why** have we been asked to do it?

A typical terms of reference could thus be as follows:

"The purpose of this report is to provide the Board of Directors of ======== with a clear picture of the company's position as at ============, in particular to identify and prioritise the main issues facing ========, respond to the issues, assess the opportunities currently available, and make appropriate recommendations.

This report relies upon information and explanations provided by the Board to date and financial information at ===========".

Again, there are very few marks available for this section of your report so it should generally be added in at the end of the exam, if you have time.

Prioritisation of key issues

In this section you identify the key issues and explain the basis of your prioritisation. You do not discuss the issues beyond that – detailed analysis and recommendations will be made elsewhere.

This section should begin with a statement linking the key issues to a SWOT analysis. For example:

'A detailed SWOT analysis of the firm has been carried out and is summarised in Appendix 1. Based on this analysis we have prioritised the key issues facing the firm as follows:'

For each key issue you should aim to do the following:

- Identify the issue and explain why it is an issue.

- Justify the basis of your relative prioritisation (so why is the number two issue below number one). As stated earlier, this assessment could include reference to the issue's urgency, size and impact on the strategic objectives of the firm.

- State the need for a management decision (in the case of a proposal being evaluated) or for management action to develop a plan (in the case of an identified problem).

 Don't forget that the issues you prioritise in your answer to requirement 1(a) should all relate to the new information provided in the unseen material.

Illustration 1 – Prioritisation statements

Imagine that the unseen information informed you that following a recent upgrade to CCIPL, there have been irregularities in the deliveries of stock to stores, resulting in some store managers complaining that stock levels are too low. Just over a quarter of CeeCee's 630 stores have now been affected.

An illustrative prioritisation statement would be:

"The most important issue to be address by the Board is the need to resolve the problems with the IT system that are resulting in lost sales, reduced profitability and damage to CeeCee's reputation.

Over a quarter of CeeCee's stores are now experiencing difficulties so the impact on the business as a whole is significant.

Shareholders will expect action to be taken urgently in order to limit the damage to the business."

This does everything that would be expected in a prioritisation statement. Most important, it:

- Explains the issue not the event
- Links back to key stakeholders (customers and shareholders)
- Gives a justification for the importance (based on impact)

Within your prioritisation section you must also ensure that:

- issues are discussed in order of priority
- all key issues appear in the SWOT analysis in Appendix 1.

You should also include a brief section on other issues to show the examiner that you have thought about them. Such a section could be worded along the lines of

"There are a number of other issues that have not been prioritised as they are not considered to merit the strategic importance of the above priorities within the scope of this report. These are........." These can then be listed in a sentence.

Main body of the report – analysis of issues

Each of the prioritised issues should have a section of their own. For example:

(4) Franchising

(5) Loss of major customer

(6) etc

Your approach to each section will depend on whether the issue is a problem to solve or a proposal to evaluate.

Problems

- The opening paragraph needs to explain the **impact** of the problem with reference to theory or real-world examples. Numbers should be used to substantiate the impact where applicable.

- Subsequent paragraphs should then deal with what **could** be done i.e. provide alternative solutions, possibly starting with 'do nothing' (used sparingly) and then moving onto other possibilities. No recommendations should be made at this stage. For each problem type issue, you must cover at least two alternative solutions.

- For each alternative solution you must give some evaluation of the option by considering advantages and disadvantages.

- Options should compared and contrasted by considering the relative weighting of the points you've made.

Proposals

- With proposals the opening paragraph should explain the logic to the proposal. This can often be done effectively using a theoretical backdrop – e.g. market development within Ansoff's matrix – and how it applies.

- In addition you could include an explanation of what the proposal is e.g. what franchising involves.

- Numerical references (e.g. possible valuations) can also be included here.

- Subsequent paragraphs could include the advantages and disadvantages of the proposal or an analysis using the suitability/feasibility/acceptability model. It is important that the risks associated with the proposal are clearly identified and discussed.

- Alternative options for achieving the same strategic goals could be considered, with a comparison being made between the options.

- Again, no recommendations should be made at this stage.

Illustration 2 – Analysis of main issues I

For the illustration we looked at earlier in this chapter, that being the irregularities in the deliveries of stock to stores, resulting in complaints that stock levels are too low, the following is an example of what could have been written to analyse the impact of the problem and to identify alternative solutions:

4 IT systems failure

4.1 Impact

The fast fashion concept relies on the ability to quickly create and supply small numbers of new products into stores. Fundamental to achieving this is a sophisticated IT system that provides seamless communication between the store and the distribution centre, the distribution centre and the suppliers and the suppliers and the designers. Failure of the IT system at any point in the supply chain will result in stores not having the right stock, in the right place at the right time.

Whilst stock outs are not viewed as a problem within the fast fashion industry, if there is too little stock in the stores, customers will become frustrated, sales will be lost and the brand will be damaged.

4.2 Alternative solutions

The alternative solutions can be split between short term and long term.

Short term

In the short term, CeeCee must focus on getting stock into the stores as a matter of urgency. The alternative options are:

Revert to manual systems for ordering

In 2004, Sainsbury's reported its first ever loss after a failed IT project left its shelves bare. As a result, Sainsbury's moved away from automated systems and reverted back to manual processes. For CeeCee, this would involve each store identifying the product lines it wishes to order, completing an order form which is then sent to the distribution centre where orders can be grouped before being passed back to suppliers.

Although this will be labour intensive, it will ensure that the correct stock is manufactured and gets into the stores in a reasonable time period.

Divert orders from other stores

In order to ensure that all stores are left with an acceptable level of stock, the logistics team could divert stock destined for unaffected stores to those who are experiencing problems. Whilst this may go some way to easing the issues in the troubled stores, it may widen the scope of the problems and result in customer dissatisfaction across the whole company. It could also impact on the level of waste stock if items are transferred to stores where they are less likely to be sold.

Longer term

In the longer term, although action will still be needed quickly, CeeCee will need to identify the cause of the problem and rectify it, as well as investigate why the daily exception reports failed to highlight the problem. Solutions include:

Handle in-house

Roberta could continue to let the team of technicians she has already assembled try to find the source of the problem. This will be the cheapest option but may result in further delays.

Outsource to a specialist supplier

CeeCee outsources some specialised design and update work to a leading global IT solutions company. Given the recent investment made in the PDA's, it is likely that some of this upgrade was outsourced to this company. Roberta could request a team of technicians from the outsourcer to be immediately assigned to uncovering the cause of the problem. This may cost a bit more (although if the fault turned out to be the IT company's, presumably nothing would be payable) but will likely result in a speedier solution to the problem.

It's important to appreciate, especially with case study, that there's more than one 'correct' way to write your answer.

Remember the above illustration is simply an example on AN answer, not THE answer.

Ethical issues

One approach for dealing with ethical issues is to discuss them within the context of contrasting stakeholder views (e.g. higher profits may be at the expense of poor working conditions, in which case there is a conflict between shareholders and employees).

The ethics section should thus contain the following:

- An opening paragraph explaining ethics in the context of stakeholders.
- For each ethical issue identify the nature of the issue, explain why it is an ethical issue, highlighting the specific nature of contrasting stakeholder views
- Provide detailed recommendations covering **what** should be done, **why** that is the best course of action and **how** the recommendation should be implemented.

You should aim to discuss two ethical issues.

Illustration 3 – Ethics

Imagine you've been presented with the following ethical issue in the unseen:

During a recent audit of a supplier, unacceptable working practices involving child labour have been discovered. The supplier manufacturers approximately 3% of CeeCee's garments.

Given below is an illustration of how this could be addressed within the ethical section in your report:

8 Ethical issues

It is important that a business should take a balanced view of the interests of its various stakeholders. Whilst it is acceptable to pursue shareholder wealth as a primary objective, this should be tempered by due consideration being given to the effect of commercial decisions on other stakeholders.

8.1 <u>Work practices at supplier</u>

This is an ethical issue because, whether knowingly or not, CeeCee is profiting from vulnerable members of society. These children are not receiving an education as a result of working. They are also too young to appreciate their rights as workers, meaning they are more likely to be exploited or have their safety endangered.

Recommendation

CeeCee cannot ignore this issue. This would risk damaging CeeCee's reputation, if the matter were discovered by the media. More importantly, it would just not be the right thing to do.

> CeeCee should issue a formal warning to the supplier and set a date (one month is suggested) by which CeeCee expects the matter to be resolved. CeeCee should work with the supplier to develop a plan to eliminate the unacceptable practices, and should carry out random checks to ensure the plan has been successfully implemented. The programme of supplier audits should also be reviewed to reduce the time between audits for all suppliers.

Recommendations

As with the prioritisation section of the report, each of the prioritised issues should have a subsection of their own here.

For each key issue you should aim to address the following:

- **What** you actually recommend the organisation does – don't sit on the fence here! For problems you need to recommend a solution. For proposals you need to recommend whether to accept it or not and, if the latter, suggest alternative courses of action.

- At least two key justifications as to **why** this is the right course of action.

- Short-term specific actions and longer-term general guidance as to **how** your recommendations can be implemented.

Try to recognise bigger issues at this stage and to link issues and recommendations together wherever appropriate.

For example, preliminary conclusions may be that all proposals are attractive, but you could then bring in issues of capital rationing and suggest which strategy should be undertaken.

 Preparing a separate recommendations section does have the benefit of allowing you to see the bigger picture and consider how your recommendations for each individual issue inter-relate with those for other issues.

However, many students may find it more efficient to write their recommendations for an issue as soon as they have finished analysing that issue (see Chapter 7 for more details). If you decide to take this approach, it is perfectly acceptable to present your recommendations for each issue immediately after your analysis, rather than grouping them altogether in a separate section of your report.

Illustration 4 – Recommendations

Back to our illustrative issue concerning the irregularities in the deliveries of stock to stores, resulting in complaints that stock levels are too low.

The following is one example of what could be written within the recommendations section:

9. Recommendations

9.1 IT systems failure

It is recommended that Jim Bold immediately contact all managers of the affected stores and asks them to compile a list of the missing orders which should be e-mailed to the logistics department and the distribution centre. These lists should then be compared with stock levels at the distribution centre and at other stores to see if stock can be transferred. The logistics department should prioritise the required movement of stock. This will ensure that what stock is available is spread around the company to ensure each store is carrying a reasonable level of stock. This may require temporary staff to be recruited to cover the additional workload.

It is further recommended that a team of buyers should be charged with renewing orders from suppliers. This should be on the basis of the orders which have correctly been received from some store manager's PDA's. This will ensure that the shortage of stock is rectified as quickly as possible.

Finally, Roberta Downs should immediately contact the IT solutions company and request a troubleshooting team to be sent to investigate the matter. Even if the outsourcer wasn't involved in the original upgrade, their expertise may help to identify the problem sooner. If the problem hasn't been rectified within two days, a manual ordering process should be implemented until the systems are fully operational.

Conclusion

The conclusion is really just finishing off the report in a professional manner in no more than five lines. One approach is as follows:

- Start by restating the key issue(s) facing the firm, as outlined in the introduction.
- Briefly summarise the main recommendations.
- Make a brief comment on the future.

For example:

'In conclusion, the main issues facing X are dealing with competitive rivalry and managing growth. Once the publicity and HR issues are resolved, X should again have a platform for high future growth.'

The conclusion could also be a useful place to mention any further information required and possible further work.

Appendices

Appendices should be at the back of the report and clearly labelled.

Typically:

- Appendix 1 will be a position analysis using a SWOT.
- Further appendices will cover calculations (and any other technical models where it was felt more efficient to display then in an appendix).

With calculations you should comment on the method used and any assumptions / limitations of your analysis.

It is not uncommon for some reports to have up to five appendices.

Furthermore, you may like to present your answer to requirement 1(b) as an appendix to your report, although this is not essential. You should follow the directions given in the requirement.

You should ensure that you refer to and discuss all of the appendices that you prepare in the relevant section of your report. All of your supporting calculations should be discussed in the financial implications section of the relevant issue.

2 Writing style
Introduction

Writing style is something that develops over time. It is influenced by your education and experiences. To some it comes easily, they enjoy words – but remember, you are not looking to win any prizes in literature.

It's about putting facts, ideas and opinions in a clear, concise, logical fashion.

Some students get very worried about their writing styles. As a general rule you should try to write as you would talk.

Logical flow

A typical point starts with a statement of fact, either given in the case or derived from analysis – 'what?'

This can then be followed by an interpretation – 'so what?'

This can then lead to an implication – 'now what?', or 'what next?'

For example:

(1) What? – The NPV is positive.

(2) So what? – Suggesting we should go ahead with the project.

(3) Now what? – Arrange board meeting to discuss strategic implications.

A similar structure can be obtained using the Socratic approach – what, why, how?

- So what?
- Why should we use it?
- How does it work?

Who is reading the report?

Failure to pitch the level correctly will inevitably result in failure to communicate your ideas effectively, since the reader will either be swamped with complexity, or bored with blandness.

The recipients of the report should also dictate the level of tact required.

Tactless	Tactful
The directors have clearly made errors	There were other options open to the board that, with hindsight, would have been beneficial
The marketing director is responsible for this disastrous change in strategy	The board should consider where this went wrong? It would appear that the marketing department may have made some mistakes

Making your report easy to read

To ensure that the marker finds your report accessible and easy to read, you should try to do the following:

- Use short words, short sentences, short phrases and short paragraphs. If you are adopting the 'what, so what, what now' approach, then you could have a paragraph containing three sentences. The next point can then be a new paragraph, also containing three sentences.

- Use the correct words to explain what you mean! For example, students often get confused between:

  - recommendations (what they should do – actions) and options (what they could do – possibilities).

  - objectives (what we want to achieve – the destination) and strategies (how we intend to achieve them – the route).

- Avoid using vague generalisations. Too often students will comment that an issue will "impact" on profit rather than being specific about whether profit will increase or decrease (or even better still, trying to quantify by how much). Other common phrases which are too vague include "communicate with" (you need to say specifically what should be discussed) and "look in to" (how should an option be looked in to?)

- Avoid unnecessary repetition. This can either be of information from the exam paper (pre-seen or unseen), of discussion within the report (in particular between what is said in one section and another) or can relate to the words that you use. Some students fall into the trap of thinking that writing a professional report means simply writing more words to say the same thing! The issue is quality not quantity.

  For example, compare the following:

'I, myself, personally'	OR	'I'
'export overseas'	OR	'export'
'green in colour'	OR	'green'

- Watch your spelling – this may seem a small and unimportant point, but poor spelling makes a document seem sloppy and may convey an impression that the content is as loose as the general appearance! Poor spelling interrupts the marker as they read your report, so there is the danger that they conclude that it did not have a logical flow.

- Recommendations – be decisive – do not 'sit on the fence' or ask for more information. Make a clear recommendation based on the information you have and justify why you have chosen that course of action.

3 Requirement 1(b)

The new CIMA syllabus in 2010 saw the introduction of a smaller, secondary requirement, worth 10% of the overall mark.

The aim of this requirement is to test students' ability to **communicate** effectively in a different format from just a simple report. It is a reflection that today's accountants have to be effective communicators regardless of the medium of that communication; they must be sensitive to the end users and be able to respond according to the situation they are in.

You should plan to spend at least 15 – 20 mins preparing your answer to part (b) of the question (see Chapter 7 for more details).

4 Content of the secondary requirement

A common mistake when tackling the second requirement (question 1 (b)) is to place too much emphasis on the format of the document, and not enough on the content.

Remember, the purpose of question 1(b) is to assess the candidate's effective communication of a particular issue or issues which will have been analysed and considered in question 1(a) to the case study exam.

It should be noted that the subject of question 1(b) may relate to one or more issues that will have been analysed and discussed within the candidate's answer to requirement 1(a). However, being the focus of the second requirement does not give any indication of the priority that should be attached to this issue / these issues.

Since the issue(s) will have already been discussed in your answer to 1(a) the purpose of the second requirement is not performing further analysis or making more recommendations. To be successful in earning high marks in part (b), you will need to extract the points that will be most important to the reader of the document and present these in an appropriate manner. By this, we don't just mean the correct format but also the tone you adopt when writing. So regardless of format, you must focus on who you are writing to, what they will be most concerned about and ensure you cover those points, and those alone.

The second requirement only scores within the logic criterion. You should therefore focus your points on giving clear advice, stating opinions and providing recommendations, along with appropriate justifications (for example, by referring to the output of key calculations).

5 The format of the secondary task

The scope of the secondary task will be restricted to either a short slide presentation, an e-mail, a draft letter, or a chart or graph.

Slide presentation

If a slide presentation is called for, your answer need only consist of the bullet points that would appear on each slide. Read the requirement carefully as guidance will be given on how many slides to prepare and the maximum number of bullets on each slide. Most likely this would be 2 slides, with a maximum of 5 bullets on each slide (or you may just be asked for 10 bullet points in total). You will not need to prepare speaker notes. You do not need to layout your answer as a slide (i.e. you don't need to draw a box). Simply noting the bullets will be sufficient.

If you are sitting the computer based exam, you should prepare your answer within your Word file (after the end of your report). You will not need, or be allowed to use PowerPoint.

Illustration 5 – Slides

A typical layout for the presentation of slides should be:

<u>**Answer to Requirement 1(b)**</u>

Slide 1:

Title

- XX
- XX
- XX
- XX
- XX

Slide 2:

Title

- XX
- XX
- XX
- XX
- XX

An e-mail

A requirement to draft an e-mail may be in response to a specific question raised by an individual within the unseen information, or perhaps even in response to an e-mail that is presented within the unseen.

Again, your answer should be presented after the end of your report (either on paper or in Word if sitting the computer exam).

You will need to ensure you give your e-mail a title and make it clear who it is to and who it is from.

Illustration 6 – An e-mail

A typical layout for the presentation of an e-mail should be:

<u>Answer to Requirement 1(b)</u>

To: xx

From: xx

Date: xx

Title: xx

Your answer to the question, using short sentences as directed in the requirement.

If you are asked to write an e-mail, then you should write short sentences (the number of which will be specified in the requirement) and NOT brief bullet points.

A letter

Exactly the same as for an e-mail but laid out in letter format. That means you should include a space for an address, a date, state who the letter is addressed to and some form summary of what the letter is regarding.

The letter should be signed off in the normal business fashion, unless you are told otherwise.

Illustration 7 – A letter

A typical layout for the presentation of a letter should be:

<u>Answer to Requirement 1(b)</u>

Address

Date

Dear xx

Title

Content of your answer, using bullet points where appropriate.

Yours sincerely

A name (don't use your own name)

A job title

A graph or chart

You may be asked to produce a chart or graph to communicate some key information, often as an attachment to another document such as an e-mail, letter or presentation.

It is important to remember that the graph or chart will contribute to some of the marks, with just as many being awarded for the content of the document to which it is attached. To score well for your graph or chart, you must ensure it has a title, that the axes are labelled, and that you include data labels for each point plotted.

Whilst it would seem more likely that this would be a requirement for those students sitting the computer only exams in March and September (who can therefore use Excel), we can't rule out that students sitting the written exam could be asked to produce such a diagram. If this was the case, graph paper will be provided.

It is recommended that you spend some time practising preparing graphs and charts (either using excel or on graph paper as appropriate) under time pressure to ensure you could complete this task in less than 15 minutes.

Illustration 8 – A graph or chart

The key elements that must be present in either a graph or a chart are:

- A title (for example, 'Product profitability')
- Clearly labelled axes ('Date' or '€m' would be examples)
- Data labels

An example of an appropriate graph looks like this:

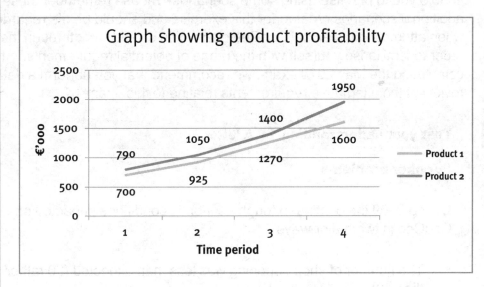

An example of an appropriate chart looks like this:

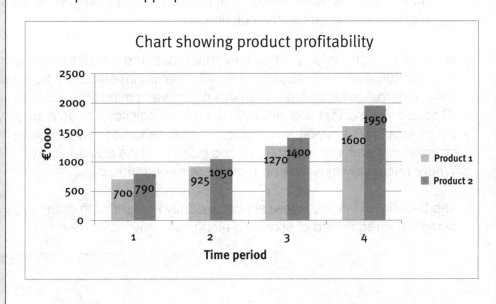

6 Next steps

In July 2010, the Examiner released a student support guide providing examples of potential question 1(b), together with suggested answers. These all related to the May 2010 (CeeCee exam) and can be accessed on the CIMA website (http://www.cimaglobal.com/Documents/Student%20docs/2010%20syllabus%20docs/T4/Support%20Guide%20%20T4%20Part%20B.pdf).

In the meantime, some test your understandings are presented below to enable you to practise using some scenarios. Please remember these are additional scenarios created for this exercise and should be dis-regarded when attempting the actual CeeCee exam. You should work through these in order to familiarise yourself with the range of potential requirements. After completing the May 2010 exam, we recommend that you perform a detailed review of the alternative requirements relating to this exam.

Test your understanding 1 – A letter

Supplier problems

During 2009 the continued tough economic conditions impacted on CeeCee in two major ways:

- The number of shops opening was less than expected (20 rather than 40)

- An increase in price based competition as customers become more 'savvy' as to where to obtain fashion at the best price while still maintaining the quality they desired.

Mid way through the year it became apparent to the Board that a review of major suppliers was required to ensure maximum efficiency from these external relationships. With this objective in mind Paulo Badeo (Operations Director) and Jim Bold (Head of Logisitcs) made a lengthy trip to Asia to visit overseas suppliers to assess the compliance with the six main criteria for selection including quality, ethics and flexibility. Where necessary existing contracts were re-negotiated.

The benefits of this visit were almost instantly realised with many orders being delivered ahead of schedule along with a reduction in costs.

An e-mail last week to all the Board from Julielle Lespere (Sales and Marketing Director) has identified that there have been a number of customer complaints resulting from garments being made from poor quality fabrics and having faulty stitching; this has impacted on the returns and the slow movement of some fashion lines. Both store managers and sales supervisors at the online shopping contact centre have had to deal with a number of irate customers who have purchased multiple items to only find that they all have the same deficiency. Rather worryingly there has been a recent report on a national popular radio station highlighting the problem more widely and twitter sites are suggesting that CeeCee is aiming to move into the 'value' sector at high street prices which only satisfies its shareholders.

Upon further investigation, the source of the problem has been traced to a major long serving and in the past, reputable supplier based in Asia; they had recently been visited by the CeeCee management team.

Required:

Draft a short letter from Paulo Badeo to the supplier, briefly informing them of the actions CeeCee will be taking and why.

Test your understanding 2 – An e-mail

New designer

Four months ago Laura Russo, the Head Designer, appointed Jake Summer as the Head of Ladies Fashion. Jake is an experienced designer and had been head-hunted from an Italian Haut Couture House known for its radical designs. He leads and inspires a team of 120 staff who are dedicated to designing the ladies wear collections of CeeCee. The terms of Jake's contract stipulated a six month probationary period.

Jake spent the first three months of his employment working alongside Laura, but over the last four weeks he has taken full control of the Ladies Fashion Design Department. The new designs are very much in the style of Jake's previous Fashion House – they are radical, cutting edge styles for young women. The new lines hit the shops two weeks ago across all 630 of CeeCee's outlets.

The sales figures over the last 7 days have been 18% below forecast. Footfall has tailed off daily over the last 8 days and is now 15% below expectations. Customer feedback is that the new designs seemed to be aimed at the teenage market and the mid-twenties young professionals, CeeCee's core market, are unimpressed with the new lines.

The stock for the next two weeks is already starting to arrive from suppliers.

Carla Celli is due to present quarterly figures to CeeCee's institutional investors next week. They will show a significant fall in revenues and production costs are 5% higher than budget.

Required:

Draft a confidential e-mail to Carla Celli suggesting control procedures to be implemented that would prevent such an issue from arising in the future.

Test your understanding 3 – A summary for presentation

Store openings and expansion outside of Europe

The latest 5 year plan has been prepared and was approved by the CeeCee Board at the end of November 2009. It includes sales from online shopping as well as the roll out of new shop openings, with 800 CeeCee shops in operation by the end of 2014. These new shop openings include expansion outside of Europe.

The Board has felt for some time that the best approach to international expansion would be to open a flagship store in a major city. If this proves successful then further stores within the country could be considered. With this in mind, Ruth Giddens, Head of Property Management, was instructed to monitor the availability of suitable locations.

At the end of 2009, Ruth reported to the Board that a retail unit had become available on Broadway, in the heart of New York's shopping district. The 2,800 square metre shop is a listed building spread over three floors.

Since then, both Ruth and Juliette Lespere, CeeCee's Sales and Marketing Director, have carried out further research and have now reported their findings to the Board (see below).

Ruth is aware of another party interested in the store and, as a result, the landlord is pressing for a decision within the month.

Report to Board

Annual revenue – all items will be priced in US dollars. It is estimated that revenue of approximately US$6,000 per square metre will be achieved.

Gross margin – Due to the size of the store, a full range of CeeCee products will be stocked including home furnishings and accessories. This will help to lift the average gross margin to 62%.

Other operating costs – Incremental operating costs associated with the store are estimated at US$3m per annum. This includes all store staff as well as additional marketing and logistics staff to support the expansion into America.

Lease costs – the landlord has quoted an annual lease charge of US$1.7m per annum, payable in advance. The lease will initially run for a period of 5 years with an option to extend thereafter.

Fit out costs – given the listed status of the building, this cost will be higher than is incurred on the average store. CeeCee use the same contractor for all of their store refurbishment programmes. The contractor has quoted €14m for the work, including all materials.

Other set up costs – It is estimated that other set up costs such as recruitment and training of approximately €1m will be incurred.

Diane Innes has advised that a suitable risk adjusted, pre-tax discount rate to appraise the project would be 10%.
The current rate of exchange between the Euro and the US dollar is €1 = $1.42.

Required:

As an appendix to your report, prepare a summary for use in a presentation to the CeeCee Board, in bullet point format, of your findings and the financial implications of the proposal to open the store in New York. The appendix should contain no more than 10 bullet points.

7 Other key tips

In order to maximise your requirement 1(b) of the T4 Part B Case Study examination we recommend the following:

(1) Make sure that you leave enough time to attempt question 1(b).

(2) Allocate approximately 15 to 20 minutes within the examination in which to prepare your answer to question 1(b) (see Chapter 7 for more guidance). Try not to leave it to the end of the exam as this increases the risk that you'll run out of time and be unable to complete this part of the requirement.

(3) Always refer to key financials (where relevant) and provide clear recommendations and action points.

(4) Practice your 'quick-fire' bullet pointing technique, identifying key factors relating to typical business issues that occur in the Case Study examination. The former case study exam (known as 'TOPCIMA' under the 2005 syllabus) has exam papers and suggested answers which can be used to gain practice and these are available on EN-gage as well as on the CIMA website.

(5) Practice preparing the various formats for answers that may be asked for in question 1(b) – using the examples in this document as a guide i.e. presentation, email, letter, graph, chart.

Test your understanding answers

Letter

CeeCee Fashion Retail
XYZ Address
Europe

A Supplier
ABC Address
Asia

Date: Today

Dear Sirs,

Following our phone conversation yesterday, you are aware that CeeCee has recently received a large number of complaints regarding poor quality fabrics and faulty stitching on a number of garments manufactured by yourselves. After a thorough investigation, we have been forced to withdraw xx product lines from our stores.

As you know, CeeCee has set criteria which suppliers must adhere to as part of our exclusive supply contract. These include both quality of production and meeting our purchase price targets.

Given that this appears to be an isolated incident, we do not propose to terminate our agreement at this stage. However, to ensure the continuation of our working arrangements, we would request that you introduce internal quality controls, including the regular and random inspection of fabrics and stitching from a sample of product lines. We expect to receive weekly reports on the outcomes of these inspections, together with samples of the lines inspected.

We hope this plan can be introduced quickly to prevent such issues arising in the future.

Yours faithfully

Paulo Badeo

Operations Director, CeeCee

Test your understanding 2 – An e-mail

Confidential E-mail

To: carla.celli@ceecee.com

From: mgt.accountant@ceecee.com

Date: Today

Re: Design department control procedures

In light of the recent issues with the new designs from Jake Summer, the following control procedures should be implemented to prevent such an issue arising in the future.

- A daily design meeting should be held where designs completed in the day are reviewed by a team of senior personnel from the design department before they are sent through to the suppliers for manufacture. This could be split into ladieswear, menswear, children's wear etc to cut down on the length of each meeting.

- Monthly meetings reviewing the product ranges as a whole should be attended by all senior design personnel. This will ensure, the products fit together and convey CeeCee's style.

- Monthly focus group meeting with a sample of customers to look at some of the designs about to be launched. This will enable feedback to be obtained before the items arrive in the shops.

- All new starters, regardless of seniority to be assigned a mentor who will work alongside them. This support should be gradually reduced over the designer's probationary period.

- Induction material should be provided showing some of CeeCee's more popular ranges throughout the life of the company. This will help give a better sense of the CeeCee brand and culture to the new recruit.

- Probationary period of six months should be standard for all new designers.

In the longer run, when we recruit new senior members of the design team in future, we should better consider how their style fits in with ours and plan a more co-ordinated launch to ensure their expertise and reputation is of benefit and not to our detriment.

Test your understanding 3 – A summary for presentation

Appendix to report

- Recommendation is to proceed with the New York store

- Large market with similar characteristics to existing markets

- Potential to quickly expand into other cities in America

- Expansion outside of Europe is a key aspect of the 5-year plan

- Listed building in a prominent location will fit with CeeCee brand

- Small negative NPV of €0.3m when assessed over five years due to high fit out costs

- When assessed over seven years (period until first refurbishment), NPV is positive at €3.9m

- Part of the cost includes establishing logistics networks in US. These would be shared across all stores when / if more open

- Benefits of key flagship store in establishing the brand have not been included in the calculation

- Neither have real options such as the future expansion into other cities

7

Managing your time in the exam

Chapter learning objectives

Upon completion of this chapter you will:

- Appreciate the importance of having a time plan.
- Be aware of the secrets behind successful time management.
- Know the key tasks to be carried out at each stage of the exam.
- Know what to look for when devising your own personal timetable.
- Be aware of how time can be wasted within the case study exam.

1 The importance of time management

Someone once referred to this exam as "the race against time" and it's difficult to imagine a more accurate description. Being able to do what the examiner is wanting is only half of the battle; being able to deliver it in the time available is another matter altogether.

For this reason, time management is a key skill required to pass the Case Study Examination. Successful time management requires two things:

(1) A tailored time plan – one that plays to your personal strengths and weaknesses; and

(2) Discipline in order to stick to it!

This chapter will provide advice to help you develop your own personal time plan, reveal the great 'robbers of time' and give top tips on things to avoid.

2 A starting point

There is not a right or a wrong time allocation to use in the exam. Instead, you must find something that works for you, and this can only be done by practising mock exams. As a starting point for developing your personal time plan, we would suggest the following allocation of time in your exam:

Stage	Action	Time
Reading	Initial read through and decision on top 4 issues	20 mins
Planning your answer	Consideration of impact / alternative solutions and content for secondary requirement	20 mins
Appendices	Preparation of SWOT analysis and all numerical appendices	25 mins
Prioritisation statement	Write the prioritisation section of your report	10 mins
Ethics	Write the ethical issues section of your report	15 mins
Key issue (1)	Write the analysis of the issue(s) to which the second requirement relates, followed immediately by writing the recommendation (20 mins in total split approximately 50:50 between analysis and recommendations)	20 mins
Requirement 1(b)	Write your answer to part (b) of the requirement	15 mins

| Remaining key issues | Cover the remaining issues (for each one write the analysis followed immediately by writing the recommendation (20 mins per issue × 3 issues) | 60 mins |
| Tidy up | Write your introduction, terms of reference and conclusion, read / spell check your report | 15 mins |

3 The different stages of preparing your answer

The above time plan will need personalising to reflect things such as your reading speed, writing or typing speed, how long you take to generate ideas, and the specifics of the unseen you're presented with. Perhaps the easiest way to personalise the time plan is to understand the actions taken at each stage and why the original suggestions have been made:

Reading time (20 minutes)

During the first 20 minutes of the exam you are only allowed to read the exam and to make notes on the exam paper itself. You are not allowed to start writing within your answer booklets or to start typing on the computer, nor are you allowed to use your calculator.

As a result you're fairly limited as to how you can use this time.

Within the exam paper, there is often at least one blank page and we would suggest that you use this to start your planning (for more details see the chapter on planning your answer). This means that for those fast readers out there, you're not left twiddling your thumbs until the reading time is over.

The key things that you need to do at this stage are:

- Read about and identify each event

- Consider what the issue is

- Evaluate the impact of the issue. Who is affected, by how much are they affected and what would happen if no action was taken?

It's important that you don't rush this stage. If you know you're quite a slow reader then it is better to do one comprehensive read that takes thirty minutes than to have to keep re-reading which could take much longer over the course of the exam. Don't be tempted to skim read as you could easily miss something significant.

Your answer to requirement 1(a) must focus on four of the key issues that have been raised in the unseen material. By the end of this first 20 minutes, you should be clear on which four issues you plan to cover, even if you haven't decided on the exact prioritisation of the issues relative to one another.

Capturing all of your thoughts and ideas at this stage can be difficult and time consuming. The chapter on planning your answer will show you how to do this effectively without wasting time.

Planning your answer (20 minutes)

The aim of this time is to further consider the impact of each of your four selected issues and to identify and evaluate alternative solutions for each. You also need to consider what the key points within your answer to the second requirement will be. This is important as it's easy to overlook this part of your answer and not give it sufficient time, either in planning or writing.

Specifically, for each of the issues you plan to cover in your report, you must:

- Further consider the impact of the issue.
- Identify the alternative courses of action.
- Consider the advantages and disadvantages of your proposals (including resource requirements and implications) – the SAF framework can be useful for this.
- Outline your recommendations thinking about *who* should do *what*, by *when* and *how.*

A key part of all of the above will be you financial analysis. You may therefore prefer to combine the planning time with the time spent preparing your appendices to ensure you properly incorporate the results of your financial analysis in your thought processes.

Planning is an essential element to passing the Case Study Exam but there is not one single right or wrong way to do it. Some people plan quicker than others and for some lucky people, a plan can be done in just five minutes. The next chapter on planning your answer will give advice on how to generate ideas and ensure you take a commercial approach.

Appendices (25 minutes)

Your SWOT should take very little time to pull together (especially if you jot a little 'S', 'W' etc in the margin of your exam paper during the reading time), so the main focus of this period will be preparing your calculations.

This can often be an area where students start to fall behind the suggested timetable. It's very easy to get bogged down in the detail and to lose track of time. So here's some key things you can do to avoid that:

(1) Check you're doing a calculation that will definitely be needed. Is it essential to allow you to fully analyse an issue or to give a firm recommendation? If not, don't do it.

(2) Spend a minute or so thinking how best to layout your calculation. You must avoid wasting time just repeating information from the exam paper but need to balance this with wanting to ensure your calculation can be clearly understood.

(3) Are there any simplifying assumptions that you can take that will speed up your calculation? Examples will include tax rates, growth rates or even something as straightforward as working in $000's.

(4) Finally, have confidence. The calculations you'll be required to do in the Case Study Exam will not be overly complex. Too often students fear calculations and convince themselves they can't do it before they even start.

At the end of preparing your appendices, you will need to finalise the order of your issues (if you haven't done so already).

Prioritisation statement (10 minutes)

If you've planned properly, this should be quite quick and easy to write. Follow the guidelines we've provided in Chapter 6 on the recommended format for your report, and in Chapter 8 on planning your answer and don't spend too long worrying about the specific words you're using. You just need 1 or 2 short paragraphs for each issue justifying why you have ranked each as 1st, 2nd etc.

Ethics (15 minutes)

The suggested plan has ethical issues being covered relatively early in the exam, primarily because the 10 marks available for this criterion should be fairly easy marks. Again though, this is only a suggestion. You may prefer to leave the ethics section until the end of the exam, instead focusing your time on covering the four key business issues within your report.

The danger is you run out of time covering other aspects and then miss out on a potential 10 marks.

As a discrete section of the report that has few links with other areas, so the choice is really up to you.

Key issues (80 minutes in total spread across the four issues and divided between analysis and recommendations)

As you will see in Chapter 6 on report writing, your discussion on the key issues will need to be broken down into analysis and recommendations.

One option is to write the analysis on all four issues and then move on to writing the recommendations. This may be preferable for some people, and does have the benefit of being able to see the bigger picture when writing your recommendations, allowing you to see that as a whole they are practical and make sense.

However, writing your recommendations in one block can lead to inefficiencies, especially as you have often forgotten about the specifics of your earlier analysis.

 To avoid this problem, you can write the analysis of one issue and then immediately move on to writing the recommendations. It does potentially create some issues relating to presentation (again, see the report writing chapter) but these are minor compared with the benefits. By moving straight to the recommendations, you continue your chain of thought and will spend less, or virtually no time, refreshing your memory on the issue. The other real benefit relates to the dangers of running out of time. The majority of value in your report is in the recommendations and if you fail to provide recommendations you are unlikely to pass the exam. This method ensures that, even if your time management doesn't go to plan, you have at least written recommendations on some of the issues. If you do decide to take this approach, you must ensure you take some time to view the bigger picture and ensure the recommendations you're giving chime with each other.

The time plan presented above suggests that you start by tackling the issue or issues to which the second requirement relates. This is not to say that this issue should always be given the highest priority in your report. It doesn't matter whether you've prioritised the issue as first or fourth, or even if it was an issue that you are only covering in the ethics section, there are real benefits to answering the second requirement early in your exam schedule. Again, there are 10 marks available for this relatively discrete part of your answer. By attempting the second requirement straight after you've tackled the issue in your report, you also avoid wasting time in having to re-familiarise yourself with the details of the issue.

One final aspect here is whether you should plan to spend an equal amount of time on each issue or whether you should weight your time towards the more important issues. Again, there is no right or wrong answer. Some people prefer to weight their time so they spend longer analysing the top two issues and then less time on issues 3 and 4. This is a personal choice but care must be taken to ensure you don't over-run and that you leave sufficient time to tackle the lower prioritised topics.

Part (b) of the requirement (15 minutes)

Part (b) of the requirement, although presented separately, will often draw upon analysis that you've performed when writing about one or more of the key business issues. It is therefore best left until after you have finished this section of your report. As noted above, there are some real advantages of completing this as soon as you've written your analysis and recommendations for the issue in your report.

An alternative option, is to leave answering part (b) to the end of the exam. This approach avoids 'breaking your flow' and can perhaps be a little easier for those sitting the paper examination, since they don't need to worry about leaving sufficient space in their exam booklet.

Either way, care must be taken to allow sufficient time to tackle this second requirement. More guidance on this can be found in Chapters 6 & 7.

Tidy up (15 minutes)

It is good practice to spend a few minutes checking your script before the end of the exam. For some this need only be 5 minutes, in which case, the time on the plan can be re-allocated to other areas. This is also a time when you can 'complete' your report by writing a short introduction, a terms of reference and a conclusion. These aspects of your report do not score many marks and should be regarded as 'nice-to-haves'.

4 Tailoring your time plan

The above plan will need personalising to reflect things such as your reading speed, writing or typing speed, how long you take to generate ideas, and the specifics of the unseen you're presented with.

Only by practising mock exams, under timed conditions, will you be able to assess your strengths and weaknesses and develop a time plan that works for you.

5 Flexibility on the day

The purpose of the plan is to give you some structure to work around in the exam. However, depending on the issues that arise in the exam, you may need to flex the timings slightly.

For example, if there are more calculations than average, you may need to spend a bit longer preparing your appendices. This is fine, provided it is only a *bit* longer. Five minutes extra on one area can easily be borrowed from another. However, if you were to spend 45 minutes on your appendices, instead of the suggested 25 minutes, you will struggle to recoup 20 minutes from somewhere else.

Equally, the time spent analysing each issue may not be equal. You may have one issue where more analysis is required (perhaps three alternative solutions have been given to you in the exam and you need to analyse all of them) and another where the options are more straight forward.

 Be prepared to be flexible but always remember your end goal is to provide reasonable analysis and recommendations on at least four issues.

6 The great time robbers

There are a number of ways in which time can be wasted or not used effectively in the Case Study Examination. An awareness of these will help to ensure you don't waste time in your exam.

- *Inactive reading*

  The initial 20 minutes reading time must be spent actively reading, processing the information and considering the impact on the organisation, how the issues link together and what could be done to resolve them. You will not have time to have a second detailed read and so these thoughts must be captured first time around.

- *Worrying unduly about the prioritisations*

  More will be said on this in Chapter 8 on planning your answer. Briefly though, whether you have an issue prioritised as number one or number two will make little difference to your overall score.

- *Placing too much focus on presentation*

  This time robber is one that has a bigger impact on those sitting the computer based exam. The temptation to change font sizes, make various words **bold** or *italics* or <u>underlined</u>, is very hard to resist. But, resist you must! There are very few (1 or 2) marks available for having a report that is well presented, and these finer details will be worth nothing at all.

- *Worrying about the words you're using / Being a perfectionist*

  Students can often spend such a long time pondering about what to write that over the course of a 3 hour exam, over half of it is spent staring into space. Again, those sitting the computer exam are often worst affected since they not only spend time pondering, but also have the ability to delete so can change their mind several times before settling on the right word combinations. It is suggested that 2,500 words (excluding appendices and the answer to requirement 1(b)) is a good script length to aim for. Anything less than this, and you will find it harder to pass the exam. Just focus on getting your points down and don't worry about whether they could have been phrased better.

- *Going into too much detail on earlier sections of your report*

  As we've said earlier, not finishing your report is a key reason for failing the Case Study Examination. One of the main reasons why students fail to finish their report is a lack of discipline when writing about an issue. They feel they have to get all of their points down rather than selecting the better points and moving on.

- *Re-reading what you've written / correcting spelling mistakes*

  Again, this is something that affects those sitting the computer exam more than those writing their answer on paper. Often students can re-read paragraphs three or more times before they move on to writing the next part of their report. Instead, try to leave the read through until your final 'tidy up' stage of writing the report. If you're sitting the computer exam, to make your report appear professional, you should ensure that you use the 'spell check' facility in Word to correct any typing errors. The CIMA marker will be reading and marking your script on screen and it is harder to read and understand the points you are making if there are many typing errors.

8

Planning your answer

Chapter learning objectives

By the end of this chapter you will:

- Understand how a structured approach can help plan your answer.

- Understand what makes an issue a key issue.

- Appreciate the impact your prioritisation will have on your overall mark.

- Have been introduced to some alternative prioritising processes.

- Have practised these processes to prioritise a set of issues relevant to the CeeCee case.

- Be aware of how to approach the analysis of a problem in order to gain judgement and logic marks.

- Have seen some useful checklists to help you "brainstorm" the impact of an issue and identify some alternative solutions in order to gain judgement and logic marks.

1 The importance of planning

In the previous chapter we saw how important it was to manage your time in the exam to ensure you're able to complete all of the necessary stages in the preparation of your answer. And for this we have suggested you devise your own personalised time plan, one that allocates an amount of time to each of the stages.

One of the stages that was outlined was 'planning your answer'. Sitting the Case Study Exam is not as straight forward as turning up, reading the requirement, and then writing your answer. With such a broad, open requirement, you must spend time planning the content of your report if you are to submit a report that scores well in all of the assessment criteria.

If you do attempt to write without any form of content plan, your report will lack direction and a logical flow, it won't fully address the key business issues, and the recommendations will lack solid justification. It is for this reason that time should be specifically allocated to planning the content of your report.

2 Using your 20 minutes reading time effectively

Given the preparation you've done before the exam, reading the un-seen can often feel like a firework display is happening in your brain; each new piece of information you read about triggers a series of thoughts and ideas.

The planning process must therefore begin as soon as you start reading the unseen information. Every second counts within the case study exam and so it's important to use all of your time effectively by capturing the thoughts as they come to you.

During this stage of the exam you should aim to:

- Read about and identify each event.
- Consider what the issue is.
- Evaluate the impact of the issue. Who is affected, by how much are they affected and what would happen if no action was taken?

At the end of the process (which may take longer than the 20 minutes reading time), you should aim to have:

- Identified which four issues you will discuss in the main body of your report. (Note: These should all be issues that have been noted in the unseen material.)

- Assigned a loose prioritisation to the issues (the final order might not be clear until after you have performed some calculations).

- Considered any linkage between the issues presented in the unseen.

- Have noted down any initial ideas/thoughts on alternative courses of action (possibly with pros and cons).

- Identified two ethical issues to discuss and advise on.

3 What is an issue?

One of the most important things you'll do when planning your report is identify the issues facing the company and prioritise them. But what do we mean by the term 'issue' and how does it differ from an 'event'?

An event is something that occurs or happens. The unseen material will typically report on a number of events which have recently occurred.

An event will often trigger an issue for the company, an issue being something that requires management action or decision:

Action – this is needed to solve a problem

Decision – this is required when assessing the viability of a strategic proposal

Thus the two basic issue types are:

- Problem

- Proposal

For example, the unseen material may tell you that a key director has resigned (the event). However, it is not the event that triggers the need for action. Instead, it is the issues which arise from the resignation, being lack of control and leadership and the concerns that key stakeholders may have over this, that bring about the need for action.

Your report must deal with the four most important issues facing the organisation as a result of the information contained in the unseen material. Your familiarisation with the pre-seen material will allow you to better assess the importance of each issue.

4 What makes an issue a key issue?

The prioritisation of your issues should be based on three key aspects:

- Impact on the organisation's strategic objectives and key stakeholders

- Urgency

- Likelihood

Of these, the impact an issue will have on an organisation is the most important.

Impact

An issue which has a high impact on the organisation should be ranked above those with a lower impact. Now, this sounds very straightforward but exactly how do we go about assessing the impact an issue will have?

 One of the best approaches is to consider each of the key stakeholders, their objectives and the effect the issue might have on those objectives. For example, shareholders will be looking for profitability, dividends and growth. Any issue that will cause profitability to reduce, either now or in the future, is going to have a high impact on them, and by association, the organisation.

Applying Mendelow's stakeholder matrix, as a general rule, any issue that increases the interest of a previously "keep satisfied" stakeholder or increases the power of a previously "keep informed" stakeholder is likely to be prioritised highly.

This approach will only be successful if you fully think through the implications of an issue. You must keep pushing each point, asking yourself "so..., so..., so..." until you get to an ultimate conclusion.

Urgency

An issue that needs dealing with urgently, or in the short term, should be ranked above those that are more longer term issues. For example, if you are told of an opportunity to win an exclusive contract, but tenders must be submitted within the next month, this would be deemed as urgent.

 Having said that, care must be taken when ranking a low impact, urgent issue against a less urgent, more significant issue. This is very commonly the situation when we have an urgent operational issue versus a less urgent strategic issue. It is not possible to give a hard and fast rule here but in general students should focus on the long-term impact if no action was taken.

A further thing to watch out for are issues that are implicitly urgent. Just because an issue doesn't have a deadline stamped on it doesn't mean it isn't urgent. For example, an issue that is damaging the reputation of the organisation will, by its nature, be urgent, because the longer it goes unaddressed, the more damage will result.

Likelihood

An issue that is more likely to happen should be ranked above one that is less likely. For example, you could be told about a threat of earthquakes within a key territory. But if the threat was assessed as low (say a 5% chance), this would not be prioritised highly, even though the effect of an earthquake would be significant.

Exercise 1 – Factors influencing prioritisation on CeeCee

As noted above, your familiarisation with the pre-seen material will allow you to better assess the potential impact an issue will have on the company and its stakeholders.

Based on your work on the CeeCee pre-seen information, identify what key factors you must consider when prioritising the issues facing CeeCee in the unseen.

5 The importance of selecting the right issues

The assessment criterion of prioritisation is worth a maximum of 5 marks to your overall score. It might therefore seem surprising that we are devoting so much time and space to the subject!

It is important to recognise that prioritisation marks are specifically awarded for the ordering of your issues and more importantly, the justification you provide of that ordering. The overall process of selecting which four issues you will discuss and in which order is however worth significantly more as it will impact on your judgement and logic marks, which together account for 40 of the 90 marks available for the main requirement.

It is therefore not surprising that this initial stage of the exam process; the reading of the material and the decision over which issues to cover, is the one where many students have the most problems.

This chapter will give some additional guidance, using examples from the CeeCee case material, to help you improve in this area.

6 Using a centralised planning sheet

To make sure the time spent now is of use to you throughout the exam, you will need consider carefully how best to document your thoughts. Within the 20 minutes reading time you are only allowed to annotate the exam paper. You can not use any other paper or start typing on your computer. Any method you adopt must be concise whilst still allowing you to capture **all** of your ideas and see the bigger picture in terms of how the issues inter-relate with one another (see additional guidance below).

Furthermore, the method must suit you! Everyone is different and what might work for one person could be a disaster for another. For example, some people prefer to work with lists, other with mindmaps.

Most people find that a combination of making notes in the margins, along with the use of a central planning sheet (to enable the bigger picture to be seen) is best. How you prepare the central planning sheet is a matter of personal preference and we've given illustrations of three different methods below. Practise each one to find out which you prefer and then tailor it further to settle on something that works for you.

Regardless of which method you end up adopting, some further tips include:

(1) Start your planning on a page torn from within the exam paper. In most cases, there will be a virtually blank piece of paper within the booklet on which you can work your magic!

(2) Never attack your exam paper with a chunky highlighter. The problem with highlighters is you can end up highlighting virtually everything (particularly in the Case Study Exam when most information provided in the unseen will be relevant) and are unable to write down any of the thoughts you have as you perform your initial read. Instead, use a normal pen and make notes in the margin of the exam paper. If you want to underline something specific, ensure you note why you thought it needed underlining. For example, you might underline a figure because you will need it to perform a calculation or you might circle a date because it indicates an urgent deadline.

(3) Always read the requirement first to ensure you identify any specific instructions. For example, are you told of an aspect that you must include in your report or is your report to be directed at a specific director or group of directors.

(4) Read about each bold heading in turn and be clear about both the event and the underlying issue. You must focus your discussions on the **issue** and not the event.

Method 1 – The ordered list

This process is ideally suited to people who prefer lists and structure.

Step 1:
- Begin by reading everything under the first bold heading. Make notes in the margins concerning the impact, urgency and size of the issue. Also jot down any ideas on alternative solutions.

- Ensure you have identified the issue and then write this in the middle of your planning sheet (use a blank page from the exam paper).

- If you think the issue also has an ethical dimension, put a star or an 'E' next to it.

Step 2:
- Read everything under the second bold heading, making notes as you did in step 1.
- To add this issue to your planning sheet, you must consider whether it should be prioritised above or below the first issue.
- To decide you will need to quickly review your notes about urgency, size and most importantly the impact of the issue on the strategic objectives of the business.
- Add this issue to your planning sheet, either above or below the first issue depending on what you decide.
- Ensure you note down your reasoning (this can be used to help write up your prioritisation section later).

Step 3:
- Repeat step 2 for all of the remaining bold headings on the exam paper.

Step 4:
- Review your list to identify any linkages. Can two issues be condensed into one because they are very similar? Could you use one issue as a potential solution for another? Will one issue impact on the recommendations you can provide on another?
- Mark the linkages on your planning sheet.

---

e.g

Illustration 1 – The ordered list

You are told of the following 3 events in the unseen information:

- A retail site in a prime location on Broadway, New York, has become available. Juliette Lespere and Ruth Giddens both believe it would be perfect as a flagship store to drive CeeCee's expansion into the USA. At least one other party is interested and the landlord is pressing for a decision;

- During a recent audit of a supplier, unacceptable working practices involving child labour have been discovered. The supplier manufacturers approximately 3% of CeeCee's garments;

- Following a recent upgrade to CCIPL, there have been irregularities in the deliveries of stock to stores, resulting in some store managers complaining that stock levels are too low. Just over a quarter of CeeCee's 630 stores have now been affected.

Required:

Prepare your planning sheet.

Suggested solution

Note: Items in italics show what has been added in each step.

Step 1 – Review of 1st bold heading

Issue	Impact
Availability of Broadway site	*Opportunity to gain foothold in new key market.*
	Growth is key to delivery of five year plan.
	Significant strategic decision.

Notes in the margin would include: implicitly urgent – other parties are interested, potential high impact if expansion was successful, needs financial evaluation.

Step 2 – Review of 2nd bold heading

Issue	Impact
Availability of Broadway site	Opportunity to gain foothold in new key market.
	Growth is key to delivery of five year plan.
	Significant strategic decision.
Use of child labour found in supply chain*	*Potential damage to reputation is exposed.*
	Failure to protect workforce – unethical.
	Rectification could lead to disruption in supply chain.

Notes in the margin would include: only 3% of garments. Internal knowledge at present. (Remember – the * denotes an ethical issue)

Step 3 – Remaining bold headings

Issue	Impact
IT systems failure	*Loss of customers (resulting in loss of revenue and falling profits) if stock not available.* *Empty shelves look bad.* *Shareholder dissatisfaction.*
Availability of Broadway site	Opportunity to gain foothold in new key market. Growth is key to delivery of five year plan. Significant strategic decision.
Use of child labour found in supply chain*	Potential damage to reputation is exposed. Failure to protect workforce – unethical. Rectification could lead to disruption in supply chain.

Notes in the margin would include: minimal damage to reputation – fast fashion concept. Impact on store manager motivation (bonus?). Big impact – ¼ of stores.

Step 4 – Linkages

Issue	Impact
IT systems failure	Loss of customers (resulting in loss of revenue and falling profits) if stock not available Empty shelves look bad Shareholder dissatisfaction.
Availability of Broadway site	Opportunity to gain foothold in new key market. Growth is key to delivery of five year plan Significant strategic decision. *Can't consider further overseas expansion if doubts over reliability of IT system.*
Use of child labour found in supply chain*	Potential damage to reputation is exposed. Failure to protect workforce – unethical. Rectification could lead to disruption in supply chain. *Could further impact on the stock issues.*

Method 2 – The extended mindmap

This process is ideally suited to those who prefer pictures and diagrams to trigger their thoughts.

Step 1:
- Read the un-seen information making notes in the margins concerning the impact, urgency and size of each issue. Also jot down any ideas on alternative solutions.

- As you read convert each event into an issue and then write the issue in a "bubble" on your planning sheet (use a blank page from the exam paper).

- If you think the issue also has an ethical dimension, put a star next to it.

Step 2:
- Keep adding each new issue you identify to your sheet. At the end you should have a page with a number of bubbles dotted about.

Step 3:
- Review your bubbles to identify any linkages. Can two issues be condensed into one because they are very similar? Could you use one issue as a potential solution for another? Will one issue impact on the recommendations you can provide on another?

- Mark the linkages on your planning sheet by connecting the bubbles.

Step 4:
- Review your notes about urgency, size and most importantly the impact of the issue on the strategic objectives of the business. Use these to decide on the order in which you should cover the issues. Place numbers next to your bubbles to indicate your decision, ensuring that you keep a note of your reasoning to help when you come to write up your prioritisation section.

Illustration 2 – The extended mindmap

You are told of the following 3 events in the unseen information:

- A retail site in a prime location on Broadway, New York, has become available. Juliette Lespere and Ruth Giddens both believe it would be perfect as a flagship store to drive CeeCee's expansion into the USA. At least one other party is interested and the landlord is pressing for a decision;

- During a recent audit of a supplier, unacceptable working practices involving child labour have been discovered. The supplier manufacturers approximately 3% of CeeCee's garments;

- Following a recent upgrade to CCIPL, there have been irregularities in the deliveries of stock to stores, resulting in some store managers complaining that stock levels are too low. Just over a quarter of CeeCee's 630 stores have now been affected.

Required:

Prepare your planning sheet.

Suggested solution

Note: Comments in the margins would be the same as for prioritisation process 1.

Step 1 – Read the unseen creating "bubbles" for each issue

Step 2 – Finish reading the unseen

Step 3 – Linkages

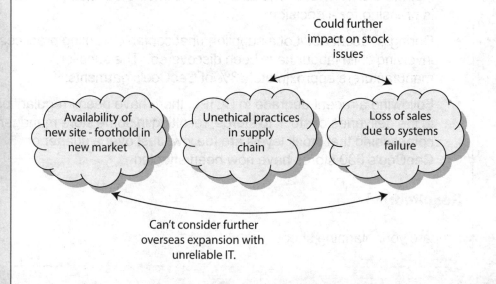

Step 4 – Order your issues

Could further impact on stock issues

Availability of new site - foothold in new market

Unethical practices in supply chain

Loss of sales due to systems failure

Can't consider further overseas expansion with unreliable IT.

2. Implicitly urgent due to interest from other parties. Growth key to delivery of 5-year plan.

3. Potential damage to reputation if exposed. Failure to protect workforce is unethical.

1. Empty shelves look bad. Loss of customers, sales and fall in profitability. Shareholder dissatisfaction.

Method 3 – Ranking using your SWOT

This process will help those who find it difficult to make the prioritisation decision.

Step 1:
- On your planning sheet (use a blank page from the exam paper), set out headings from strengths, weaknesses etc. As you read the unseen information making notes in the margins concerning the impact, urgency and size of each issue. Also jot down any ideas on alternative solutions.

- Convert each event into an issue and then write the issue on your planning sheet under the appropriate heading.

- If you think the issue also has an ethical dimension, put a star next to it.

Step 2:
- Keep adding each new issue you identify to your sheet. At the end you should have a virtually complete SWOT.

Step 3:
- Review your SWOT to identify any linkages. Can two issues be condensed into one because they are very similar? Could you use one issue as a potential solution for another? Will one issue impact on the recommendations you can provide on another?
- Mark the linkages on your planning sheet.

Step 4:
- Review your notes about urgency, likelihood and most importantly the impact of the issue on the strategic objectives of the business. For each issue decide whether each criteria is high, medium or low. When you've assessed each you should be able to see the order in which your issues should be placed.

Illustration 3 – Using your SWOT

You are told of the following 3 events in the unseen information:

- A retail site in a prime location on Broadway, New York, has become available. Juliette Lespere and Ruth Giddens both believe it would be perfect as a flagship store to drive CeeCee's expansion into the USA. At least one other party is interested and the landlord is pressing for a decision;

- During a recent audit of a supplier, unacceptable working practices involving child labour have been discovered. The supplier manufacturers approximately 3% of CeeCee's garments;

- Following a recent upgrade to CCIPL, there have been irregularities in the deliveries of stock to stores, resulting in some store managers complaining that stock levels are too low. Just over a quarter of CeeCee's 630 stores have now been affected.

Required:

Prepare your planning sheet.

Suggested solution

Note: Items in italics show what has been added in each step. Comments in the margins would be the same as for prioritisation process 1.

Step 1

	Urgency	Likelihood	Impact
Strengths			
Weaknesses			
Opportunities *Availability of Broadway site – expansion into new market*			
Threats			

Step 2

	Urgency	Likelihood	Impact
Strengths			
Weaknesses *IT systems failure resulting in low stock and lost sales*			
Opportunities Availability of Broadway site – expansion into new market			
Threats *Use of child labour found in supply chain* – potential damage to reputation*			

Step 3

	Urgency	Likelihood	Impact
Strengths			
Weaknesses IT systems failure resulting in low stock and lost sales.			
Opportunities Availability of Broadway site - expansion into new market. *(Can't consider overseas expansion if doubts over IT system)*			
Threats Use of child labour found in supply chain* - potential damage to reputation. *(Could further impact on stock issues)*			

Step 4 – Grade each issue based on urgency, likelihood and impact.

	Urgency	Likelihood	Impact
Strengths			
Weaknesses IT systems failure resulting in low stock and lost sales	*High – need to get stock into stores urgently and resolve long-term to ensure doesn't happen again*	*High – already happening*	*High – ¼ of all stores affected*
Opportunities Availability of Broadway site - expansion into new market (Can't consider overseas expansion if doubts over IT system)	*High – implicit urgency brought about by interest from other parties*	*Medium – difficult to assess because still early stages. Financial evaluation needed*	*Medium - US is likely to be large market. Could be key to achieving growth plans*
Threats Use of child labour found in supply chain* – potential damage to reputation (Could further impact on stock issues)	*Medium – any unethical practices should be curtailed once unearthed*	*Low – chances of damage to reputation is low, especially now it has been discovered and provided action is taken*	*Low – supplier is relatively small (3% of garments)*

Given the above assessments, you should rank the IT systems failure as the first issue followed by the availability of the Broadway site and then the unethical behaviour of the supplier.

Whilst these methods do have similarities, they also have subtle differences that bring about advantages and disadvantages.

Method one places the emphasis on the prioritisation decision whereas method two emphasises the identification of linkages between issues. Method three can help the prioritisation process but can feel rather robotic and can result in an ordering that might not reflect true commercial reality. Unfortunately in the Case Study Examination, not everything fits into a nice little box!

The following test your understandings will allow you to practise each of the processes using relatively simplistic scenarios. This will help you to gain a better understanding of which process best suits you.

Test your understanding 1

For the purposes of this exercise only, imagine you have been told of the following events in the un-seen information:

- Six months ago CeeCee opened its first shop in Asia, located in Tokyo. On the day of opening 25,000 customers visited the store. However, since then customer numbers have dwindled rapidly. Sales are only 50% of budget. Customer feedback indicates that the shoppers do not like the fashion – which they feel is too European.

- Juliette Lespere, the Sales and Marketing Director, has proposed launching a new clothing range under the label of Suzie Q (a leading, globally recognised designer). The relationship would initially last for 6 months. Juliette proposes a European-wide marketing campaign (TV, magazines and billboards). She is looking for a marketing campaign budget of 0.5% of annual sales revenue. Carla Celli is against the idea.

- An investigative journalist has found several large bags of slashed and cut new clothing (end of line) in an alleyway behind CeeCee's flagship store in Milan. This destroyed clothing was going to be dumped in land fill. Typically, end-of-line stock is either sold through market stalls or given to charities. La Stampa, the leading Italian newspaper, has published a feature article on this appalling waste.

- In order to improve profit margins in 2010, the Board have implemented some changes in pay and working practices across all 630 of CeeCee's shops. Firstly , staff salaries have been frozen for the next 2 years. Weekend working, which had been voluntary for staff, is now compulsory. Staff must work 6 days per calendar month on a Saturday or Sunday. Diane Innes (FD) calculates that these changes will cut costs by €150 million in 2010. Shop floor staff morale has plummeted and the customer experience is already being adversely affected by this.

- There has been a fire in the Central Distribution Centre. 10% of stock, valued at €10 million, has been destroyed. The Fire Department have commented that evacuation procedures were somewhat chaotic. Many members of staff have complained that they were unsure on evacuation routes within the centre.

- The Operations Director (Paulo Badeo) has tendered his resignation. This came as a complete surprise to all of the board. He has not chosen to give details of his reasons for leaving or what he intends to do next. There is six months notice in his contract.

Required:

Prepare the prioritisation section of your report. Also identify two ethical issues that you could cover in your report.

Test your understanding 2

For the purposes of this exercise only, imagine you have been told of the following events in the un-seen information:

- A proposal has been put forward to acquire Orihuela SA, a clothing manufacturer based in Spain, which employs 3,500 staff, and turns over €560m with a negligible profit before tax. The sellers are asking for €1,800m.

- Delays are now expected in the approval process for new leases on retail units in some countries as a result of new health and safety regulations brought in for EU member states. There is a possibility that much less than the planned 20 new stores will be opening in 2010.

- There has been recent media coverage over the actions of a group of senior management whilst on a business trip in Prague. Newspaper coverage has suggested that the group had misbehaved themselves after consuming too much alcohol at a fashion fair in the Czech Republic.

- Staff turnover in the last six months has increased by 20% in one of the European operations. The board is considering increasing the rates of pay of staff by 5% or improving the holiday and medical benefits on offer. The country provided €100m of the overall turnover of CeeCee in 2009.

- Laura Russo has resigned this morning giving one months notice (as stipulated in her contract). She is leaving to join Competitor 1 in the pre-seen (page 8) as the Head of Design.

- A major international supermarket chain Setco, has recently announced its intention to launch a wide range of "fast fashion" for sale via its European network of stores. It claims that it will be creating 1,000 new jobs as a result. Setco operates in virtually all of the European countries in which CeeCee operates.

- A new advertising campaign for an established product line has been suggested by a member of the Board. The campaign will be the same for all countries and involves an aspect of nudity on the part of the models in the advertisements

Required:

Prepare the prioritisation section or your report and advise on the two ethical issues to be covered.

7 Using your planning time effectively

Once you get past the initial 20 mins reading time, you are able to write on additional pieces of paper, use your calculator and, if applicable, start typing on your computer.

Given that you're now able to do a lot more, the next stage in the process is to plan your answer in more depth. Having decided on the four issues you plan to cover in your report, you will need to:

- Further consider the impact of the issue

- Identify some alternative courses of action

- Assess the advantages and disadvantages of the proposals (including resource requirements and implications) (potentially using the SAF framework)

- Have a brief outline of your recommendations

Again, there are a number of methods that can be used and by working through several practice mock exams you will be able to find a method that works for you. For those of you sitting the computer-based exam, you are able to plan within your word document, by setting up your key headings and jotting brief notes and bullet points on your ideas. A real danger to watch out for is spending time preparing a plan which you then don't refer to whilst writing up your script; planning on the computer does at least help to avoid this.

The time plan presented in the last chapter suggests you should spend a further 20 minutes performing this more in-depth planning. It also suggests 25 minutes should be spent preparing your appendices, primarily your SWOT analysis and any calculations you need to perform. In reality, you might find it easier to view this as 45 minutes in total, tackling each issue in turn by performing any calculations and considering the content of your report. When considering the impact of an issue, and when evaluating the alternative courses of action, it will be important to integrate the results of your financial analysis and so completing this alongside your planning will help you do this.

At the end of the process, you should aim to have:

- Completed any necessary calculations

- Expanded on the impact of each issue by considering key stakeholders

- Identified alternative courses of action and made some notes on the advantages and disadvantages of each

- Identified technical models and examples from the real world that will help to support the points you're making (you should be aiming for five of each, spread over the issues)

- A plan for answering the second requirement

- An idea of the recommendations you'll be making

Within this time it is unlikely that you'll know precisely what your recommendations will be. Very often these ideas will form as you write up your analysis. However, it is good to have a brief idea of what you're ultimately going to suggest as this will give your report a better flow, and gives you a chance to see the bigger picture and ensure your recommendations don't conflict with one another.

Some additional guidance

(1) This is perhaps the hardest part of the exam; as soon as you tell your brain it needs to come up with some ideas, it very often refuses to co-operate! Detailed below are some useful prompts that can be used to analyse different broad types of issues (problems or proposals). By reviewing these and using them during mock exams you can really help your brain to deliver ideas when you need it to.

(2) Don't simply view technical models and diversity points as something that must be included to tick a box. Instead *use* the models to help analyse the issues or suggest solutions.

(3) If you start looking at an issue and are stuck for ideas, don't waste time staring into space. Move on to the next issue and you'll find the creative juices soon start flowing.

8 Generating ideas

According to the examiner: "Business awareness will prevent you from making unrealistic comments and will enhance the commercial and professional judgement that you display throughout the report. The Judgement criterion is the main area of weakness for many candidates. What is required to gain marks is realistic clear discussions and recommendations that are commercially viable and professionally assessed."

It all sounds quite straightforward, doesn't it? Unfortunately, the reality can be quite different since it is often difficult to get the mind generating information and ideas under pressure, so a structured approach can help with the "brainstorming" process and result in a much clearer discussion within your report.

We noted earlier that the issues you'll cover in your report will fall into one of two basic types of:

- Problem; or
- Proposal

Having identified the type of issue, the idea is that you can use a certain structure for the analysis that will help to generate ideas and think about what is needed in the final report.

The structure to use is broadly based upon Johnson, Scholes & Whittington's 3 stage planning model, which we referred to in Chapters 1 and 3.

	Problem	**Proposal**
Strategic analysis	Impact of the problem	The logic of the proposal and analysis of it
Strategic choice	Alternative solutions	Alternative methods
Strategic implementation	Recommendations	Recommendations

These next sections will look at the structured approach for both issue types in detail.

9 The analytical structure of a problem

When you write your report you will be aiming to explain the impact of the problem, generate a range of possible solutions to that problem, and present your recommendations. It therefore follows that when planning your report, you should direct your thoughts in a similar way.

The impact of the problem

Your analysis should explain the areas of the business that may be affected by the problem and the likely impact if nothing is done about this problem.

You will already have considered the impact (and urgency and likelihood) of each issue when deciding on your prioritisations. Now, we need to consider the impact in more depth.

You may find that the problem impacts upon a range of areas of the business such as:

- Stakeholder interface (S for stakeholders)
- Business strategy (S for strategy)
- Short and long term operations (O for operations)
- Financial implications for cash and profit reporting (F for financial)

Together we have SSOF and we can use these headings as a checklist to work through; considering each area in turn to identify the full impact.

Stakeholders

Applying Mendelow's stakeholder matrix will be particularly relevant here.

The first key stakeholder to consider are shareholders. Any issue with a significant financial impact (see below) will have a direct impact on shareholders; the key question is how they might react to the issue. Arguably the impact may be greater in a listed company, as the shareholders are able to easily dispose of their shares if they are unhappy at the situation or don't feel it is being managed well.

The impact of an issue on customers and employees will also be critical, especially for those businesses who compete via a differentiation strategy. Media involvement can heighten the impact on either of these stakeholder groups, leading to greater reputational risk. Unhappy employees can lead to unhappy customers (especially within a service providing company) or can lead to operational issues (see below).

Strategy

To assess the impact of an issue on strategy, it is helpful to think of the following:

Core competence	– a product or process attribute that gives buyers and consumers reason to buy / use our product. **The advantage.**
Threshold competence	– a product or process attribute that, if not present, gives buyers and consumers reason NOT to buy / use our product. **The disadvantage.**

Any issue affecting competencies can present an opportunity to enhance strategy or may force the company to amend it.

If the pre-seen material provides information on future strategies, you will also need to consider the impact of the issue on the company's ability to implement these.

Operations

Events can create the issue of crisis management which if not dealt with, could severely damage the brand or even possibly lead to the closure of the business.

Operational issues tend to have a short-term impact, which if not addressed will turn into longer-term strategic issues. Common areas to watch out for are the impact on reputation, the impact on capacity and delivery and the impact on HR.

Financial

Many issues within the Case Study Exam will have a financial impact; it will up to you to quantify the effect (where relevant). Similar to operations, this effect may be both in the short-term and the longer-term, and whilst you might not be able to quantify both, you should at least recognise them. For example, an issue reducing profitability now may have a longer-term impact on the ability of the company to finance growth strategies.

Alternative solutions

The aim here is to highlight what could be done (not should but could). This is perhaps the hardest part of the exam for students and is an area well worth spending some time planning.

You will need to explain a range of possible solutions that could be deployed for the areas that may be affected, and again, the SSOF labels we saw above can help.

Stakeholders

Again, an application of Mendelow's stakeholder matrix can help, this time when identifying alternative courses of action.

To deal with some issues stakeholder support is often important when trying to find and implement solutions. With other issues, you won't get their support but you will need to manage the interface.

For this reason your suggested solutions must address how key stakeholders should be handled and how they should be communicated with. It is impossible to cover all stakeholders when writing your answer so the two key interfaces to deal with are the "keep satisfieds" and the "keep informed".

"Keep satisfieds"

Who are they?	Management tools / Potential solutions
• Bankers • Institutional shareholders • Private shareholders with substantial holdings • Regulatory authorities • National governments • Local governments • Unionised labour force • Highly skilled labour • Customers where high% of total revenue	• Face to face meeting with high profile commitment from our side. i.e. senior managers or key directors. Important as it shows that we are taking the matter seriously and with key staff at the meeting, decisions can be made there and then without having to report back • Periodic meetings as normal course of business • Regular formal reporting with KPIs within the stakeholder bespoke format • Frequent communication between lower level staff • Quality audits as specified • Multi functional and cultural interface team – dedicated resource with PR involvement • Feed-forward control with segregation of duty – check before not after the event • External consultants – expertise but at a price

"Keep informed"

Who are they?	Management tools / Potential solutions
• Staff – skilled & unskilled • Customers with small % of total revenue • Customers where product is of low value • Consumers • General public in some instances	• Email – periodic newsletter • Website with news and FAQ • Post • Media – press releases / magazine articles / TV interviews / obituaries • Company meetings – whole unit / division / department / operating unit • "Rumour mill" • Internal PR department • External consultants to provide specific management expertise • Open transparent processes • Physical security issues – separation of groups/use of third parties i.e. Police/internal staff or "external consultant"

Strategy

Many events will create the need to amend the organisation's strategy, planning or defend their advantage. With such an issue your alternative courses of action may need to cover:

- the ways in which the strategy should be changed (consider things such as the marketing mix (price, product, place, promotion), scenario planning, competitor analysis);

- suggestions of how that change can be implemented (consider things such as benchmarking, balanced scorecard, cultural change).

Many issues involving a change in strategy will be in the form of a 'multiple proposal'. This is where you're told about a problem and then two or three potential solutions are outlined for you. This reduces the importance of identifying the solutions and changes the emphasis towards analysing the options suggested.

Operations

The alternative solutions to address the operational impact of an issue can often be divided into short-term and long-term. The short-term involves dealing with the crisis (putting the fire out) while the longer-term sees adjustments made to minimise the chances of a similar event happening again in the future.

In the short term action will be needed to address:

- Stakeholder management – reassurance to all groups using techniques already discussed

- HRM – for example dealing with changing of the staff resource or issues relating to industrial relations and fraud

- Operations capacity – how to overcome problems of capacity constraint

In the longer-term to prevent repetition, amendments to the systems of internal control will be needed. E.g. new fire alarm system having seen one of the factories burn down.

Financial

Alternative courses of action will likely focus on:

- Ways to plug any gap in forecast profits (this could be via cost control or expansion into a new area)

- Where to obtain further finance (possibly to fund an expansion strategy or if the business hasn't been doing well).

- What to do with surplus funds (consider further investing or returning money to shareholders).

Once you get going and the confidence increases, hopefully many other points will come to mind especially ones that the examiner has given you some clues to in the pre and unseen materials.

Recommendations

Often you won't be a position to fully determine your recommendations at this stage. However, it doesn't do any harm to have a brief consideration of them. The clearer you are about your recommendations before you start writing, the better the flow of your report will be.

Things to consider at this stage include:

- What might the implication of a recommendation be?
- What resources will be needed and are they available?
- If not, how could it be obtained?

By asking these things now, it may help to reveal advantages and disadvantages of some of the alternative solutions you've identified.

10 The analytical structure of a proposal

When analysing a proposal in your report, you should aim to cover three areas:

(1) The logic of the proposal

(2) An analysis of the proposal - financial and business impact

(3) Alternatives

Logic

The logic requires an explanation of the strategic reasoning behind a proposal

For example: "Franchising is a form of strategic alliance and an alliance is created when two organisations join forces for the short to medium term for mutual strategic benefit. One party provides the expertise that the other lacks and vice-versa. McDonalds international growth strategy is based in many cases on alliancing, they provide fast food expertise whilst their partner provides local knowledge and cultural awareness"

Analysis

The analysis can be undertaken in two ways. Both use the Johnson, Scholes & Whittington framework for assessing the viability of a given strategy. This requires an assessment of the suitability, feasibility and acceptability of the proposal.

Firstly, one could simply present the advantages and disadvantages of the given proposal. Very useful if not all SFA areas are identifiable and can be combined with common sense.

Secondly, one could simply use the three headings of suitability, feasibility and acceptability and deal with the pros and cons under each of those headings.

Proposals vary and some lend themselves more to advantages and disadvantages whilst others are better dealt with using an SFA heading. It is suggested that you are familiar with both approaches.

Whichever approach you take, it is important to ensure the risks of the proposal are clearly identified.

Alternatives

The "alternatives" section is a final paragraph which highlights alternative courses of action to the one proposed. This won't be relevant to all proposals and is very much a 'nice to have' rather than essential.

The idea is that perhaps the same strategic outcome could be achieved in a different way. Therefore, to fully evaluate a proposal we should compare it against other ways in which that outcome could be achieved.

11 Using technical models to help your analysis

Don't forget that during the exam you will need to select no more than five technical models that you will apply within your report. The models and frameworks need to do more than just aid the analysis of the material (as was the case with the pre-seen material); they now need to support the analysis of the issues and recommended actions. This means you should choose the models that are most appropriate to the scenario you're dealing with.

Don't just view technical models as something you have to fit into your report. Choose what is the most relevant to the scenario and to help analyse the new issues presented to you in the unseen material.

The best way to use a model is either:

- To help explain the impact of an issue (for example, the resignation of a director may result in a majority shareholder moving from a 'keep satisfied' classification under Mendelow's Matrix to a 'key player' classification, as they will be concerned about the Board's ability to successfully manage any issues within the business. Action must be taken quickly to reassure the shareholder and demonstrate the strength of the Board.)

- To help evaluate a potential solution. Examples would include using Johnson, Scholes & Whittington's suitability, feasibility, acceptability framework to evaluate an opportunity or using Porter's Generic Strategies to show how an option would damage the organisations competitive strategy, or an NPV calculation to appraise an potential investment.

- To set the scene. Common examples include the use of financial ratios to comment on the performance of the organisation or reference to competitive strategy using Porter's Generic Strategies.

Having used the model when planning your answer it then becomes very easy to refer to the model within your report.

Models can, but do not have to be, detailed in an appendix. The most common models that benefit from being presented in an appendix are the SWOT analysis and your calculations. The danger of doing too many models in appendices is that you spend a lot of time writing them all out and then fail to cover all of the issues in your report because you run out of time. Often models such as Mendelow's and Ansoff's are better just referred to and applied in the main body of your report since a drawing of the four quadrants adds little value to the overall discussion. Bear this in mind during this planning stage and consider whether you do need to prepare an appendix or not.

Finally, if you do refer to a model in the body of your report, you are best to include the name of the model (for example, "Analysing the stakeholders using Mendelow's Matrix, we would classify the majority stakeholder as a 'keep satisfied' as they have high power but low interest"). However, you do not need to provide any background to a model or explain the theory behind it.

12 Using real world awareness to help your analysis

During the exam you will need to include no more than five comments relating to the real world. As with the technical models, your comments need to do more than just aid the analysis of the material, they now need to support the analysis of the issues and recommended actions. This means you should choose the facts and observations that are most appropriate to the scenario you're dealing with.

To score your diversity marks, each comment you make must be applied or 'used'. Too often, students drop in a random observation without commenting on the relevance. Like with technical models, you can ensure you capture the marks by using your understanding of the industry to help think through the impact of an issue or to help identify or evaluate alternative solutions. If these points are integral to your planning they will easily be integrated into your report.

You can refer to and use your real world observations at any point within your report. You do not have to give great detail on the source of the information although, if you can remember the source, it is best to quote it. If not, a comment such as "industry research shows that ..." makes it clearer that you are bringing in some real world examples.

13 Planning your ethical issues

Don't forget to spend some time within this planning period to consider your ethical issues. Ethical issues within the exam can either be problems or opportunities and can therefore be planned using much the same thought processes as outlined above.

However, one additional factor that must be explained within your script is the ethical nature of the issue. You must clearly explain why you consider it to be an ethical issue. Often this will arise from a conflict of interest between stakeholders or perhaps where the organisation may be perceived as owing a duty of care to, or acting unfairly towards a particular person or group.

Note: You should be careful not to confuse ethical issues with legal issues. If the organisation is or is considering doing something that is illegal, it will be far more than just an ethical issue.

When planning your answer to the ethics section of you report, you must ensure you cover the above, as well as giving brief consideration to the alternative courses of action and then ultimately providing detailed recommendations on what should be done.

You must ensure that the recommendations provided in the ethics section fit alongside the wider recommendations you are making for the other issues in the report. One common failing noted by the examiner is that the recommendations on key business issues will sometimes conflict with the ethical ones, and this is why it can be beneficial to give some brief consideration to your recommendations at this early stage. Be careful not to place too much importance to 'doing the right thing'. Yes, every business wants (or should want) to act ethically but at the end of the day, they may not be able to if it threatens the future performance of the business.

14 Requirement 1(b)

You should also spend some time during this 45 minutes giving some consideration to requirement 1(b). You don't need to decide on all of the points you plan to cover but should at least think about the user of the document, what their objectives might be, the tone your document will need to take and whether there are any key points that you've already identified in your planning that must be included.

15 The planning process – an overview

In summary therefore, we would suggest you follow a 6 step approach to your planning:

Within the 20 minutes reading time:

Step 1 –	Read about the event,	Note down your thoughts and ideas in the margin
Step 2 –	Consider what the issue is	Relate back to key stakeholders and profitability
Step 3 –	Evaluate the impact of the issue.	Use SSOF to help trigger thoughts. Make notes on a centralised planning sheet

Within the 20 minutes planning time:

Step 4 –	Identify some alternative courses of action	Expand your plan (either on paper or on screen) building on the SSOF headings.
Step 5 –	Analyse the alternatives (including resource requirements and implications)	Use technical models and real world awareness where relevant.
Step 6 –	Outline your recommendations thinking about **who** should do **what**, by **when** and **how**	Think through the implications of your suggestions and consider the bigger picture.

Don't forget, you may wish to group your planning time in with the time spent preparing your appendices and specifically performing financial analysis. The output of your calculations may be key to planning what you're going to say in your report.

By working through these steps, you will have an outline of the content of your report. This will not only ensure your report makes more sense and has a logical flow, it will also save you time. If you've ever tried to do two things at once you'll know that although it can be done, it'll take you longer to complete each task than if you had just focused on one task at a time. Trying to think and write at the same time is a good example. By doing the majority of your thinking up front you will be far more efficient when you write your report.

Test your understanding answers

Exercise 1 – Factors influencing prioritisation on CeeCee

Key aspects to consider when prioritising issues in the CeeCee case:

- CeeCee is a listed company and the majority of shares are held by institutional shareholders. Their interest in the company will be low when times are good and they do not have the power to influence the strategy of the business. However, if issues arise affecting either profitability, the ability of the Board to run the company or the brand image of the company, this interest will increase. Equally, they do have the power to push for the removal of the Board as a whole or any individual member of the Board. As a result, any issue that will move a shareholder into a key player position must be regarded as a key issue.

- CeeCee's success is primarily based on its reputation for up to the minute fashion styles (including both quality of design and speed of delivery) and excellent customer care. The brand image is strong and we are told of other key factors, all of which contribute to this image, on page 4 of the pre-seen. Anything that threatens this image or reputation should be regarded as a key issue. If customers stop spending, profits will fall and so shareholders will become dissatisfied.

- Finally, as mentioned above, excellent customer care is viewed as a cornerstone of CeeCee's success. A crucial element of this care is the staff employed by CeeCee. Therefore, anything affecting the motivation of staff, or anything that might reduce the level of care they provide (e.g. issues with training or recruitment), should also be regarded as a key issue.

Test your understanding 1

3. Prioritisation of issues

The following issues have been prioritised from the SWOT analysis (Appendix A)

3.1 The first priority is to address the erosion of the customer experience, a critical success factor of CeeCee, caused by the fall in staff morale when working practices changed. This is the most important issue to address as it is impacting upon the whole of the business already and will quickly adversely affect CeeCee's reputation for excellent customer service, thus leading to a fall in sales.

3.2 The second issue is to deal with the loss of talent and leadership if Paulo Badeo leaves the organisation. The ability of this fast fashion organisation to operate smoothly will be seriously undermined if this key player leaves the business. Additionally, Paulo works closely with Carla and his departure will unsettle the Board affecting its effectiveness. The six month notice period gives the Board a small amount of time to successfully resolve this problem.

3.3 Thirdly, the Board should decide whether to market a clothing range under the name of Suzie Q. The alliance with Suzie Q will impact on all 630 of CeeCee's shops. This will require an expensive marketing campaign to be undertaken and as such represents a significant shift in CeeCee's business strategy. The issue is ranked as third because it is less urgent than the top two issues.

3.4 The fourth issue is to address the reasons behind the shop in Tokyo falling below budget, and then take appropriate action. Whilst it could be argued that this is only one outlet (hence its ranking of fourth), if CeeCee is to expand into Asia, then it is important that this first store in the region succeeds.

3.5 Other issues

Another business issue, although not viewed as key, is dealing with the bad publicity in the Italian newspaper. It appears that this is a one-off incident and in the long run CeeCee's reputation should not be affected by one newspaper report. Of course, CeeCee should ensure that this is a one-off incident that will not re-occur. The ethical aspect of this issue is dealt with below.

Note: The above would all appear within the prioritisation section of your report. As an addition, for this exercise, we've included below details on the two ethical issues which you should have flagged to be covered in the ethical issues section of your report. These include:

(1) *The lack of professional behaviour that CeeCee has shown towards its staff causing chaos during the evacuation at the Distribution Centre. These poor health and safety procedures need to be addressed to ensure the safety of staff.*

(2) *The ethical conflict arising from CeeCee destroying clothes rather than giving them to charities or selling them off cheaply. Their action has been to the detriment to certain members of the population.*

Test your understanding 2

3. Prioritisation of issues

A SWOT analysis can be found in appendix A and the main issues arising are prioritised below.

Top priority will be to deal with the threats arising from the recent unexpected resignation of Laura Russo. This has been given the highest priority since the role of Head Designer has a significant impact on the quality of the product and the perceptions for the future of the main stakeholder groups. As such the potential impact on the basis of competitive advantage is likely to be substantial. The level of urgency is increased given the one month notice period and that she is going to work for a competitor. This needs to be dealt with before any consideration of strategic proposals and problems.

Second priority relates to assessing the viability of the proposed acquisition in Spain. It is prioritised as it involves an acquisition of an existing Spanish company for a substantial amount of cash and as such this will have significant impact on finances and the growth strategies of the company. A swift decision will be necessary before a competitor becomes interested.

Third priority links to dealing with the concerns that are likely to be arising from the possible delay in opening of the new retail units. This has been prioritised as this event could well hinder the growth strategy in 2010 and beyond and as such impacts on the ability to deliver the results that have been promised to the market place. At present, the delays are only a possibility and so this has been prioritised below the first two issues.

The final priority relates to the consideration of possible changes in business strategy and planning processes as a result of the entry of Setco into the European market for fast fashion. Given the size, reputation and coverage proposed, this could impact upon our ability to achieve growth targets in the long term.

Note: *The above would all appear within the prioritisation section of your report. As an addition, for this exercise, we've included below details on the two ethical issues which you should have flagged to be covered in the ethical issues section of your report. These include:*

(1) *The proposed TV advertising campaign which may contain a level of nudity. This could be perceived by society as unacceptable and unnecessary and it could cause offence to some people.*

(2) *The Directors and senior managers are representatives of the organisation and their actions whilst attending a recent fashion fair could be perceived as reckless and inappropriate.*

CeeCee: The unseen material

Chapter learning objectives

By the end of this chapter you will:

- Have reviewed the unseen material for the May 2010 CeeCee case study exam.

- Have had a chance to practise the techniques outlined in Chapters 3 through to 8.

1 A chance to practise

This chapter contains the unseen material for the May 2010 CeeCee case exam.

We would strongly recommend that before looking at the case writer's sample answer (presented in the next chapter), you prepare your own answer to this exam.

Whether you attempt this under timed conditions is entirely up to you. If this is the first full exam you have tackled you might like to take slightly longer, ensuring that you're happy with each stage of the process as you go. However, writing your answer within the 3 hours and 20 minutes time allocation will give you a chance to practise the essential time management skills.

2 The requirement

ANSWER THE FOLLOWING QUESTIONS

You are the Management Accountant of CeeCee.

Carla Celli, the CEO, has asked you to provide advice and recommendations on the issues facing CeeCee.

Question 1 part (a)

Prepare a report that prioritises, analyses and evaluates the issues facing CeeCee and makes appropriate recommendations.

(Total marks for Question 1 part (a) = 90 Marks)

Question 1 part (b)

As an Appendix to your report, prepare a summary for use in a presentation to the CeeCee Board, in bullet point format, of your findings and the financial implications of the proposal to franchise CeeCee shops in Asia. This Appendix should contain no more than 10 bullet points.

(Total marks for Question 1 part (b) = 10 Marks)

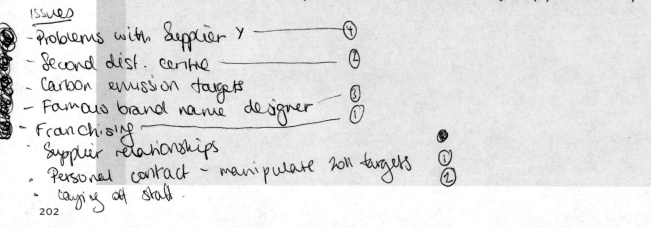

3 The CeeCee unseen material

The final accounts for the year ended 31 December 2009 showed that CeeCee achieved the forecast operating profit, before finance costs and tax, of €634 million.

The latest full year forecast for 2010 shows that the planned operating profit of €690 million should be achieved.

Problems with Supplier Y

Supplier Y, based in Eastern Europe, manufactures knitwear only for CeeCee. It has been manufacturing men's and ladies' knitwear for CeeCee for the past 9 years. It is one of CeeCee's many suppliers of knitwear, although the majority of CeeCee's knitwear is imported to Europe from suppliers in Asia.

CeeCee's IT systems are integrated with Supplier Y's systems for ordering and delivery of products. Supplier Y upgraded its IT systems 3 weeks ago and since then many of its IT systems have experienced severe problems. Supplier Y has failed to action several recent orders placed through CeeCee's automated IT ordering system. Additionally, Supplier Y has invoiced CeeCee for items which have not been manufactured or delivered.

Roberta Downs, the IT Director, has informed Supplier Y that it has a further 14 days to sort out its IT problems. If the IT problems are not resolved, she has stated that CeeCee will terminate the contract with Supplier Y. The contract is worth €20 million each year. She has stated that CeeCee needs to maintain direct contact with its suppliers as part of the fast fashion model and cannot work with suppliers which have unreliable IT systems.

Proposal to open a second distribution centre

All transportation of CeeCee products from manufacturer to shops is out-sourced. In the year ended 31 December 2009, the cost of CeeCee's out-sourced transportation of all products was €30 million. As is usual in this industry, CeeCee legally takes ownership of all products from the moment they leave CeeCee's suppliers' factories.

The transportation cost of €30 million includes shipping costs and air freight transportation costs for the 30% of products manufactured in Asia, as well as all road transportation around Europe. The transportation costs within Europe include transportation to, and from, CeeCee's current distribution centre in Northern Europe as well as transportation to all of its shops in Europe. Of the 70% of products manufactured in Europe, the majority are manufactured in Eastern Europe. These manufactured products are then transported in bulk to CeeCee's current distribution centre in Northern Europe.

CeeCee owns its current distribution centre. The current distribution centre is conveniently located near to a large shipping port and an airport, both of which receive products which have been manufactured for CeeCee in Asia. However, the current distribution centre is not well placed for the bulk of the products that are manufactured in Eastern Europe. Some products are transported across several European countries to the current distribution centre and then transported back across the same countries to CeeCee's shops in Eastern Europe.

Due to the increased cost of fuel and other road haulage costs, CeeCee has been advised that the cost of its out-sourced road transportation is expected to rise by 20% each year, for the foreseeable future.

Jim Bold, the Head of Logistics, has put forward a proposal to open a distribution centre in Eastern Europe. CeeCee would rent this proposed distribution centre, which could become operational by January 2011.

Some details of the proposal, prepared by Jim Bold, are as follows:

Out-sourced transportation costs	Transportation cost savings are forecast to be €4.2 million in 2011, rising by 20% each year.
Rental costs	€0.6 million per year, fixed for a 2 year period. Minimum rental period would be 2 years. After 2 years, rental costs are forecast to rise by 10%. The second distribution centre would be located in Eastern Europe, within 300 miles of 75% of CeeCee's European suppliers. The second distribution centre will not handle any of the products shipped from Asia. The current distribution centre will still handle all products imported from Asia and a small volume of products manufactured in Europe.
Location of distribution centres	The second distribution centre would be located in Eastern Europe, within 300 miles of 75% of CeeCee's European suppliers. The second distribution centre will not handle any of the products shipped from Asia. The current distribution centre will still handle all products imported from Asia and a small volume of products manufactured in Europe.
Employees and staff costs	The second distribution centre will require 80 employees and have annual staff costs of €1.8 million. The current distribution centre will require only 60 of its current 130 employees. 70 employees would be made redundant before the end of December 2010 at a forecast cost of €1.0 million. The staff costs at the current distribution centre will fall by €2.0 million per year from 2011.

IT costs	The one-off cost of the required changes to CeeCee's IT systems and the cost of new IT equipment for the second distribution centre is €1.6 million and will be incurred before 1 January 2011.
Other operating cashflows	The new distribution centre will incur €0.2 million per year in other operating cashflows. The current distribution centre incurs €0.8 million in other operating costs, which includes depreciation. These costs will remain unchanged.
Sub-letting of unused space at CeeCee's current distribution centre	There will be a large amount of unused space at CeeCee's current distribution centre which CeeCee owns, that it hopes it will be able to sub-let. CeeCee does not anticipate sub-letting this space until January 2012 at the earliest, at a rental income of €1.2 million per year.
Inventory costs	The impact of having 2 distribution centres is that this will increase inventory holdings by 3 days overall on a continuing basis. Some products will go straight to the second distribution centre and then subsequently move into the current distribution centre before reaching shops, slowing down the time taken from supplier to shop. Inventory at the end of December 2009 was €280 million based on 94 days inventory.
Carbon emissions	The proposal is forecast to reduce CeeCee's carbon emissions by 18% from its current levels.

You should evaluate this proposal over a 3 year period, using CeeCee's pre-tax cost of capital of 8%. Ignore tax. Ignore inflation except for cost increases stated in the table above.

Paulo Badeo, the Operations Director, is concerned that this proposal may not incorporate all of the factors that should be considered when changing CeeCee's distribution system. He has asked you to review the other business factors that should be considered in addition to the NPV evaluation of this proposal.

Carbon emission targets

Paulo Badeo has a close friend, Ralf Lenz, who is a member of the European Union (EU) commission responsible for setting carbon emission reduction targets for EU based companies. Paulo Badeo has been unofficially advised in confidence by Ralf Lenz that targets for reductions in carbon emissions for each company, over the next 10 years, will be based on the actual carbon emissions each company generates in 2011. Therefore, 2011 will become the base year against which target reductions will be measured.

Ralf Lenz has also advised Paulo Badeo in confidence that there will be financial penalties for companies which do not meet the legally imposed percentage reductions in carbon emission targets for each year after 2011.

Paulo Badeo has passed this information onto his fellow members of the CeeCee Board.

Proposal to appoint a famous brand name designer

Laura Russo, the Head Designer, is currently negotiating a 3 year contract with a famous global designer, Ben Eastwood, who has his own brand label. Ben Eastwood will design a small range of clothes exclusively for CeeCee 4 times a year over the 3 year contract period. These clothes will sell at the usual CeeCee pricing levels. Other High Street shops which have had "top brand name" designers have attracted new customers to their shops.

The total number of clothing products to be manufactured using the new Ben Eastwood designs will be limited to 0.5 million items in each of the 4 design collections per year to maintain exclusivity. The average price per item is forecast to be €30, generating additional sales revenue of €60 million per year. This will produce post-tax cash flows of €25 million for each year of the 3 year contract period.

Diane Innes, the Finance Director, has asked you to suggest a range of values for the fee that could be payable to Ben Eastwood for each year of the proposed 3 year contract period and to discuss the factors affecting the level of the fee that CeeCee might have to pay.

Franchising proposal

The CeeCee Board meeting in early May 2010 approved the planned expansion of CeeCee shops into Asia. The planned expansion is to open 150 shops in the 4 year period ending in December 2014, with 800 shops open in total, in Europe and Asia, by this date (as shown in Appendix 4 to the pre-seen material).

Juliette Lespere, the Sales and Marketing Director, is keen for CeeCee's expansion into Asia to happen faster and has stated that in addition to opening new shops managed by CeeCee, it could also franchise.

Franchising is where independent owners run a shop (or several shops) and products are supplied by CeeCee, using CeeCee's current designs and manufacturing suppliers. The owner of the franchised shops, called the franchisee, would be responsible for locating a suitable site, all capital expenditure, running the shop and all of its operating costs. The franchised shop staff are employees of the franchisee.

CeeCee would support all franchisees by providing marketing and IT support as well as access to its sales and inventory IT systems. The franchisee would be under strict contractual arrangements to conform to the CeeCee "house style" and not to sell any products that CeeCee had not supplied.

The table below excludes all capital expenditure relating to the shops CeeCee will manage and also excludes the capital expenditure for the shops that will be franchised. However, the operating profit figures shown for CeeCee managed shops are stated after the relevant depreciation charges for these managed shops. The average capital expenditure incurred for the opening of a new shop is forecast to be around €4.4 million per shop.

Juliette Lespere's franchising proposal is for a reduced number of CeeCee managed shops to be opened over the 4 year plan period, with 100 new CeeCee managed shop openings rather than 150. This reduced number of shop openings would be offset by 150 franchised shop openings in Asia only, over the next 4 years. This would result in 900 shops open in total by 31 December 2014, rather than 800 shops in the agreed 5-year plan.

The franchising proposal, compared to the agreed 5-year plan, is summarised below.

	Financial years ended 31 December			
	2011	2012	2013	2014
Original agreed 5-year plan (per Appendix 4 of pre-seen material)				
Average number of shops (end 2014 is 800 shops in total)	661	687	726	775
	€ million	€ million	€ million	€ million
Total operating profit	780	896	1,045	1,237

Juliette Lespere's Franchising proposal:				
Average number of shops:				
CeeCee managed shops (end 2014 is 750 shops in total)	661	685	711	737
Franchised (end 2014 is 150 shops in total)	15	50	90	130
Total (end 2014 is 900 shops in total)	676	735	801	867
	€ million	€ million	€ million	€ million
Average operating profit per CeeCee managed shop	1.18	1.30	1.44	1.60
Average estimated operating profit for CeeCee per franchised shop (based on franchise fees payable to CeeCee from franchisees less marketing and IT support costs)	0.70	0.70	0.80	0.90

The average operating profit figures for each franchised shop shown in the table above represents the revenue from franchising fees that CeeCee would charge the franchisees, less the cost of marketing and IT support provided to franchisees. It does not represent the operating profit which the franchisees could achieve by operating franchised shops.

Juliette Lespere has stated that she has already gained considerable interest from possible franchisees. Juliette Lespere has discussed her ideas for franchising with some of CeeCee's shop managers in Europe. Over 50 shop managers have expressed an interest to her in resigning from CeeCee and becoming a franchisee in Asia.

Diane Innes has asked you to calculate for each of the remaining 4 years of the plan period, and in total for the 4 years, the following:

- The total operating profit from the reduced number of CeeCee managed shops and franchised shops

- The difference between the total operating profit generated from the reduced number of CeeCee managed shops plus franchised shops compared to the original 5-year plan.

10

CeeCee: Walkthrough of the exam

Chapter learning objectives

By the end of this chapter you will:

- Have completed the initial reading and planning for the May 2010 case study exam.

- Be more familiar with the approaches and techniques discussed in Chapters 3 through to 8.

1 The aim of a walkthrough

The purpose of this chapter is to help cement many of the techniques we've shown you in the previous chapters. By breaking down the preparation of the report into the various stages we've outlined in Chapters 7 and 8, we can demonstrate what needs to be completed at each stage and show the sort of thought processes you will need to use in the exam.

2 Reading time – the first 20 minutes

Remember, the aim of the first 20 minutes is to read through the unseen material, absorbing information about each of the events and considering the issue and the impact of that issue.

Whilst reading, you should also start to form some opinions about which issues are more important than others.

Any ideas that come to mind about potential solutions should also be noted (although not forced – we have more time for this later) along with ideas for useful and relevant technical models and real world comments that could be used to help analyse the issue or identify solutions.

Finally, each issue should be marked as either a strength (unlikely), weakness, opportunity or threat, or a combination (such as an opportunity as well as a threat). This will help speed up the preparation of the SWOT analysis once the writing / typing time commences.

Also remember that within the 20 minutes reading time you are only allowed to annotate the exam paper. You can not use any other paper or start typing on your computer. The method you adopt for recording your thoughts must be concise whilst still allowing you to capture **all** of your ideas and see the bigger picture in terms of how the issues inter-relate with one another

In Chapter 8 we showed you some useful approaches to documenting your thoughts at this stage of the exam. What follows in this chapter is a sample of one of these documents. **Note:** This not **the** correct (CIMA published) answer. It is **an** answer but others could be equally as valid (both in content and style). Also note, that this is more detailed than you would perhaps prepare in the exam. Much of what has been written in the third column would more efficiently be noted by you in the margins of the exam paper on exam day rather than written separately onto a central planning sheet.

Sample output from 20 minutes reading time

The issues below have been presented based on priority order rather than the order in which they appear in the unseen. This is following the 'ordered list' approach outlined in Chapter 8; as each new issue has been read about, the thoughts have been positioned on the planning sheet based on whether an issue has a greater or lesser impact than the issues already covered. The urgency of each issue has also been considered when deciding on the order of the issues.

Issue	Impact	Other comments / notes (on exam day you should make these notes on the exam paper in the margins)
Proposal to franchise CeeCee shops in Asia	Fundamental change to current business plan – shareholders may be sceptical Faster expansion than agreed in 5-year plan Higher operating margins than forecast Reasonably urgent given level of interest expressed. Control of franchisees CeeCee has no experience of managing franchisees	Key opportunity – more shops in Asia by 2014 No experience of managing shops in Asia or of franchising (weakness). Threat from loss of control / damage to brand. Franchising widely used in industry (Zara, Mango) Legal restrictions re entry to markets overcome Reduced capital spend and lower risk but lower profitability. Needs financial evaluation Pros and cons of franchising
Proposal to open a second distribution centre	Operational savings may be possible Costs will increase if proposal not implemented – reduced profitability	Financial evaluation needed Opportunity to reduce costs Extra 3 days stock holding and impact on fast fashion model

		Lengthen lead time – damage to CSF in 'fast fashion' Not such a significant impact as franchising proposal.	Speed to market = CSF. Risk of losing sales to competitors (competitive rivalry, threat from value chains). More difficult to quantify. Opportunity to reduce carbon emissions – linkage of issues Ethical view point on redundancies within a growing business. Might not be able to sub-let space in current distribution centre – threat.
Proposal to appoint a famous brand name designer		Could generate additional revenues and profits Adds to differentiation through good publicity Small range of clothes so not as significant.	Opportunity if exclusive agreement. Loss of sales if Ben signed with a competitor. Asked for range of values for the fee payable – need to evaluate likely profit (prepare calculations). Small range will create exclusivity - should ensure all clothes sold. Risk of designs not selling sits with CeeCee Common strategy (H&M – Stella McCartney) Threat – behaviour of designer can reflect on CeeCee (TopShop – Kate Moss)

Problems with Supplier Y	Against good CSR principles of handling suppliers Unfair to threaten termination (ethical issue as well) Disruption to supply chain if contract terminated	<u>Business issue</u> Reliant of suppliers to deliver fast fashion (weakness?). Importance of IT in supply chain (especially in fast fashion business model) Could lead to supply issues – threat Raises questions over professionalism of Y – lack of sufficient testing indicates poor management Fairly easy to replace (€20m contract per annum). <u>Ethical issue</u> Terminating contract could force Y into liquidation (100% exclusive to CeeCee) Heavy handed given one problem in 9 year relationship
The need to reduce carbon emissions	Link with proposal for second distribution centre – delay in this could make it easier to reach targets and therefore avoid fines. Advice was received unofficially so potentially unethical to act upon it – inside information.	<u>Business issue</u> Threat of potential fines <u>Ethical issue</u> Acting on information provided in confidence – 'inside information' – risk of manipulation Target will be harder to meet if second distribution centre implemented immediately. Integrity of all Board members jeopardised by Paulo sharing his information.

Summary

To summarise the output from the initial reading time. (**Note:** You will not need to do this in the exam.)

Top four issues:

(1) Franchise proposal.

(2) Second distribution centre.

(3) Famous brand name designer.

(4) Problems with Supplier Y.

Ethical issues:

(1) Proposed treatment of Supplier Y.

(2) Reductions in carbon emissions.

Key new SWOT entries:

Weaknesses:

- Current problem with Supplier Y could create stock availability issues due to fast turn-around.
- CeeCee has no experience of franchising or operating in Asia.

Opportunities:

- Franchising proposal increases speed of growth in Asia (more shops in Asia by 2014).
- Reduced operating costs from opening a second distribution centre.
- Reduced carbon emissions from opening a second distribution centre.
- New Ben Eastwood designs.

Threats:

- Franchising – loss of control.
- Lower profitability at franchised shops.
- Supplier Y IT problems creating supply issues.
- Carbon emissions fines in the future.

3 Planning and calculations – the next 45 minutes

Before you start writing your report you must continue the planning process to expand on the impact of each of your top four issues and identify and evaluate alternative courses of action. You also need to perform any calculations that might be necessary to advise on a particular issue. You don't need to form your recommendations at this stage although any ideas you have should be noted down.

Techniques that may help you plan your answer further were covered in Chapter 8.

In this chapter we've given some notes on each issue to help show the sort of things you might have come up with. It is unlikely that you will have time in the exam to make such detailed notes. Remember, all you need to do is note down enough to prompt you when writing up your report. We've also outlined some thoughts on the calculations and provided some examples.

Issue 1 – Proposal to franchise CeeCee shops in Asia

Let's start by looking at the financial evaluation of the proposal.

	Financial years ended 31 December				Total
	2011	2012	2013	2014	
Original agreed 5-year plan (per Appendix 4 of pre-seen material)	€ million	€ million	€ million	€ million	€ million
Total operating profit	780	896	1,045	1,237	3,958
Juliette Lespere's Franchising proposal: Operating profit from managed stores:					
Number of CeeCee managed shops × average operating profit per owned shop	780	891	1,024	1,179	
Operating profit from franchised stores:					
Number of franchised stores (average) × average operating profit per franchised shop	11	35	72	117	
Total operating profit under new proposal	791	926	1,096	1,296	4,109
Difference from original plan	**+11**	**+30**	**+51**	**+59**	**+151**

In total, this gives additional operating profit of €151 million over the four-year period.

Further evaluation of this proposal could be effectively performed using the suitability, feasibility, acceptability framework of Johnson, Scholes & Whittington. Planning your answer under these headings therefore makes sense.

Suitability

- Expansion outside of Europe is a key part of the five-year plan.

- Asia could be a difficult market to crack due to barriers to entry (franchise relationship would overcome this) and cultural differences (different tastes and preferences) (a good technical tool to apply here would be a PEST analysis).

- Local knowledge of franchisee would help to reduce risks.

- Expansion may be easier to achieve into other regions such as the US, although these markets are already more developed with greater competitive rivalry.

- Asia is a high growth market as the younger professional population seek to adopt western styles.

- Opportunity to speed up growth. Would result in 900 stores in total, 100 more than planned. Extends the reach of the CeeCee brand.

Feasibility

- Lower capital outlay than owned store expansion (plan was to spend 150 × €4.4m =) €660m, this will fall to (100 × €4.4m =) €440m, a saving of €220m) – this then facilitates a faster expansion than could be achieved alone.

- There may be issues around attracting suitable franchisees.

- Could also lead to the loss of some existing store managers – we're told that Juliette has discussed the proposal with them (whether she should have done so can be questioned) and that 50 are interested. How many of these would be able to raise the finance is a different matter.

- It would free up management time as the day to day operations would fall to the franchisee. It would be necessary to establish a small department to liaise with the franchisees and ensure some control is maintained (monitor / audit).

Acceptability

- Per the financial evaluation, the proposal would lead to additional operating profit of €151 million over the four-year period.

- Reduced risk of failure due to lower capital investment.

- No current experience of managing shops outside of Europe or of managing franchisees.

- There is a risk of brand damage if the franchisees not controlled properly although this is reduced due to franchise operation being restricted to Asia (meaning any problems are less likely to transfer back to the European market).

- Possible loss of intellectual property rights (IPRs) if franchisees 'copied' clothes or sold the designs to other retailers – need controls and restrictions in place.

- Risk of loss of experience amongst current store manager team - performance of existing stores could decline.

Requirement 1(b)

Requirement 1(b) relates to the franchising proposal so at this point it is worth quickly considering what aspects from the above should be included. This doesn't have to be comprehensive at this stage – your thoughts will develop as you write up the issue.

However, initial thoughts are that reference should be made to:

- The recommendation (probably 'go for it').
- Additional operating profit.
- Increased number of stores - 100 more than planned (additional brand reach).
- Reduced finance required for expansion.
- Key pros and cons of franchising.

Issue 2 – Proposal to open a second distribution centre

As another proposal type issue, you may want to also analyse this in terms of its suitability, feasibility and acceptability. An alternative approach would be to consider the advantages and disadvantages. When writing up your answer, don't feel that you have to use these headings. They are more headings to prompt thoughts at this stage of the process.

We'll begin by considering the financial impact:

	T0	T1	T2	T3
	€ million	€ million	€ million	€ million
Transportation costs (€4.2m rising by 20%)		4.2	5.0	6.0
Rental costs		(0.6)	(0.6)	(0.7)
Staff costs - second distribution centre		(1.8)	(1.8)	(1.8)
Staff costs - current distribution centre (incl redundancies)	(1.0)	2.0	2.0	2.0
IT costs	(1.6)			
Other operating costs		(0.2)	(0.2)	(0.2)
Sub-letting of unused space			1.2	1.2
Inventory costs (€280m ÷ 94 days × 3 days)	(8.9)			
Total pre-tax cash flows	(11.5)	3.6	5.6	6.5
Discount rates @ 8%	1	0.926	0.857	0.794
Present value	**(11.5)**	**3.3**	**4.8**	**5.2**

Net present value = €1.8 million.

Advantages	Disadvantages
Positive NPV suggests project would increase shareholder wealth via cost savings in the business. However, this includes revenue from sub-letting the existing facilities which is by no means certain.	Compared to operating profit of €690 million per annum the amount is insignificant.
Reduction in carbon emissions and lower transportation costs (transportation costs will rise by 20% per year if no action is taken).	Three day lengthening in lead time will threaten fast fashion concept and CeeCee may lose sales to competitors. Increasing size of value retailers means they are able to deliver within shorter lead times, eroding CeeCee sustainable competitive advantage (Porter's Generic Strategies would be a good technical model to apply).

	Maybe investigate further as sense would suggest the second distribution centre should speed things up, not slow them down.
Diversity point could relate to Zara's operations (4 core distribution centres)	Stock holding will increase by nearly €9m.
	Making 70 people redundant when the company is growing will damage morale amongst the workforce.

Issue 3 – Proposal to appoint brand name designer

Again, this proposal can be analysed using the SAF model or by considering advantages and disadvantages. Don't forget to address the specific request from Diane, and suggest a range of values for the fee that could be payable to Ben Eastwood. Also, try to consider any ways to avoid any disadvantages or any potential blockages that may prevent the advantages being realised.

Advantages	Disadvantages
Provides a basis for a competitive advantage (provided the agreement restricts Ben's ability to work for other high street retailers)	Brand reputation could be damaged if styles are too extreme or if Ben misbehaves (as seen with TopShop and Kate Moss)
Limited number of items will enhance exclusive feel	Risk of unsold items rests with CeeCee
Increase in sales revenue of €60 million (approx 2%)	
Strategy has been very successful for real life companies (H&M)	

Fee suggestions

€60 million revenue at the usual gross margin (2009: 60%) implies gross margin of around €36 million from the items (assuming they were all sold). This represents the maximum that could be paid to Ben. However:

- This does not take account of transport and distribution costs, nor any of the other overheads associated with selling the goods

- CeeCee assumes all the risk of unsold items

- The gross margin may be higher on these items due to the exclusive nature.

- Market forces will need to be considered (if CeeCee doesn't offer enough, Ben could go to a competitor).

- Suggested fee level is to pay the designer 50% of the gross margin of these products which would be €18 million. However, negotiate upwards from, say, €5 million.

Other factors

- Will need to ensure designs are suitable for CeeCee customer base – could include clauses in the contract

- Will need to ensure the contract prevents Ben from working with any of CeeCee's competitors

- Break clauses could be included around Ben's actions and how they reflect on CeeCee.

Issue 4 – Problems with Supplier Y

Being a problem type issue, it is important that your planning addresses not only the impact of the problem but also evaluates some alternative solutions. Additionally, this problem creates both business and ethical issues and it will be important that the ultimate recommendations you make balance both aspects.

The notes relating to impact have already been included on the central planning sheet above. We'll therefore focus on the potential solutions here.

Alternative solutions

Solution	Factors to consider
Terminate contract if problems not resolved in 14 days	Should be fairly easy to replace supplier Y with one who has reliable IT (Y is one of many suppliers – contract is only worth €20m per annum) (could apply Porter's Five Forces model).
	Least hassle approach for CeeCee.
	Won't resolve short-term supply issues.
	That the problem has occurred could be a reflection of poor management and could indicate that further problems might be expected.

Work with Y to resolve the problems	Shows respect to the long-term relationship and nine years of problem free trading.
	Is the ethically correct action (the 'right thing to do') - without this contract, Y may be forced into liquidation and employees will lose jobs.
	Recognises that this is a one off IT upgrade, not an issue that is likely to frequently re-occur.
	Could result in additional cost (and therefore reduced profit) for CeeCee.

Other general factors to consider:

- Short-term action may be required to ensure supply problems don't escalate. Perhaps they could revert to manual ordering (or at least manual confirmation) until the problem is resolved. The invoicing problems will need to be investigated.

- Support could be provided by CeeCee on a chargeable basis. CeeCee could send their IT experts to Supplier Y to help solve the problem.

- Good relationships with suppliers are essential to the delivery of fast fashion.

Ethical issues

The planning relating to the ethical issue regarding the proposed treatment of supplier Y has been covered above.

Reduction in carbon emissions

Ethical issue is whether to act on the information that has been provided in confidence.

If deliberately delayed the development of a second distribution centre, could make reaching targets much easier and reduce the potential for fines if targets are missed.

However, this is not going along with the spirit of the new targets. Would not be viewed as being 'the right thing to do'.

Alternative is to take no action based on the information; to in effect 'ignore' it and consider with all decision making without considering the ability of CeeCee to reach these targets.

Technical and diversity marks

The above points will allow you to score judgement and logic marks but don't forget about other criteria within the assessment matrix. Crucially, there are marks available within technical, application and diversity that will be gained throughout your whole report. It is therefore useful, at the end of your planning, to make sure you have identified the five technical models that you plan to include (and which issues you will apply them to) and the five real world diversity points you will use to support your arguments. This will ensure you don't forget to include them when it comes to writing up that section of your report. In this case we have:

Technical models:

(1) SWOT (general for prioritisation)

(2) PEST (franchising proposal)

(3) SFA (franchising proposal)

(4) Porter's Generic Strategies (designer)

(5) Porter's Five Forces (supplier Y)

Diversity points:

(1) Zara / Mango use of franchising

(2) Use of central distribution centres (Zara)

(3) H&M (Stella McCartney) for successful strategy regarding designers

(4) TopShop (Kate Moss) for potential risk associated with designer names

A further diversity point is required. This can be gained in the introduction (suggestion would be economic climate in Europe making expansion to other markets more attractive).

11

CeeCee: A review of a sample answer

Chapter learning objectives

By the end of this chapter you will:

- Have reviewed a sample answer and made a comparison between this and your own answer in order to identify areas for you to improve.

- Be more aware of what scores marks under each of the assessment criteria.

- Appreciate the characteristics of a good script.

1 Sample answer

Presented in this chapter is a sample script for the CeeCee case exam. It was sat under exam conditions in 3 hours and 20 mins.

The script is above average length at just over 4,000 words excluding appendices. It would score highly, with a mark of 70% (35 credits). The CIMA suggested answer is far more comprehensive than this sample answer, and is available on the CIMA website.

The script has been presented as it was submitted. The layout has been preserved as much as possible and spelling and punctuation errors from the original document have been retained.

Against the script is a detailed analysis of where marks were scored and where they were lost. Commentary is given on both strong and weak areas and includes identification of where and how the candidate could have improved their marks.

Report

To: Carla Celli, CeeCee CEO
From: Management Accountant
Date: 27 May 2010
Subject: Review of issues facing CeeCee

Contents Page
1.0 Introduction
2.0 Terms of Reference
3.0 Prioritisation of Issues
4.0 Proposal to franchise CeeCee shops in Asia
5.0 Proposal to open a second distribution centre
6.0 Famous brand designer
7.0 Problems with Supplier Y
8.0 Ethical issues
9.0 Recommendations
10.0 Conclusion

Appendices

Appendix A SWOT Analysis
Appendix B Franchising proposal
Appendix C Distribution centre
Appendix D Summary for presentation to the CeeCee Board on the proposal to franchise CeeCee shops in Asia.

1.0 Introduction

The economic recession in 2009 has affected a number of retailers badly with shoppers having less disposal income to spend on luxury goods, this has seen a number of companies going into administration such as MFI, Adams & USC to name just a few in the UK alone.

CeeCee have performed extremely well in the same period and have managed to achieve the forecast operating profit of €614m in 2010.

CeeCee operate a differentiation strategy as identified by Porter by creating the feeling of exclusivity amongst their ranges which allows them to charge a premium for the products. This strategy has allowed CeeCee to fend off attacks from the large value retailers such as Primark & supermarket chain Tesco who both adopt a cost leadership strategy and retain their market share which prepared them well for the recession.

2.0 Terms of Reference

I am the Management Accountant appointed to write a report to the CEO which prioritises, analyses and evaluates the issues facing CeeCee and makes appropriate recommendations.

I have been asked to prepare a summary of points for presentation to the CeeCee Board on the proposal to franchise CeeCee shops in Asia and this is included in Appendix 6 to this report.

Although the title page, introduction and terms of reference are all areas of your report that attract few specific marks, submitting a report where these are just left blank does detract from the overall professionalism and will not make a good impression on your marker. You are inadvertently telling them that you had difficulties managing your time in the exam.

Try to ensure these sections are completed even if it is just a brief one line comment.

In this case though, the student has been able to produce more than this, including some real world awareness (problems with recessionary environment) and using a technical model (Porter's Generic Strategies) to help show why CeeCee has remained successful. This would therefore gain one technical mark, one application mark, and one diversity mark.

3.0 Prioritisation of Issues

The following issues have been prioritised in relation to the SWOT analysis in Appendix A.

3.1 Franchising Issue

The first issue that needs to be considered is the Franchising proposal, this is a change to the current strategy but there are huge opportunities to be gained by expanding the company outside of Europe. This issue has been prioritised above all others as there is the potential to significantly improve the company's operating profit and achieve better growth than is expected in the 5 year plan.

Try to avoid using general words such as "huge". If you can quantify the effect, do so. Also here, the reference to "opportunities to be gained" could have been more specific.

Students often resort to using emotive words like "significantly" as they feel it makes their report appear more professional. It doesn't and words like this should be avoided.

The link back to operating profit and growth is good.

3.2 Proposal to Open a Second Distribution Centre

The second issue is a new business strategy; this will impact on the time it takes for goods to arrive in shops and has the potential to affect one of CeeCee's core competencies. This proposal will compliment the expansion plans as extra capacity is bound to be needed to support this. The current distribution centre is coping well at present and that is why this issue is viewed as being less urgent than the issue above.

This section has explained very clearly the linkage between this issue and the franchise opportunity. It has also given a reasonable explanation for the relative positioning (why this is below the first issue).

However, the concern about the damage to a core competence could have been better explained; "has the potential to affect" is a bit vague and would have been better communicated as "the core competence of quick turnarounds in fast fashion could be lost".

3.3 Collaboration with Brand Name Designer

The third issue is a new proposal that has the potential to generate new revenue streams for CeeCee. This issue has been classed below the others as it is deemed to have less of an impact on the overall company.

This paragraph lacks a little depth but does cover the core impact of generating additional revenue. The attempt at justifying the relative positioning could be improved by explaining why the issue has less of an impact than the other issues rather than just stating it does.

3.4 Problems with Supplier Y

The fourth most important issue that needs to be dealt with is the IT problem currently being faced by Supplier Y. At the moment this is only affecting one supplier but this has the potential to spread to other suppliers and could end up compromising CeeCee's competitive advantage as contact with suppliers is a core competence. This has been prioritised below issue three as this is one of many knitwear suppliers so the impact on CeeCee is low at present.

3.5 Other Issues

Other issues such as the carbon emission targets and the staff redundancies at the current distribution centre have been considered in the ethics section.

The suggestion that this issue could spread to other suppliers shows that the student failed to read the unseen in sufficient detail. It is important to read the unseen carefully as the significance of an issue can easily be affected by just one or two words.

This section would score as a clear pass for prioritisation (4 out of 5). The order of the issues is acceptable, since the examiner deemed it was necessary to rank the franchising proposal in the top 1 or 2 issues in order to gain pass marks in Prioritisation.

However, the justification for the ranking was vague in places and so the section would not have scored full marks.

4-Franchising Proposal

Impact

The franchising proposal has the potential to turn CeeCee into a global brand and at the same time exceed the expectations of the five year plan as more shops will be open in 2014 than forecasted.

Franchising has worked very successfully for some of ceecee's competitors such as Zara who at the end of 2009 had about 10% of all shops as Franchises.

This strategy as identified by Ansoff is a Market development strategy, it allows ceecee to offer it's current range of products in new markets and so increase the area in which the brand will be recognised.

This proposal has a number of advantages and disadvantages which have been discussed below.

This section has some very good elements including the real world awareness of how other companies have successfully used franchising as a mechanism for growth (1 diversity mark would be awarded).

Perhaps the only let down is that the technical model (Ansoff's) has not been fully applied; it leaves the reader asking the question, "why have you told me that?". A technical mark would be awarded but the associated application mark would not be given.

Advantages of Proposal

From looking at appendix B it is clear that at the current projections show the Franchising strategy will generate an additional €150m of operating profit by the end of 2014 when compared to the 5 year plan. This will sit well with the shareholders as it will increase their wealth as it is likely to see an increase in dividends if ceecee stick to the current level and it will also be likely to increase the market value of the company as ceecee will be exceeding expectations.

This analysis is good and picks out most of the key advantages to the proposal, whilst also bringing in some real world awareness.

A clear reference is made to the appendix and the results of the calculations are discussed, together with the implications (shareholder satisfaction). The application marks for the calculations would be high (4 marks).

Another advantage of this proposal is that there will be less capital expenditure needed as the majority of the costs will be borne by the franchisee. This will allow ceecee to expand even quicker as there will be additional cashflow available to fund the expansion.

Another advantage is the fact that this proposal will allow ceecee to break into markets that may not have been accessibly by direct investment. Zara have experienced a number of difficulties breaking into the Middle East due to government restrictions but by following this strategy a number of these barriers to entry are eliminated.

Significantly, for each advantage noted, a detailed explanation about why it is an advantage, or how the proposal results in the advantage, is provided.

Disadvantages

Firstly ceecee have no experience of operating outside of Europe, designer trends historically have been different in Asia to Europe and so it will mean a number of adjustment will be needed not only to clothing styles but also to the sizes being manufactured.

Franchising runs the risk of damaging the brand reputation of the company if appropriate controls are not imposed on the franchisee, ceecee relies on its brand name as an alternative in part to marketing and any damage to this could affect the global brand name of ceecee and impact on the results throughout Europe.

Again, this is a sound analysis of the disadvantages. Significantly, when dealing with such an issue, it is easy for a student to simply regurgitate the generic disadvantages of a franchising strategy, without bringing in the specifics of the scenario. This student has not done this. Note how each paragraph clearly explains the point being made.

There is likely to be significant costs incurred for the franchisee, it costs a Mango franchisee €500,000 to initially start a franchise and with the current economic climate and the banks reducing lending it may be difficult for the franchisees to raise the finance necessary to open up the stores.

Being one of the more important issues, there would be a greater allocation of judgement marks for this section of the report than there would for other, less important issues. This would score as a clear pass for judgement (6 marks) as it gives a good evaluation of the advantages and disadvantages (each paragraph presented is of sufficient depth to be awarded a judgement mark). The score would have been higher if more discussion had been given on alternative ways of achieving the expansion.

5-New Distribution Centre

The new distribution centre is likely to be key in any future expansion plans ceecee has and so from the offset the idea seems to be in line with the objectives of the company.

This section is very brief and fails to address the many different ways in which this strategy will impact on the company (cost savings, logistics and carbon emissions).

This proposal will be analysed using Johnson Scholes & Whitttons framework of suitability, feasibility & acceptability.

The technical model has been used and applied well, meaning marks would be gained (even if the name of the model is incorrect).

Suitability

This looks at how the proposal fits with the organisations current strategic goals and objectives. As mentioned above a new distribution centre will be needed if ceecee continues to expand as the current distribution centre will soon be at full capacity. Ceecee's expansion plans are based on expanding outside of Europe as can be seen from the earlier franchising issue which questions the location of the new distribution centre as this is also based in Europe, although currently this centre is located close to the current shops this may not be the case within the next 4 years.

A good linkage between issues has been made. However, this candidate has failed to recognise the importance of the speed to market and how this CSF would be damaged under the proposal. This is a significant oversight.

Feasibility

This criteria looks at whether ceecee have the relevant resources and competencies available to carry the project through to a close. Jim bold has revolutionised the ceecee logistics system since his employment and this experience should mean that the new distribution centre although complex should not cause too many problems for Jim. There is also a need for new staff to work at the distribution centre and with the current economic environment there should be no problem in recruiting the staff needed to operate the centre. There are also limited financial burden as the new premises are going to be leased rather than bought.

Under the feasibility heading, the SAF model has been applied well and many different resources requirements have been explored.

Acceptability

This looks at how acceptable the project will be to the various stakeholders within ceecee. From a purely financial aspect this project has a positive NPV of €12.4m and so it is likely to be acceptably to the shareholders as it will increase their wealth. If we look at this from an employee point of view though this is likely to be totally unacceptable as the new distribution centre will mean redundancies are needed at the current distribution centre. If we look at this by using Mendelows Matrix of stakeholds which bases the finding on the relevant levels of power and interest on their own we would class employees as keep informed with high interest but low power, however if employees collaborate and bring in unions they move into the key player sector as they have a greater deal of bargaining power. Once employees are not happy it could lead to severe consequences for the company, as has been seen recently when British Airways staff staged a strike it effectively brought the whole company to its Knees and has caused significant brand and reputational damage. If this were to happen at ceecee the strike action could suspend the supply chain and would lead to significant losses.

The use of Mendelow's matrix seems a little 'shoe-horned' into the answer, as does the diversity point relating to British Airways, since a strong union presence would be unusual within this industry. A technical mark would be awarded but with no associated application marks.

Alternative solution

An alternative solution would be to look to open a distribution centre in Asia which would complement the five year plan of entering the new market and would have a positive impact on ceecee's carbon footprint.

This is a valuable addition to the analysis.

Despite some reasonable points being made under feasibility and acceptability, and the suggestion of an alternative approach, this section would score as a marginal fail due to the omission regarding the speed to market. This is a key factor that was viewed by the Examiner as an essential element that should have been identified and discussed.

6-Famous Brand Collaboration

The proposal has been implemented by a number of ceecee's competitors such as Topshop who have employed Kate Moss to design a range of clothes for there stores. This has had a positive impact on performance and has also increased the profile of the company due to the popularity of designers in the media.

This shows an excellent application of real world awareness and a diversity mark would be awarded.

The proposal has the potential to generate additional revenue of €60m per year and will improve post tax cash flows significantly.

The fee payable to the designed should be made up of a fixed fee with additional royalty payments being due depending on the success of the clothing. This way the designer will be retained and will be motivated to achieve designs that are going to fly off the shelves.

This reads more like a recommendation rather than an alternative.

This proposal will give ceecee a wider audience and will help to promote the brand across the world as media coverage targets audiences all over the planet. This should help ceecee to become known in Asia where it is planning its franchises and it should also create additional publicity throughout Europe when it is currently a well know brand. The only downside of this would be if the designer started to attract media attention for the wrong reasons, this has been seen for a number of retailers and could lead to some negative publicity being generated.

This proposal would also be likely to inspire ceecee designers and would give them motivation as the would be working along side Ben Eastwood which would increase their job satisfaction, it could also cause some designers to feel overlooked and may not be acceptable to all of them.

As a result the analysis seems to focus more on a discussion of whether CeeCee should appoint a famous brand designer rather than a range of values for the fee as was asked for by Diane Innes.

This is the weakest section of the report and perhaps reflects the time pressure that was starting to build. The analysis provided was superficial and lacked detail in key areas, specifically comments on the range of fees that could be paid to Ben Eastwood, which had been specifically requested in the unseen material. It would score as a marginal fail with perhaps only two judgement marks in total.

7-Problems with supplier Y

At the moment this supply problem is only affecting one supplier but if further supplier upgrade their IT systems this could start to escalate and any disruption in the supply chain could lead to a loss of competitive advantage as shops are likely to get low on stock which would result in lower sales and damage to the brand image.

Although this is a potential risk, no comment has been made about the likelihood of other suppliers upgrading (and the comments made by the student suggests this could happen imminently). This therefore appears to be a bit tangential.

Sainsbury's a large value retailer experience IT problems back in 2004 when they implemented a new £3billion system, it was necessary for them to revert to manual stock takes and it resulted in goods being left in the warehouse and ultimately led to the company experiencing its first loss in the company history.

Good use of the comparison with Sainsbury's – this would score a diversity mark.

Currently Roberta has come down hard on this supplier and only given them 14 days to rectify the situation and threatened them with termination of the contract. The following are alternative suggestion on how to deal with this supplier.

This final paragraph adds no value as it is simply a regurgitation of information from the unseen material.

<u>*Divert Orders to other Suppliers*</u>

Supplier Y is one of many Knitwear suppliers, in order to ensure there is no disruption to the supply chain it is an option to divert the orders to one of the other Knitwear supplier , ceecee currently has 350 exclusive suppliers and it is likely to find enough who have spare capacity to meet the increase in production. This option would mean there would be minimal disruption to the supply chain; porter identified 5 primary functions which needed to be done well to have an effective supply chain, inbound logistics being one of them. This option would also reduce the pressure on the supplier and ensure no rogue invoices were being produced. This option does not however solve the problem; the issue will still exist as there will be no improvement to the IT system.

A reasonable suggestion, the feasibility of which has been questioned.

The student has also made a clear distinction between the short-term and long-term.

Send IT Consultants out to the supplier

Ceecee is reliant on good relationships with suppliers and it is important to keep these intact, it is an option that Ceecee could send some of its own IT consultants out to the supplier to see if they can work together to solve the problem, they may also need to call on the outsourced It consultants if the problem is outside of their own remit. This option would not immediately solve the problem and would still lead to a delay in the supply chain; however it would give ceecee the experience to deal with this type of problem if it occurred in the future and would increase the time taken to deal with any further IT problems in the future. This option will also mean that additional costs are incurred but it will ensure a good working relationship is kept with the supplier.

Revert back to the old system

Ceecee could try to encourage the supplier to revert to the old system until the problem is located, this would immediately ensure business as usual was restored and it would mean that the supplier would not be faced with their contract being terminated. This may not sit well with the supplier as it is likely they have incurred significant cost in the upgrade and will be reluctant to see this go to waste. This option would however be the quickest as long as the supplier still had access to operate the old system which it would if it was running a parallel implementation.

Some other sensible suggestions have been made, all of which have been evaluated with a range of advantages and disadvantages.

> Three decent alternative courses of action have been analysed well; this section would score as a clear pass for judgement with around 4 judgement marks.

8-Ethics

An ethical issue arises when there is conflict between Stakeholder groups over what is seen as acceptable or unacceptable behaviour by the company.

This sentence is a 'nice-to-have' but would not earn any specific marks.

Ceecee is currently facing the following Ethical issues.

<u>*Carbon Emissions Targets*</u>

Paulo has recently been advised about the new financial penalties being implemented from his friend at the EU, which has raised a number of ethical issues. As the targets are being based on the carbon emissions in 2011 there is the opportunity for Paulo to act without integrity by reducing the focus on Carbon emissions to ensure that the targets that will be set will not be difficult to meet.

A very good explanation of the ethical dilemma that would score highly for the ethics analysis.

Paulo has advised the Board of the targets so he does seem to be acting with professional behaviour but it is important that the actions taken do not cause ceecee to change its CSR policies.

The exact opposite of this could be argued. Paulo has jeopardised the integrity of other Board members by sharing the information.

Jeroon de Joost should continue to implement the energy efficient lighting scheme that is expected to be finished in 2010. As this was included in the 2009 CSR report there is no change of strategy so ceecee will still be acting responsibility. A report should be made to the directors on the progress of th strategy to ensure it is completed on schedule. This should reduce emissions and ensure any targets set will take these measures into account. Zara have recently opened an energy efficient store in Athens that produces 120tonnes less co2 each year than its other stores, ceecee could look into some high profile stores like this with its expansion into new markets.

None of these recommendations relate specifically to the ethical issue regarding whether action should be taken based on the information supplied. Furthermore, the diversity point appears to have been shoe-horned in. This section would therefore score low marks for the advice given.

Problems with Supplier Y

Ceecee uses exclusive suppliers and as such the action threatened to supplier Y from Roberta Downs shows a lack of compassion as if ceecee terminated the contract it would effectively cause the supplier to go out of business and result in many redundancies.

Instead of ceecee seeing its suppliers in this way it should ensure relationships are built to maintain the long term relationships. Any redundancies made by a large organisation will generate negative publicity and will work against the company.

It would have been acceptable to address this ethical issue alongside the business issue in the main body of the report.

The explanation of the ethical issue could be better (although one mark would be earned for the recognition that it would force the company out of business). More detail was needed on why this action is not the 'right thing to do'.

It isn't clear whether the student is saying this will act against CeeCee or Y.

It is recommended that the communication between ceecee and supplier Y is increased in this difficult time and to ensure integrity ceecee should advise supplier Y that the relationship is not at risk of being terminated. By working together and ensuring the supplier stick to the ceecee code of conduct ceecee can be seen as a brand who take care of their suppliers and are concerned for the welfare of their staff.

This will also fit with ceecee good csr responsibilities as being a responsible employer.

The recommendations given could be improved if more specific details had been provided (e.g. what should the be communicating about, and how).

The justification for the recommendation (that CeeCee would be seen as a brand who takes care) is missing the point. Businesses should not take action to resolve ethical issues purely because of how it will look.

As they stand, these recommendations are too bland to score any more than one mark.

This candidate would score a pass for ethics with a mark of 6. Two issues are identified, both contain an reasonable explanation of the ethical dilemma although the recommendations given lack detail in places.

Recommendations

9.1 Franchising Proposal

It is recommended that the franchising proposal is implemented as soon as possible, this has been chosen ahead of the traditional expansion plan included in the five year plan as it will significantly increase the operating profit over the next 4 years, these benefits will be noticed as early as 2011 when it is expected there will be an increase of operating profit of €10.48m (Appendix B) when compared to the five year plan. Although this proposal does contain some risks it has already been successful for ceecee's competitors and the financial gain makes the risk less severe.

This is an excellent recommendations section. For this first issue, the recommendation is clearly stated and a good justification is provided as to why this is the right course of action.

This is then followed by some very specific details regarding who should do what, by when in order to implement this plan.

The new proposal should be communicated to the shareholders and at the same time it should also be highlighted has this strategy has been so successful for both Zara & Mango. Carla I think it would be best if you contacted the Institutional shareholders in person and Juliette should also post a message on the company website outlining the plan to franchise.

I think Juliette should immediately contact an agent in Asia who can start to market the ceecee franchise model and identify potential franchisees. It is very important that the franchisees come from a solid financial background and it is advice that stringent checks take place before any agreements are signed.

As Ceecee do not have any experience of operating a franchise it is advisable to employ someone with the relevant experience, I would advice that Alan Howard immediately contact the agencies to identify potential candidates who would be able to bring experience in this field to ensure the project is a success.

Paulo Badeo should also contact our suppliers in Asia to ensure that they are made aware of the new developments and will be able to increase production to meet the expected increase in design and garment size requirements. The problem identified earlier about the different fashion trends is likely to be less of a problem as Asia has become far more westernised in recent years and their acceptance of fashion trends has increased.

The Franchising proposal should be monitored and if possible benchmarked against Zara of Mango who have already successfully rolled out their Franchise models.

9.2 New Distribution Centre

It is recommended that this proposal is not implemented at this time.

Although the proposal has a positive NPV there are a number of factors that do not make it acceptable at the current time. One of the main reasons this should not be implemented is due to the fact that it increases the time it take for clothes to get from suppliers to shops. Speed to shops is one of ceecee's core competencies and any proposal should not cause damage to these but instead improve the competence and make it harder for competitors to copy.

It is recommended that Jim Bold is tasked with looking into a new distribution centre in Asia instead of a further one in Europe. The potential benefits would be that transportation costs are reduced which will also sit well with Jeroon de Joost when the new carbon emission targets are introduced in 2011. This option is also likely to increase the speed it take to get garments from suppliers to the shops which will give ceecee threat all important competitive advantage and ensure it fends off attack from its competitors.

This is another excellent set of recommendations that includes the linkage of issues. This shows that the candidate has clearly seen the bigger picture. It is a shame that the importance of the speed to market was not discussed in more detail earlier in the report.

9.3 Collaboration with Ben Eastwood

It is recommended that the collaboration with Ben Eastwood is implemented immediately and we should aim to have the first collection in the shops by the end of June to take advantage of the increased sales due to people in Europe taking their summer holidays.

The fee that should be negotiated with Ben should represent the increase in turnover that is expected. e need to ensure we make the offer acceptable to both parties and it is important that we act quickly to ensure Ben does not get snapped up by one of our competitors. I recommend a base fee of €250,000 for each collection with additional royalty payments being made after each collection has been finished. Laura Russo should open negotiations with Ben immediately. This royalty fee will be dependent on the success of each collection and it is advised that Alan Howard do some research to identify the fees our competitors pay their famous designers, we should match and if possible better the offer of our competitors to ensure Ben does not leave ceecee.

Ben is a globally recognised designer and his influence should help us to break into the Asian market successfully, it is advised that Ben is used on our Marketing strategy in the Far East to ensure that the brand is a success in Asia.

This recommendation is not as strong as the others, primarily due to the weaknesses within the analysis.

Most significantly, the fee base seems to appear from nowhere and has little justification. It could have been improved with some limits to support the negotiations.

On the plus side, at least a specific fee has been noted which is more than many candidates managed on this exam.

This shows an excellent linkage of issues, again reflecting that the student has viewed the company's position as a whole.

There should also be the opportunity for some of our designers to work with Ben on the new lines to increase our own designers experience and to ensure that they do not feel as if they are being overlooked. Ian Howard should speak with Laura Russo about implementing a scheme which gives our designers the chance to have a secondment with Ben for one of the season's collections he produces.

9.4 Problems with Supplier Y

This problem has the potential to impact on the whole supply chain if other suppliers follow Y and upgrade their own systems. It is therefore important that we find the root of the problem.

It is recommended that the short term solution is to divert all orders away from supplier Y we should have enough capacity with other suppliers to cover the extra production. Paulo Baddeo should contact the suppliers he believe are able to cover the extra load immediately to reduce the impact this problem is having on the supply chain.

I think that we need to work with supplier Y to come to the root of the problem therefore it is my advise that we do not impose the deadline set by Roberta as it is important to maintain a good working relationship with Y. I think that Paulo also contact supplier Y to advise that we want to work with them to find out what the problem is.

Again, plenty of justification and detail make these a strong set of recommendations.

An attempt has been made to address both the short-term operational and longer-term strategic issues. However, the practicalities of the recommendations haven't been fully thought through (for example, for transferring orders to other suppliers it has been noted that 'we should have enough capacity' yet there is no foundation for this comment.

We then need to send out a team to supplier Y so that the problem can be identified and rectified, we need input from both sides so it is important the we stress to supplier Y that this will not affect our long term working relationship. Roberta should set up this team and if needed contact our external IT consultants to attend the meeting to ensure this problem is identified in the shortest possible time. Ceecee should also aim to claim back as many of the costs incurred by ceecee from the issue with supplier Y this should not be discussed until the problem is resolved to ensure there are no further delays.

Once the problem has been resolved it is advised that supplier Y is used as a supplier at the same levels it was prior to the problem.

In the longer term it is important that we send a memo to all our suppliers to highlight the problems incurred and how the situation was rectified, it may be that the software used was not compatible and if this is the case the suppliers should be advised of alternative software to use. I think it is important that we also stress in this memo that our supply chain is at the core of the ceecee business and any interruptions are very costly so in future any system upgrades should not be implemented without appropriate testing and if possible parallel running to ensure there is always a backup system in case of failure.

This is a simple preventative measure to ensure the risk of future problems arising is minimised.

Of the 30 logic marks available, 20 relate to the first requirement to prepare a report. Those 20 marks are further broken down between the issues, with the more important issues having a higher allocation of marks. This report would score well on virtually all issues, with the exception of the designer proposal. Overall, the candidate would score a clear pass.

10-Conclusion

Ceecee has a number of exciting opportunities that will enable it to grow from a European brand into a global brand. This is good news for the future of ceecee and it is likely to have a positive impact on the Market Value of the company once these initiatives are set out in detail to the market. Ceecee has a bright future and with careful management can grow to rival market leaders in the fast fashion industry such as Indetex (Zara).

This conclusion does enough in the context of the overall report.

A conclusion is a 'nice to have' and is certainly not an essential element of the report. A few lines such as we see here is perfectly acceptable.

Appendix A

SWOT

Strengths

- *Good IT & Logistics system allowing smooth running of fast fashion model*
- *Achievement of Planned operating profit in 2009 despite difficult trading conditions*

Weaknesses

- *Problems with Supplier Y*
- *Has not yet achieved global brand as still no shops outside of Europe*

Opportunities

- *Collaboration with Famous Brand Designer – Ben Eastwood*
- *Franchising Proposal to expand outside of Europe*
- *New Distribution Centre in Eastern Europe*

Threats

- *Continued threat from Value retailers gaining market share*
- *Juliette Lespere being poached by Franchisees*

> The SWOT contains all of the key business issues but does not reflect the ethical issues regarding the treatment of supplier Y and the carbon emissions targets. It also fails to recognise the franchising proposal as a threat as well as an opportunity. The marks under the application criteria would therefore be slightly reduced to 2.

Appendix B - Franchising proposal

€m

Year	2011	2012	2013	2014	
Operating profit from CeeCee shops	779.98	890.5	1023.84	1179.2	
Operating profit from Franchise shops	10.5	35	72	117	
Total operating profit	790.48	925.5	1095.84	1296.2	
Operating profit from 5 Year plan	780	896	1045	1237	
Difference between franchise and 5 year plan	**10.48**	**29.5**	**50.84**	**59.2**	**150.02**

This calculation is reasonably well set out and, most importantly, the calculations are correct. However, the lack of workings could have let the student down if errors had been made. Despite this, the calculation would still score highly within application.

Appendix C - NPV of second distribution centre

€m

Year	0	1	2	3
IT Costs	-1.6			
Transportation cost savings		4.2	5.0	6.0
Staff cost savings & redundancies	-1.0	0.2	0.2	0.2
Other operating cash flows		-0.2	-0.2	-0.2
Revenue from subletting			1.2	1.2
Net cash flows	-2.6	4.2	6.2	7.2
DF @ 8%	1	0.926	0.857	0.794
Present value	**-2.6**	**3.9**	**5.3**	**5.8**
NPV	**12.4**			

This calculation is reasonably well set out but does have a number of elements missing (rental costs and staff costs for the second distribution centre and most importantly the cash flow impact of the additional 3 days of inventory holdings). The omission of the inventory costs was a serious flaw in this answer. There is also an error on the staff cost savings. Marks would be deducted for these oversights. Equally, there was no attempt to re-evaluate assuming the revenue from sub-letting could not be achieved.

Question 1(b)

The following summary has been prepared to look at the proposed franchise of ceecee shops in Asia.

Business Aspects

- *Franchising has already been successfully implemented by a number of ceecee competitors e.g. Zara, Mango.*

- *Economic Crisis threatening banks ability to lend to Franchisees which could be a stumbling block, ceecee could guarantee the franchisees but this would increase risk of the project.*

- *Possibility of Brand erosion if tight controls are not Imposed*

- *Entry Barriers reduced as foreign ownership not permitted in some Asian countries*

- *Market development strategies are riskier as there is less experience of the new market.*

- *Ceecee would be recognised as a global brand rather than just recognised in Europe.*

- *Collaboration with Ben Eastwood should generate good publicity and Brand awareness to compliment the franchise.*

Financial Implications

- *Increase in operating profit of €150m by 2014*

- *Lower Capital Expenditure requirements as Franchisees take on these costs.*

- *Expansion outside of Europe is likely to have a positive effect on ceecee's share price and therefore improve Market Capitalisation.*

Some good points have been made, many of which go above and beyond what was noted in the answer to question 1(a). However, the summary fails to reach a clear recommendation and so would be marked down for this. Also, the section on financial implications is fairly limited and there is no recognition that the profitability of franchised stores is lower than owned stores. It would score 6 out of 10.

CeeCee: CIMA Examiner's post exam guidance

Chapter learning objectives

By the end of this chapter you will:

- Have reviewed the examiner's post exam guidance to better understand what is required under each of the assessment criteria and appreciate the common errors and omissions made by candidates who sat this exam.

1 How to use the post exam guidance report

After each exam sitting, the Examiner releases a post exam guidance report and these are available on the CIMA website for all past exams (they are published about 5 weeks after each exam).

You should read this document thoroughly to learn more about:

- What is required to score well under each of the assessment criteria.

- What common errors and omissions were made by the candidates who sat this exam.

- How to learn from other people's errors!

2 Post exam guidance report for the May 2010 CeeCee case

The main purpose of this report is to give help to candidates who were not successful in the May 2010 examination of the CeeCee retail fashion case. It is also intended to provide guidance to prospective candidates who plan to take future T4 Part B case study examinations. This report explains the basic rationale behind the case and the suggested approach to each of the assessment criteria. It also provides a brief marking guide, general comments by the Examiner and a statement of common errors, including omissions, which were made by candidates.

This case was concerned with CeeCee, a fashion retailer, founded in 1989 based in Europe, which prided itself on being a differentiator providing up to the minute fashion styles through a business model known as "Fast Fashion". CeeCee had 44,000 employees and operated in 18 different countries in Europe.

The company began by selling "look alike" clothing ranges which were popular with young professional women and had expanded into menswear, children's clothing and home furnishings. CeeCee, listed on a European stock exchange, achieved an operating profit of €616 million in the year to 31 December 2008 and achieved its forecast operating profit for the year to 31 December 2009 of €634 million. The full year forecast for the year ending 31 December 2010 was for an operating profit of €690 million.

The candidate was asked to (a) prepare a report that prioritised, analysed, and evaluated the issues facing CeeCee and to make appropriate recommendations and (b) prepare a summary as an appendix of findings and financial implications relating to one of the issues contained in the unseen material.

The T4 assessment matrix has 9 criteria, each of which carries between 5 and 30 marks. It should be noted that the Logic criterion has 30 marks associated with it, 20 marks for recommendations given in the answer to part (a) and 10 marks for the answer to part (b). It is important that the candidate earns high marks in the Judgement and Logic criteria as each of these carry 20 marks within part (a). It is also important that the candidate undertakes sufficient analysis to provide a sound base for discussion of the issues from which appropriate and logical recommendations can be made. The analysis should include appropriate financial and numerical calculations particularly those which are discernable from the unseen examination material.

The main issues contained in the unseen material covered the areas of:

- A proposal to franchise CeeCee shops in Asia
- A proposal to open a second distribution centre
- A proposal to appoint a famous brand name designer
- Problems being encountered with a particular supplier (Y)

There were other areas which candidates could have discussed (and which were given credit in the marking) but it was critical that the issues relating to the possible franchise of CeeCee shops in Asia and the proposal to open a second distribution centre were fully addressed in the answer.

Format of answers

The format of candidates' answers to part (a) was generally good. Candidates generally began with an introduction leading to very brief terms of reference, prioritisation of issues, followed by discussion of those issues. Ethical issues were then discussed and advice given and then recommendations were made on the issues which had been prioritised. Finally, most candidates provided a brief conclusion. The appendices were usually contained in an Excel file or in a separate answer book, although some were shown in the Word document or the main answer book. Either way is acceptable. One point worthy of note is that some candidates waste time producing a Position Audit which discusses the contents of the appendices. A position audit is not required in the examination. It is better that candidates reserve their comments for the main discussion section of their report.

It was noticeable that some candidates did not address part (b) at all, possibly because of time pressures. This was a dangerous omission, given that part (b) is worth 10% of the marks.

Discussion of general candidate performance under each assessment criteria

T4 Assessment Criteria

	Maximum marks available
Analysis of Issues (25 marks)	
Technical	5
Application	15
Diversity	5
Strategic Choices (35 marks)	
Focus	5
Prioritisation	5
Judgement	20
Ethics	5
Recommendations (40 marks)	
Logic	30
Integration	5
Ethics	5

<u>Analysis of issues</u>

PART (a):

Technical:

Rationale:

The purpose of this criterion is to assess the use of relevant theoretical techniques and frameworks and the provision of calculations to aid the analysis of the case material.

Suggested Approach:

It is recommended that candidates present their technical knowledge either in the form of appendices to the main report (in an Excel spread sheet or in a separate answer book or at the end of the report itself) or referred to within the report where relevant. Some candidates prefer to present their appendices at the beginning of the report which is also acceptable.

Marking Guide:

Marks are awarded for technical models and theories which are relevant to the case. It is usually appropriate to limit the technical knowledge displayed to 5 separate items.

Commentary:

Most candidates were able to display sound technical knowledge principally comprising a SWOT analysis, the Johnson, Scholes and Whittington SAF framework, a Mendelow matrix and a range of other strategic planning approaches. This was appropriate in this case study. As usual, most candidates performed well under this criterion.

Common errors:

Very few errors were made under this criterion other than some mixing up of the names of individual theorists, for example ascribing Ansoff's Growth Vector matrix to Professor Michael Porter.

It is important that candidates think about which models can be realistically applied to the actual case material rather than simply producing ones that are well known to them and hope they prove to be appropriate. For example, it is always appropriate to produce a SWOT analysis. It would be expected that the main issues to be discussed in part (a) of the answer will feature somewhere within the SWOT analysis. The purpose of the SWOT is to assist the candidate to identify the main issues affecting the organisation in the case. A SWOT analysis does not need to be very long. It should be long enough to enable the candidate to state what are the main issues contained in the case which must be addressed within the report. It would be very rare for a case study not to have something under each of the SWOT headings.

Application:

Rationale:

The point of the Application criterion is to assess how well candidates use the techniques, frameworks and calculations to support the analysis of the issues in the unseen material and their subsequent recommended actions.

Suggested approach:

Candidates are advised to ensure that they apply relevant models, techniques and frameworks correctly, given the case material. Thus it is important that rather than just regurgitating the model or framework, it is presented in such a way so that it conveys information which is relevant to the case. It is then expected that candidates use this information in their discussion of the issues. This also applies in respect of calculations, which should also be relevant to the information given in the particular case. The use of NPV analyses to evaluate an investment proposal is a well used technique which candidates should be familiar with and should be able to prepare accurately.

Marking guide:

Marks are available for the relevant application of techniques, models, frameworks and supporting calculations but only if the candidate applies them to the specific case. Marks were awarded for the application of models to the case material and for relevant calculations. Candidates who carried out sufficient numerical analysis were well rewarded. There was plenty of scope in this case to obtain high marks under Application if candidates had grasped the opportunity. In particular, marks were available for the evaluation of the franchise proposal, the second distribution centre and for calculating a range of possible fee payments to Ben Eastwood, the famous brand name designer. Failure to undertake any of these calculations meant that you were not meeting the requirements of the question as in all three issues, some calculations were required within the unseen material.

Commentary:

Most candidates provided a SWOT analysis although there were some candidates who did not. It was apparent that some candidates pre-prepared their SWOT analysis based on the pre-seen material and did not update it in the light of the unseen material. Such SWOT presentations earned very few marks as often the key issues were not included. You should ensure that all the prioritised issues are included in the appropriate quadrant of your SWOT. The SWOT should have included the opportunity offered by franchising shops in Asia but also that this presented threats, in particular the potential loss of control and the lower profitability offered by the franchised shops compared with those owned by CeeCee.

Common errors:

Some candidates' SWOTS omitted the franchising proposal as a threat.

There were numerous errors in the calculations. Some candidates failed to provide the original 5 year planned operating profit when considering the franchise proposal, despite this being given in Appendix 4 of the pre-seen material. Others failed to calculate the operating profit for CeeCee managed shops, the operating profit expected from franchised shops and then adding them together to arrive at an overall total. Others failed to calculate the difference between the total estimated operating profit for the managed plus the franchised shops and the forecast operating profit contained in the 5 year plan. Some candidates carried out an NPV calculation of the franchise proposal. This was technically incorrect as the profit from the owned shops was net of depreciation. Unless the depreciation was accounted for, the resulting NPV would have been erroneous as it would have been calculated on profits rather than cash flow. Candidates were given credit for the profit calculations they arrived at. What was indefensible was the deduction of the capital costs of opening new shops from revenue to arrive at a profit figure or increasing the revenue of the franchised shops by the capital costs saved. This shows basic lack of knowledge and understanding.

There were some errors within the NPV calculation relating to the second distribution centre. Most candidates did not know how to deal with the inventory costs. These should have been included within the calculation of the NPV as a one-off cost in year 0. The unseen material stated that these will be ongoing "on a continuing basis" and so the inventory costs should not have been shown as a recovered item in year 3. At least candidates who did treat the inventory costs in some way in the NPV received some credit, even if it was wrong. This put them ahead of the candidates who did nothing with it at all. It was surprising how many candidates were unable to prepare accurate NPV calculations which included costs and savings in the relevant years.

Finally, many candidates made no attempt at calculating a range of fees for Ben Eastwood. Those who did often failed to recognise that the absolute top amount that could be paid to him was €36 million per year, being the estimated cost to CeeCee before tax. It was unreasonable to suggest that this amount be paid to Ben Eastwood as that would leave no profit for CeeCee, but it does at least identify the absolute upper limit of the payment that could be made.

Diversity:

Rationale:

This criterion seeks to assess knowledge and understanding of relevant real life situations in the same or similar context as that in which the case is set. It also assesses the recognition of commercial or organisational issues relevant to the situation contained in the case whether or not they occur within the same industry.

Suggested approach:

Candidates should seek to introduce relevant examples at the point where they discuss the issue in their answer. Typically, this may occur in the introduction, the prioritisation section, discussion of the issues, ethics or within the recommendations. The main point is that candidates should seek to bring in the relevant example at the point which enables them to elaborate or emphasise the issue which is being considered within the answer.

Marking guide:

Essentially, there is one mark available for each relevant example given, providing it is clearly stated why it is relevant. This is an important point that candidates should note. There are no marks for simply name dropping. The candidate needs to explain why the example is relevant to the point being made. It is possible to quote the same organisation more than once if the examples given support different points.

Commentary:

This was generally satisfactory. These included references to many organisations which are engaged in the retail fashion industry and those which operate franchises.

Common errors:

There were few errors as such. The one main suggestion to candidates would be not to overdo it. Giving strings of examples which illustrate the same point is a waste of time as markers will only give credit for a single example which relates to the issue being considered and discussed.

Strategic choices

Focus:

Rationale:

This criterion requires candidates to select the issues that are regarded as the most important and which will be discussed further within the answer.

Suggested approach:

This is not a section of the report as such. Marks are awarded based on the issues which are contained and discussed within the report.

Marking guide:

There are five marks available for this criterion even if there are not 5 separate issues identified. It is for the candidate to determine which are the most relevant issues in the case to be discussed.

Commentary:

Most candidates were able to identify separate issues and received good reward.

Common errors:

There were no common errors associated with this criterion which, as usual, was well handled by candidates in the main. It should be noted though, that a candidate who prioritises an issue and then fails to discuss it will not receive credit for that issue under the Focus criterion. Poor time management that results in few issues discussed will have the effect of restricting marks awarded in Focus and other criteria.

Prioritisation:

Rationale:

Under this criterion, the candidate is required to rank the issues and to state clearly and concisely the justification for that ranking. The ranking should reflect the impact of the issues on the particular organisation, which may include its urgency.

Suggested approach:

The priorities should be presented early in the answer under their own heading. The priorities should be set out with the issues ranked as either 1st, 2nd, 3rd etc. Each should be justified with a concise explanation of its position.

Marking guide:

High marks are awarded if the candidate presents the most important issues with a good rationale as to why they are ranked as main priorities. It should be noted that markers do give credit to candidates who make a case for prioritising issues differently from those contained in the suggested answer. However, given the impact on profit of the franchising proposal and the effect a second distribution centre would have on CeeCee's logistics, it was clear that these should have been given prominence within the prioritisation section.

Commentary:

On the whole, candidates are now well versed in producing their rankings and generally manage to present their prioritised issues. The SWOT analysis, if carefully carried out, should help to clarify which are the most important issues to be addressed.

Common errors:

Some candidates failed to recognise the importance of the franchise proposal although most identified it as the top or second most important issue. Some candidates regarded carbon emissions as an issue which was acceptable although it might have been better considered under the Ethics criterion or as lower priority.

Judgement:

Rationale:

This criterion assesses the candidates' exercise of commercial and professional judgement in discussing the key issues which were prioritised.

Suggested approach:

It is important that the candidate discusses the impact the prioritised issues have on the organisation and what alternative actions, with reasons, could be taken to address them. This should include relevant supporting analysis drawn from the "Application" criterion. So for example, if a calculation is made within an appendix, then it should be used in support of the point being made in this section of the report. It is appropriate for candidates to make reference to their SWOT analysis when they discuss the issues highlighting its importance.

Marking guide:

Marks are awarded for discussing the different aspects of an issue and also for providing appropriate alternative approaches to resolving it. Clearly, the alternative approaches will receive higher marks if they are accompanied with a cogent rationale as to why they are being put forward.

Commentary:

Good analysis is critical to sensible commentary in Judgement. In most instances, the numerical analysis should support the case the candidate makes under the Judgement criterion. Without sufficient analysis, including discussion of the numerical analysis, the candidate is likely to make shallow remarks which cannot be substantiated. For example, failure to calculate the effect of the franchise proposal or the NPV for the second distribution centre is likely to lead to superficial commentary. There remain a number of candidates who after making such calculations, often to a high standard, then seem not to know what to do with the information they have produced in support of their argument. An employer not only wants a qualified accountant to be able to make relevant calculations but also to be able to interpret their meaning.

Common errors:

The main errors are listed as follows:

- Simple repetition of the case material without any additional analysis

- Discussion of issues not raised in the pre-seen or un-seen material which may have originated in a mock exam.

- Lack of depth in many answers, for example omission of discussion of the risks for CeeCee franchising in Asia

- Poor use of supporting analysis and calculations

- Failure to consider alternative approaches to resolving the issues

- Failure to discuss all the issues prioritised

- Wasting time on some issues not included in the unseen material for example Juliette Lespere being headhunted by a competitor

- Confusion between profit and cash as the increase in expected overall profit from the franchise proposal does not equate to cash flow

- Failure to recognise the possible impact of the franchise proposal or Ben Eastwood's appointment on CeeCee's IPR

- Failure to take account of the complications surrounding some of the issues, for example the impact the opening of the second distribution centre would have on CeeCee's logistics. The increase in inventory days would have a dramatic adverse effect on their fast fashion model and yet most candidates failed to recognise this or considered the 3 day delay to be immaterial

- Misunderstanding the inventory issue, the second distribution centre will increase inventory days, not reduce them

- Simple acceptance, without question, of why some products need to pass through both distribution centres

- Failure to discuss the NPV calculations prepared

- Incorrect derivation of the NPV for the second distribution centre

- Failure to consider a range of fees for Ben Eastwood despite being asked for this

- Failure to consider the cost of support to Supplier Y. Offering support is laudable, but should Y be asked to pay for this?

- Failure to recognise the need for CeeCee to have strong IT links with its suppliers

- Stating that Supplier Y should not be trusted due to incorrect invoicing and a lack of understanding of how invoices would be prepared and the data which would be needed to substantiate the invoices

- Failure to recognise the serious impact on Supplier Y's cash flow if invoice payments were delayed

- Failure to recognise the need for good communication, especially to staff once decisions had been made

- Making reference to non-existent appendices

- Over reliance on pre-learned material.

Ethics:

Rationale:

The candidate is required to use judgement to identify and analyse the ethical issues and state why these issues have ethical implications.

Suggested approach:

This section is normally coupled with the recommendations on how to resolve the ethical issues. It is perfectly acceptable to provide the answer in one section or it could be split over two as presented in the Assessment Criteria. The reason it is split in the Assessment Criteria is because the business issues usually have an ethical dimension associated with them. It is therefore appropriate for the ethical issues to be discussed alongside the business dimension. It is for the candidate to choose the method with which he or she feels most comfortable.

Marking guide:

Marks are awarded for recognising the ethical issue and then it is crucial to explain why it is considered to be an ethical issue.

Commentary:

On the whole, candidates were able to identify the ethical issues, particularly relating to carbon emissions, the treatment of Supplier Y and the potential redundancies if the second distribution centre is opened.

Common errors:

Generally, the ethical issues were reasonably well handled. Candidates were mostly able to identify them and provide a reasonable explanation of why the issue might be considered to be ethical although this was not always the case. There were some issues raised that were not ethical for CeeCee, for example the fact that a member of the EU Commission has revealed some inside information to a CeeCee Board member is ethical in so far as how CeeCee reacts to it. The fact that the EU Commission member has revealed the possible information is an ethical issue for the EU, not for CeeCee. Advice that the CeeCee director concerned should have no further relations with the EU staff member or be disciplined for receiving such information seems inappropriate. Advice that the CeeCee director should keep such information to himself in future is more realistic.

Recommendations

Logic:

Rationale:

This criterion tests whether the candidate is able to make well-justified recommendations for each of the prioritised issues.

Suggested approach:

It is important that the candidate ensures that there is strong reasoning for the recommended course of action. The recommendations should follow on from the weight of arguments and choices of possible actions in a logical manner. There is no one absolutely correct way of presenting the recommendations. Most candidates present them towards the end of the report, which is completely acceptable. Essentially, it is expected that the candidates will present their recommendations, provide a justification of why these courses of action are being recommended and then state what should be the follow-on actions.

Marking guide:

Marks are awarded not just for the recommendations themselves but also, crucially, for the rationale and strength of argument supporting them and for explaining what the organisation should do next to make the recommendation happen. Clearly the bulk of the marks available will relate to the main issues contained in the case.

Commentary:

The recommendations made by candidates were often weak and frequently commercially unrealistic. While most candidates provided recommendations, they were often not supported by an appropriate rationale, or any rationale at all. Failure to carry out sufficient analysis of the issues usually results in discussion which is weak and superficial leading to poor unjustified recommendations. It was also evident that there were time management problems encountered by some candidates with the recommendations being short. It is well to remember that this criterion carries 20 marks and is very important. The recommendations should follow the analysis and discussion and therefore sufficient time should be allowed for the recommendations to be provided. This should take the form of a firm recommendation which is followed by the justification for it. This will usually marshal the discussion around the issue and then candidates should state what follow-on action is required.

Common errors:

Many recommendations sections were short and failed to adequately address the options raised on key issues earlier in the report. As in previous diets, it was apparent that some candidates failed to recognise that a significant input was required in order to gain a good mark, or simply ran out of time and did not provide detailed and fully justified recommendations.

Frequently, the recommendations only repeated what had been suggested in the earlier discussion. Candidates should explain why they have chosen a particular recommendation, especially if they have discussed alternatives. The main areas where improvements could be made as well as those mentioned above were:

- The provision of an adequate rationale for a recommendation. There are good arguments both for pursuing and not pursuing the franchise. Similarly, there are good arguments for and against the second distribution centre. It is for the candidate to make a reasoned argument in support of his / her recommendation. Note, there may not be an absolute right or wrong recommendation for each issue.

- See the scale of the issues relating to the franchise proposal and the second distribution centre. In fact, the second distribution centre would have a minimal affect on CeeCee's cash flow, but would have a large impact on the logistics due to the increase in inventory. It would have been reasonable to recommend going ahead with the second distribution centre providing the inventory days were not increased.

- Recognition of the need for carefully drafted contracts with franchisees and the need to appoint a franchise manager. Some candidates assumed that Juliette Lespere had aspirations to become a franchisee herself.

- Recognition of the different aspects of some issues when each required a recommendation, for example the issue relating to Supplier Y in terms of what should CeeCee do immediately and in the longer term.

- Recommending that Ben Eastwood be appointed and then recommending a range of fees which could be paid to him.

- Reference to a fee structure by suggesting a range of fees for Ben Eastwood that might be applied.

- An explanation of the action or steps which need to be taken to implement the recommended courses of action.

In essence, the recommendations are a very important part of the answer and candidates should allow sufficient time to address them fully.

Integration:

Rationale:

The marks are all available for the overall functionality and quality of the report in part (a).

Suggested approach:

This is not a section of the report, but a holistic view of its entirety. As a guide therefore it is important that candidates present a report which is clear, sectionalised, addresses the main issues with good analysis and discussion and makes suitable recommendations based on the weight of evidence presented.

Marking guide:

Reports are deemed to be highly professional, sound, satisfactory, inadequate or poor. The whole 5 marks are available for a highly professional report and 0 or 1 mark for a poor report.

Commentary:

The quality of the analysis, discussion and recommendations in the reports was variable. Good answers tend to divide the report into the following distinct parts:

- Table of contents
- Brief terms of reference
- A brief introduction
- Prioritisation of the key strategic issues
- A detailed analysis of the issues

- Ethical issues (which may be in one section or split across the detailed analysis and the recommendations)
- Recommendations
- Appendices

It is important to effectively integrate the different parts of the report. So, for example, the recommendations should include the evidence base supporting them by reference to the earlier analysis which may be drawn from the main body of the report or the appendices.

A low mark will be awarded in Integration if the key issues are not properly addressed, or indeed are not discussed at all. Further, a low mark will apply in Integration if analysis is not sufficiently carried out, for example if the numerical analysis, requested by the Finance Director, was ignored or the discussion of the issues was vague and generally superficial in its nature and did not specifically relate to the unseen case material.

Common errors:

Some reports simply did not address the main issues and did not provide sufficient depth of analysis or reasoning behind the recommendations to warrant a high mark.

Ethics:

Rationale:

This criterion judges candidates on their recommendations and reasoning for each of the ethical issues identified.

Suggested approach:

This section follows on from the identification and explanation of the ethical issues. It may either be contained in one complete section or split over two as presented in the Assessment Criteria.

Marking guide:

Marks are awarded for the quality and depth of advice on the ethical issues raised.

Commentary:

Candidates tended to give sensible advice on the issues raised in the report although this was often too brief or vague and there were some instances where candidates did not provide any advice at all.

Common errors:

There are no common errors to report on the advice given for ethical issues other than to say that most andidates could increase their marks if they explained the reasoning for their advice in sufficient depth, rather than simply providing a statement of the advice they are offering. The issue of inappropriate ethical issues was considered earlier in this PEG. It is also worth noting that there may be more than one element of advice that should be given, for example there were two distinct ethical issues associated with the provision of insider information relating to potential limits for carbon emissions. Candidates need to be consistent in their advice under the criteria of Ethics and Logic. For example, it is not sensible to recommend in Logic that Supplier Y be replaced and then in Ethics to state that this same supplier should be supported.

PART (b):

Rationale:

The purpose of part (b) is to test candidates' ability to communicate in a competent professional way their analysis, findings and financial implications relating to a particular issue contained in the unseen material. It is important that candidates grasp that this part relates to one issue only, not all the issues in the case. Some candidates, very few, prepared the answer to part (b) as if it related to all the issues in the case, rather than just franchising.

Suggested approach:

Candidates should consider carefully the purpose of the communication, for whom it is intended and the salient points that he or she wishes to communicate. This means that the candidate needs to think carefully about what are the major points which need to be included in the communication. Thought also needs to go into the effectiveness of the communication which means that it should have clarity, be to the point and not be ambiguous. You should also follow the instructions or requirement for part (b), which in this case also asked for the financial implications of the franchising proposal.

Marking guide:

Marks are awarded on the strength of the communication provided. There are marks available for commentary on the strategic importance of an issue and the inclusion of relevant financial or numerical information where appropriate, the benefits and disadvantages of a particular course of action and a recommendation.

In this particular case, the issue related to the proposal to franchise shops in Asia. This was clearly a major strategic issue and gave the opportunity for the candidate to use appropriate numerical information within the communication. This was an ideal place to make reference to the profitability expected and the capital expenditure implications for CeeCee. However, the candidate should also have considered the other non financial issues, such as the potential for high growth and the need for suitable partners. These should have been balanced with the risk of loss of control and the lower margins expected from franchised shops compared with those owned solely by CeeCee. Where candidates made reference to more than the franchising issue, marks were applied to franchising and then consideration given to whether the overall result would have changed if the candidate had just concentrated on franchising and earned more marks. Candidates were given the benefit, if appropriate, by the display of strength in part (a).

Commentary:

This was the second time such a requirement has been included (the first being in March 2010) and the general level of communication was not strong and therefore disappointing. Typical answers made reference to the financial implications of the franchising proposal, the speed of growth and the need for suitable partners. Most candidates did not include a clear recommendation and many failed to progress beyond the superficial provision of numerical analysis. Many candidates thought that repeating information contained in the case was adequate, especially relating to the financial analysis. The question had specifically asked for the financial implications and therefore it was expected that the results of appropriate calculations should have been included. Effective communication is an essential skill of a Chartered Management Accountant and therefore candidates should ensure that they address this part of the examination fully.

Common errors:

The common errors in May were largely the same as in March being:

- Failure to actually do the appendix as required.
- Failure to provide a clear recommendation.
- Bullet points were in excess of the required maximum of 10.
- Bullet points which were too long and consequently lost their message.
- Insufficient attention to the strategic aspects of the decision sometimes as a result of poor earlier analysis.
- Omission of any financial analysis.

VYP: Pre-seen material

Chapter learning objectives

By the end of this chapter you will:

- Have a chance to practise the familiarisation techniques outlined in Chapter 3 on another past T4 case study – this time the pre-seen material for the November 2010 case set in the television industry.

1 The purpose of another case

As was noted throughout much of the first half of this study text, there is not necessarily a right or wrong way of tackling the T4 case study exam. The key to your success will be identifying the techniques that work for you, and this can only be done by practising.

The remainder of this text therefore presents a further T4 past case study, V & Y Productions (VYP), which is set in the TV programme making industry. By attempting to apply some of the techniques you've learned so far to this new case, you will be able to hone your approach, improve your commercial thinking and give yourself the best possible chance of passing this exam.

2 A reminder of the pre-seen approach

In Chapter 3 we outlined a generic set of steps that can be followed when familiarising yourself with the pre-seen material.

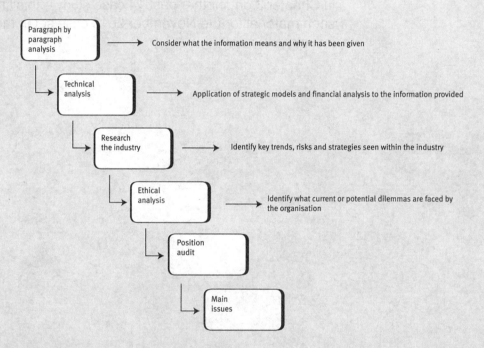

You should consider each of the steps when reading the pre-seen material for VYP presented in section 3 below.

After reading this pre-seen material, you should work through the mini-exercises, presented in section 4, to ensure you have a good level of familiarisation with this case. You should attempt to complete all of the exercises before you move onto the next chapter.

3 The VYP pre-seen information

Background and industry definitions

A large number of independent television (TV) production companies have been making TV programmes for transmission by TV broadcast companies in the UK and Europe for the last 30 years. Independent TV production companies are generally referred to as "indies".

Some independent TV production companies specialise in their choice of programme content, such as comedy, drama, current affairs or documentaries. Independent TV production companies are usually commissioned by a TV broadcast organisation to make a series of programmes, to meet specific criteria and for an agreed fixed contract price.

TV broadcast organisations include the BBC, ITV, Channel 4, Channel 5 and Sky in the UK and other commercial broadcast organisations in other European countries. All of the programmes that these broadcast organisations transmit to the viewing public come from 3 sources. These 3 sources are:

(1) "In-house" productions – where programmes are produced by their own production teams. "In-house" productions generally include news programmes, sports and events.

(2) "Acquired" programmes – which are programmes originally created for another broadcaster. Typically these include USA-made TV programmes and films.

(3) "Third party content providers" – this includes the range of programmes made by independent TV production companies.

Some of the TV broadcast companies in Europe are listed companies, whereas others are state-owned organisations. In the UK, the BBC is funded through a licence fee and it has an obligation to commission a minimum percentage of its programmes from independent production companies. It is currently exceeding the minimum percentage of commissioned programmes.

This case study is based on the third category above, concerning the production of TV programmes by an independent TV production company.

The definition of an independent TV production company (an "indie") is a company which does not have a licence to broadcast programmes, but which is commissioned by TV broadcast companies to make TV programmes for transmission (both for transmission on terrestrial channels and satellite channels).

The ability to make successful TV programmes is a mixture of good ideas, good production skills and the ability to sell the programme ideas to TV broadcasting companies. It is a very entrepreneurial industry which attracts highly skilled and artistic people. Many of the independent TV production companies are small businesses which are owned and managed by experienced TV production people. Most of these companies are private limited companies and are not listed. The shares are usually fully owned by the founder (s) of the company. Some independent TV production companies are highly geared, as debt has been used extensively to finance TV programme-making operations as well as to finance the capital expenditure required for the purchase of high technology programme-making equipment.

A small number of TV production companies are larger and have established a good brand reputation by consistently making highly popular TV programmes. Many of these larger TV production companies (referred to as 'super-indies') make a large number of long-running series of TV programmes.

The total value of commissioned programmes in the UK was over £2.0 billion in 2008, an increase of 2.5% in value terms from 2007. For example, the BBC commissions its programmes from a range of independent TV production companies, and it commissions around 37% of its programme output from "indies". The remaining output comprises programmes it makes itself and acquired programmes.

Some of the independent TV production companies have an international division which sells its completed programmes, or the programme format, to TV broadcast organisations in other countries. However, the ability of the TV production companies to sell the programme, or the programme format, depends on who holds the intellectual property rights (IPRs). It is usual for the TV broadcast company which commissioned the programme in the first place to own the IPRs for the initial broadcast of the programme as well as secondary rights for repeat broadcasts in the home geographical region (such as the UK). The independent TV production company usually owns all (or part) of the IPRs for sales made to TV broadcast companies elsewhere in the world. In addition, the broadcast company may also own the IPRs (or share the IPRs) for other media apart from television, such as the programme website, books and merchandise including toys and T-shirts. The international sale of programmes is explained further on page 10.

V and Y Productions Ltd

V and Y Productions (VYP) is an independent TV production company (an "indie"). The company was established in 2003 by two experienced TV programme directors who previously both worked directly for TV broadcast companies in the UK.

VYP is based in the UK and it makes TV programmes commissioned by the BBC, ITV, Channel 4 and Channel 5. VYP is not listed on either a main stock exchange or the Alternative Investment Market (AIM).

The aim of VYP is to make successful programmes for profit.

The 2 founders of the company, Steve Voddil and John Young, are both experienced programme makers, who have held programme director roles when they worked as employees for TV broadcast companies. They both wanted the freedom to do what they do best, which is to make TV programmes. The company was established in 2003, with only 12 employees, but now employs 60 people directly and outsources much of the routine TV production work to other small specialised companies. The outsourced companies provided VYP with the equivalent of around 400 person years of work in the year ended 31 March 2010. More details are shown in the section headed "Programme-making" on page 8.

The key employees in the company, who own shares in VYP, in addition to Steve Voddil and John Young, are Raj Shah and Paul Maas who are Directors of Videotape (VT) Editing, Janet Black, who is the Finance Director and Les Fisher, the Business and Legal Affairs Director.

A summary of VYP's key personnel is shown in **Appendix 1**.

The reputation of VYP is intrinsically linked to its people, especially Steve Voddil and John Young. They both are actively involved in winning new commissioned programmes from the broadcasting company, and they work alongside the relevant TV programme director who is proposing the programme idea. In this industry it is the people and their reputation and track record that determines the company's success.

VYP enhanced its reputation last year with several new series of programmes which were considered to be successful in terms of audience viewing figures. During the last 3 years VYP has won several TV programme awards which recognised the content of its programmes was excellent or innovative. VYP has established a reputation for the production of documentaries which allow the general public to make their views known on topical issues.

VYP generated total revenues of £28.6 million in the financial year ended 31 March 2010, which was almost 39% growth in total revenues from the previous year. This resulted in VYP having a market share of commissioned TV programmes in the UK of around 1.4%. There are hundreds of small independent TV production companies making programmes, and therefore this is a reasonable share of the market. This places VYP within the top 20 companies making TV programmes in the UK.

An extract from VYP's Statement of Comprehensive Income is shown in **Appendix 2**.

Programme commissioning

Programme commissioning is concerned with the stages that are undertaken by an independent TV production company, such as VYP, with any of the broadcast companies for which it wishes to make TV programmes. In the past there were some TV production companies which made "pilot", or trial, programmes in order to sell the programme concept. This is rarely done now due to cost. All of the TV programmes made by VYP are commissioned and contracted with a broadcast company before the production of the programme commences. The risk of a series of programmes being poorly accepted by its viewers lies entirely with the broadcast company which commissioned the series of programmes. This results in broadcast companies being cautious about which TV production companies, and which style of programmes, they decide to commission.

There are 3 steps in the process of getting a programme, or a series of programmes, commissioned. These are:

(1) Programme proposal submission. VYP will submit a programme proposal to the chosen broadcast company for approval of the programme content. This proposal will detail the genre of the programme (drama, comedy, documentary etc), the programme content and the number of programmes in a series. A re-commissioning of programmes (where a previous series has already been commissioned, made and transmitted) will often be approved quickly if the previous, or first, series was successful. Success is usually determined by externally audited audience rating figures.

(2) Business approval. VYP will submit to the relevant broadcast company the detailed budget for making the programme, or series of programmes, for approval. Broadcast companies do not negotiate these proposed costs on a line-for-line basis if the total cost falls within their "cost per hour" criteria for the genre of the proposed programmes. The factors that will influence approval of the budget will be the style of the programme and whether outside filming will be required, the location of any filming, as well as the fees required for any famous actors for the programmes. A new influence on costs is the use of computer generated imaging or computer graphics.

(3) Contract approval. This stage is reached when all aspects of the programme content and the budgets for the programme(s) have been approved by the broadcast company. It is only after contracts have been signed with the respective broadcast company that VYP can start to make the programme and the contracted revenue is paid to VYP. For most commissioned programmes, the full contracted revenue is paid to VYP soon after contracts are agreed.

When VYP has agreed a contract with a broadcast company for a commissioned programme, or series of programmes, then the actual costs incurred in the making of the programme are the responsibility of VYP. The profit, or loss, for each programme is determined by the difference between the contracted commissioned revenue and the actual costs incurred by VYP in the making of the programme. This therefore puts the emphasis of cost control with VYP.

In terms of cash flow, most of the broadcast companies fund part, or all, of the contracted commissioned revenue at the time the programme is commissioned. In other words, the broadcast company funds the programme production and pays for the finished programme before it is made. There are some exceptions, for example, when a programme is commissioned and is not expected to go straight into production.

There has been an increasing trend for broadcast companies to delay funding for commissioned programmes, which has put VYP and other independent production companies under cash flow pressure. However, usually the funding for making the programmes is provided within weeks of the contracts being signed for new commissioned programmes.

The elapsed time from approaching a broadcast company through to signing contracts varies considerably. It is usual for the process to take 8 to 12 weeks. For larger, more expensive programme proposals, the process can take far longer. The minimum time is usually 6 weeks.

The time taken from signing contracts for a commissioned programme to completion of the finished programme also varies considerably. The average time is around 6 months. Some programmes take only 2 months, whereas others, such as some documentary or drama programmes, take over 1 year to complete the production of the entire commissioned series of programmes.

Some programmes require a script to be written, such as scripted comedy programmes or drama programmes. VYP will not outsource script writing until the programme is commissioned. Therefore, the making of scripted programmes takes longer, as the programme cannot go into production until the script is complete and been agreed. There is also the problem that the required actors may not be immediately available.

The broadcasting of programmes by the broadcast company which commissions them also varies and is outside the control of VYP. The contract is fulfilled when VYP hands over the finished programme on the required media (usually on a broadcast quality videotape).

The fee paid for commissioned programmes varies by the programme genre and also the anticipated transmission time of the programme by the broadcast company. Programmes that are transmitted in "Peak" viewing times can command a higher fee. "Peak" viewing times in Europe are defined as 17.30 to 24.00 every evening.

There is higher commissioned revenue for making programmes that are to be transmitted in "Peak" times, because higher numbers of viewers are watching TV at these times. Additionally, there are greater advertising revenues generated by the commercial channels at "Peak" viewing times. Almost all of VYP's programmes are made for transmission in "Peak" viewing times.

It is the responsibility of each of VYP's programme directors to come up with ideas for new programmes and to develop these ideas with either of the 2 Managing Directors, Steve Voddil and John Young. It is vitally important that Steve Voddil and John Young nurture the artistic and visionary skills the programme directors have in identifying suitable programmes to make.

After the programme director has firmed up on the idea, the programme proposal is put before the monthly VYP commissioning committee, which is chaired by Sara Mills, as Head of Programme Commissioning. She has huge experience of what type of programme she can approach a broadcast company with, to try to get it commissioned. Sara Mills is always very nervous about new programme proposals, as there is a fine line between what is innovative and what will attract the majority of viewers. It is always a balancing act, for example, between new types of humour in a comedy programme and ensuring that the audience will be amused, rather than offended.

When a programme idea has been developed into a workable format for a programme, then the programme director will work with Sara Mills and her small team to get the idea ready in a detailed proposal format. This detailed proposal will then be used to market the programme idea to one of the broadcast companies. A detailed programme budget will be prepared to cover all aspects of the making of the programme. This will show details of all of the outsourced work and outsourced facilities, for which standard daily rates will be used for estimating purposes. It will also include the costs associated with VYP's programme-making employees and the use of VYP's in-house facilities which will be used for making the programme.

Programmes made by VYP

VYP produces 4 programmes genres. These are:

(1) Documentaries – defined as programmes which are informative to the viewing audience.

(2) Drama series – these are a series of programmes, usually transmitted once a week, which have regular characters and tell a continuing storyline.

(3) Scripted comedy programmes – defined as programmes which are intended to amuse and entertain the viewing audience, and which retain the same characters but have a variety of short storylines each week.

(4) General entertainment programmes – these vary considerably from quizzes, to cookery programmes to comedy.

VYP established its reputation in comedy and entertainment with several series of popular programmes. It has made several series of documentary programmes and some have won TV awards many times over the last 7 years. Broadcast companies have identified that there has been a renewed interest from viewers for documentary programmes in Peak viewing time. The specific requirement from broadcast companies is for documentary programmes to be both informative and entertaining. VYP has gained some new commissions for documentary programmes as it is experienced in this area of TV programme-making.

During the last year VYP was commissioned to make 2 drama series. Prior to these 2 drama series, VYP had not made this genre of programme. These drama series have been popular and have attracted high numbers of viewers. VYP incurred large initial costs with these 2 new series of programmes, which resulted in lower margins than had been planned. This is shown in **Appendix 4**.

In the last financial year ended 31 March 2010, VYP has completed a total of 197 programmes, varying in length from 26 minutes to 58 minutes. The average revenue per hour achieved by VYP in the last financial year was around £225,000. The 197 programmes completed in the year ended 31 March 2010, represented a total of 121.3 hours of broadcast time, and included a range of commissioned series of programmes.

The analysis of programmes completed, by each of the 4 genres, in the financial year ended 31 March 2010 is shown in **Appendix 3**.

The profit, or loss, made on each programme is recognised when each programme is completed (rather than the completion of the commissioned series of programmes) and this occurs when each programme is sent to the broadcast company which commissioned it. When the programme is actually transmitted is not relevant to VYP for accounting purposes. However, any additional revenues payable to VYP for repeat transmissions are recognised in VYP's accounts when the revenues become due, in accordance with the contract for each commissioned programme.

Commissioned programmes revenue per hour

A key statistic for TV broadcast companies is the "cost per hour" of programmes transmitted. This is defined as the cost per hour of output from the TV broadcast companies' perspective. This is the same as the "revenue per hour" from the viewpoint of VYP, which makes some of the programmes for the TV broadcast companies.

The commissioning revenue for each programme will be determined by 2 factors:

- The genre of the programme being commissioned
- The length of each commissioned programme

Programmes are made to "fit" into a 30 minute or 60 minute "transmission slot". Depending on whether the broadcast company is going to insert advertising breaks or programme promotion trailers into the programme, the finished contracted length of a programme will usually be between 26 minutes and 29 minutes long for a 30 minute transmission slot and between 52 minutes and 58 minutes long for a 60 minute transmission slot.

The indicative commissioned revenue per hour is the amount that each of the broadcast companies is willing to spend and it is determined by the genre of the programme. For example, a documentary will be expected to have commissioning revenue per hour of between £100,000 and £300,000 for a programme to be broadcast in Peak viewing times. In contrast, the indicative commissioning revenue for a scripted comedy programme is between £200,000 and £400,000 per hour. Therefore for illustrative purposes, if the commissioned revenue for a programme is £300,000 per hour and the contract is to make a programme that is 26 minutes long, the contracted revenue will be £130,000 per programme (i.e. £300,000 / 60 minutes x 26 minutes).

The control of programme-making costs, to ensure that the costs do not exceed the contracted commissioned revenue to VYP, lies entirely with VYP. The commissioned revenue is considered by the broadcast company to be adequate to provide a profit to VYP of around 10% on commissioned revenue

If a programme, or series of programmes, is successful, the TV broadcast company which commissioned the programme is likely to commission a second or subsequent series of programmes. This is called re-commissioning. The fees payable to VYP for re-commissioned programmes tend to be 10% to 20% lower than the original fees. This is to reflect the savings represented by factors such as:

- The studio "sets" having already been designed and made
- Ideas and research having already been conducted
- Experience from making the programmes in the previous series leading to further efficiencies on subsequent programmes.

VYP finds re-commissioned programmes a challenge to be able to keep within the reduced budget and to maintain programme standards. However, re-commissioned programmes represent a growing proportion of VYP's revenues.

VYP's equipment, manpower and premises

VYP, as a small independent TV production company, cannot afford to fully equip itself to make TV programmes at its own rented premises. This would not be cost effective due to the high cost of equipment. Therefore VYP does not own any studios or employ any videotape (VT) crews for VT filming, although VYP does have 4 VT editing suites and employs VT editors to work with programme directors, editing together the final finished programme.

VYP's skills lie with its creative and artistic programme-making people. These employees are skilled programme makers who contract to bring in the required people to help with the making of a programme and hire the required facilities. Therefore, VYP outsources much of the actual programme-making to other people, some of them are freelance individuals and some are small specialised companies.

As soon as a programme, or series of programmes, is commissioned, VYP will recruit the array of freelance and outsourced skills which are required to make those programmes. These freelance people and facilities will be hired only for the specific time required to make the programme and then their short-term contracts will end. Everything is focused on the skills and facilities required to make each commissioned programme.

Of VYP's 60 employees, 16 are involved in HR, finance, administration and contract handling work. The remaining 44 employees are directly involved in programme-making activities. These 44 employees include all of the Executive Directors of VYP.

The success of VYP is based on nurturing creativity and solid personal relationships with key members of staff. Programme directors and producers receive performance bonuses based on several factors, including meeting agreed programme-making budgets, but more importantly on the success of their programmes. Any programme nominated or receiving an award results in bonuses payable and performance related bonuses are additionally payable for repeat commissions and also for viewing figures exceeding those expected for the genre of the programme. It is important that programme makers are rewarded well in order to retain their skills and keep them loyal to VYP.

Over the last 7 years only a handful of programme directors and producers have left VYP, and these have all been by mutual agreement. The remaining programme-making employees have grown in confidence as the company has grown. Steve Voddil, in particular, is excellent at fostering and building team spirit. The positive atmosphere at VYP is a strength of the company.

The one area that the programme directors felt should be retained "in house" is videotape (VT) editing. A VT editor is a skilled individual who can help contribute to the success of the programmes using his experience and intuitive skills of what to leave in, or edit out, of the finished programme. The VT editor reviews all of the VT recorded for each programme, often 10 times the length of the required finished programme. The VT editors that VYP employs work closely with the programme directors to achieve the desired finished programme. It is logistically convenient to have this function within VYP's offices.

The company initially had just 2 VT editing suites and outsourced the rest of the VT editing. During 2009, a further 2 editing suites were purchased and installed at VYP's offices as its existing editing suites were almost always fully utilised. Sometimes, due to high demand at certain times, external VT editing suites need to be hired by VYP on a daily basis.

The company rents its single Head Office which provides office space for its employees, as well as for the 4 VT editing suites.

Programme-making

Like many independent TV production companies, VYP's success lies with the people involved in all stages of making a programme. This starts with the programme concept and the programme genre. There are many considerations that will influence the type of programme and its cost profile, such as:

- Will the programme be recorded in a TV studio, or will outside "filming" be involved? It should be noted that all outside "filming" no longer uses "film", but instead uses broadcast quality VT and the use of a VT crew, although it is commonly referred to as "outside filming"

- Will the programme involve the use of actors or famous personalities, whose fees will affect the overall costs considerably?

- Will there be extensive use of computer imagery or graphics?

VYP employs TV programme directors and producers to make its TV programmes. However, the bulk of TV programme-making is outsourced to experienced freelance people.

The programme director is the creative head and leads the team making the programme and who sometimes (but not always) has initiated the original programme idea.

The programme producer, and his or her production team, manages the production work for the programme. This involves planning the work and resources required and arranging for all of the bookings of outsourced people and outsourced facilities, such as studios and VT crews for outside filming. The producer and his staff manage the programme budget, supported by Janet Black's finance staff.

The finished quality of VYP's programmes is influenced by the skills of the programme director, whereas the cost of the programme is managed by the producer. There is often a conflict between what the programme director wants and what the producer can afford. It is the producer who manages the agreed programme budget and the outsourced production staff, in order to make the programme idea come to fruition within budget.

VYP outsources many of the constituent parts of making the TV programmes it has had commissioned, to outsourcing specialist companies. VYP tends to work with the same freelance people and some small companies work exclusively for VYP.

During the financial year to the end of March 2010, VYP outsourced the equivalent of around 400 person years of work to a range of external specialised freelance individuals and small companies.

For programmes that require the use of a TV studio, VYP rents a suitably sized and equipped studio. Studios are usually rented by the day, but sometimes block-bookings are made for some of the comedy and drama programmes that it makes. VYP's bookings department will hire the most suitable studio available at the lowest cost for the exact day, or days, that it is required. For example, in the UK, a programme that VYP has been commissioned to make for Channel 5 could be made in a studio hired from the BBC. There are no rules concerning where the programme is made. VYP's bookings department will always try to maximise studio facilities to meet the needs of the programme, whilst minimising the cost of hiring the studio facilities.

Studio time is very expensive and furthermore setting up of a studio with all of the necessary programme specific sets and lighting is time consuming. Therefore, VYP often block-books a studio for several days at a time, or even for 2 weeks at a time. For example, for a scripted comedy or a general entertainment programme, VYP will always plan to complete all of the studio work for at least one 26 minute programme in one day in the studio. For a drama series, a studio will be booked for several weeks and all of the studio work is recorded with scenes from programmes often being recorded out of sequence. Therefore in a block period, all of the studio scenes are recorded and will be edited together at the end, after all outside VT filming has been completed.

Computer graphics

Computer graphics are used widely in TV programmes and VYP has a small number of highly skilled employees who enjoy the challenges of finding innovative and often amusing ways to grab the audience's attention at the start of its programmes.

The use of computer graphics within documentary programmes, in particular, has appealed to the commissioning TV broadcast companies as well as their viewers.

VYP has a computer graphics software package and has skilled graphics technicians who can create many effects. For certain specialised computer graphics effects, the technicians use outsourced specialist facilities to produce the desired effects. The graphics technicians who are employed by VYP are keen for the company to invest in a new software package.

Programme costing

Unlike accounting in most companies, which is focused on sales and costs incurred on a monthly basis, accounting and cost control in VYP is all orientated on a project basis. This is where each commissioned programme (or series of programmes) is controlled and reported on as a separate project. Costs are reported on the basis of costs incurred for each commissioned programme(s) in the month and cumulatively, irrespective of the financial year. Forecast costs for completion of the programmes are also prepared. In this way, all costs for the programme can be monitored against budget.

VYP holds weekly programme management meetings, as well as monthly management meetings, in which finance and TV production staff are involved, with a view to ensuring that the costs for each commissioned programme remain within budget. There have been some instances over the last year where the agreed programme budget was exceeded. This was due to poor control by the programme producer and his production staff over the bookings required for outsourced freelance programme-making people and outsourced facilities. Furthermore, the inaccurate forecasting of the remaining work and costs to complete the programmes, prepared by the programme producer and his production staff, resulted in the cost over-runs not being identified until the programmes were completed.

International sales of programmes by VYP

Most of the programmes that VYP makes are commissioned by TV broadcast companies which retain the intellectual property rights (IPRs) for transmission in the UK. However, VYP usually own the IPRs for sale of the programme in its finished format for the rest of the world. Much depends on the broadcast company which commissioned the programme and the actual contract. Sometimes, the revenue for international sales of the programme are shared with the broadcast company which commissioned the original programme, even though it is VYP's people who generate the interest and actually sell the programme to a broadcast company elsewhere in the world.

Alternatively, it is possible to sell the international IPRs for the programme format. This usually involves allowing the use of the same set design or the style of the programme. The purchaser of a programme format would be a broadcast company in another country, such as Australia, which will then write its own scripts, and have its own presenters, but will make the programmes using the acquired IPRs for the programme format.

VYP did not sell its programmes internationally until 2007. Tom Harrison, the Head of International Sales, had previously worked for another independent TV production company and was head-hunted into VYP to generate international sales. He has been successful in achieving sales of programmes and programme formats to several countries, including the USA.

In the financial year ended 31 March 2010, Tom Harrison achieved international sales of £1.3 million. His contract of employment includes a performance related bonus of 5% of all contracted international sales revenues.

The expenditure that VYP incurs in respect of international programme sales include legal costs in connection with the contracts for the sales and travel and staff costs for Tom Harrison and his small support team. The international sales of VYP programmes generate a high profit margin.

VYP's IT systems

VYP runs a nominal ledger and fixed assets register which uses a popular accounting software package. The finance department raises sales invoices for programmes immediately they are commissioned. The revenue for commissioned programmes is treated as a prepayment in the accounts until the programme is completed.

The programme producer is responsible for the programme budget. Each programme, or series of programmes, has a project number to which all costs are coded and reported against, as in project costing. VYP's employee costs for programme-making employees are chargeable against the relevant programmes based on the number of days they work on each programme. The costs for programme-making employees are charged based on the overall cost per day for each type of employee. The employee cost per day charges are reviewed annually. All Head Office overhead costs that are not allocated directly to programmes are charged to programmes based on a standard charge, allocated on the basis of the number of production days for each programme.

The company has a standard purchase ledger package that interfaces directly with the nominal ledger. The bookings for freelance people or outsourced facilities must commence with the completion of a purchase order, authorised by the producer for the relevant programme. All invoices are then matched with the original order, and where the actual charges agree to the original order, the paperwork is processed within the finance department without having to trouble the programme producer for further authorisation.

At the end of each accounting period, reports on the actual programme costs for the month and cumulative costs for the programme are emailed to each of the programme producers. This report also shows the detailed programme budget against each of the cost headings. The reports are used for 2 purposes:

- To prepare a list of cost accruals for work completed to date, but which has not yet been invoiced to VYP.

- To allow each producer to check and closely monitor actual programme costs against budget.

VYP uses a database system for the submission of forecast costs. This allows the producers to input the forecast costs that will be incurred to the end of the completion of each programme, with an analysis of costs by month. The finance department uses this data to prepare financial forecasts for each financial year as well as a forecast for each commissioned programme, irrespective of whether or not it spans a financial year end. The emphasis of cost control is against the agreed budget for each programme or series of programmes rather than against annual budgets.

As programmes are commissioned and contracted, each producer will have several programme budgets that he or she is responsible for. The value of the total budget each producer controls varies continuously by month and between financial years, as everything is dependent on the individual programme budgets. The producer controls the budgets for programmes currently being made. Most of VYP's producers manage their planning and control of programme costs using spreadsheets.

Reduced commissioning revenues

In the current economic environment, the revenues generated for the commercial TV broadcast companies from advertising have been substantially reduced. This has affected the commissioning revenues that the commercial TV broadcast companies are prepared to pay independent TV production companies, including VYP, for commissioned programmes. Additionally, the BBC, which is not funded by advertising revenue in the UK, has reduced its programme commissioning revenues in order to meet internal funding constraints.

Over the last year VYP has seen a reduction in the commissioned revenue per hour for programmes of a comparable composition and genre compared to the previous year. For example, the average commissioned revenue per hour for documentary programme in the year ended 31 March 2010 was £184,100 (as shown in Appendix 3), whereas in the previous year it was around £215,000 per hour, a reduction of over 14%.

Furthermore, the revenues for re-commissioned programmes (second and subsequent series) which is usually 10 to 20% lower than the first series, has also been reduced. VYP has seen a reduction of 20 to 25% in the last 3 series of programmes that it has recently had re-commissioned.

However, VYP has been able to cut the level of fees that it pays to some of the artists and presenters used in its programmes. This has generated savings which have been used to finance other parts of the programme budget.

Programme directors and production staff are frustrated that the level of cost reduction has led to economies and efficiency savings which have affected the finished quality of the programme. However, some of the TV broadcast companies have countered this argument, stating that the viewing public will not necessarily notice the difference in programme quality.

Overall, VYP has seen its average operating profit margin on commissioned revenue fall from 10.1% in the year ended 31 March 2009 to 9.4% in the year ended 31 March 2010.

The analysis of margins by programme genre is shown in **Appendix 4**.

Cost reduction and quality targets

Both Steve Voddil and John Young are aware of the falling margins achieved in the last financial year ended 31 March 2010. Operating profit margins fell to 9.4 % as a direct result of lower commissioning revenues. This has occurred across most programme genres. VYP is aware that it needs to work even harder to secure contracts for new commissioned programmes as well as to secure commissions for returning series of programmes. VYP also recognises the need to make its programmes to tighter programme budgets.

The reduction in commissioning revenues puts VYP under increasing pressure to make cost effective programmes. However, the programme directors argue that not all of the emphasis should be based on cost effectiveness, as VYP needs to maintain its reputation for delivering high quality programmes.

The Joint Managing Directors, Steve Voddil and John Young, consider that the best way forward in this competitive market is to do what they set out to do when the company was established 7 years ago. That is to create innovative programme ideas that will appeal to its target audiences. In this way the programme is likely to be successful in terms of audience viewing figures. Making successful programmes profitably is VYP's main aim. If programmes are successful then VYP is more likely to secure future programme commissions and also be well positioned for securing re-commissions for subsequent series of programmes.

Share ownership

VYP is a private limited company and is not listed on any stock exchange. It has 10 million shares in issue, each of £1 par value. The shares are held as follows:

	Number of shares held at 31 March 2010	Percentage shareholding
	Million	%
Steve Voddil	3.0	30
John Young	3.0	30
Raj Shah	1.0	10
Paul Maas	1.0	10
Les Fisher	1.5	15
Janet Black	0.5	5
Total	10.0	100

The company has an authorised share capital of 20 million shares.

The company is now generating reasonable profits and strong cash flows. The VYP Board declared dividends for the first time during 2009. A total dividend of £0.9 million was paid to the equity shareholders during 2009.

Both of the Managing Directors are keen for some of the other key employees to share in the profits of the company. They are considering whether a few more of the senior employees should become shareholders in VYP.

The company is now generating reasonable profits and strong cash flows. The VYP Board declared dividends for the first time during 2009. A total dividend of £0.9 million was paid to the equity shareholders during 2009.

Both of the Managing Directors are keen for some of the other key employees to share in the profits of the company. They are considering whether a few more of the senior employees should become shareholders in VYP.

Charity and community work undertaken by VYP

Steve Voddil has been involved for many years in making documentary programmes concerning natural disasters around the world, as well as documentaries about the plight of child labour. Having seen these upsetting images first hand, he was determined to do something more than simply report them through the media of TV. He has convinced the Board of VYP to donate money on a regular basis to several recognised charities that support his chosen causes. During the last financial year, VYP donated a total of £128,000. This is included in operating costs.

John Young is concerned that there are few positions available in TV now for young people to gain training or an insight into how TV programmes are made. He has set up a scheme which allows school children access to view VT filming of certain programmes several times each year. The scheme involves schoolchildren from 20 schools across the UK. This scheme costs VYP around £24,000 each year in total. It has generated much interest and 2 young people who were particularly interested in making TV programmes are currently studying for degrees in media and journalism. VYP is keeping a close eye on their progress and may offer them a full-time junior position with the company when they graduate.

Appendix 1

VYP's key personnel

Non-executive Chairman – Ravi Patel

Ravi Patel, aged 48, has worked with Steve Voddil and John Young for many years and is a trusted friend and experienced TV producer. He has taken on the Non-executive Chairman role as he brings a wealth of experience and knowledge of the industry. He has been an advisor to the founders and current Joint Managing Directors for the last 7 years.

Joint Managing Directors – Steve Voddil and John Young

Steve Voddil

Steve Voddil, aged 39, worked for one of the commercial broadcast companies for 10 years following his undergraduate degree in journalism. He has always had a flair for identifying a different angle to make a documentary programme, which catches the viewers' attention. He was a programme director of in-house made programmes for a broadcast company for several years. After winning several awards for his documentaries and establishing his reputation in the industry, he was determined to set up his own business. However, he was too busy making programmes to take this step and it was not until he met John Young, that he decided to establish VYP 7 years ago.

John Young

John Young, aged 43, came from a similar background to Steve Voddil, except that he trained and worked for a TV broadcast company, initially as a graphic designer and later as a programme director. He was frustrated working for this TV broadcast company which did not allow him the freedom to make decisions on programme formats and content. He felt that he was in the role as programme director which should have allowed him control over the programme, but in practice he had limited authority. His area of experience was in scripted comedy programmes, where the quality of the script usually determined the success of the programme, rather than his skills as a programme director. He wanted to make a move into programme-making on his own to further satisfy his creative desires. He is very artistic and creative and has also won TV programme awards and admits that he is no good at managing budgets. Following a chance meeting with Steve Voddil in 2002, and subsequent planning meetings, they both formed the idea of establishing VYP as an independent TV progamme-making company, which became operational in 2003.

Finance Director – Janet Black

Janet Black, aged 36, is a CIMA qualified accountant who has worked in a number of industries and was the Finance Director for a small music video production company before she joined VYP. She was recruited based on a recommendation by the Non-executive Chairman, who had heard of her tough reputation. Janet Black has to work alongside talented artistic people, most of whom have a weak understanding of the financials and who often are not interested in controlling costs. This was just the type of person that Steve Voddil and John Young recognised they needed for the company they were setting up. They recruited Janet Black and gave her a small shareholding in the company. She has proved her worth over the last 7 years and has instilled good financial control over VYP's programme-making. Janet Black has responsibility for all finance and administration functions. This includes the booking managers, who book all of the outsourced people and facilities required for making programmes. Her small finance team works closely with the production team for each programme to closely monitor and control costs against the agreed programme budget.

Directors of Videotape (VT) Editing – Raj Shah and Paul Maas

VYP currently employs 4 VT editors, but the senior 2 VT editors joined VYP when it was formed as they had previously worked closely with Steve Voddil and John Young on several programmes. The Joint MD's had identified the skills that these 2 editors possessed and their ability to produce exceptionally good finished programmes. Raj Shah and Paul Maas were both given small shareholdings in VYP when the company was formed.

Business and Legal Affairs Director – Les Fisher

Les Fisher, aged 48, has worked in the entertainment business for over 20 years and brings a wealth of experience to the company. When VYP was first established it outsourced all of its legal work, but as the company grew it was clear that it needed in-house legal expertise to manage the many contracts that VYP generates. VYP has contracts with a variety of entities, including the broadcast companies that commission the work, the artists and presenters involved with the programmes and also the many contracts with outsourcing companies and freelance individuals. It is common in this industry to have in-house legal expertise to protect the company from all of the problems that can occur and to ensure that all contracts are as "water-tight" as possible. He has 2 legal assistants who process much of the paperwork, but VYP programme directors are not allowed to commit to anything, in legal or business terms, before Les Fisher has seen and approved the contract. When Les Fisher joined VYP in 2005 he insisted on having an equity stake in the company.

Human Resources Director – Ralph White

Ralph White, aged 45, works part-time for VYP and outsources all aspects of HR and payroll to a specialised company. The outsourcing of the HR functions has worked extremely well and allows VYP to maintain a small number of employees which helps it to maintain flexibility in this industry. Ralph White works closely with the programme producers to identify and hire skilled freelance people required to work on specific programmes.

Head of International Sales – Tom Harrison

Tom Harrison, aged 28, is responsible for selling TV programmes or the format of programmes to overseas broadcast companies. The sale of programmes internationally generates much publicity for VYP and generates additional income. Tom Harrison joined VYP in 2007 and in the last financial year he generated sales of £1.3 million.

Head of Programme Commissioning – Sara Mills

Sara Mills, aged 35, had previously worked for one of the UK's commercial TV broadcast companies in the opposite role, where she used to select programmes to be commissioned from independent TV production companies. When Steve Voddil and John Young decided to establish VYP, they knew the importance of having an experienced person to deal with all of the details concerning programme commissioning, including understanding of programme budgets and programme concepts. As programme makers, both Steve Voddil and John Young recognised that she had an excellent grasp of details and a better understanding of the financial aspects of programme-making than they did. Sara Mills has been excellent at helping the company to achieve growth in programme commissions each year. She has recently approached Steve Voddil and John Young to ask whether she can participate in the company's success as she does not consider that her skills are being fully recognised and rewarded.

Programme Directors

VYP employs 14 programme directors. These programme directors are talented, highly paid individuals who are the creative driving force behind the programmes that they create. Most of the time, the programme idea originates from the programme director. The programme directors see the idea through from original concept to getting the programme commissioned, and then through to the final edited version of each programme. The director works alongside almost all of the production people and is the senior person involved with the making of each programme.

Appendix 2

Extracts from VYP's Statement of Comprehensive Income

	Year ended 31 March 2010	Year ended 31 March 2009
	£000	£000
Sales revenue	28,610	20,620
Operating costs	25,228	18,116
Operating profit	3,382	2,504
Finance costs (net)	133	145
Tax expense (effective tax rate is 30%)	975	708
Profit for the period	2,274	1,651

Appendix 3

Analysis of programmes and revenues for programmes completed in financial year ended March 2010

Programme genre	Number of different types of programme	Total number of programmes completed	Total number of programme hours	Average commissioning revenue per hour	Total revenue
				£000	£000
Documentaries	6	45	36.4	184.1	6,700
Drama series	2	23	16.0	426.3	6,820
Scripted comedy	4	90	41.4	251.4	10,410
General entertainment	6	39	27.5	122.9	3,380
Totals / averages	18	197	121.3	225.1	27,310
International sale of programmes					1,300
Total revenue					28,610

Appendix 4

Analysis of margins by programme genre

	Year ended 31 March 2010			Year ended 31 March 2009		
Programme genre	Revenues	Operating profit	Margin %	Revenues	Operating profit	Margin %
	£000	£000		£000	£000	
Documentaries	6,700	660	9.9%	6,900	694	10.1%
Drama series	6,820	520	7.6%	0	0	–
Scripted comedy	10,410	985	9.5%	9,840	1,005	10.2%
Entertainment	3,380	407	12.0%	2,970	300	10.1%
Totals / Average	27,310	2,572	9.4%	19,710	1,999	10.1%
International sale of programmes	1,300	810	62.3%	910	505	55.5%
Totals	28,610	3,382	11.8%	20,620	2,504	12.1%

4 Improving your familiarisation

Hopefully you've read the above information with the pre-seen familiarisation approach in mind, and have asked yourself lots of questions as you've been reading. You should now complete the following exercises in order to improve your familiarisation with the material.

Familiarisation exercise 1 – SWOT

Prepare a SWOT analysis on VYP.

(**Note:** You will benefit from first preparing a PEST analysis and a Porter's Five Forces analysis.)

Familiarisation exercise 2 – Financial analysis

In most cases we have a full set of financial statements. In VYP we only have a summary income statement for this year and last (appendix 2) together with some analysis of programmes and revenues (appendix 3) and of margins by programme genre (appendix 4).

Perform financial analysis on these three appendices, using calculations that you deem relevant, and comment on your findings.

Familiarisation exercise 3 – Mendelow's Matrix

Assess VYP's stakeholder relationships using Mendelow's Matrix. Consider the power and interest that each stakeholder has.

Familiarisation exercise 4 – CSFs

Identify the critical success factors in the industry and assess whether VYP has the resources required to meet those CSFs.

Familiarisation exercise 5 – Risk analysis

Identify the main risks facing the organisation using the following headings:

- Business risks
- Financial risks
- Political and legal risks
- Technology risks
- Economic risks
- Reputation risks

Familiarisation exercise 6 – Identifying ethical issues

Question	Your response
Comment on VYP's approach to CSR	
Are there any areas of dubious business ethics or questionable personal ethical behaviour that can be identified from the pre-seen?	
What ethical issues face TV production companies in the real world?	

Test your understanding answers

Familiarisation exercise 1 – SWOT

Strengths	Weaknesses
• Reputation and experience of senior staff - especially Steve Voddil, John Young and Sara Mills • Strong reputation in documentary genre as evidenced by industry awards • Innovation • High revenue growth (39% growth in 2010 to give revenue of £28.6m, making VYP a "top 20" company)) • Strong growth in revenue and margins from international sales and Low staff turnover • Charity and community work undertaken	• Possible motivational issues re key staff - e.g. Sara Mills has expressed a desire for share ownership • Falling margins for comedy and documentaries. These are now below the industry assumed figure of 10%, potentially due to a mixture of reduced commissioning revenue per hour and some poor cost control. • Primitive MIS - e.g. no integration between budgeting, cost control and reporting.
Opportunities	**Threats**
• Listing (Full market or AIM) • Bring some outsourced activities inhouse - e.g. buy a studio • Invest more in growing international sales as these have the highest margins • Invest more in making entertainment programmes as these have the highest margins for VYP's commissioned work. • Invest in a new integrated MIS • Move into making feature films / adverts / pop videos / etc	• Loss of key staff - e.g. poaching or staff setting up their own companies • High competitive rivalry - hundreds of competitors • TV broadcast companies reducing the level of commissioned revenue • Misjudging viewer reaction to more "risky" programmes - e.g comedy programmes being seen as offensive rather than funny. This could damage reputation. • Get sued over IPR - e.g. claims that one of our programmes has copied the ideas from another.

Familiarisation exercise 2 – Financial analysis

From appendix 2:

- Revenue growth of 38.7% is very impressive given competition and state of the economy (recession and fall in advertising revenues for broadcasters)

- Operating margin has fallen from 12.1% to 11.8%. As this point we do not know why but later we are told about pressure from broadcasters to reduce fees.

- Net margin has remained fairly consistent at around 8%

- In summary a healthy growing business. The only concerns at this stage are falling margins.

- We do not have enough information to analyse working capital management, liquidity, ROCE, gearing, etc

From the information in appendices 3 and 4:

A summary of VYP's performance in each key genre is:

Area	Your response
Documentaries	- An area that is currently very popular and one that VYP is very good at, as evidenced by awards. - Currently represents 23.4% of total revenue - However, appendix 4 shows falling margins (10.1% to 9.9%) and revenue (drop of 2.9%) from 2009 to 2010. We do not know (yet) why this is the case but later on in the pre-seen the main cause is given as lower revenue per hour due to broadcasters seeing their advertising revenues falling (note how neither of these movements is that significant). - Documentaries also have the second lowest revenue per hour at £184,100

Drama	• A new area for VYP but viewer response so far has been favourable
	• Already contributed 23.8% of revenue
	• Dramas have the highest revenue per hour presumably to reflect the higher costs of using known actors / actresses and set design.
	• Lowest margins at only 7.6% reflect initial set-up costs and possible cost overruns / difficulty budgeting in a new genre - we would expect margins to be higher in 2011
	• Individual projects are much larger than with other genres – e.g. revenue per programme for drama was nearly £297k compared with £149k for documentaries, £116k for comedy and £87k for entertainment. (appendix 3). Thus winning one extra commission could have a major impact on revenue and profits.
Scripted comedy	• An area where VYP established its reputation and still its largest revenue earner (36.4% of total revenue)
	• 2010 has seen falling margins (10.2% to 9.5%) but increased revenue (growth of 5.8%), possibly indicating VYP has cut prices to secure commissions.
Entertainment	• Increasing margins (10.1% to 12.0%) and revenue (growth of 13.8%).
	• Highest margins for commissioned work, possibly because programmes will be viewed at peak time, thus commanding higher fees, yet production costs are likely to be more modest than say with a drama.
	• Suggest that VYP tries to win more commissions in this genre.

International sales	• Huge margins (62.3%) as expected due to minimal additional costs to sell on finished programmes.
	• Increasing margins from 55.5% to 62.3%.
	• High growth of 43%
	• Together these indicate that international sales is an area VYP should pursue further.

Specifically, the fall of 14% in revenue per hour for documentary programmes can be compared to the drop in margin for documentaries from 10.1% to 9.9%. This would indicate that VYP has done a brilliant job of limiting the damage of the fall in revenue, presumably through cost cutting and designing projects with a lower cost budget.

Familiarisation exercise 3 – Mendelow's Matrix

	Low Interest	High Interest
Low Power	• Viewers - while they are very interested in a particular programme, they are generally unaware of who made it.	• Suppliers for outsourced services • Non-key employees
High Power	• OFCOM • Broadcasters	• Key employees

In summary key relationships that need to be managed are:

• keeping and motivating key staff

• maintaining strong relationships with broadcasters, delivering quality programmes on time to avoid their interest increasing, turning them into a key player able to (albeit indirectly) influence the business

• maintaining ethical standards in the programmes we produce to ensure that the pursuit of innovation does not lead to questionable content, which could increase the interest of OFCOM (and as with broadcasters, turn them into a key player).

Familiarisation exercise 4 – CSFs

CSF	Organisation
Keeping and motivating key staff	• To date there is no evidence that VYP had suffered staff losses - if anything, it has successfully headhunted staff (e.g. Tom Harrison) • Furthermore we are told that Steve Voddil is excellent at fostering and building a team spirit • As for motivation, many key staff have shares and there appears to be a range of bonus schemes in place (e.g. Tom gets 5% of international sales revenue, programme directors and producers get bonuses linked to hitting budgets, viewing figures, winning awards and recommissions). We do not have sufficient information to benchmark these schemes. • However, there is a potential problem in as much as Sara does not feel her skills are being fully recognised and rewarded.
Making programmes that viewers want to see	• While we don't have viewing figures we are told that VYP enhanced its reputation last year with several new series of programmes which were considered to be successful in terms of audience viewing figures.

CSF	Organisation
Cost control	• We are told that there have been some cost overruns due to poor cost control over outsourced services. • We can also see that operating margins have fallen from 12.1% to 11.8%. However, given the 14% drop in revenue per commissioned hour for documentaries, it seems that VYP has demonstrated excellent cost control to stop margins falling by more.
Having a good reputation and strong brand name	• VYP has a good reputation, is a "top 20" company and has won many awards
Ensuring that you retain IPR on international sales as these have particularly high margins	• We are not told the detail of the IPR aspects of VYP's contracts. However, the growth in international sales would suggest that this is not a problem.
Getting programmes recommissioned for second or third series	• We are not told how many programmes or series get recommissioned or what the mix of total revenue is between original work and recommissioned work. • However, we are told that recommissioned programmes represent a growing proportion of VYP's revenue, indicating some strengths in this respect.
Getting programmes commissioned in the first place	• We do not know VYP's "hit rate" in converting proposals into commissioned work. • However, we are told that Sara's expertise includes knowing exactly what broadcasters are looking for.

Familiarisation exercise 5 – Risk analysis

Risk area	Your response
Business risks	• Competitive rivalry • Loss of key staff • Broadcasters lowering prices further.
Financial risks	• Exchange rate movements could affect international sales and profits • Interest rate movements could affect finance costs, currently £133k. (**Note:** We do not know the level of debt finance or VYP's gearing level)
Political and legal risks	• It is vital that contracts are reviewed carefully to ensure VYP is protected - especially in the area of IPR.
Technology risk	• VYP may miss out on opportunities if it fails to keep up to date with respect to digital editing, distributing via streaming, internet sales, etc.
Economic risk	• VYP is exposed to the state of the economy in the sense that Broadcasters advertising revenue is strongly cyclical.
Reputation risk	• It only takes few programme failures to seriously damage VYP's reputation. • Similarly if VYP is sued for copying other companies' ideas could damage its image.

Familiarisation exercise 6 – Identifying ethical issues

Question	Your response
Comment on VYP's approach to CSR	• Charitable donations to help stop child labour • Schemes to give schoolchildren access to TV production • No mention of carbon footprint of production (e.g. flying to exotic locations for filming)
Are there any areas of dubious business ethics or questionable personal ethical behaviour that can be identified from the pre-seen?	• Issue of IPR raised but no indication of bad practice.
What ethical issues face TV production companies in the real world?	• Copying ideas from other companies • Headhunting staff • Programme content of documentaries – e.g. distorting the truth to make a good story, invasion of privacy, libel and slander, use of children, "digging for dirt", bugging phonecalls, etc • Programme content of cutting edge comedy and entertainment – e.g. offensive content

VYP: Summary of the pre-seen material

Chapter learning objectives

By the end of this chapter you will:

- Understand the key issues facing the organisation.
- Have considered the big picture perspective of the case.

General background

V and Y Productions (VYP) is an unquoted, independent TV production company established in 2003 by two experienced directors, Steve Voddil and John Young. VYP is based in the UK and makes programmes commissioned by the BBC, ITV, Channel 4 and Channel 5.

The two founders are both experienced programme makers and have experience of working for TV broadcast companies but wanted to make TV programmes of their own. VYP employs 60 people directly and outsources much of the routine TV production work to other small specialised companies.

The reputation of VYP was based solidly on the calibre of its staff. The two founders are actively involved in winning new commissioned programmes and work alongside the relevant TV programme directors who propose programme ideas.

Other key members of staff include:

- Sara Mills (Head of Programme Commissioning). Sara and the relationships she has with broadcasters are key to winning programme commissions. She has an excellent understanding of the programme budgets and concepts and has been key in helping the company achieve growth in programme commissions each year. Sara has recently asked Steve and John whether she can participate in the company's success; she does not currently own any shares in the company.

- Tom Harrison (Head of International Sales). Tom has been with VYP since 2007 and in that short period he has built the international sales department from nothing to sales of £1.3m in the year end 31 March 2010. Tom is paid a bonus of 5% of all contracted international sales revenue. International sales generate a high profit margin of 62.3%.

Over the last three years, VYP has won several TV programme awards and has established a reputation for the production of documentaries which allow the general public to air their views on topical issues.

In the last financial year, VYP generated total revenues of £28.6 million, representing growth of nearly 39% from revenue earned in the previous year. VYP hold a market share of about 1.4% of commissioned TV programmes in the UK, which places them in the top 20 companies making TV programmes in the UK.

The overall aim of VYP is to make successful programmes for profit. It has four programme genres being documentaries, drama series, scripted comedy programmes and general entertainment programmes.

One of the founders has convinced the Board to donate money on a regular basis to several recognised charities. The other founder has set up a scheme which allows school-children to view videotape filming of some programmes.

Commissioned revenue and production costs

Once VYP has agreed a contract with a broadcast company for a commissioned programme, or series of programmes, then the actual costs incurred in the making of the programme are the responsibility of VYP. The profit, or loss, for each programme is determined by the difference between the contracted commissioned revenue and the actual costs incurred by VYP in the making of the programme. This therefore puts the emphasis of cost control with VYP. The commissioned revenue is considered by the broadcast company to be adequate to provide a profit to VYP of around 10% on commissioned revenue.

If a programme, or series of programmes, is successful, the TV broadcast company which commissioned the programme is likely to commission a second or subsequent series of programmes. This is called re-commissioning. The fees payable to VYP for re-commissioned programmes tend to be 10% to 20% lower than the original fees. VYP finds re-commissioned programmes a challenge to be able to keep within the reduced budget and to maintain programme standards. However, re-commissioned programmes represent a growing proportion of VYP's revenues.

In the current economic environment, the revenues generated for the commercial TV broadcast companies from advertising have been substantially reduced. This has affected the commissioning revenues that the commercial TV broadcast companies are prepared to pay independent TV production companies, including VYP, for commissioned programmes.

Over the last year VYP has seen a reduction in the commissioned revenue per hour compared to the previous year. For example, the average commissioned revenue per hour for a documentary programme has reduced by over 14%. Furthermore, VYP has seen a reduction of 20 to 25% in the last 3 series of programmes that it has recently had re-commissioned, compared with the usual 10% to 20% experienced in the past.

VYP holds weekly programme management meetings, as well as monthly management meetings, in which finance and TV production staff are involved, with a view to ensuring that the costs for each commissioned programme remain within budget. There have been some instances over the last year where the agreed programme budget was exceeded. The company has a standard purchase ledger package that interfaces directly with the nominal ledger. However, a database system is used for the submission of forecast costs and most of VYP's producers manage their planning and control of programme costs using spreadsheets.

Programme production

VYP employs TV programme directors and producers to make its TV programmes. However, the bulk of TV programme-making is outsourced to experienced freelance people. VYP does not own any studios or employ any videotape (VT) crews for VT filming, although VYP does have 4 VT editing suites and employs VT editors to work with programme directors, editing together the final finished programme. As soon as a programme, or series of programmes, is commissioned, VYP will recruit the array of freelance and outsourced skills which are required to make those programmes.

VYP has a computer graphics software package and has skilled graphics technicians who can create many effects. For certain specialised computer graphics effects, the technicians use outsourced specialist facilities to produce the desired effects. The graphics technicians who are employed by VYP are keen for the company to invest in a new software package.

The Industry

VYP is a top 20 company in a highly competitive industry with hundreds of rival indies. Broadcasters exercise considerable buyer power as has been seen by recent cuts in commissioned revenue per hour offered following a fall in advertising revenues.

Critical success factors include innovative ideas, good production skills, having creative staff and the ability to sell programme ideas to broadcasters. Gaining recommissions and being able to sell programmes internationally can also contribute significantly to the bottom line. In the case of the latter, IPR are particularly important.

Key trends within the industry include:

- A high number of mergers and acquisition, both horizontal and vertical, including the creation of so-called 'super-indies' such as Endemol and TalkbackTHAMES.

- The switch to digital and the resulting increase in the number of television channels. However, only the public-service broadcasters have set targets for the quantity of first-run originations.

- Relaxation of regulations relating to product placement within TV programmes. This is opening up additional funding methods which can be used to help fill the funding gap following pressure on the broadcasters to cut costs.

- The use of computer graphics (and computer generate imagery) to enhance programmes (as well as the reputation of the production companies).

- The sale of format into different territories has been big business. The UK TV production industry total international sales amounted to £439m in 2009 and now accounts for 41% of the world market.

Existing and future strategy

VYP has tried to be a differentiator, focusing on innovative ideas and successful pitches to broadcasters. Recent developments have included making dramas (first done in 2010) and selling internationally (started in 2007 by Tom Harrison).

Little information is given regarding future strategies.

Headline Financials

Positives:

- Overall revenue growth of 38.7% to £28,610k

- International sales revenue grew by 42.9% to £1,300k

- Expansion into drama genre generated revenues of £6,820k with an operating margin of 7.6%

- Operating margin on international sales grew from 55.5% to 62.3% (highest margin in the product portfolio)

- Operating margin on entertainment programmes increased from 10.1% to 12.0%

Negatives:

- Overall operating margins fell from 12.1% to 11.8%

- Documentary revenues fell by 2.9% to £6,700k

Test your understanding 1 – Prioritisation on VYP

Based on your familiarisation with the VYP pre-seen information, identify what key factors you must consider when prioritising the issues facing VYP in the un-seen.

Test your understanding answers

Test your understanding 1 – Prioritisation on VYP

Key aspects to consider when prioritising issues in the VYP case are:

- The success of VYP is down to its reputation. Specifically, this reputation is based on:
    - its people, especially Steve Voddil and John Young. Both are actively involved in winning new commissioned programmes;
    - successful programmes. The content of programmes have been recognised as excellent and innovative, as evidenced by awards won and audience viewing figures;
    - specialisation. VYP's is best known for the production of documentaries which allow the general public to make their views known on topical issues

    Therefore, anything that could damage their reputation must be regarded as a key issue

- It is vitally important that the artistic and visionary skills of the programme directors are nurtured. Only a handful of programme directors and producers have left VYP over the last 7 years and we're told that Steve Voddil in particular is excellent at fostering and building team spirit. Other key personnel will include those involved in generating ideas, production and those who sell the ideas to the TV broadcasting companies. This would include the 4 VT editors, Sara Mills (Head of Programme Commissioning) and Tom Harrison (Head of International Sales) as well as the programme directors.

    Since its people are so key to the company's reputation, any disruption amongst staff, in particular the key personnel, must be regarded as a key issue.

- A key threat is the reduction in commissioning revenues that is having a direct impact on the bottom-line. As a small, independent, unlisted company, significantly squeezed margins can lead to bankcruptcy. Although having a good reputation and artistic staff will help to reduce the impact of this threat, tight cost control will also be necessary to ensure the long-term viability of the business.

    Any indication of a lack of cost control or of costs spiralling must be viewed as a key issue.

15

VYP: The unseen material

Chapter learning objectives

By the end of this chapter you will:

- Have reviewed the unseen material for the November 2010 VYP case study exam.

- Have had a chance to practise the techniques outlined in Chapters 3 through to 8.

1 A chance to practise

This chapter contains the unseen material for the November 2010 VYP case exam.

We would strongly recommend that you prepare your own answer to this exam before looking at the the review of a sample answer (presented in Chapter 17).

Whether you attempt this under timed conditions is entirely up to you. If this is the first full exam you have tackled you might like to take slightly longer, ensuring that you're happy with each stage of the process as you go. If you do, the walkthrough presented in the next chapter may help you. However, writing your answer within the 3 hours and 20 minutes time allocation will give you a chance to practise the essential time management skills.

2 The requirement

ANSWER THE FOLLOWING QUESTIONS

You are the Management Accountant of VYP.

Steve Voddil and John Young, the joint Managing Directors, have asked you to provide advice and recommendations on the issues facing VYP.

Question 1 part (a)

Prepare a report that prioritises, analyses and evaluates the issues facing VYP and makes appropriate recommendations.

(Total marks for Question 1 part (a) = 90 Marks)

Question 1 part (b)

In addition to your analysis in your report for part (a), Janet Black, the Finance Director has asked you to draft an email, which she intends to send to all of VYP's programme producers. Your email should persuade VYP's programme producers of the need for improved IT systems in order to achieve better control of direct programme-making costs.

Your email should contain no more than 10 short sentences.

(Total marks for Question 1 part (b) = 10 Marks)

3 The unseen material

Selection of outsourced companies

In order to maintain flexibility, VYP outsources most of the actual programme-making to a range of small TV production companies or freelance individuals. VYP has a small bookings department comprising 3 experienced bookings managers who are responsible for making all bookings of outsourced people and facilities. The booking managers work closely with the directors and producers of each programme to ensure they match the needs of the programme to the wide range of outsourcing companies available to TV production companies.

One of VYP's producers has recently identified that one small outsourcing company, which is used for the supply of various items of equipment used in programmes, is being booked much more often than previously. This outsourced company provides an excellent service but is slightly more expensive than some of its rivals. On investigation, he has discovered that all 3 of VYP's bookings managers have been making bookings with this company after receiving a range of personal gifts, which is normal practice in this industry.

TV presenter taken ill

VYP has been commissioned to make 12 documentary programmes for delivery in December 2011. The commissioned revenue is contracted to be £200,000 per programme, with total revenue of £2.4 million for the series. The programmes are to be filmed in a variety of cities throughout the world, where the presenter interviews local people and local business people about their attitudes to specific global brands. The programmes are considered to be controversial and could attract much publicity. The broadcast company has advanced the full commissioned revenue of £2.4 million to VYP, in order to fund the making of the programmes.

4 of the 12 programmes have been partially completed and the production team was due to fly to another 2 cities with the programme presenter next week. However, the presenter has become ill and has advised that he will not be able to complete the series. Les Fisher, VYP's Business and Legal Affairs Director, has stated that the contract with the presenter states that no fee is payable, even for the 4 programmes partially made. However, VYP has incurred costs to date of £0.6 million (excluding the presenter's fee) on the 4 partially completed programmes. Sara Mills, the Head of Programme Commissioning has approached the TV broadcast company which commissioned the series and has explained the problem. The TV broadcast company is not sympathetic and has suggested 2 alternatives:

- The TV broadcast company has agreed that an alternative presenter may be used, entirely at VYP's cost. The TV broadcast company has insisted that the same presenter is used for the entire series of 12 programmes.

  Or

- The series of 12 programmes is cancelled and that VYP refunds the cash advance for the entire commissioning revenues of £2.4 million back to the broadcaster. The broadcast company has stated that it would be reluctant to commission further documentary programmes from VYP if this series is cancelled.

The programme director proposes to book a different presenter to complete the remaining 8 programmes. Furthermore, as the 4 partially completed programmes have not yet been edited, the director is planning to replace all of the sequences that showed the original presenter with the new presenter. New sequences could be filmed with the new presenter (not on location) and these sequences could be inserted into the 4 programmes already partially made. The production team has forecast that around £2.0 million will be required to complete the remaining 8 programmes including all of the extra work with the proposed new presenter being edited into the first 4 programmes.

VT filming proposals

Currently all outdoors videotape (VT) "filming" work is outsourced to 2 different companies, which provide experienced VT crews for filming outdoor scenes for programmes. VYP has worked with one of the outsourced VT companies, Tee, for several years and Tee provides almost all of its VT film crew requirements. Tee is a key outsourcing company and it works exclusively for VYP. Following initial talks, there is a proposal for VYP to acquire Tee, which is also an unlisted company. Tee's Managing Director has supplied the following information:

Number of VT crews	15
Number of VT crew days per year	210
Financial information from accounts for last financial year ended 31 December 2009:	£ million
Revenue	3.78
Profit after finance costs and tax	0.85

VYP currently pays an average outsource hire fee for each VT crew of £1,200 per day. VYP currently uses around 3,500 VT crew days per year on all of its existing programmes. VYP anticipates growth in the use of VT filming work following some recent programme commissions.

Janet Black has asked you to suggest a price that could be offered to acquire Tee and to comment on the other factors affecting the proposed acquisition of Tee. An appropriate proxy P/E ratio for a similar unlisted company is considered to be 4. Tee's Managing Director has indicated that he wants a realistic price for his company as well as a seat on the Board of VYP and shares in VYP. As a result of the proposed acquisition of Tee, it is forecast that VYP will save £1.4 million each year compared to its current total cost of outsourcing of £4.2 million. Both the forecast saving and the cost of outsourcing are forecast to rise by 10% from the first year. There are 2 alternatives to acquiring Tee, which are:

(1) To carry on outsourcing. This is forecast to rise by 10% from the first year.

(2) To take all VT filming work in-house, by purchasing the required VT equipment and recruiting experienced people. To equip the required number of crews to meet growth in VT filming, the capital cost of the equipment would be £7 million and the total operating costs are forecast to be £2.2 million in the first year, rising by 10% after the first year. Assume that there is no residual value for the equipment after year 3. VYP is considering trying to recruit some of Tee's employees.

You should evaluate these alternative proposals over 3 years. VYP's pre-tax cost of capital is forecast to be 9%. Ignore taxation.

Proposal to re-commission a new series of "Leah"

VYP had been commissioned in July 2009 to make 12 drama programmes called "Leah" which were completed on time and delivered to the broadcast company in May 2010. They are currently being transmitted once a week and have attracted much publicity across various media and have achieved high viewing figures. The programmes cost slightly more to make than had been budgeted, due to the extensive use of outside VT sequences. The total commissioned revenue for the first series was £2.60 million (just under £217,000 per programme). The total cost of making the 12 programmes was £2.37 million, providing a return to VYP of 8.8%.

The broadcast company has now approached VYP, with a proposal to re-commission a second series of "Leah". The broadcast company would like to commission a series of 24 programmes which will be transmitted twice a week. The broadcast company has stated that the re-commissioning revenue for 24 programmes would be £4.16 million and that this is the maximum that it is prepared to pay. The broadcast company needs a decision within the next week.

The programme's producer has prepared the following data for each programme:

	Relevant number of days	Cost per day £
Scriptwriter's fees	3	2,000
Studio time (including all related costs including lighting, cameraman etc)	2	30,000
Outsourced VT crew	8	1,200
Outsourced freelance programme-making people	10	1,000
VT editing (in-house)	4	500
VYP programme-making employees (excluding in-house VT editing)	16	1,100
Other direct programme costs	16	300

Artists' fees:
Forecast total fees per programme = £35,000
VYP Head Office overhead costs:
Assume allocation to be £8,000 per programme
Contingency for unforeseen costs:
Forecast at 10% of total programme costs

Steve Voddil and John Young have stated that VYP requires a return on commissioned revenue of not less than 9% for re-commissioned programmes. The programme's producer is concerned about the final style of the programme but considers that it could be possible to record all of the scenes set in the studio for all 24 programmes in one studio session over several weeks. This would enable VYP to make savings in the number of studio days. He forecasts that 8 studio days and 8 person days of VYP programme-making employees could be saved over the total series of 24 programmes.

Janet Black has asked you to prepare the following:

- A budget for the total costs for each programme and for the 24 programme series

- The operating profit and the return on commissioned revenue before, and after, any savings in the number of studio days and VYP programme-making employees

- The operating profit and return on commissioned revenue for the series of 24 programmes after the above savings in studio days and VYP programme-making employees, assuming overhead costs for the company do not increase from the present level if this series is re-commissioned.

Documentary series

VYP has been commissioned to make a series of 4 documentary programmes about children's lives around the world and the education differences between countries. One of VYP's programme directors and an outsourced VT film crew have just returned from filming a documentary which included the use of child labour in a range of countries. The child workers were often making goods for global retail companies, which have not adequately checked their suppliers' factories.

The outsourced VT film crew included a young VT cameraman, Greg Jackson, who was very upset at the images he filmed and the various dangers the children faced. He was worried about what he saw and he has contacted Steve Voddil directly, and met with him yesterday to express his concerns. Greg Jackson has asked for VYP to take immediate action to contact the global companies who indirectly employ the child labour to ask them to intervene. However, Steve Voddil and VYP's programme director have stated that this is outside the scope of VYP's programme-making responsibilities and that when the programme is broadcast, in around 6 months' time, it will be in the public domain.

Cost control

VYP has grown considerably over the last 7 years and it has failed to invest in IT solutions. Much of the programme planning and forecasting of costs by programme producers are done manually or using spreadsheets. Sometimes, the programme-making people discover that a booking has not been made for outsourced facilities or freelance programme-making people until the last minute. This usually results in higher costs. Additionally, it can also result in not being able to hire exactly what the director wants. Many of VYP's competitors use IT solutions to help them plan all aspects of their TV production work.

Janet Black considers that cost control in VYP is weak. Many of VYP's producers are under pressure to complete their programme and they are not as focussed on costs as they should be. The programme producers usually spend up to the programme budget. However, in the last few months 35 out of 50 completed programmes have exceeded their agreed programme budgets. Janet Black's accountants meet with each programme production team each month to help to prepare a forecast of costs for the remainder of each of the commissioned programmes. The accountants often find that some costs have been omitted by production staff, including the costs relating to bookings which have already been placed through the company's purchase order system.

Janet Black is concerned that VYP now needs improved IT systems in order to achieve better control of direct programme-making costs.

4 What to do now

Now that you have read the VYP November 2010 unseen material you should have a go at preparing your own answer for this case. You can now either:

- work through the next chapter if you feel like you need some more help before you attempt your answer; or you can

- attempt your own answer using the unseen material.

You should complete your answer before you refer to the sample answer in Chapter 17.

16

VYP: Walkthrough of the exam

Chapter learning objectives

By the end of this chapter you will:

- Have completed the initial reading and planning for the November 2010 VYP case study exam.

- Be more familiar with the approaches and techniques discussed in Chapters 3 through to 8.

1 The aim of a walkthrough

As we did with CeeCee, the purpose of this chapter is to help cement many of the techniques we've shown you in the previous chapters and again, we've broken down the preparation of the report into the various stages we've outlined in Chapters 7 and 8.

However, in order to develop your techniques, we've presented this walkthrough as a series of mini-exercises, rather than simply presenting some ideas of thoughts you could have had. Each exercise does still have a suggested answer, which you can compare your thoughts against, but you should aim to complete each exercise yourself before reviewing the answer.

2 The first 20 minutes

Remember, the aim of the first 20 minutes is to read through the unseen material, absorbing information about each of the events and considering the issue and the impact of that issue.

Whilst reading, you should also start to form some opinions about which issues are more important than others.

Any ideas that come to mind about potential solutions should also be noted (although not forced – we have more time for this later) along with ideas for useful technical models and real world comments that could be used to help analyse the issue or identify a solution.

Finally, each issue should be marked as either a strength (unlikely), weakness, opportunity or threat. This will help speed up the preparation of the SWOT analysis once the writing / typing time commences.

Exercise 1 – The first 20 minutes

In Chapter 8 we showed you some useful approaches to documenting your thoughts at this stage of the exam. Using one of these approaches, or a similar approach that you think may work for you, prepare a central planning sheet and annotate the un-seen information with any initial thoughts you may have.

3 Planning and calculations

Before you start writing your report you must continue the planning process to expand on the impact of each of your top four issues and identify and evaluate alternative courses of action. You also need to perform any calculations that might be necessary to advise on a particular issue.

Techniques that may help you plan your answer further were covered in Chapter 8.

In the answers to the following exercises we've given some notes on each issue to help show the sort of things you might have come up with. It is unlikely that you will have time in the exam to make such detailed notes. Remember, all you need to do is note down enough to prompt you when writing up your report. We've also outlined some thoughts on the calculations and provided some examples.

Exercise 2 – Planning and calculations: Re-commission of "Leah"

Prepare calculations and then plan your answer that addresses the proposal to re-commission a new series of "Leah".

Exercise 3 – Planning and calculations: TV presenter

Prepare calculations and then plan your answer to address the illness of the TV presenter.

Exercise 4 – Planning and calculations: Cost control

Plan your answer to address the problems regarding cost control.

Also plan your answer to requirement 1(b) by considering which key points you may want to include and the tone your e-mail should take.

Exercise 5 – Planning and calculations: VT filming

Prepare calculations and then plan your answer to address the VT filming proposals.

Exercise 6 – Planning: Ethical issues

Plan your answer to address the ethical issues of:

- The documentary series with child labour scenes
- The selection of outsourced companies.

Technical and diversity marks

The above points will allow you to score judgement and logic marks but don't forget about other criteria within the assessment matrix. Crucially, there are marks available within technical, application and diversity that will be gained throughout your whole report. It is therefore useful, at the end of your planning, to make sure you have identified the five technical models that you plan to include (and which issues you will apply them to) and the five real world diversity points you will use to support your arguments. This will ensure you don't forget to include them when it comes to writing up that section of your report. In this case we have:

Exercise 7 – Summary of technical models and diversity points

Prepare a summary of the five technical models and five diversity points you plan to use in your answer.

(Remember – you won't need to formally write these out in an exam situation but you should get into the habit of reviewing your plan as a whole to ensure you have everything covered).

Test your understanding answers

Exercise 1 – The first 20 minutes

What follows is an example of a central planning document that could have been prepared. **Note:** This is not **the** correct answer. It is **an** answer but others could be equally as valid (both in content and style). Also note, that this is more detailed than you would perhaps prepare in the exam. Much of what has been written in the third column would more efficiently be noted in the margins of the exam paper rather than written separately onto a central planning sheet.

The issues below have been presented based on priority order rather than the order in which they appear in the unseen. This is following the 'ordered list' approach outlined in Chapter 8; as each new issue has been read about, the thoughts have been positioned on the planning sheet based on whether an issue has a greater or lesser impact than the issues already covered. The urgency of each issue has also been considered when deciding on the order of the issues.

Issue	Impact	Other comments / notes
Proposal to re-commission a new series of "Leah"	24 programmes so a sizeable commission. High profile commission given popularity of first series. Opportunity to further enhance reputation.	Decision needed within a week so fairly urgent. Key opportunity. Programme budget needs to be prepared. Decision needed on whether return on commissioned revenue is sufficient. Use of outside VT sequences – link to VT filming proposals issue. Studio time seems to be key driver.

TV presenter taken ill	Failure to deliver could impact on reputation – could lead to loss of future commissions. Fairly significant impact on profit and cash flows Delivery is 1 year away but a decision will be needed fairly urgently to ensure on time delivery.	Financial evaluation needed. Opportunity to complete the series with a new presenter. Threat to reputation if series is cancelled. Sunk costs of £0.6m. Need to consider broadcaster's perspective.
Cost control	Pressure from falling margins makes this important as without good cost control VYP may be unable to compete effectively and still be profitable. 35 out of 50 programmes exceeded budget means this would have a widespread impact.	Internal rather than external so less important than issues above. Threat of reduced commissioned revenue and falling operating profit margins. Opportunity to invest in IT to achieve better control. Weakness - lack of IT solutions makes cost control difficult. Will require a change in culture - difficult to achieve.
VT filming proposals	Could be a fundamental change to the way VYP operates. No real urgency - lower prioritisation	Opportunity to acquire Tee. Link to cost cutting and pressure on margins. Need to evaluate v carrying on outsourcing or bringing in-house. Been asked to suggest a price for Tee.

Selection of outsourced companies	Business issue – VYP may be paying more for outsourced work than is necessary leading to reduced profitability. Ethical issue – booking managers should not be influenced by gifts or other enticements but should focus on the needs of the programmes	Clearer guidelines needed. Controls needed to identify such transactions (Weakness). Link back to issues regarding cost control and VT filming proposals.
Documentary series with child labour scenes	Ethical issue – having knowledge of such practices yet not taking action against them: should VYP intervene. Business issue – could damage reputation	Failure to act could reflect badly on VYP.

Summary

To summarise the output from the initial reading time. (**Note:** You will not need to do this in the exam).

Top four issues:

(1) Proposal to re-commission a new series of "Leah"

(2) TV presenter taken ill

(3) Cost control

(4) VT filming proposals

Ethical issues:

(1) Documentary series with child labour scenes

(2) Selection of outsourced companies

Key new SWOT entries:

Weaknesses:

• Poor control over programme-making costs

• Lack of IT solutions makes cost control difficult

• Poor control over bookings managers

Opportunities:

- Proposal for the re-commissioning of "Leah"
- Proposal to acquire Tee
- To improve cost control by investing in IT solutions
- To complete the documentary series with a new presenter

Threats:

- Reduction in commissioned revenue and falling operating margins
- Damage to reputation if documentary series cancelled.

Exercise 2 – Planning and calculations: Re-commission of "Leah"

Let's start by looking at the financial evaluation of the proposal.

	Relevant number of days	Cost / day	Total cost / prog	Total cost for 24 progs	Revised units	Total cost with saving for 24 progs	Marginal cost with savings for 24 progs
		£	£'000	£'000		£'000	£'000
Script writers	3	2,000	6.0	144.0		144.0	144.0
Studio time	2	30,000	60.0	1,440.0	40	1,200.0	1,200.0
Outsourced VT crews	8	1,200	9.6	230.4		230.4	230.4
Outsourced freelance prog makers	10	1,000	10.0	240.0		240.0	240.0
VT editing	4	500	2.0	48.0		48.0	48.0
VYP prog making employees	16	1,100	17.6	422.4	376	413.6	413.6
Other direct prog costs	16	300	4.8	115.2		115.2	115.2
Artists fees			35.0	840.0		840.0	840.0
VYP head office costs			8.0	192.0		192.0	0
			153.0	3,672.0		3,423.2	3,231.2
Contingency	10%		15.3	367.2		342.3	323.1
Total cost			168.3	4,039.2		3,765.5	3,554.3
Commissioned revenue			173.3	4,160.0		4,160.0	4,160.0
Profit			5.0	120.8		394.5	605.7
Return on comm. revenue			2.9%	2.9%		9.5%	14.6%

On the back of these calculations, other points to note in the planning of your answer could include:

- Revenue is substantially lower than the first series (£173k v £217k). This is a 20% decrease (at the top end of the 10 – 20% fall mentioned in the pre-seen). There may be scope for negotiation although they have stated this is the maximum they are willing to pay.

- Total cost of the first series was £2.37m or £197,500 per programme. Considerable savings will be required if a profit is to be made on the second series.

- Cutting costs too much could damage the look and feel of the programme, which in turn could reflect badly on VYP (link to Porter's Generic Strategies).

- Joint MD's want a return of not less than 9% – this would seem unlikely given the first series only delivered 8.8%. Might there be any learning curve effects?

- It's not worth doing the series if a profit can't be made – the stated aim of VYP is "to make successful programmes for profit".

- There could be longer term implications on VYP if the proposal is rejected. Further re-commissions may not be requested.

- Based on the assumptions provided, a return of 2.9% would not be sufficient in the eyes of the joint MDs.

- If the savings suggested can be realised, a margin of 9.5% may be possible - need to assess how realistic these savings might be.

- Incremental basis of appraising projects would suggest that head office costs should be ignored. This 'marginal costing' approach further increases the return to 14.6%. However, this approach cannot be taken for all programmes or else the head office costs would not be covered by profit. Why should "Leah" be treated any differently?

A good way to help analyse this proposal would be using the headings of Johnson, Scholes & Whittington's suitability, feasibility, acceptability model.

Exercise 3 – Planning and calculations: TV presenter

This is an example of a "multiple proposal" type issue; one that begins with a problem but the unseen material makes some proposals on how the problem can be resolved. Here, you're given two potential options: use an alternative presenter or cancel the series.

You should begin by considering the financial impact of the options:

Option A: Use an alternative presenter

	£ million
Income	2.4
Expense incurred	(0.6)
Expense to go	(2.0)
Net profit pre-tax	(0.2)

Option B: Cancel the series

Sunk costs of £0.6 million could be lost as there would be no incremental revenue.

Other factors to consider could include:

- Reputational damage from letting down the broadcaster – may lead to difficulties winning further work. Makes the option of cancelling commercially unrealistic.

- Broadcaster could be viewed as key player per Mendelow's Matrix – will need to consult with them

- Relevant costing should ignore the sunk cost and consider incremental revenue of £2.4m v additional cost of £2m.

- Controversial nature of this series could lead to valuable publicity.

- May want to question the accuracy of the £2m forecast costs to complete – could these be reduced?

- May be able to pay lower fees to the replacement presenter if they are less "high-profile".

Exercise 4 – Planning and calculations: Cost control

Being a problem type issue, it is important that your planning addresses not only the impact of the problem but also evaluates some alternative solutions.

Impact

- Producers won't always have a financial background and so this increases the importance of a reliable IT system.

- IT system hasn't grown with the business.

- Could lead to de-motivation amongst production staff if they are being expected to drive down costs (without compromising quality) but don't have the tools to do that.

- Competitors are gaining an advantage through the use of IT.

Alternative solutions

Solution	Factors to consider
Stay with existing systems	A straw man option. Clearly not viable given everything noted above.
Invest in an IT system	An obvious alternative so the focus of analysis should be on how best to use IT and where to direct the investment. • Bespoke package or off the shelf? If competitors use IT effectively this might suggest that off the shelf solutions are available. These will be cheaper but might not meet all of VYPs requirements. • All producers and finance staff will require training – need to consider who should deliver this and the timing of it • The culture of the organisation will need to be changed – will need a change agent and a driver. Training will also need to cover this. Without a change in culture the IT system won't be fully effective. • May need to appoint an IT manager (or outsource). IT Manager will help to ensure the right package is selected in the first place. However, it will bring additional cost. • IT system installations are notoriously problematic, an experienced project manager may be worthwhile.

Required 1(b)

The purpose of the e-mail is to persuade the programme producers of the need for improved IT. Since they are not financing the investment, the arguments should not purely hinge around financial viability for the company; it must focus on the benefits for the producers themselves. This will include greater ease of control, on-time delivery of programmes and allowing them to better control costs, thereby reaching targets and earning bonuses.

The implementation of new IT systems will represent quite a cultural change for the producers and so the steps that could be taken to minimise the impact of this should be covered.

Exercise 5 – Planning and calculations: VT filming

This is another example of a "multiple proposal" type issue. In this case you're given two potential options: purchase Tee or bring the VT filming in-house. Don't forget that there is nothing stopping VYP continuing as they are, outsourcing to a third party. This should therefore be viewed as the base case.

We'll begin by considering the financial impact of the options:

A	Carry on outsourcing - Base Case	Yr	0	1	2	3
			£m	£m	£m	£m
	Cost of outsourcing (3,500 days × £1,200) growing @ 10%			(4.62)	(5.08)	(5.59)
	Discount rate @ 9%			0.917	0.842	0.772
	Discounted cash flow			(4.24)	(4.28)	(4.32)
	NPV	(12.84m)				

B	Purchase Tee					
	Investment (4 × £0.85m)		(3.4)			
	Costs of outsourcing (3,500 days × £1,200) growing @ 10%			(4.62)	(5.08)	(5.59)
	Savings (£1.4 m growing at 10%)			1.54	1.69	1.86
	Total cash flows		(3.4)	(3.08)	(3.39)	(3.73)
	Discount rate @ 9%		1.000	0.917	0.842	0.772
	Discounted cash flow		(3.4)	(2.82)	(2.85)	(2.88)
	NPV	(11.95m)				

C	VT filming work in house					
	Investment		(7.0)			
	Total operating costs (growing by 10 %)			(2.2)	(2.42)	(2.66)
	Discount rate @ 9%		1.000	0.917	0.842	0.772
	NPV	(13.11m)				

If carrying on outsourcing is regarded as the 'base case', the acquisition of Tee could increase shareholder wealth by £0.89m (£12.84m - £11.95m). Taking the VT filming in-house would reduce shareholder wealth by £0.27m.

Other factors to consider could include:

- Existing close working relationship between Tee and VYP (3,150 days - approx 90% of VT filming work in total).

- Vertical integration would bring additional fixed costs and business risk (could also apply Ansoff's in terms of related diversification).

- If the acquisition was to succeed VYP would need to ensure it retained the existing staff (maintain expertise).

- Should review the age and quality of the assets being purchased.

- No urgency associated with the decision.

- May help to reduce costs (link to cost control issue).

- Outsourcing brings additional flexibility.

- Bringing the work in-house seems to combine the worst of both worlds - increased risk and lack of expertise.

- £7m investment to bring the filming in-house may be difficult to raise.

Exercise 6 – Planning: Ethical issues

You must not forget to spend some of your planning time giving further consideration to the ethical issues you've identified. In your report, you will need to include:

- A clear explanation of the ethical issue

- Brief coverage of some alternative solutions

- Detailed recommendations covering **what** should be done, **why** this is the best course of action and **how** it should be implemented.

It wouldn't be expected that you'd cover all of these within your planning phase (in particular you might not get on to the detailed recommendations) but a brief consideration of the options available will be of benefit.

We'll look at each of the ethical issues in turn.

Selection of outsourced companies

The ethical issue is that booking managers should not be influenced by gifts or other enticements but should focus on the needs of the programmes. Such actions could be seen as bribery and, although quite commonplace within several industries, should not be viewed as acceptable.

Potential action could include:

- Update the company guidelines so all employees clearly know what is and isn't acceptable. This could completely prohibit the acceptance of all gifts (removes any ambiguity) or could place a limit of the maximum monetary value that would be deemed as acceptable.

- Enforce disciplinary procedures for anyone found to be breaking the guidelines.

- Provide training to all booking managers on how to handle such offers

- Specific set criteria against which all outsourced companies should be selected. These should include both cost and suitability to meet the needs of the programme.

Documentary series with child labour scenes

As noted, the ethical issue here is whether VYP should intervene to try to stop the use of child labour.

Potential action could include:

- Provide details of findings to the head offices of the global companies whose products VYP has filmed and ask them to take action. However, the companies involved may request specific evidence.

- Supply copies of extracts of the film to the companies and request a response. This may require permission from the broadcaster since they have commissioned the documentary.

- Publicising the names of the global companies to raise press interest. This may raise publicity for the programme but could make the companies very defensive meaning the issue doesn't get fully addressed.

- Do nothing and simply complete the programmes for broadcast in 6 months' time. The easiest option but not the ethically 'right' thing to do.

Exercise 7 – Summary of technical models and diversity points

Technical models:

(1) SWOT (general for prioritisation)

(2) SFA ("Leah")

(3) Porter's Generic Strategies (general intro and "Leah")

(4) Mendelow (TV Presenter)

(5) Ansoff's (VT Filming proposal)

Diversity points:

(1) The rise of super-indies and vertically integrated production companies (VT Filming)

(2) Reported reductions in programme budgets (80% in indies reporting a fall) (cost control)

(3) IT systems implementation (e.g. SAP) and associated difficulties (cost control)

(4) Harry Potter: death of Richard Harris and how filming was amended (TV Presenter illness)

A further diversity point is required. This can be gained in the introduction (suggestion would be decline in advertising revenues as a result of economic climate and the pressure this is placing on commissioning revenues).

VYP: A review of a sample answer

Chapter learning objectives

By the end of this chapter you will:

- Have reviewed a sample answer and made a comparison between this and your own answer in order to identify areas to improve.

- Be more aware of what scores marks under each of the assessment criteria.

- Appreciate the characteristics of a good script.

1 Introduction

Presented in this chapter is a sample script for the VYP November 2010 case exam. It was sat under exam conditions in 3 hours and 20 mins.

The script is a bit shorter than average, at approximately 2,800 words excluding appendices. It has been presented as it was submitted. Layout has been preserved as much as possible and spelling and punctuation errors from the original documents have been retained.

Against the script is a detailed analysis of where marks were scored and where they were lost. Commentary is given on both strong and weak areas and includes identification of where and how the candidate could have improved their marks.

Before you read this script you should have attempted you own answer (in either 3 hours and 20 minutes or perhaps in a greater time to see what you can achieve without time pressures). Do not 'cheat' and look at this answer – as the purpose of writing your own answer is to see what YOU can achieve! When you have completed your answer, only then should you read this sample answer – which scored highly at 74%. You can then check your script against this sample to see what you did right, what you did wrong and most importantly, what you may have missed out of your answer.

2 Sample script

Report: analysis, prioritisation & recommendation of key issues facing VYP
Date: 25th November 2010
To: Joint MD's
CC: Janet Black
From: Management Accountant

Introduction
The issues that the organisation faces include the power of customer & VYP's influences over its suppliers (Porters Five Forces – covered in more detail in the relevant sections below). Although, VYP is clearly a differentiator (Porters Generic Strategies) cost control is an important general issue & is a key factor in deciding whether Leah re-commission is accepted or not.

> Although the title page, introduction and terms of reference are all areas of your report that attract few specific marks, submitting a report where these are just left blank does detract from the overall professionalism and will not make a good impression on your marker. You are inadvertently telling them that you had difficulties managing your time in the exam.
>
> Try to ensure these sections are completed even if it is just a brief one line comment.

Prioritisation Statement

The following issues have been prioritised with regard to the SWOT analysis in Appendix A.

Issue 1: Leah

This opportunity has been deemed to be the top priority as a response is required within the next week. Additionally, the margins can only be achieved by careful control & better planning of costs. This is likely to require strong planning around other portfolio activity & could result in other activity being planned around it, this could benefit from the IT changes.

It is a large volume commission based on last year's output 24 programmes out of 197 programmes would represent 12% of programmes

Additionally, this represents a consolidation of an entry into a new genre which could itself drive further commissions.

Issue 2: TV presenter

Whilst still a pressing issue, given the broadcast date is more than 12 month hence this is ranked slightly lower than the Leah issue. Whilst, Sara Mills has been open & communicated with the broadcaster the prospective risk of losing future commissions as well as the current series profit risk elevates this issue above the other issues.

Issue 3: VT filming proposals

This is lower ranked as it is not business critical. It is ranked above the cost control issues as a 3rd party supplier has been engaged & from a relationship perspective VYP should look to maintain good relations.

Issue 4: Cost control

This is an opportunity born out of the current weakness of VYP's cost control processes. However, this does not have external or operational survival impacts & is therefore lowest ranked.

Other issues have been captured as ethical issues.

> This section would score 5 out of 5 for prioritisation. The order of the issues is in line with the examiners view and clear justification has been provided for the positioning of each issue based on both impact and urgency.

Analysis

Issue 1: Leah
This opportunity has been assessed under the Suitability, Feasibility, Acceptability framework as designed by Johnson, Scholes et.al.

Suitability

Given, the success of last year's foray into drama – the follow up with a re-commission would stamp VYP's authority on this genre in that market. It is therefore desirable to see the emphasis of success that this repeat would bring.

It is likely that the scrip-writers already have creative ideas that have spun out of the original commission & this is likely to be positive for their moral & being a fulfilling project. These people are likely to be nearer the top of Maslow's hierarchy of needs where comfort & safety are over-taken by ambition & fulfilment.

Feasibility

VYP need to ensure that it has sufficient man-power, studios & relevant actors available to be able to stage the next 24 in the series. If an actor is away for the relevant filming on a bush-tucker trial for instance it may not be able to accept the filming if the character is integral. Work-around's around possible e.g. Robin of Sherwood in the 1980's used a replacement Robin (Jason Connery) in some its repeats.

The positive cash flows usually associated with re-commissioning should mean that cash is available.

Acceptability (figures are extracted from Appendix C)

If the cost control is implemented & the prospective cost saving is delivered then even if the contingency is burnt the return would be 9.5% - higher than the 9% threshold.

VYP need to consider the risk of that this is not delivered giving only a 2.9% return. At the other end of the scale if the contingency is not spent a return of 18% is possible. Some organisations do not hold contingency at a project level as it encourages it to be spent or alternatively hold some only at a project level but still require a change request process to exceed the projects non-contingent budget. A good example is Lloyds Corporate Banking which has adopted this hybrid approach.

Programme & series returns are more fully examined in Appendix C.

Being one of the more important issues, there would be a greater allocation of judgement marks for this section of the report than there would for other, less important issues. This section would score as a marginal pass. Key omissions are:

- No discussion of a marginal costing approach or the consideration of the contribution earned towards the allocated overheads of £192k

- No discussion of whether the allocation of overheads was suitable for decision making purposes

However, there was good application of the SAF model and of Maslow's hierarchy of needs, as well as the use of some real world examples relating to Robin Hood and Lloyds Corporate Banking.

Issue 2: TV presenter

With only a limited number of customers that VYP sells to in the domestic market the risk of zero commissions going forwards is a real risk. This is a clear example of how customer power in Porters Five Forces is enacted. Both options result in a loss to the organisation (see Appendix B)

Programmes cancelled

Advantages

- *this is easy to implement*
- *resources that were being used can be "free'd up" to work on other projects*

Disadvantages

- *there is a real risk of losing future commissions from the broadcaster – given VYP have only a few domestic customers (BBC, ITV, C4 & C5) this could seriously damaged revenues & profitability*
- *not completing a project could have contagion effect – resulting in other broadcasters not giving commissions to VYP*

Programmes re-scheduled

Advantages

- *positive message for staff who have been putting time & effort into a project – they will see some fruit for their labours*
- *positive marketing message that VYP are committed to delivery & can overcome obstacles*

Disadvantage

- still a loss to the organisation

VYP might look to consider insurance for external events not just sickness. In considering the end to end process by project the key risk areas can be identified & potentially insured against. Many organisations took insurance out in the event that a consortium of their employees won the lottery & all quit their jobs at the same time.

This section would score as a marginal fail as the issue and the alternative solutions have not been examined in sufficient depth. Key omissions are:

- the need to find an appoint a presenter urgently

- the risk of cost over-runs making the loss for this series even larger

- the need to maintain programme quality

- the reputational damage if the series were cancelled

Issue 3: VT filming proposals (figures referred to in appendix D)

The purchasing of Tee assessed at a "fair price" of £3.4m would not bring a positive NPV based on the initial purchase price vs. the incremental cost savings.

Other issues include:

- *the need to raise cash to finance the purchase – it is difficult to get corporate loans in the current financial environment*

- *giving out shares to the Tee MD would dissolve ownership control, voting rights & margins enjoyed by the other shareholders*

The investment in equipment of £7m & subsequent cost savings is even more financially disadvantageous.

The question as to how an organisation that has profits of only £850k can afford equipment that would cost VYP £7m needs to be addressed – either Tee is not sustainable in the long-term or the figures around the £7m have been over-estimated.

The margin at 22% is significantly higher that VYP's of less than 10%. VYP could use its power over its supplier (Porter 5 forces) to force the cost down in much the way that Tesco did with its purchase power under Terry Leahy.

Again, the commentary here is a little superficial, although some sensible comments are made regarding the other issues to consider and the margin comparison with VYP. The query over how Tee can afford equipment that would cost VYP £7m is ill thought-out as it failes to recognise that the profit is after depreciation costs relating to the equipment and that Tee would have a rolling programme to replace equipment so would not need to invest £7m all in one go.

The section also fails to note that VT filming is not a core activity for VYP, who outsources much of its programme making. This should lead the candidate to question why VYP would consider taking the function in-house. How VYP would manage this activity should also have been questioned.

Overall this section would score half marks.

Issue 4: Cost control

Improved cost control is always desirable in a business. In VYP this focus will draw producers & directors focus back to the core objectives of producing successful programmes at a profit.

Do nothing

There is an argument that although margins have reduced if the costs of charitable donations were added back in the overall margin (excluding international sales) would be only slightly below the industry expectations of 10%. However given VYP is a Top20 company it might be expected that the margins should be slightly better than average.

The new IT systems will cost money to purchase & this will reduce company profits were there to be no benefits. Additionally, the purchase would use cash.

Poor cost controls lead to lower profit & in not address systemic or process driven issues there is a danger of continual margin reductions & lower profitability.

Cost control is important for the organisation as without it the opportunity to achieve the desired margin in "Leah" could be missed & potentially VYP might not accept the proposal.

Invest in new IT systems

There is a precedent to purchasing new IT systems in that the competition already have implemented – VYP may do well to adopt a fast-follower principle & do likewise.

There are a number of tools that are on the market from the ubiquitous Microsoft Planning, "Plan-IT" / Mercatus (bespoke) systems used in House of Fraser. Alternatively a modular semi-bespoke system that integrates mechanism might be used such as Sun Micro Systems or Siebel time-recording used in the Financial Services Compensation Scheme.

Some technology investments are modular to allow for component upgrade as & when necessary. This avoids wholesale purchases which can be more expensive & disruptive.

VYP in considering any investment should be quite clear about the elements that they are buying. It might be that a simple basic solution is all that is required, rather than a top end software package that costs much more to purchase.

VYP should look to consider the approximated net benefits of the purchase to ensure that it is getting value for money. A mechanism that integrates with current systems & perhaps enhances current budgeting activities with an easy to understand user-interface would be most desirable.

Cultural / process changes

VYP could look to implement non-system changes to improve cost control.

Example 1: the current purchase order system does not have final invoice sign-off by the producer. The consequences are that a bill for 5 days work if initially 5 days were commissioned would be settled even if only 4 days work on a time & materials basis was used. A simple improvement would ensure that invoices have to be approved by producers / directors where relevant.

Example 2: improved planning. This is not just an IT system but also a mind-set that needs to be changed. It is important to change the mind-set of the programme-making people to understand that completion of the programme without regard to cost is not acceptable. Bonuses could be set so that a bonus is not payable if the production goes over budget.

> This is a very good section that would score full marks under judgement. Unfortunately though, as a lower prioritised issue, there are fewer judgement marks available when compared to the higher prioritised issues (4 marks v 8 marks).

Ethics

Issue 1: Documentary series

The issue is that due to scheduling the injustices that are being carried out remain unreported for 6 months & potentially unknown by the global retailers.

The recommendation is that Steve speaks carefully with Greg Jackson & respects his concern – part of his empathy demonstrates that he is human & this is likely to be a big benefit in future projects. He should be assured that negative personal impacts of filming is not the first time this has happened: a documentary that saw a Komodo dragon slowly killing its prey over many days has also had negative impacts on the camera crew.

Greg should be assured that the impact of filming & its subsequent broadcast is itself action that could result in a reduction of the human injustices.

Steve could also discuss with the broadcaster the possibility of bringing forward the documentary on the grounds that in six months it could be less topical & that there is a real sense of injustice being carried out.

There could also be an additional angle in filming or obtaining the global suppliers responses there is both early communication to the global retailers & also additional content for the programmes.

Issue 2: Selection of outsourced companies

The issue is that whilst accepted practice to receive gifts it is not necessarily good practice. Although not comparable on scale it is similar to the jet fighter "bungs" that were supplied to the Saudi Royal Family by BAE systems. Additionally, there are suggestions but not proof that this has influenced supplier selection.

There is also a business issue as margins are going to be eroded if the more expensive supplier is being used.

It is recommended that a gift register is established so that all gifts >£5 received by all personnel are recorded to ensure that there is a fair transparent control in place.

It is recommended that the buyers in question are talked to on an individual basis by Steve or John about the need to ensure that the best price is obtained. A process to ensure that procurement of outsourcing is justified in the business case as to why the supplier & not another one is selected should resolve any fears of unfair selection.

In relation to the documentary series, the candidate has missed the ethical issue here – which is what to do NOW with the knowledge of the use of child labour, and the ethical responsibility that VYP should notify either the global companies whose suppliers are using child labour or to contact the relevant authorities.

Regarding the selection of outsourced companies, no mention has been made of a code of conduct and the need for clear rules and / or disciplinary action if further gifts are accepted.

Overall this section is fairly weak, especially when it comes to the recommendations. It would score 5 out of the possible 10 marks.

Recommendations

Issue 1: Leah

It is recommended that Leah be accepted as a re-commission subject to strict cost control implementation & contingent upon ensuring that time-frames & central actors are available.

The producer, director & management accountant should be assembled as a small project team. The producer / director needs to ensure about casting availability prior to agreeing with the broadcasters. It is recommended that only a 5% contingency is given & then any expenditure over and above the non-contingent budget needs to be approved by a centrally controlled change-request process. This better manages the risk of cost over-runs & could lead to greater margin successes than are currently being anticipated. The producer needs to be given ownership for delivering the studio / people cost savings & in conjunction with the management accountant agree that this is reasonable up front & monitor progress towards achieving the target.

Issue 2: TV presenter

This is a no win situation, but it is the degree to which VYP loses that is at stake. The clear recommendation is to re-shoot the programmes that have already been shot with a new presenter & complete the series. Early communication of this intention by a board member will ensure that VYP's continued commitment to quality & delivery is underlined. This is because from a financial perspective this is the least loss situation.

Additionally, from a reputational perspective & counter the risk a zero commissions from what is a limited market place this is the least risk solution. Further work to mitigate the losses should be undertaken but not at the risk of quality & not to any greater degree that margin enhancement would be covered by analysis on other projects.

The project team should be assembled & taken through the logic of the decision & informed of the challenges ahead to ensure that there is team buy-in. Len Fisher should look to seek out the cost of insurances to advice what risk premium is payable to transfer the risk of this or other outside events impacting on profitability.

Issue 3: VT filming proposals

The recommendation is that VYP continue to use Tee as an outsourcing company. Given the relatively strong margins that Tee seems to be reporting & VYP's relative power it is suggested that the prices that Tee charge for its services are re-negotiated downwards. If Tee is not willing to reduce its margins then VYP can look elsewhere in the market for other suppliers.

It is suggested that this is undertaken by a board member perhaps including the executive chairman where sensitive strategic discussion don't get in the way of operational continuity.

Issue 4: Cost control

The recommendation is that VYP need to invest in an appropriate IT system in the medium-term & in the short-term improved Purchase processes, procurement opportunities investigated & post project cost reviews implemented. Janet Black should change the procurement process to ensure that programme-makers sign-off on all invoices. This not only solves a process issue but also re-enforces the need for cost control & gives the programme-makers more accountability & responsibility.

The relationship manager should re-negotiate the contract with Tee to reduce cost by c£400k a year or if this proves not possible seek out an alternative supplier who can provide the quality of service at lower margins.

Janet Black should put before the board a proposal with alternative solutions to select a software provider. The proposal should consider the estimated cost savings, possibly the pay-back period of the purchase.

Of the 30 logic marks available, 20 relate to the first requirement to prepare a report. Those 20 marks are further broken down between the issues, with the more important issues having a higher allocation of marks.

This section would score as a clear pass, gaining around 13 of the 20 marks available. Not all of the recommendations are supported by clear justifications (this is especially true with the recommendations on Leah) and not all suggestions consider the reaction of other stakeholders and the implications of what is being suggested (particularly true on Tee).

However, a strength of these recommendations is the extent of detail provided on the specific actions needed to be taken.

Appendix A

SWOT

Strengths
Drama programmes success has resulted in a request for re-commissioning

Weaknesses
Current IT systems
Current cost control processes
Procurement processes

Opportunities
Option of purchasing Tee - or other filming proposals to reduce costs

Threats
Risk that broadcaster will not recommission

> The SWOT does not include two key threats relating to the reduced commissioning revenues and the threat to VYP's reputation if the documentary series were to be cancelled (due to the ill presenter). The candidate would gain 1 technical mark, but only 1 application mark (instead of the maximum 3 available for the SWOT).

Appendix B - TV Presenter

		£ks
A Alternative Presenter	Income	2,400
	Expense incurred	(600)
	Expense to go	(2,000)
	Net profit pre-tax	(200)
B Programmes cancelled	Income	0
	Expense incurred	(600)
	Expense to go	0
	Net profit pre-tax	(600)

> The costs incurred to date are sunk costs and are irrelevant to future decisions. This is not clearly highlighted within these calculations. The differential impact between cancelling the series and appointing a new presenter is +£0.4m (i.e. £0.6m loss - £0.2m loss) and it is this differential that should have driven the decision.
>
> Failure to highlight this cost the candidate one application mark.

Appendix C - Leah

	Cost per unit	Days / prog	Cost / prog	24 progs	unit saving	cost saving	re-stated cost
Script writers	2,000	3	6,000	144,000			144,000
Studio time	30,000	2	60,000	1,440,000	(8)	(240,000)	1,200,000
Outsourced VT crews	1,200	8	9,600	230,400			230,400
Outsourced freelance prog makers	1,000	10	10,000	240,000			240,000
VT editing	500	4	2,000	48,000			48,000
VYP prog making employees	1,100	16	17,600	422,400	(8)	(8,800)	413,600
Other direct prog costs	300	16	4,800	115,200			115,200
Artists fees	35,000	1	35,000	840,000			840,000
VYP head office costs	8,000	1	8,000	192,000			192,000
			153,000	3,672,000			3,423,200
Contingency	10%		15,300	367,200			342,320
Budget for programme			168,300	4,039,200			3,765,520

	No savings	With savings	Zero contingency
Revenue £ks	4,160	4,160	4,160
Cost	(4,039)	(3,766)	
Operating profit	121	394	737
Margin	2.9%	9.5%	18%

> These calculations are substantially correct and so would score highly. The return of 18% with zero contingency was not required and earned no marks.
>
> However, these calculations omit what was required in respect of removing the £192k of overhead costs to show the marginal costs. This would have produced costs without overheads of £3,554,300 and generated a return of 14.6% (see calculations in previous chapter). Application marks have therefore been lost.

Appendix D - VT Filming proposals

Hurdle rate 9%

A Carry on outsourcing - Base Case		Yr	0	1	2	3
Day rate	1,200			4,200,000	4,620,000	5,082,000
No. days	3,500					
	4,200,000					
Growth	10%					

B Purchase Tee - incremental cost / benefits only						
Earnings	850,000	Investment	(3,400,000)			
PE	4	Savings		944,444	1,038,889	1,142,778
Turnover	3,780,000					
Percentage margin	22%	NPV	(776,691)			

C VT filming work in house		Investment	(7,000,000)			
incremental costs / benefits only		On-going costs		(2,200,000)	(2,420,000)	(2,662,000)
		Cost savings		4,200,000	4,620,000	5,082,000
		Net savings		2,000,000	2,200,000	2,420,000
Cost growth	10%	NPV	(1,444,758)			

> The calculations in parts A & C are correct and would score highly. The incremental approach (of considering the continued use of Tee on an outsourced basis) is perfectly acceptable, although not the only way in which these calculations could have been attempted.
>
> In part B, whilst the P/E valuation is correct, the calculation of the savings is incorrect (see previous chapter for correct calculations in this area).

2nd Requirement

Email

From: Janet Black
To: VYP programme producers
CC: John Young; Steve Voddil; Management Accountant
Subject: Need for improved IT systems

Given the recent spate of programmes that have exceeded the project budget (35 out of last 50 projects) there is clearly a requirement to better control budgets.

Inevitably, there is a cost associated with purchasing software & any hardware upgrades but if the benefits can be demonstrated to outweigh the costs the purchase is a logical conclusion.

The purchase would help programme producers to better plan costs for a specific project to give a rolling dynamic view or estimates to completion & estimates at completion.

Support from the management accountant would help identify & report variances to previous plans.

An integrated solution would ensure that booking of limited resources such as video-tape is controlled through a scheduler. The opportunities to reschedule usage with other projects or identify pinch-points & hire externally at a cheaper price at an earlier stage will become apparent.

The purchase would force a more systematic approach to the planning process & then force users to identify what resources are required for how long.

Prior to purchase I suggest that we involve a select group of Producers to ensure that we get the best fit for the organisation. Additionally, this time can be used to ensure that the user-interface will be satisfactory & easy to learn – to this end please can I have volunteers for a trial.

This is a good attempt and would score 7 out of a possible 10 marks. Significantly, it contains:

- Short sentences (as directed in the requirement)

- An explanation of the need for change

- An explanation of the benefits to programme producers.

VYP: CIMA Examiner's post exam guidance

Chapter learning objectives

By the end of this chapter you will:

- Have reviewed the examiner's post exam guidance to better understand what is required under each of the assessment criteria and appreciate the common errors and omissions made by candidates who sat this exam.

1 How to use the post exam guidance report

After each exam sitting, the Examiner releases a post exam guidance report and these are available on the CIMA website for all past exams.

You should read this document thoroughly to learn more about:

- What is required to score well under each of the assessment criteria.
- What common errors and omissions were made by the candidates who sat this exam.
- How to learn from other people's errors!

2 Post exam guidance report for the Nov 2010 VYP case

The main purpose of this report is to give help to candidates who were not successful in the November 2010 examination of the VYP TV production company case. It is also intended to provide guidance to prospective candidates who plan to take future T4 Part B case study examinations. This report explains the basic rationale behind the case and the suggested approach to each of the assessment criteria. It also provides a brief marking guide, general comments on the candidates' scripts and a statement of common errors, including omissions, which were made by candidates.

This case was concerned with V and Y Productions (VYP), a television production company, established in 2003 based in the United Kingdom, which makes programmes commissioned by the BBC, ITV, Channel 4 and Channel 5. VYP is not listed on either the main stock exchange or the AIM.

The two founders were both experienced programme makers and had experience of working for TV broadcast companies but wanted to make TV programmes of their own. VYP employed 60 people directly and outsourced much of the routine TV production work to other small specialised companies.

The reputation of VYP was based solidly on the calibre of its staff. The two founders were actively involved in winning new commissioned programmes and worked alongside the relevant TV programme directors who proposed programme ideas.

Over the last three years, VYP had won several TV programme awards and had established a reputation for the production of documentaries which allowed the general public to air their views on topical issues.

In the last financial year, VYP generated total revenues of £28.6 million, representing growth of nearly 39% from revenue earned in the previous year. VYP held a market share of about 1.4% of commissioned TV programmes in the UK. This placed VYP in the top 20 companies making TV programmes in the UK.

The overall aim of VYP was to make successful programmes for profit. It had four programme genres being documentaries, drama series, scripted comedy programmes and general entertainment programmes.

One of the founders had convinced the Board to donate money on a regular basis to several recognised charities. The other founder had set up a scheme which allowed school children to view videotape filming of some programmes.

The unseen material required candidates to (a) prepare a report that prioritised, analysed and evaluated the issues facing VYP and make appropriate recommendations and (b) in addition to the analysis in the report, to draft an email to all of VYP's programme producers on behalf of the Finance Director to persuade them of the need for improved IT systems in order to achieve better control of direct programme-making costs. The email was restricted to 10 short sentences. The requirement for part (a) was worth 90 marks and part (b) was worth 10 marks.

The T4 assessment matrix has 9 criteria, each of which carries between 5 and 30 marks. It should be noted that the Logic criterion has 30 marks associated with it, 20 marks for recommendations given in the answer to part (a) and 10 marks for the answer to part (b). It is important that the candidate earns high marks in the Judgement and Logic criteria as each of these carry 20 marks within part (a). It is also important that the candidate undertakes sufficient analysis to provide a sound base for discussion of the issues from which appropriate and logical recommendations can be made. The analysis should include appropriate financial and numerical calculations, particularly those which are discernable from the unseen examination material which is rewarded in Application.

The main issues contained in the unseen material covered the areas of:

(1) Proposal to re-commission a new series of 24 drama programmes called "Leah"

(2) TV presenter taken ill

(3) Cost control

(4) Videotape (VT) filming proposals

There were other areas which candidates could have discussed (and which were given credit in the marking) but it was critical that the issues relating to the proposal to re-commission a new series of 24 drama programmes was fully addressed in the answer as this represented such a large proportion of VYP's revenue.

Format of answers

The format of candidates' answers to part (a) was generally good. Candidates usually began with an introduction leading to very brief terms of reference, prioritisation of issues, followed by discussion of those issues. Ethical issues were discussed and advice given and then recommendations were made on the issues which had been prioritised. Finally, most candidates provided a brief conclusion. The appendices were usually contained either in an Excel file or at the end of the report. Non computer based candidates' scripts usually presented their appendices in a second answer book. Some candidates provided their appendices at the beginning of their report, which is also acceptable. Part (b) was often included as an appendix to the report, which is acceptable. It is worth emphasising again that a position audit is not required in the examination. It is better that candidates' reserve their comments for the main discussion section of their report.

It was noticeable again, that some candidates did not address part (b) at all, possibly because of time pressures. This was a dangerous omission, given that part (b) is worth 10% of the marks. It is surprising that such omissions were made as this is now the fourth examination in which part (b) has been required and reference has been made to it in each of the previous post examination guidance reports.

Discussion of general candidate performance under each assessment criteria

T4 Assessment Criteria

	Maximum marks available
Analysis of Issues (25 marks)	
Technical	5
Application	15
Diversity	5
Strategic Choices (35 marks)	
Focus	5
Prioritisation	5
Judgement	20
Ethics	5
Recommendations (40 marks)	
Logic	30
Integration	5
Ethics	5

Analysis of issues

PART (a):

Technical:

Rationale:

The purpose of this criterion is to assess the use of relevant theoretical techniques and frameworks and the provision of calculations to aid the analysis of the case material.

Suggested Approach:

It is recommended that candidates present their technical knowledge either in the form of appendices to the main report (in an Excel spreadsheet or at the end of the report itself in a separate answer book) and referred to within the report where relevant. Some candidates prefer to present their appendices at the beginning of the report which is also acceptable.

Marking Guide:

Marks are awarded for technical models and theories which are relevant to the case. It is usually appropriate to limit the technical knowledge displayed to 5 separate items.

Commentary:

Most candidates were able to display sound technical knowledge principally comprising a SWOT analysis, the Johnson, Scholes and Whittington SAF framework, the Mendelow Matrix and a range of other strategic planning approaches. These were appropriate in this case study. As usual, most candidates performed well under this criterion. It was noticeable that many candidates were more discerning over their use of strategic planning models, limiting their use to a few relevant models which is welcomed.

Common errors:

It is important that candidates do proceed to apply the models they cite. Some candidates still produce models which they then do not use within their analysis of the issues. It is always appropriate to produce a SWOT analysis. It would be expected that the main issues to be discussed in part (a) of the answer will feature somewhere within the SWOT analysis. The purpose of the SWOT is to assist the candidate to identify the main issues affecting the organisation in the case. A SWOT analysis does not need to be very long. It should be long enough to enable the candidate to state what are the main issues contained in the case which must be addressed within the report. It would be very rare for a case study not to have something under each of the SWOT headings. Analytical models such as Johnson, Scholes and Whittington's SAF framework are regularly used within the report and this is satisfactory.

Application:

Rationale:

The point of the Application criterion is to assess how well candidates use the techniques, frameworks and calculations to support their analysis of the issues in the unseen material and their subsequent recommended actions.

Suggested approach:

Candidates are advised to ensure that they apply relevant models, techniques and frameworks correctly, given the case material. Thus it is important that rather than just regurgitating the model or framework, it is presented in such a way so that it conveys information which is relevant to the case. It is then expected that candidates use this information in their discussion of the issues. This also applies in respect of calculations, which should be relevant to the information given in the particular case.

Marking guide:

Marks are available for the relevant application of techniques, models, frameworks and supporting calculations but only if the candidate applies them to the specific case. Marks were awarded for the application of models to the case material and for relevant calculations. Candidates who carried out sufficient numerical analysis were well rewarded. There was plenty of scope in this case to obtain high marks under Application if candidates had grasped the opportunity.

In particular, marks were available for calculating the following requirement of the Finance Director in respect of Leah as set out in the unseen material:

- A budget for the total costs for each programme and the 24 programme series

- The operating profit and the return on commissioned revenue before, and after, any savings in the number of studio days and VYP programme-making employees

- The operating profit on commissioned revenue for the series of 24 programmes after the savings in studio days and VYP programme-making employees, assuming overhead costs for the company do not increase from the present level if the series is re-commissioned.

This last bullet point referred to calculating the marginal cost of the Leah programmes and the contribution that could be made towards VYP's fixed overhead costs. This was an area poorly attempted, or not attempted at all by many candidates but is a very relevant technique especially in difficult economic times.

In addition, candidates should have analysed the three VT filming proposals, being acquiring Tee (a VT company to which VYP outsourced work), to carry on outsourcing its VT work or to take in-house all the VT filming work which VYP requires to be done.

A further calculation could have been made relating to the costs and potential benefits to VYP of either cancelling the commission for the 12 documentary programmes following the illness of the presenter or to carry on and make all 12 programmes, recognising the potential loss on the contract.

Commentary:

Most candidates provided a SWOT analysis. It was still apparent that some candidates pre-prepared their SWOT analysis based on the pre-seen material and did not update it in the light of the new issues raised in the unseen material. Such SWOT presentations earned very few marks as often the key issues, as presented in the unseen material, were not included. The candidate should ensure that all the prioritised issues are included in the appropriate quadrant of the SWOT. The SWOT should have included the threats posed by the reduced commission revenue as exemplified by the Leah re-commission and the reputational damage to VYP if they cancelled the 12 part documentary series as a result of the presenter falling ill.

Common errors:

Some candidates' SWOT analyses omitted some or all of the issues identified above, in particular the reduction in commissioning revenue.

While on the whole most candidates applied the technical models and theories they cited, some did not. Candidates are reminded that the models and theories are useful only if they are applied to the case material.

There were a whole range of errors relating to the calculations made by candidates as follows:

- The first and foremost shocking error was made by too many candidates believing that the total loss on the documentary series to which VYP was liable would be the costs incurred to date, £0.6 million plus the return of the advanced revenue for the whole series of £2.4 million giving a "total loss" of £3 million. This is not acceptable from someone who is intent on joining the accounting profession as it demonstrates a lack of understanding of first principles. VYP had spent £0.6 million against the cash advance of £2.4 million at the time the company was considering cancelling the series. This would have meant that the whole £2.4 million would need to be returned, but they had only spent £0.6 million of that cash advance and this was the maximum loss they would have incurred. The other £1.8 million had not been spent on producing the series. Even if VYP had spent the remaining £1.8 million, the sum of £2.4 million would still not have been a book loss. Candidates with better understanding recognised that this loss could be mitigated by completing the series and was estimated to reduce to a loss of £0.2 million. The even better candidates recognised that the difference of £0.4 million (being the difference between the £2.4 million advance and the expected future cash costs of £2 million) represented an opportunity gain for VYP as they were at that point committed to a loss of £0.6 million which was an unrecoverable sunk cost. Recognition was given to candidates who correctly stated that the return of the £2.4 million might cause some cash flow difficulties for VYP, given that they had already spent £0.6 million of this advance.

- With respect to Leah, it was surprising how many candidates either failed to do exactly as requested by the Finance Director or only did part of what was asked for. For example, the Finance Director asked for a budget for the "total costs for each programme and for the 24 programme series". Many candidates did one and not the other. Other candidates did not then proceed to calculate the operating profit and the return on commissioned revenue after the savings and even fewer calculated the operating profit and return after the savings assuming the overhead costs do not change. This last item, relating to overheads remaining static, was a clear opportunity and broad hint for candidates to show their knowledge of basic management accounting and to discuss the effect of overheads on costs. However, many candidates failed to prepare any calculations on the contribution towards fixed costs and therefore did not earn the marks available. It is an important aspect of management accountancy to recognise which costs are relevant to the decision making process.

- Other issues relating to Leah were that many candidates seemed incapable of undertaking what was a very straight forward budgeting exercise. One particular error which was made was failing to recognise that a contingency applied to total programme costs would be reduced if some of those costs were taken out.

- With regard to the VT filming proposals, it was mentioned above that many candidates failed to recognise that there were in fact three options available to VYP. It remains a surprise that candidates are unable to undertake straightforward PV and NPV calculations especially given that they have encountered more complicated NPV calculations at the Strategic Level. Some candidates took the wrong discount rate, others were confused about timing differences. Many candidates were unable to accurately value Tee using the P/E ratio which was given. A lot of candidates reduced the P/E ratio by a factor even though the unseen material clearly stated that this was "an approximate P/E ratio for a similar unlisted company". Therefore, no reduction was necessary. Some candidates multiplied the revenue by the P/E ratio instead of the earnings. It seems that many candidates know the mechanics but do not apply their knowledge to the circumstances and blindly follow a mechanistic approach. This implies lack of understanding. It also seems that some candidates simply regard a capital investment appraisal calculation itself as a mechanical exercise and are conditioned to expect there to always be positive and negative cash flows. In fact the in-house alternative only had negative cash flows associated with it, yet some candidates were insistent on presenting the cash flows each year as positive in-flows when they were in fact the opposite. The candidates who took the current outsourcing present value as a benchmark, and compared the alternatives of acquiring Tee or taking VT filming in-house against that benchmark, were well rewarded for their clear understanding of the principle involved.

Many of these errors are not acceptable at this level. Candidates must understand that the marker will seriously doubt a candidate's competence if presented with such errors. It implies that the candidate is numerically incompetent and errors of this nature cannot be condoned. These were not difficult or complicated calculations and employers expect their accountants to be sufficiently competent to undertake them accurately.

Diversity:

Rationale:

This criterion seeks to assess knowledge and understanding of relevant real life situations in the same or similar context as that in which the case is set. It also assesses the recognition of commercial or organisational issues relevant to the situation contained in the case whether or not they occur within the same industry.

Suggested approach:

Candidates should seek to introduce relevant examples at the point where they discuss the issue in their answer. Typically, this may occur in the introduction, the prioritisation section, discussion of the issues, ethics or within the recommendations. The main point is that a candidate should seek to bring in the relevant example at the point which enables him or her to elaborate or emphasise the issue which is being considered within the answer.

Marking guide:

Essentially, there is one mark available for each relevant example given, providing it is clearly stated why it is relevant. This is an important point that candidates should note. There are no marks for simply name dropping. Additionally, general discussion of many real life companies in the introduction will not attract more than one mark, as they have not been related to the issues raised in the unseen material. The introduction should be relatively brief. The candidate needs to explain why the example is relevant to the point being made. It is possible to quote the same organisation more than once if the examples given support different points.

Commentary:

This was generally satisfactory. These included references to many organisations which are engaged in the TV production industry.

Common errors:

There were few errors as such but a surprising number of candidates failed to provide any industry examples at all. There are many examples of "indies" which regularly feature in the media spotlight.

Strategic choices

Focus:

Rationale:

This criterion requires candidates to select the issues that are regarded as the most important and which will be discussed further within the answer.

Suggested approach:

This is not a section of the report as such. Marks are awarded based on the issues which are contained and discussed within the report.

Marking guide:

There are five marks available for this criterion even if there are not 5 separate issues identified. It is for the candidate to determine the most relevant issues in the case that should be discussed. As it happened, there were four distinct issues, excluding the ethical issues, in the unseen material.

Commentary:

Most candidates were able to identify separate issues and received good reward.

Common errors:

There were no common errors associated with this criterion which, as usual, was well handled by candidates in the main. It should be noted though, that a candidate who prioritises an issue and then fails to discuss it will not receive credit for that issue under the Focus criterion. Poor time management that results in few issues discussed will have the effect of restricting marks awarded in Focus as well as other criteria such as Judgment and Logic.

Prioritisation:

Rationale:

Under this criterion, the candidate is required to rank the issues and to state clearly and concisely the justification for that ranking. The ranking should reflect the impact of the issues on the particular organisation, which may include its urgency.

Suggested approach:

The priorities should be presented early in the answer under their own heading. The priorities should be set out with the issues ranked as either 1st, 2nd, 3rd etc. Each should be justified with a concise explanation of why the candidate has ranked it in such a position.

Marking guide:

High marks are awarded if the candidate presents the most important issues with a good rationale as to why they are ranked as main priorities. It should be noted that markers do give credit to candidates who make a case for prioritising issues differently from those contained in the suggested answer. The main issues for this case were clearly the re-commission of the Leah programmes and the TV presenter being taken ill part way through the documentary series. These two issues had the largest impact on VYP's revenue and reputation. It was expected that these two issues would feature as the highest priorities in the candidates' answers.

Commentary:

On the whole, candidates are now well versed in producing their rankings and generally manage to present their prioritised issues in an appropriate form. The SWOT analysis, if carefully carried out, should help to clarify which are the most important issues to be addressed.

Common errors:

It was surprising how many candidates did not consider the re-commissioning of Leah to be a major priority, despite its major impact on VYP. The re-commissioning revenue represented around 15% of its total revenue in 2010 and even with the costs as forecast should have produced an operating margin of just under 3%. This was lower than required but what was available to put in its place if the re-commission was turned down? With savings and cautious budgeting and control, it was possible for VYP to increase the operating profit on the re-commission.

Judgement:

Rationale:

This criterion assesses the candidates' exercise of commercial and professional judgement in discussing the key issues which were prioritised.

Suggested approach:

It is important that the candidate discusses the impact the prioritised issues have on the organisation and what alternative actions, with reasons, could be taken to address them. This should include relevant supporting analysis drawn from the "Application" criterion. So for example, if a calculation is made within an appendix, then it should be used in support of the point being made under the relevant heading within this section of the report. It is important that the financial implications of alternative actions, for each of the issues, are discussed. It is appropriate for a candidate to make reference to his or her SWOT analysis when discussing each of the issues, highlighting their importance.

Marking guide:

Marks are awarded for discussing the different aspects of an issue and also for providing appropriate alternative approaches to resolving it. Clearly, the alternative approaches will receive higher marks if they are accompanied with a cogent rationale as to why they are being put forward.

Commentary:

The Judgement criterion is extremely important as it provides the facility for candidates to express their full analysis of the issues contained in the case. It is essential that sufficient time and effort is put into carrying out this fundamental analysis. It is not sufficient for a candidate to simply repeat the facts of the case and regard that as his or her analysis. The facts of the case should be used as evidence to support the commentary on the issues. It is essential that candidates state the impact of a particular issue, citing evidence. For example, the re-commissioning of Leah would represent 15% of the total revenue earned in 2010 and therefore would have a major effect on VYP's reputation, organisation and management of resources.

Once the impact has been stated then the candidate should consider the alternative actions which could be taken by the organisation in the case study and bring in relevant analysis in support of each item. So, taking the Leah example again, it would be expected that the candidate identified the margin which would be made under the normal costing model and how this might be improved. It would then be expected that the candidate discussed how savings might be made without affecting quality and the need for tight budgetary control. It would also be appropriate for the candidate to explain what the potential consequences for VYP would be if it turned the re-commission down.

Common errors:

The main errors are listed as follows:

- Simple repetition of the case material without any additional analysis.

- Disappointingly little analysis of the cost control issues affecting VYP.

- Too much time spent on the shortcomings of the current cost control systems in place without discussion of what to do about them.

- Very little discussion on the impact overheads have in costing and pricing. Pricing was not actually an issue in this particular case but the effect of overheads on the Leah issue, in particular, was very important. This case provided a golden opportunity for a candidate to express his or her understanding of cost behaviour, fundamental to Chartered Management Accounting, and its impact on operating profit.

- Prioritising issues and then not discussing them, possibly due to shortage of time but also due to fundamental lack of analysis. This is exemplified by VT filming being prioritised, but then no financial analysis being undertaken and no subsequent discussion. This usually means that the candidate was not able to carry out the fundamental financial analysis and therefore had little or nothing to say.

- Worse than this though are the candidates who fail to carry out the financial analysis but still proceed to discuss the issue with apparent authority making sweeping statements with no substance to back them up.

- Failure to recognise that there were in fact three options relating to VT filming: carry on outsourcing, acquiring Tee or bringing VT filming in-house. Some candidates were confused that there were three options available. Acquiring Tee was not the same as bringing VT filming in-house.

- Making reference to non-existent appendices.

- Over reliance on pre-learned material, especially those which may have appeared in mock examinations.

It is essential that the candidate concentrates his or her mind on the issues contained in the actual case and the unseen material and does not become confused with issues that have either occurred in a previous diet or a mock examination. If the issues are fully considered, with good numerical analysis where appropriate, it is not difficult to produce some alternative approaches which might be adopted by the organisation in the case and for the benefits and disadvantages of each to be expressed. This then naturally leads to the candidate being able to produce a rationale for his or her later recommendations. There is no single right answer to the issues and credit is given for recommendations which are logically supported with a clear rationale, even if these do not correspond with the suggested answer. However, to do this effectively, the candidate must have first analysed the issues in depth. It is this lack of in-depth analysis which causes most candidates to fail the examination.

Ethics:

Rationale:

The candidate is required to use judgement to identify and analyse the ethical issues and state why these issues have ethical implications.

Suggested approach:

This section is normally coupled with the recommendations on how to resolve the ethical issues. It is perfectly acceptable to provide the answer in one section or it could be split over two as presented in the Assessment Criteria. The reason it is split in the Assessment Criteria is because the business issues often have an ethical dimension associated with them. It is therefore appropriate for the ethical issues to be discussed alongside the business dimension. It is for the candidate to choose the method with which he or she feels most comfortable.

Marking guide:

Marks are awarded for recognising each of the ethical issues and then it is crucial to explain why they are considered to be ethical issues.

Commentary:

On the whole, candidates were able to identify the ethical issues which were the selection of outsourced companies and the documentary series which highlighted child labour practices around the world.

Common errors:

Generally, the ethical issues were reasonably well handled. Candidates were mostly able to identify them and provide a reasonable explanation of why the issue might be considered to be ethical although this was not always the case. There were some issues raised that were not ethical per se, the main example being the non-payment to the presenter who had fallen ill. This is not an ethical issue, but a business issue. It was made clear in the case that no fee was payable to the ill presenter and therefore there was no obligation on VYP to make any payment. If VYP chose to do so then that was a matter for the company as a purely business transaction in order to maintain its own reputation. An equally valid argument could be made for VYP to adhere to the contract and not make any payment. An ethical obligation is one where an organisation has a moral duty to do something. This was not a moral obligation, it was a contractual agreement and there was no obligation on VYP to make any payment whatsoever.

Another ethical issue raised by some candidates was VYP's possible employment of Tee's staff if they chose to bring VT filming in-house. It is normal business practise for companies to recruit staff from competitors and other companies and so it is difficult to see how this would be an ethical issue. It would be courteous for VYP to inform Tee if it chose to establish its own in-house provision.

Some common errors relating to the filming of child workers included a complete misunderstanding in that some candidates thought VYP itself was employing child labour.

Recommendations

Logic:

Rationale:

This criterion tests whether the candidate is able to make well-justified recommendations for each of the prioritised issues.

Suggested approach:

It is important that the candidate ensures that there is strong reasoning for the recommended course of action. The recommendations should follow on from the weight of arguments and choices of possible actions in a logical manner. There is no one absolutely correct way of presenting the recommendations. Most candidates present them towards the end of the report, which is perfectly acceptable. Essentially, it is expected that the candidates will present their recommendations, provide a justification of why these courses of action are being recommended and then state what should be the follow-on actions.

Marking guide:

Marks are awarded not just for the recommendations themselves but also, crucially, for the rationale and strength of argument supporting them and for explaining what the organisation should do next to make the recommendations happen.

Commentary:

To re-iterate what was said under the Judgement criterion, recommendations will be given credit even if they do not accord with those in the suggested answer. There is often no single right answer. It is the rationale for the recommendation which is important. The follow-on actions must be consistent with the recommendations. Further, candidates must understand that recommendations must be consistent with each other and with recommendations on ethical issues where appropriate.

Most candidates provided recommendations, but they were often not supported by an appropriate rationale or any rationale at all. It was also evident that there were time management problems encountered by some candidates with the recommendations being very brief. It is well to remember that this criterion carries 20 marks and is very important. The recommendations should follow the analysis and discussion and therefore sufficient time should be allowed for the recommendations to be provided.

Common errors:

- Time management issues with some recommendations being very short. Candidates must recognise that the recommendations section of the Logic criterion carries 20% of the available marks for the examination and is very important. This therefore justifies 36 minutes worth of the available time being spent on the recommendations.

- Generally poor justification of the recommendations made which merely repeated what had been said in the earlier discussion. It is expected that the justification should draw together the earlier discussion in justifying the recommendation made, not simply repeat the benefits and disadvantages of each approach. It is for the candidate to synthesise the benefits and disadvantages into a coherent explanation of why a particular course of action is being recommended.

- Generally weak rationale which does not really address the issue. To simply suggest that allocating finance staff to producers will not of itself help VYP to reduce costs. It might enable costs to be better monitored. However, it is also necessary to provide clear guidance to both the producers and the finance staff as to what levels of authority each is given before referring expenditure proposals to senior staff in the organisation. It is also incumbent on the finance staff to be able to interrogate costs with a view to identifying areas where savings can be made. Therefore some guidance on such issues as budgeting techniques and analysis of expenditure patterns of peaks and troughs would have been appropriate. A further example was the recommendation which simply stated "invest in IT" to overcome the cost control issues. Too frequently there was no consideration given to how this would be managed and by whom or how planning and resources should be managed to achieve a successful implementation of a new IT system.

- Recommendation to acquire Tee with no justification or explanation of how the acquisition could be financed, managed or how the two companies would be successfully integrated.

- Recommending that the cash advanced for Leah could be used to acquire Tee. These funds were committed to producing the Leah re-commission.

In essence, the recommendations are a very important part of the answer and candidates should allow sufficient time to address them fully.

Integration:

Rationale:

The marks are all available for the overall functionality and quality of the report in part (a).

Suggested approach:

This is not a section of the report, but a holistic view of its entirety. As a guide therefore it is important that candidates present a report which is clear, sectionalised, addresses the main issues with good analysis and discussion and makes suitable recommendations based on the weight of evidence presented.

Marking guide:

Reports are deemed to be highly professional, sound, satisfactory, inadequate or poor. The whole 5 marks are available for a highly professional report and 0 or 1 mark for a poor report.

Commentary:

The quality of the analysis, discussion and recommendations in the reports was variable. Good answers tend to divide the report into the following distinct parts:

- Table of contents
- Brief terms of reference
- A brief introduction
- Prioritisation of the key strategic issues
- A detailed analysis of the issues
- Ethical issues (which may be in one section or split across the detailed analysis and the recommendations)
- Recommendations
- Appendices including part (b).

It is important to effectively integrate the different parts of the report. So, for example, the recommendations should include the evidence base supporting them by reference to the earlier analysis which may be drawn from the main body of the report or the appendices.

A low mark will be awarded in Integration if the key issues are not properly addressed, or indeed are not discussed at all. Further, a low mark will apply in Integration if analysis is not sufficiently carried out, for example, the discussion of the issues was vague and generally superficial in its nature and did not specifically relate to the unseen case material.

Common errors:

Some reports simply did not address the main issues or provide sufficient depth of analysis or reasoning behind the recommendations to warrant a high mark. There was often a lack of flow of discussion within the report and contradictions between the recommendations provided to the business and ethical issues.

Ethics:

Rationale:

This criterion judges candidates on their recommendations and reasoning for each of the ethical issues identified.

Suggested approach:

This section follows on from the identification and explanation of the ethical issues. It may either be contained in one complete section or split over two as presented in the Assessment Criteria.

Marking guide:

Marks are awarded for the quality and depth of advice on the ethical issues raised.

Commentary:

Candidates tended to give sensible advice on the issues raised in the report although this was often too brief or vague and there were some instances where candidates did not provide any advice at all.

Common errors:

The main common error was that some candidates failed to provide any advice on the ethical issue raised. It is essential that advice is given on how the ethical dilemma may be resolved. The advice itself should be ethical. So, for example, advising that the bookings managers should be dismissed for accepting bribes is not ethical if there has been no proper investigation carried out. It is debateable whether it is ethical in an industry where such actions are common if proper guidance has not been provided beforehand.

Regarding the filming of child labour, some candidates advised that VYP should not report their findings to anyone, as it is outside their remit, and others suggested that government and international agencies should be notified, including the United Nations. This is too vague and does not directly address the issue. Too few suggested that the international firms benefiting from the supplies manufactured by children should be contacted directly and given an opportunity to respond to provide balance in the programme. Some candidates rather than dealing with the issue stated that VYP should not film such sequences in the future. Others thought that VYP should destroy the film sequences as they would be distressing to viewers without considering VYP's moral obligation to portray honestly what they had filmed.

Candidates could increase their marks under this criterion by explaining the reasoning for their advice. Also, the advice provided by students is often brief and more marks would be gained if the candidate gave fuller advice. Candidates need to be consistent in their advice under the criteria of Ethics and Logic.

PART (b):

Rationale:

The purpose of part (b) is to test candidates' ability to communicate in a competent professional way their analysis, findings and financial implications relating to a particular issue contained in the unseen material. It seems that candidates have recognised that this part relates to one issue only, not all the issues in the case. It will only ever relate to a single issue in the case study.

Suggested approach:

Candidates should consider carefully the purpose of the communication, for whom it is intended, and the salient points that he or she wishes to communicate. This means that the candidate needs to think carefully about the major points which need to be included in the communication. Thought also needs to go into the effectiveness of the communication which means that it should have clarity, be to the point and not be ambiguous. Candidates should follow the instructions or requirement for part (b). In this case the requirement asked for an email to be drafted, on behalf of the Finance Director, which persuaded programme producers of the need for improved IT systems to achieve better control of direct programme-making costs.

Marking guide:

Marks are awarded on the strength of the communication provided. There are marks available for commentary on the strategic importance of an issue and the inclusion of relevant financial or numerical information, the benefits and disadvantages of a particular course of action and a recommendation where appropriate.

Commentary:

Candidates should recognise that if the guidance states "10 short sentences" that is what is required, not a page of script. Neither is a series of short bullet points acceptable, although it is clear that some candidates ran out of time and hurried their answer to this part of the examination. It was disappointing that some candidates chose not to attempt part (b) at all. It is dangerous not to attempt it as it is worth 10% of the marks available.

Common errors:

The common errors were:

- Failure to address the email correctly indicating who it is from, to whom it is addressed and its subject.

- Failure to discuss IT systems and instead to concentrate on improved manual procedures.

- Failure to explain why improved IT systems were needed.

- Failure to explain how an improved IT system would help programme producers.

It should be recognised that employers have made it clear to CIMA that they seek candidates who are not only competent in accountancy but are able to communicate effectively. This is the main reason why part (b) exists in the T4 case study examination. It should be remembered that an email is regarded in law as an official form of communication and it should be treated with the same respect as would be a formal letter.

19

What to do next to practise

Chapter learning objectives

By the end of this chapter you will:

- Have read through a summary of the key points contained within this text book.

- Be aware of what your next steps should be to help prepare for your exam.

- Be ready to tackle one or two recent T4 case study exams, which are included in the appendices.

1 A summary of the key points

Now you've worked through two practice past case studies, the purpose of this chapter is to remind you of the key pieces of information and tips about how to approach the case study. It will also ensure you understand what further steps you should now take in order to properly prepare yourself for your actual exam. Let's start with a summary of all the really important stuff.

2 The assessment criteria

You won't pass the exam unless you understand what the examiner is looking for and how your script will be assessed. You will earn marks under nine separate assessment criteria, each of which is noted below along with a quick summary of how to earn the marks in each area.

Criterion (marks)	What you need to do
Technical (5)	A SWOT should be the starting point, and should include all of your prioritised issues and the impact they have on the company.
	You need to use four more models in your report. Other examples: ratios, Ansoff, PEST, Porter's Five Forces, Porter's Generic Strategies, BCG, Product lifecycle, balanced scorecard, motivation theories, suitability/feasibility/acceptability, etc
Application (15)	Use/apply the above techniques / technical knowledge.
	Prepare relevant accurate calculations presented in your appendices.
Diversity (5)	Show real-world awareness for both the industry dealt with in the scenario and situations and events that impact a business in general e.g. franchising, acquisitions, etc.
	Aim to include five points in total throughout your report.
Focus (5)	Select the issues that are regarded as the most important.
Prioritisation (5)	Using your SWOT, identify four key issues from the unseen material. Following the approach:
	• Clearly identify the issue
	• Justify the prioritisation of the issue.
	You must ensure it is CLEAR why you have prioritised each issue.

Judgement (20)	Discussion of the four key issues in greater detail.
	Assess the significance (impact) of each of the issues.
	Evaluate any options and consider alternative courses of action.
	Discuss your financial analysis for each issue where you have prepared calculations.
Ethics (5 + 5)	Identify two ethical issues. Explain/justify the issues. Give practical, justified recommendations.
Logic (30)	20 marks for your report (requirement 1 (a)) – Clear recommendations should be given for the four key issues first and then any other areas discussed in the report.
	You should cover **what** should be done, **why** you consider that this is the best course of action and **how** it should be implemented.
	10 marks for question 1 (b) - Identify the key areas of advice / opinions and convey succinctly in an appropriate tone. Include financial implications and your recommendation on the issue(s).
Integration (5)	Does the report cover the main issues and flow from identification to recommendation?
	Is your report complete?

3 Familiarisation with pre-seen material

Familiarisation with the pre-seen material and the industry in which the organisation operates will underpin your ability to assess the impact of the issues presented in the unseen material. It will also equip you to identify and evaluate alternative courses of action.

The best approach to familiarising yourself with the material can be summarised as:

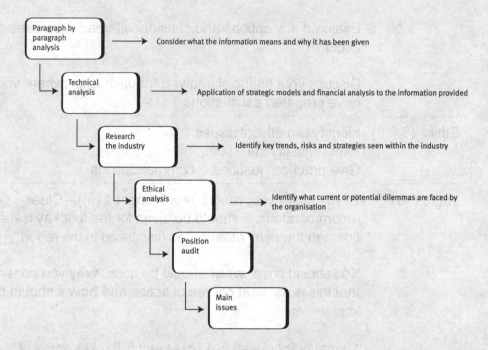

4 Time management

Your ability to answer the question set will not only require a sound knowledge and good technique; it will require a disciplined management of your time in the exam. A suggested starting point would be:

Stage	Action	Time
Reading	Initial read through and decision on top 4 issues	20 mins
Planning your answer	Consideration of impact / alternative solutions and content for secondary requirement	20 mins
Appendices	Preparation of SWOT analysis and all numerical appendices	25 mins
Prioritisation statement	Write the prioritisation section of your report	10 mins
Ethics	Write the ethical issues section of your report	15 mins
Key issue (1)	Write the analysis of the issue(s) to which the second requirement relates, followed immediately by writing the recommendation (20 mins in total split approximately 50:50 between analysis and recommendations)	20 mins

Requirement 1(b)	Write your answer to part (b) of the requirement	15 mins
Remaining key issues	Cover the remaining issues (for each one write the analysis followed immediately by writing the recommendation (20 mins per issue × 3 issues)	60 mins
Tidy up	Write your introduction, terms of reference and conclusion, read / spell check your report	15 mins

5 Answer formats

Requirement 1(a) will ask you to prepare a report that prioritises, analyses and evaluates the issues facing the organisation and makes appropriate recommendations.

A recommended structure for your report would be:

Section number	Title
1.0	Introduction
2.0	Terms of reference
3.0	Prioritisation of key issues
4.0 – 7.0	Analysis of issues
8.0	Ethical considerations
9.0	Recommendations
10.0	Conclusion

Requirement 1(b) will test your ability to communicate effectively in a different format from just a simple report. This communication document requires you to place yourself in the position of the reader of the document, and ask what pieces of information will be most important to them. You will need to present this information in the format specified using a tone appropriate to the scenario.

The scope of requirement 1(b) is limited to a presentation, an e-mail, a letter or a graph / chart (most often as an attachment to another document such as an e-mail, letter or presentation).

6 Next steps

You are now well underway in your quest for success in the T4 Case Study Examination. However, there is still much more work to be done.

- If you still feel uncertain about any of the processes covered in this text you may want to sit some further practice cases. One option is to attempt either the March 2010 CeeCee exam or the September 2010 VYP exam as this will avoid the need to familiarise yourself with a further set of pre-seen material. Both of these can be downloaded from MyCIMA or from the EN-gage portal (access to which accompanies this book). An alternative option is to work through either or both of the two additional cases presented in the appendices of this text: September 2011 Papy (sustainable trading in the supermarket industry) or March 2012 Jot (toy industry).

- You will need to familiarise yourself with the pre-seen material relating to the real T4 case study that you plan to sit. Remember, this can be downloaded from the CIMA website at least six weeks prior to the exam. To help with this, you may wish to consider purchasing CIMA Publishing's Case Analysis Workbook for your particular pre-seen material. This can be ordered from www.cimapublishing.com

- You need to practise mock exams based on your actual pre-seen. These can be accessed by attending a course with a tuition provider. Alternatively, one mock exam is included in the CIMA Publishing Case Analysis Workbook and further exams are sometimes available to purchase from open access forums.

Practice might not make perfect when it comes to the Case Study Exam but it does definitely lead to progress. The time you invest now will not be wasted.

Good luck in your exam.

T4 – Part B Case Study Examination

Wednesday 31 August 2011

Instructions to candidates

You are allowed three hours to answer this question paper.
You are allowed 20 minutes reading time **before the examination begins** during which you should read the question paper and, if you wish, make annotations on the question paper. However, you will **not** be allowed, **under any circumstances**, to begin using your computer to produce your answer or to use your calculator during the reading time.
This booklet contains the examination question and both the pre-seen and unseen elements of the case material.
Answer the question on page 17, which is detachable for ease of reference. The Case Study Assessment Criteria, which your script will be marked against, is also included on page 17.
Maths Tables and Formulae are provided on pages 23 to 26.
Your computer will contain two blank files – a Word and an Excel file. Please ensure that you check that the file names for these two documents correspond with your candidate number.

© The Chartered Institute of Management Accountants 2011

Sustainable trading in the supermarket industry

The supermarket industry

There are many large international companies which operate supermarkets in a range of countries around the world using globally recognised brand names. Most of the supermarket chains have a large market share in their home country and have expanded to other countries both by acquisition and by organic growth. There have been many acquisitions of smaller supermarket chains in order to achieve greater economies of scale and to expand the promotion of the supermarket brand globally.

Most of the large supermarkets sell a wide range of products with food items comprising less than 75% of revenues. Non-food items include household and electrical goods as well as clothing and shoes.

The trend in the past was to build and operate larger and larger stores with the view that most people would make the journey to a large supermarket to shop. However, over the last decade there has been a reversal in this trend with the opening (mainly through acquisition) of smaller "convenience" stores enabling people to shop locally. A small "convenience" store is defined as a small retail store which is open long hours offering a limited range of food and household products and is located in city centre or suburban residential areas. Within city centres, these convenience stores have generated increasingly high sales levels. This has encouraged supermarket chains to operate a portfolio of smaller "convenience" stores as well as large supermarket stores.

Some global food retailers operate a range of brands and have a portfolio of several types of stores, ranging from very large "hypermarkets" to smaller "convenience" local stores. A "hypermarket" is defined as a very large retail store which combines a grocery supermarket and a department store, situated at out-of-town locations and generally having a sales area of over 20,000 square metres.

The global supermarket industry is highly competitive and most brands compete primarily on price. There have been many changes in the way supermarkets operate over the last decade. These innovations include internet shopping, wider ranges of organic produce, wider ranges of non-food products and the expansion of "own brand" products and "value" ranges. "Own brand" products are food and household products which display the brand name of the store selling it rather than that of the company which made it. "Value" ranges are defined as goods sold at substantially lower prices than other comparable products under "own brand value range" labels, so that the target customers consider that they are getting exceptional value for money.

Background information on sustainable trading

Sustainable trading is defined as "a trading system that does not harm the environment or deteriorate social conditions while promoting economical growth" (source: European Union (EU) website).

Sustainable trading is also often related to the reduction in carbon emissions which is acknowledged to be an important factor linked to climate change. It is now argued that climate change is one of the greatest threats facing mankind.

Climate change is being caused by the build up of greenhouse gases (GHGs) in the atmosphere from human activities, primarily the burning of fossil fuels, to provide the energy for the goods and services that we use every day.

There are several gases that contribute to the greenhouse effect and the best known is carbon dioxide. These other gases have different effects, and are usually measured and reported as the equivalent amount of carbon dioxide. For the purposes of this case, all gases are described as "GHGs" or "Carbon emissions" although they include the equivalent amount of other harmful gases.

The supermarket industry has been slow to react to the need for sustainable trading as there has been a period of intense price competition and the focus of most supermarkets has been on maintaining customer loyalty and profitability. All global supermarket chains measure and report a range of statistics concerning their sustainability or "green" credentials, but some have not incorporated sustainability into their strategic plans.

Currently, around 2,500 organisations globally now measure and disclose their carbon emissions and climate change strategies. It is recognised that retail businesses can play an important role in tackling climate change but many businesses are slow to respond to the challenges. In a recent survey, it was found that 85% of Chief Executives believe that companies do integrate the measurement of sustainability into their businesses. However, only 64% of Chief Executives considered that their companies do so effectively. Clearly there is enormous scope for improvement by companies to monitor and improve their levels of sustainable trading.

A recent assessment of 500 global companies which have set themselves carbon emission reduction targets shows that only 19% of these companies have shown significant carbon emission reductions. The opinion of researchers demonstrates that the response of companies to make significant reductions is "not equal to the global sustainability challenges faced". Therefore there is huge scope for large reductions in carbon emissions if companies are focussed on achieving real change in the way that they operate.

Carbon credits

Carbon credits and carbon markets are part of the international attempt to reduce the growth of carbon emissions, which is primarily carbon dioxide. One carbon credit is equal to one tonne of carbon dioxide (or equivalent gases). One tonne is equivalent to around 1,000 kilograms (kg). All measurements of carbon emissions in this case study are shown in kg.

Carbon credits were created following the Kyoto Protocol in 1997 which aims to reduce carbon emissions. Since that date more than 180 countries have ratified their agreement to reduce the volume of carbon emissions.

Papy supermarkets

The Papy supermarket brand was formed in the early 1950's in a European country and was initially a family-run business. It was listed on the stock exchange of its home country in 1960. The number of stores operated by the Papy group has grown considerably since.

The Papy supermarket chain now operates in its home European country as well as in 7 other European countries. It does not currently operate outside of Europe. Its Board considers that there is plenty of room for the company to grow within Europe, where its supply chain is established and works efficiently. It does not offer Internet shopping at present.

A summary of Papy's key personnel is shown in **Appendix 1** on pages 9 and 10.

The Papy chain had 1,156 stores operational at 31 December 2010. These stores generated total sales revenues of over €12,900 million in the financial year ended 31 December 2010. The operating profit was €658 million.

Within the portfolio of 1,156 stores, 414 stores are large supermarkets, with an average store size of 2,800 square metres. The remaining 742 Papy stores are small convenience stores.

A summary of Papy's stores and statistics is shown in **Appendix 2** on page 11.

Papy's recent history

Over the last 10 years, trading conditions have been very competitive, but Papy has shown an increase in profits and earnings per share (EPS) each year. The company has not opened many large supermarkets in the last 10 years, but it has expanded the number of small convenience stores from 360 to 742 stores at 31 December 2010.

The company operates a dual pricing policy whereby some products are slightly higher priced at the small convenience stores, although still competitively priced. Customer numbers have increased across all stores in the last 5 years. Furthermore, the number of customers who regularly shop at Papy stores, as measured by loyalty card usage, has increased.

During 2010, the average sales revenue of all customers has shown a small increase when expressed as revenue per visit. For example, in supermarket stores, the average sales revenue per customer per visit was €121.10 in the year ended 31 December 2010, which is a small increase on the revenue per customer per visit of €118.75 for the year ended 31 December 2009.

Financials and shares

Papy generated sales revenue of €12,911 million in the financial year ended 31 December 2010, with a gross profit of €2,608 million (20.2%). Its operating profit was €658 million, a margin of 5.1%, up from 4.9% in the year ended 31 December 2009, due to both a small growth in the gross margin and a small reduction in the administration costs as a percentage of sales revenue.

The earnings per share (EPS) for the year ended 31 December 2010 was €4.544 (year to 31 December 2009 EPS was €4.219). This is an increase of 7.7%.

An extract from the accounts for Papy is shown in **Appendix 3** on page 12.

Papy's Cash Flow Statement for the year ended 31 December 2010 is shown in **Appendix 4** on page 13.

There are 100 million shares in issue and 200 million authorised shares. The majority are held by large investors including institutional investors and the founding family has retained only around 5% of the shares.

Papy operates an employee share scheme which rewards all of its employees with free shares dependent on the achievement of individual store profitability targets as well as the achievement of a range of group financial targets. Papy's employee share scheme currently purchases shares already in issue to meet the requirements for shares given to employees. The total cost of shares given to Papy's employees is included in administrative expenses in the Statement of Comprehensive Income.

Sustainable trading

There are many facets to sustainable trading in the supermarket industry. Some of Papy's competitors, especially the largest global supermarket companies, have already started to address the need to become more sustainable companies. The facets of sustainable trading include the following:

- Reductions in energy consumption
- Reduction in carbon emissions
- Use of alternative sources of power
- Reduction in waste and improved levels of recycling
- Reduction in the volume of free plastic carrier bags given to customers
- Being a responsible employer and improving the well-being of employees
- Providing training to employees to enhance their career development

- Paying a fair price to suppliers
- Sourcing products from suppliers which are also trying to be responsible and sustainable in the ways in which they operate
- Sourcing of paper and wooden products from recycled sources as well as from companies which operate sustainable forests
- Inspecting the working conditions at supplier sites and taking action where they do not meet company standards
- Selection and assistance to Papy's supply chain companies to enhance their sustainable trading credentials
- Reviving local rural life with the opening of convenience stores in small communities.

Competitor analysis

Papy is operating in a competitive market in a total of 8 European countries. It is difficult to assess Papy's overall market share across the European countries in which it operates. However, in its "home" country, Papy has a market share of around 19% and it is within the top 3 supermarket chains, based on sales revenues, in this country.

The table below compares some key performance indicators of Papy against 3 of its competitors based on data extracted from the annual accounts and report for the latest available financial year.

	Papy	Competitor 1	Competitor 2	Competitor 3
Revenue (total group) € million (see Note 1 below)	12,911	53,900	64,020	11,820
Operating profit margin	5.1%	5.9%	3.4%	4.8%
Number of stores – Europe only (end of year figures)	1,156	2,576	5,420	1,046
Market share in "home" country (see Note 2 below)	19.0%	22.9%	28.9%	22.0%
Change in market share over last year	+ 0.3%	+ 0.1%	+ 0.8%	+ 0.2%
Free disposable plastic bags (shown as per square metre of sales area)	549	506	266	580
Carbon emissions (GHGs) (shown as kilograms (kg) per average square metre of sales area)	1,042	681	243	1,005

Notes to the table above:

1. Revenue figures for each of the competitors include revenues generated from Internet shopping and revenues generated outside of Europe.

2. Market share in "home" country reflects a different "home" country for each of the competitors.

Recent Boardroom changes

Tobias Otte had been Papy's Chief Executive for 12 years. However, due to poor health over the last 2 years, he had not given his full attention to the need for changes within the Papy group. The most notable area where Papy has fallen behind its competitors is in the monitoring and targeted reduction of energy and carbon emissions.

Tobias Otte retired in March 2011 and the in-coming Chief Executive, Lucas Meyer, is renowned for his ability to bring about change within the companies for which he has worked. His first action on arrival was to obtain Board approval for a new Board position of Corporate Affairs Director. He was then instrumental in recruiting Arif Karp, who had been working as a consultant advising companies on how to reduce carbon emissions and to improve the performance measures for these companies' corporate social responsibilities.

An extract from a recent press announcement by Papy's new Chief Executive is shown in **Appendix 5** on page 14.

Arif Karp joined Papy on 20 June 2011. He is currently establishing the range and the quality of the data currently being collected by Papy and assessing the integrity of the data. He plans to form a team to prepare and implement new proposals.

Corporate Social Responsibilities

Papy has made significant progress in many of the areas of its Corporate Social Responsibilities and in the last year it has had some major achievements but the group still faces many challenges. Papy's CSR responsibilities have been split into 5 sections which are:

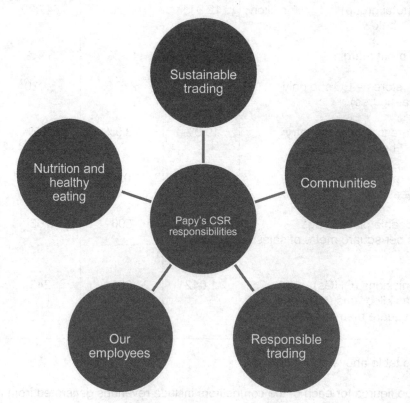

Sustainable trading

The biggest challenge facing Papy, as well as many other companies worldwide in a wide range of industries, is sustainable trading and the impact of its operations on the environment and on climate change. Papy currently has targets for its carbon emissions, which are measured as "carbon emissions in kilograms (kg) per square metre of sales area".

Papy is also reducing its waste materials and is improving the volume and range of materials that it recycles. Papy is committed to reducing the volume and types of packaging for its products in order to reduce waste.

The availability of free disposable bags at checkouts is being discouraged and customers in some countries have been offered free re-usable shopping bags. Papy has reduced the weight and the type of plastic used in the manufacture of its carrier bags and is actively encouraging customers to re-use bags, including a credit to customers' loyalty cards for re-using carrier bags.

Some of Papy's current sustainability measures are shown in **Appendix 6** on page 15.

Communities

In respect of the communities in which Papy operates, it has established a range of community and school projects and supports a range of charities. Additionally, Papy's employees are encouraged to participate in community projects, both voluntarily and through paid secondments, to lend Papy's skills to enhance community and charitable projects.

Responsible trading

Papy would like to be considered as a responsible retailer which treats its suppliers and its customers fairly. During the last year, Papy expanded its range of ethically sourced products, both "Fair Trade" labelled products and other ethically sourced products. "Fair Trade" labelled products are defined as those produced by an organised social movement which helps small-scale farmers in developing countries to obtain better trading conditions than they could achieve individually, and ensures a fair price is paid to producers in order for them to earn a living wage.

Papy only procures fish from suppliers which meet the criteria set out in the international fishing industry's guide to responsible purchasing practices.

In a survey of Papy's supply chain, over 90% of suppliers considered they are treated with respect by Papy and that a fair price was negotiated. Some of Papy's suppliers have entered into longer-term contracts than in the past, in order to reflect Papy's commitment, loyalty and support to agricultural producers worldwide. Papy also inspects the working conditions at supplier sites to ensure compliance with its policy for suppliers' working conditions.

Employees

Papy has almost 97,000 full-time equivalent (FTE) employees. Papy values its employees and has many dedicated training centres to enhance their skills. Papy is developing more managerial level employees in each of the countries in which it operates, in order to help to build upon its successful expansion. It has also been training its employees in order to raise their awareness of environmentally-friendly actions.

Nutrition and healthy eating

Nutrition and healthy eating is another important CSR responsibility in which Papy is keen to find and promote the right message to help its customers make more healthy eating choices. Papy has expanded its ranges of healthy eating products and 100% of products are labelled with nutritional values.

IT systems

Papy has a range of sophisticated and integrated IT systems which range from logistics to finance systems. Papy's procurement IT systems are linked to over 70% of its suppliers. Orders are tracked from supplier to distribution depots and onto each store location using the latest scanning IT solutions.

Because of Papy's significant growth throughout Europe in recent years and the increase in the number of stores in operation, Papy's IT Director, Ziad Abbill, has needed to invest heavily in IT hardware and software solutions. This ensures that the IT capacity is more than adequate to cope with the forecast growth in the volume of goods procured, control of inventory (which is so important in the food retailing industry as products have a short shelf life) and retail transactions.

To meet the requirements of consumer legislation, Papy's computerised tills need to ensure all special offers, both group and local store offers, are correctly reflected in prices charged to its customers.

Ziad Abbill is currently having discussions with Arif Karp on the possible need for an Environmental Management System (EMS). This type of IT system would be used to capture and report on a wide range of non-financial data. This could help Papy's management team to track and report on a range of issues concerning sustainable trading.

Carbon emissions

The Papy chain of supermarkets generates carbon emissions in many ways and reports these under sustainable trading within Papy's CSR responsibilities (shown on page 6). Papy's carbon emissions are generated in the following ways:

1. Heating, cooling and lighting at stores and distribution depots
2. Moving products to the stores
3. Construction of new stores

Furthermore, carbon emissions are generated by suppliers in Papy's supply chain. Additionally, Papy's customers generate their own carbon footprint by travelling to and from Papy stores and also in the way they use the products bought and dispose of its packaging. Arif Karp also recognises that the majority of the carbon emissions which are generated in the manufacture or processing of the products that Papy sells, originate from its supply chain. He would like to educate and encourage Papy's suppliers in order to assist them to reduce their carbon emissions.

Until recently, Papy's Board has set targets for reductions in carbon emissions in an unstructured way with no real definition of what actions are required in order to make significant reductions. Therefore, whilst the spirit of reductions has been embraced by Papy's management team, there has been no overall strategy developed in order to achieve the reductions. Whilst there has been a range of initiatives, which include more efficient logistics for deliveries to stores, reduced packaging and the increased use of rail transportation rather than road, there has not been an integrated approach on a large scale to tackle and reduce Papy's carbon emissions.

The new Chief Executive, Lucas Meyer, wants to change the way in which the Papy chain of stores operates, so that it can reduce its carbon emissions and become a more sustainable retailing company. Therefore, Arif Karp considers that Papy needs to set targets for the coming years and to plan how reductions in carbon emissions could be achieved.

Papy's key personnel

Non-executive Chairman - Dmitry Baludia
Dmitry Baludia, aged 58, became Non-executive Chairman in January 2010. Prior to this he held an executive position on the Papy Board as Operations and Logistics Director. He was instrumental in Papy's expansion into the 7 European countries in which it now operates. He has worked for Papy for over 22 years. Prior to this he held a senior role in another food retailing company.

Chief Executive - Lucas Meyer (newly appointed)
*   - Tobias Otte (retired)*

Tobias Otte, aged 55, was the Chief Executive of Papy for 12 years and he retired due to ill-health in March 2011 after a period of poor health over the last 2 years.

Lucas Meyer, aged 47, was appointed Chief Executive on 1 May 2011. He previously held the role of Chief Executive for a major European clothing retailer for 4 years. Prior to this role he had been the Finance Director for a global sportswear brand. The Board considers that his experience in non-food retailing will bring new knowledge to Papy. He is also known for his ability to bring about change and to introduce new ideas in the companies he has worked for. The new Chief Executive believes that the Papy group of supermarkets has not been taking its Corporate Social Responsibility seriously enough. He has been key in the creation of a new Board role of Corporate Affairs Director.

Operations and Logistics Director - Rafael Lucci
Rafael Lucci, aged 42, has worked for Papy for only 5 years. He joined as the Operations and Logistics Manager in one of the European countries that Papy expanded into 5 years ago. He has proved himself to be a good manager and has worked closely with Ziad Abbill, the IT Director, to introduce new IT solutions to improve operational efficiency and to save costs. He was promoted to his current position in January 2010 when Dmitry Baludia became Non-executive Chairman.

Corporate Affairs Director – Arif Karp
Arif Karp, aged 43, was appointed to this new role on 20 June 2011, in order to initiate change within Papy. Arif Karp was previously in the role of a consultant for a leading global consultancy company which advised companies on how to reduce carbon emissions and to improve their performance measures in respect of their corporate social responsibilities. This consultancy company agreed to allow him to take up this position at Papy without serving all of his notice period, as it believed that he would bring good publicity for the consultancy group with the work that he will undertake at Papy. He has worked with Lucas Meyer in his previous role and they have a good respect for each other's skills.

Finance Director – Abdul Yarkol
Abdul Yarkol, aged 55, has been Papy's Finance Director for 8 years after a member of the founding Papy family retired. He has been frustrated at the lack of leadership over the last 2 years, due to the ill-health of the now retired Chief Executive, Tobias Otte.

IT Director – Ziad Abbill
Ziad Abbill, aged 38 and the youngest Board member, has been on the Papy Board for 2 years. He has proved himself as a committed, highly motivated individual who has overseen a number of significant changes in Papy's IT systems. He is well liked and respected as he has the ability to listen to the needs of the system's users.

Marketing Director – Karen Wagnes
Karen Wagnes, aged 52, was appointed to the Papy Board 6 years ago having held various managerial roles in marketing and store management for Papy in the preceding 6 years. She had previously worked in a marketing role for a competing supermarket company.

Papy's key personnel (continued)

Human Resources Director – Simona Papy
Simona Papy, aged 45, joined the Papy Board 3 years ago. She is a member of the founding Papy family and has worked in many roles throughout the company including a period as store manager at one of the largest of the Papy chain of supermarkets. In this role she identified the importance of staff motivation and took a post-graduate course in Human Relations. She worked in a senior role in the HR department for several years before she was appointed, on merit, as HR Director, when the previous HR Director left the company.

Non-executive directors
Papy has 7 Non-executive directors

CSR Manager – Suzanna Nec
Suzanna Nec, aged 54, has worked for Papy for over 30 years and has been the CSR Manager reporting to the Papy Board for the last 12 years but is not a Board Director. She has been involved in a period of great change for the company and has many skills to offer. However, the new Chief Executive, Lucas Meyer, did not consider that she had the skill set required to be appointed to the new role of Corporate Affairs Director. She reports directly to Arif Karp.

Summary of Papy's stores and statistics

	Year ended 31 December 2009	Year ended 31 December 2010	Year ended 31 December 2011
	Actual	Actual	Latest full year forecast
Number of stores:			
Start of year			
Supermarkets	400	406	414
Small convenience stores	700	716	742
Total	1,100	1,122	1,156
New store openings:			
Supermarkets	6	8	8
Small convenience stores	30	32	22
Total	36	40	30
Closures:			
Supermarkets	0	0	0
Small convenience stores	14	6	4
Total	14	6	4
End of year:			
Supermarkets	406	414	422
Small convenience stores	716	742	760
Total	1,122	1,156	1,182
Average for the year			
Supermarkets	403	410	418
Small convenience stores	708	729	751
Total	1,111	1,139	1,169
Total sales area (all stores) (square metres)			
- end year	1,351,600	1,381,800	1,409,600
- average for the year	1,340,800	1,366,700	1,395,700
Average sales revenue per square metre of sales area €	9,427	9,447	9,468
Average sales revenue per FTE employee €	132,293	133,356	133,771

Extract from Papy's Statement of Comprehensive Income,
Statement of Financial Position and Statement of Changes in Equity

Statement of Comprehensive Income	Year ended 31 December 2010	Year ended 31 December 2009
	€ million	€ million
Revenue	12,911.0	12,640.0
Cost of sales	10,303.0	10,099.0
Gross profit	2,608.0	2,541.0
Administrative expenses	1,950.0	1,921.0
Operating profit	658.0	620.0
Finance income	17.3	14.9
Finance expense	69.4	72.3
Profit before tax	605.9	562.6
Tax expense (effective tax rate is 25%)	151.5	140.7
Profit for the period	**454.4**	**421.9**

Statement of Financial Position	As at 31 December 2010		As at 31 December 2009	
	€ million	€ million	€ million	€ million
Non-current assets (net)		**3,247.0**		**3,396.0**
Current assets				
Inventory	1,072.0		1,086.0	
Trade receivables	336.0		322.0	
Cash and cash equivalents	603.9		480.0	
Total current assets		2,011.9		1,888.0
Total assets		**5,258.9**		**5,284.0**
Equity and liabilities				
Equity				
Share capital	100.0		100.0	
Share premium	635.0		635.0	
Retained earnings	1,369.4		1,105.0	
Total Equity		2,104.4		1,840.0
Non-current liabilities				
Long term loans		870.0		1,020.0
Current liabilities				
Trade payables	2,133.0		2,283.3	
Tax payables	151.5		140.7	
Total current liabilities		2,284.5		2,424.0
Total equity and liabilities		**5,258.9**		**5,284.0**

Note: Paid in share capital represents 100 million shares of €1.00 each at 31 December 2010

Statement of Changes in Equity For the year ended 31 December 2010	Share Capital	Share premium	Retained earnings	Total
	€ million	€ million	€ million	€ million
Balance at 31 December 2009	100.0	635.0	1,105.0	1,840.0
Profit	-	-	454.4	454.4
Dividends paid	-	-	190.0	190.0
Balance at 31 December 2010	**100.0**	**635.0**	**1,369.4**	**2,104.4**

Cash Flow Statement

	Year ended 31 December 2010	
	€ million	€ million
Cash flows from operating activities:		
Profit before taxation (after Finance costs (net))		605.9
Adjustments:		
Depreciation	541.0	
Finance costs (net)	52.1	
		593.1
(Increase) / decrease in inventories	14.0	
(Increase) / decrease in trade receivables	(14.0)	
Increase / (decrease) in trade payables (excluding taxation)	(150.3)	
		(150.3)
Cash generated from operations		1,048.7
Finance costs (net) paid	(52.1)	
Tax paid	(140.7)	
		(192.8)
Cash generated from operating activities		855.9
Cash flows from investing activities:		
Purchase of non-current assets (net)	(392.0)	
Cash used in investing activities		(392.0)
Cash flows from financing activities:		
Repayment of loans	(150.0)	
Dividends paid	(190.0)	
Cash flows from financing activities		(340.0)
Net increase in cash and cash equivalents		123.9
Cash and cash equivalents at 31 December 2009		480.0
Cash and cash equivalents at 31 December 2010		603.9

Press report on Papy's announcement to become more sustainable

Date: 24 June 2011

The new Chief Executive of Papy, Lucas Meyer, announced yesterday his intention for the Papy chain of supermarkets to change the way in which it operates, in order to become a more sustainable business.

He stated "the Papy chain will incorporate sustainability in its strategy and it will also promote the need for a more sustainable attitude in the food retailing business, both to customers and to its own supply chain". He further commented "Papy should take a greater responsibility for the effect it has on the environment in which it operates".

Lucas Meyer further stated that "with fossil fuel due to run out in 40 years time there has never been a greater need for action. We can no longer wait for Governments to legislate to force change upon us. We should not be complacent and wait for our competitors to spur us into taking actions".

He continued by stating "We, at Papy, are going to make changes in the way that we operate that will affect our supply chain and our customers. However, we feel that the changes we will make in the coming months, and years, are the right way to operate a business in the long-term. We are confident that our loyal customers will see that what we plan to do will help Papy to trade in a much more sustainable way. We aim to reduce carbon emissions and make changes in order to become a business that can maintain its long-term presence in this industry".

Lucas Meyer added "in order to survive in the competitive food retailing market we must change. Innovation is the key to our future success".

By the end of trading on 23 June 2011, Papy's share price had risen to €38.80 per share.

Some of Papy's current Sustainability Indicators for the period 2008 to 2010

Energy consumption

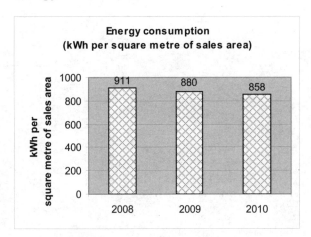

The reported measure is the average kilowatt hours (kWh) divided by the total number of square metres of sales area.

Free disposable plastic bags

The reported measure is the number of free disposable plastic bags purchased by Papy and given to customers at checkouts, divided by the total number of square metres of sales area.

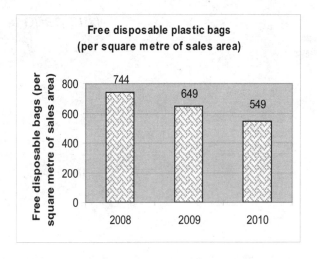

Carbon emissions

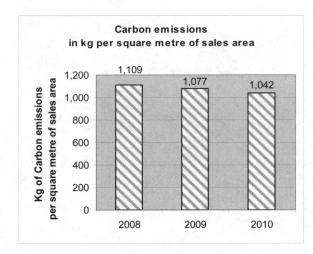

This is the consolidated total of all carbon emissions in kilograms (kg) (including Papy's stores' and warehouses' energy consumption and the transportation of products to stores) divided by Papy's average sales area (in square metres) for each year.

The reported measure is carbon emissions in kilograms (kg) per square metre of sales area.

This measure excludes carbon emissions generated by Papy's supply chain.

End of pre-seen material

This page is blank

Additional (unseen) information relating to the case is given on pages 19 to 22.

Read all of the additional material before you answer the question.

ANSWER THE FOLLOWING QUESTION

You are the Management Accountant of Papy.

Lucas Meyer, Chief Executive, has asked you to provide advice and recommendations on the issues facing Papy.

Question 1 part (a)

Prepare a report that prioritises, analyses and evaluates the issues facing Papy and makes appropriate recommendations.

(Total marks for Question 1 part (a) = 90 Marks)

Question 1 part (b)

In addition to your analysis in your report for part (a), Lucas Meyer, Chief Executive, has asked you to prepare a presentation to the Papy Board, on the savings in carbon emissions that could be achieved by the replacement freezer cabinet proposal and the solar panels proposal.

Your presentation should contain no more than 5 bullet points, including your recommendation, and 1 graph (a column chart or a bar chart or a line chart).

This graph, as an attachment to your presentation, should show Papy's carbon emissions expressed as "kilogram (kg) per square metre of sales area" for each of the 5 years 2009 to 2013. Your graph should include the savings in carbon emissions that could be achieved if Papy were to implement both of the above 2 proposals.

(Total marks for Question 1 part (b) = 10 Marks)

Your script will be marked against the T4 Part B Case Study Assessment Criteria shown below.

Criterion	Maximum marks available
Analysis of issues (25 marks)	
Technical	5
Application	15
Diversity	5
Strategic choices (35 marks)	
Focus	5
Prioritisation	5
Judgement	20
Ethics	5
Recommendations (40 marks)	
Logic	30
Integration	5
Ethics	5
Total	**100**

This page is blank

New team established

Arif Karp, Corporate Affairs Director, has been tasked to establish a multi-disciplinary team to help Papy become more sustainable and to reduce carbon emissions. This new team includes you, the Management Accountant, as well as representatives from marketing, store management and logistics. He is still selecting some team members.

Carbon emissions targets

Papy's published carbon emissions for the last 2 years, measured in kilograms (kg), are:

	2009 Published	2010 Published
Published levels of carbon emissions (kg million)	1,444	1,424
Actual total sales area (square metres)	1,340,800	1,366,700
Published carbon emissions (kg per square metre)	1,077	1,042

At a recent Board meeting, Arif Karp, advised that his initial research had identified that the published levels of carbon emission figures for 2009 (1,444 million kg) and 2010 (1,424 million kg), shown above, are understated and should be increased by 5%.

Lucas Meyer, Chief Executive, stated at this Board meeting that he considers that the forecast figures, shown in the table below, are far too high. Papy's latest forecast for carbon emissions, which have been revised for the understatement of 5% identified by Arif Karp, are as follows:

	2011 Forecast	2012 Forecast	2013 Forecast
Forecast levels of carbon emissions (kg million)	1,427	1,351	1,274
Forecast total sales area (square metres)	1,395,700	1,425,400	1,457,000
Forecast carbon emissions (kg per square metre)	1,022	948	874

The forecast figures in the table above exclude the effects of the 2 proposals set out below.

Lucas Meyer proposes a target reduction in carbon emissions for 2012 based on a 25% reduction from the revised 2010 levels (that is 1,042 kg per square metre which needs to be updated for the understatement). Lucas Meyer's proposed target for 2013 is based on a reduction of 15% from the new 2012 target. All targets are based upon the measurement of "carbon emissions per square metre of sales area".

Lucas Meyer has assured the Board that financing for capital investment projects to reduce carbon emissions will be given a top priority. Lucas Meyer has asked Arif Karp to identify suitable investment projects to help deliver his proposed target reductions in carbon emissions.

The terms of Arif Karp's employment includes a performance related bonus linked to the level of the reduction in Papy's carbon emissions and waste materials over the next few years.

Arif Karp has asked you to calculate the revised level of carbon emissions for 2009 and 2010 and the new target levels of carbon emissions, based on Lucas Meyer's proposed target reductions, for 2012 and 2013. He has also asked you to comment on whether the new 2013 target is attainable with the proposals set out on the next 2 pages.

Proposal to change freezer cabinets

The freezer cabinets in Papy's supermarkets and small convenience stores include several different models and sizes procured from a small range of manufacturers. They also vary as to when they were purchased and installed. Papy's usual policy is to replace them every 8 years.

There has recently been a 2 month trial in 30 supermarkets using low carbon technology freezer cabinets, supplied by one of Papy's existing freezer cabinet manufacturers. This trial confirmed that these freezer cabinets would result in a substantial reduction in energy usage and carbon emissions.

The proposal is to replace the current freezer cabinets in a substantial number of Papy stores during the rest of this year, so they are all fully operational from 1 January 2012 onwards. Papy has sufficient cash available to finance the capital costs of this proposal.

Relevant data for this proposal is:

- To change the freezer cabinets at 400 supermarket stores

- To change the freezer cabinets at 100 small convenience stores

- Electricity costs would be reduced by €60,000 each year for each supermarket store and by €18,000 each year for each small convenience store.

- Capital costs would be €200,000 for each supermarket store and €50,000 for each small convenience store.

- Reduction in carbon emissions due to the proposed new freezer cabinets is forecast to be 110,000 kg each year for each supermarket store and 30,000 kg each year for each small convenience store.

Some of the existing freezer cabinets that will be removed are not fully depreciated. The net book value is €25.0 million and it is forecast that they would have no realisable value.

The trial showed a small drop in the volume of sales of frozen food products, as customers have to open the glass doors to access the frozen food products with the new freezer cabinets, rather than simply reaching into the freezers as previously. The forecast gross margin for sales of frozen food products for each supermarket store is €560,000 for each year. This figure is forecast to remain unchanged over the next 5 years.

The trial data showed the following reduction in the gross margin for each supermarket store:

- 60% of supermarket stores showed a fall of 3%
- 30% of supermarket stores showed a fall of 5%
- 10% of supermarket stores showed no change

It is forecast that sales volumes for all of the 400 supermarket stores will fall in accordance with the trial information shown above but that sales volumes for all of 100 small convenience stores will remain unchanged.

It should be assumed that capital expenditure is eligible for 100% tax relief, received 1 year in arrears at the tax rate of 25%. All other cash flows are eligible for tax relief at the tax rate of 25% and that tax is paid, or refunded, 1 year in arrears. The Finance Director has set a criterion for the appraisal of this proposal, and has stated that for acceptance of this proposal the undiscounted payback should be less than 5 years. However, the Finance Director has some reservations about the appropriateness of this appraisal method.

Proposal for solar panels

Arif Karp would like most of Papy's supermarket stores that are located in southern Europe, which experience high levels of sunshine, to be fitted with solar panels on the roofs of these supermarket stores in order to generate solar powered electricity. Depending on the location of the store, it is forecast that up to 30% of each of the store's electricity requirement could be produced by the solar panels. This would save electricity costs and also reduce the stores' carbon emissions. Solar panels will not currently be installed for any small convenience stores.

It is proposed that 200 supermarket stores that are located in Southern Europe would have solar panels installed over a 2 year period, at the rate of 100 supermarkets each year.

The proposal generates an NPV of €91 million at a risk adjusted post-tax cost of capital of 9% when evaluated over a 10 year period. The discounted payback period is within 8 years.

The capital cost of installing solar panels for each supermarket store is €3 million.

It is proposed that the capital cost will be funded by new debt. Abdul Yarkol, Finance Director, considers that Papy's gearing (defined as debt to debt plus equity) is significantly lower than some of its competitors, which have gearing ratios of around 40%. He is currently in negotiations with banks but other sources of finance may also be required.

There is some discussion in Arif Karp's team as to whether Papy should invest in solar panels for as many as 200 supermarket stores in the next 2 years or whether Papy should wait. The technology for solar panels is improving, allowing a greater amount of electricity to be generated by each solar panel. Improved solar panel technology, which could be 20% more effective than the current technology, is likely to be commercially available in 2017.

Arif Karp wants this proposal to invest in solar panels for 200 supermarket stores to proceed as soon as possible. He considers that any investment undertaken now could easily be upgraded to use the newer technology solar panels as they become available.

The reduction in carbon emissions as a direct result of this investment is forecast to be an average of 900,000 kg for each year for each supermarket store.

For simplicity, it should be assumed that if this proposal is approved, then the capital expenditure for the solar panels for the first 100 supermarket stores will be incurred in 2011. The benefits from the electricity savings and carbon emission reductions from these 100 stores with solar panels will begin in 2012. The second 100 supermarket stores will be installed in late 2012 and the carbon reductions will begin in 2013.

Measurement of waste materials

Papy currently measures waste materials, including packaging materials for products delivered to stores, by volume. However, Arif Karp considers that the weight of waste materials would be a more helpful measurement. The statistics for waste materials for last year and the latest forecast figures for 2011 and 2012 are as follows:

Waste materials from all stores	2010 Actual	2011 Forecast	2012 Forecast
By volume (millions of cubic metres)	450	430	409
By weight (kg million)	110	95	70

Papy publishes an annual Corporate Social Responsibility report which includes statistics on sustainability issues, including waste materials. Arif Karp proposes that all statistics for waste material reduction should be based on weight, and not volume.

Management of change

Arif Karp has requested all store managers to collect a new range of non-financial data effective from 1 September 2011. This data is to be submitted monthly, on spreadsheets, to his team for collation and analysis. Arif Karp would like to implement a dedicated IT system for capturing this non-financial data. However, many of Papy's senior management team have not replied to any of his requests concerning the sources of information for data for this proposed new IT system and the general response is that they are too busy. Therefore, Arif Karp has appointed external consultants to help to specify the requirements for this new IT system. These external consultants have expertise in IT systems but lack specialist knowledge of the supermarket industry.

Many employees either do not know, or understand, what Arif Karp and his team are trying to achieve. Most employees are focused on their specific job responsibilities and in meeting the current financial targets. They do not understand the reasons for change and are resistant to taking on the extra work that store managers have passed to them to do.

Currently targets include a range of measures, including waste reduction and speed of products to stores, but principally targets have been financial measures such as revenues and operating profit for each store. Some of the senior management team, as well as some store managers, are sceptical about the cost of the initiatives being considered and that the demands of reducing carbon emissions will raise costs. They believe that the pressure to deliver increased profits will ultimately take precedence over reductions in carbon emissions. They further believe that this is just a temporary phase for Papy and that Arif Karp will be unable to deliver substantial reductions in carbon emissions, and that he will consequently leave Papy.

Arif Karp is frustrated about the lack of support given to him and his team from both the senior management team, including some Board members, as well as store managers. He recognises the urgency in changing attitudes within Papy in order to meet revised carbon emission targets and become more sustainable.

You should discuss what actions are required in order to help bring about change in employees attitudes and to minimise employees' resistance to change.

Cancellation of 2 supplier contracts

As part of a review of sales and the level of waste from unsold fresh produce, Papy has established that sales have reduced for a small range of fresh products supplied under 2 contracts. The level of waste currently being experienced has eroded Papy's gross profit margins for these products significantly.

Rafael Lucci, Papy's Operations and Logistics Director, is proposing to cancel these 2 contracts when they expire in 3 months time. These 2 contracts are with farming co-operatives in Africa which produce fresh fruit under the "Fair Trade" label. The "Fair Trade" label is defined as an organised social movement which helps small-scale farmers in developing countries to obtain better trading conditions than they could achieve individually, and ensures that a fair price is paid to producers in order for them to earn a living wage.

End of unseen material

APPLICABLE MATHS TABLES AND FORMULAE

Present value table

Present value of 1.00 unit of currency, that is $(1 + r)^{-n}$ where r = interest rate; n = number of periods until payment or receipt.

Periods	Interest rates (r)									
(n)	1%	2%	3%	4%	5%	6%	7%	8%	9%	10%
1	0.990	0.980	0.971	0.962	0.952	0.943	0.935	0.926	0.917	0.909
2	0.980	0.961	0.943	0.925	0.907	0.890	0.873	0.857	0.842	0.826
3	0.971	0.942	0.915	0.889	0.864	0.840	0.816	0.794	0.772	0.751
4	0.961	0.924	0.888	0.855	0.823	0.792	0.763	0.735	0.708	0.683
5	0.951	0.906	0.863	0.822	0.784	0.747	0.713	0.681	0.650	0.621
6	0.942	0.888	0.837	0.790	0.746	0705	0.666	0.630	0.596	0.564
7	0.933	0.871	0.813	0.760	0.711	0.665	0.623	0.583	0.547	0.513
8	0.923	0.853	0.789	0.731	0.677	0.627	0.582	0.540	0.502	0.467
9	0.914	0.837	0.766	0.703	0.645	0.592	0.544	0.500	0.460	0.424
10	0.905	0.820	0.744	0.676	0.614	0.558	0.508	0.463	0.422	0.386
11	0.896	0.804	0.722	0.650	0.585	0.527	0.475	0.429	0.388	0.350
12	0.887	0.788	0.701	0.625	0.557	0.497	0.444	0.397	0.356	0.319
13	0.879	0.773	0.681	0.601	0.530	0.469	0.415	0.368	0.326	0.290
14	0.870	0.758	0.661	0.577	0.505	0.442	0.388	0.340	0.299	0.263
15	0.861	0.743	0.642	0.555	0.481	0.417	0.362	0.315	0.275	0.239
16	0.853	0.728	0.623	0.534	0.458	0.394	0.339	0.292	0.252	0.218
17	0.844	0.714	0.605	0.513	0.436	0.371	0.317	0.270	0.231	0.198
18	0.836	0.700	0.587	0.494	0.416	0.350	0.296	0.250	0.212	0.180
19	0.828	0.686	0.570	0.475	0.396	0.331	0.277	0.232	0.194	0.164
20	0.820	0.673	0.554	0.456	0.377	0.312	0.258	0.215	0.178	0.149

Periods	Interest rates (r)									
(n)	11%	12%	13%	14%	15%	16%	17%	18%	19%	20%
1	0.901	0.893	0.885	0.877	0.870	0.862	0.855	0.847	0.840	0.833
2	0.812	0.797	0.783	0.769	0.756	0.743	0.731	0.718	0.706	0.694
3	0.731	0.712	0.693	0.675	0.658	0.641	0.624	0.609	0.593	0.579
4	0.659	0.636	0.613	0.592	0.572	0.552	0.534	0.516	0.499	0.482
5	0.593	0.567	0.543	0.519	0.497	0.476	0.456	0.437	0.419	0.402
6	0.535	0.507	0.480	0.456	0.432	0.410	0.390	0.370	0.352	0.335
7	0.482	0.452	0.425	0.400	0.376	0.354	0.333	0.314	0.296	0.279
8	0.434	0.404	0.376	0.351	0.327	0.305	0.285	0.266	0.249	0.233
9	0.391	0.361	0.333	0.308	0.284	0.263	0.243	0.225	0.209	0.194
10	0.352	0.322	0.295	0.270	0.247	0.227	0.208	0.191	0.176	0.162
11	0.317	0.287	0.261	0.237	0.215	0.195	0.178	0.162	0.148	0.135
12	0.286	0.257	0.231	0.208	0.187	0.168	0.152	0.137	0.124	0.112
13	0.258	0.229	0.204	0.182	0.163	0.145	0.130	0.116	0.104	0.093
14	0.232	0.205	0.181	0.160	0.141	0.125	0.111	0.099	0.088	0.078
15	0.209	0.183	0.160	0.140	0.123	0.108	0.095	0.084	0.079	0.065
16	0.188	0.163	0.141	0.123	0.107	0.093	0.081	0.071	0.062	0.054
17	0.170	0.146	0.125	0.108	0.093	0.080	0.069	0.060	0.052	0.045
18	0.153	0.130	0.111	0.095	0.081	0.069	0.059	0.051	0.044	0.038
19	0.138	0.116	0.098	0.083	0.070	0.060	0.051	0.043	0.037	0.031
20	0.124	0.104	0.087	0.073	0.061	0.051	0.043	0.037	0.031	0.026

Cumulative present value of 1.00 unit of currency per annum, Receivable or Payable at the end of each year for n years $\left[\dfrac{1-(1+r)^{-n}}{r}\right]$

Periods	Interest rates (r)									
(n)	1%	2%	3%	4%	5%	6%	7%	8%	9%	10%
1	0.990	0.980	0.971	0.962	0.952	0.943	0.935	0.926	0.917	0.909
2	1.970	1.942	1.913	1.886	1.859	1.833	1.808	1.783	1.759	1.736
3	2.941	2.884	2.829	2.775	2.723	2.673	2.624	2.577	2.531	2.487
4	3.902	3.808	3.717	3.630	3.546	3.465	3.387	3.312	3.240	3.170
5	4.853	4.713	4.580	4.452	4.329	4.212	4.100	3.993	3.890	3.791
6	5.795	5.601	5.417	5.242	5.076	4.917	4.767	4.623	4.486	4.355
7	6.728	6.472	6.230	6.002	5.786	5.582	5.389	5.206	5.033	4.868
8	7.652	7.325	7.020	6.733	6.463	6.210	5.971	5.747	5.535	5.335
9	8.566	8.162	7.786	7.435	7.108	6.802	6.515	6.247	5.995	5.759
10	9.471	8.983	8.530	8.111	7.722	7.360	7.024	6.710	6.418	6.145
11	10.368	9.787	9.253	8.760	8.306	7.887	7.499	7.139	6.805	6.495
12	11.255	10.575	9.954	9.385	8.863	8.384	7.943	7.536	7.161	6.814
13	12.134	11.348	10.635	9.986	9.394	8.853	8.358	7.904	7.487	7.103
14	13.004	12.106	11.296	10.563	9.899	9.295	8.745	8.244	7.786	7.367
15	13.865	12.849	11.938	11.118	10.380	9.712	9.108	8.559	8.061	7.606
16	14.718	13.578	12.561	11.652	10.838	10.106	9.447	8.851	8.313	7.824
17	15.562	14.292	13.166	12.166	11.274	10.477	9.763	9.122	8.544	8.022
18	16.398	14.992	13.754	12.659	11.690	10.828	10.059	9.372	8.756	8.201
19	17.226	15.679	14.324	13.134	12.085	11.158	10.336	9.604	8.950	8.365
20	18.046	16.351	14.878	13.590	12.462	11.470	10.594	9.818	9.129	8.514

Periods	Interest rates (r)									
(n)	11%	12%	13%	14%	15%	16%	17%	18%	19%	20%
1	0.901	0.893	0.885	0.877	0.870	0.862	0.855	0.847	0.840	0.833
2	1.713	1.690	1.668	1.647	1.626	1.605	1.585	1.566	1.547	1.528
3	2.444	2.402	2.361	2.322	2.283	2.246	2.210	2.174	2.140	2.106
4	3.102	3.037	2.974	2.914	2.855	2.798	2.743	2.690	2.639	2.589
5	3.696	3.605	3.517	3.433	3.352	3.274	3.199	3.127	3.058	2.991
6	4.231	4.111	3.998	3.889	3.784	3.685	3.589	3.498	3.410	3.326
7	4.712	4.564	4.423	4.288	4.160	4.039	3.922	3.812	3.706	3.605
8	5.146	4.968	4.799	4.639	4.487	4.344	4.207	4.078	3.954	3.837
9	5.537	5.328	5.132	4.946	4.772	4.607	4.451	4.303	4.163	4.031
10	5.889	5.650	5.426	5.216	5.019	4.833	4.659	4.494	4.339	4.192
11	6.207	5.938	5.687	5.453	5.234	5.029	4.836	4.656	4.486	4.327
12	6.492	6.194	5.918	5.660	5.421	5.197	4.988	7.793	4.611	4.439
13	6.750	6.424	6.122	5.842	5.583	5.342	5.118	4.910	4.715	4.533
14	6.982	6.628	6.302	6.002	5.724	5.468	5.229	5.008	4.802	4.611
15	7.191	6.811	6.462	6.142	5.847	5.575	5.324	5.092	4.876	4.675
16	7.379	6.974	6.604	6.265	5.954	5.668	5.405	5.162	4.938	4.730
17	7.549	7.120	6.729	6.373	6.047	5.749	5.475	5.222	4.990	4.775
18	7.702	7.250	6.840	6.467	6.128	5.818	5.534	5.273	5.033	4.812
19	7.839	7.366	6.938	6.550	6.198	5.877	5.584	5.316	5.070	4.843
20	7.963	7.469	7.025	6.623	6.259	5.929	5.628	5.353	5.101	4.870

FORMULAE

Valuation Models

(i) Irredeemable preference share, paying a constant annual dividend, d, in perpetuity, where P_0 is the ex-div value:

$$P_0 = \frac{d}{k_{pref}}$$

(ii) Ordinary (Equity) share, paying a constant annual dividend, d, in perpetuity, where P_0 is the ex-div value:

$$P_0 = \frac{d}{k_e}$$

(iii) Ordinary (Equity) share, paying an annual dividend, d, growing in perpetuity at a constant rate, g, where P_0 is the ex-div value:

$$P_0 = \frac{d_1}{k_e - g} \text{ or } P_0 = \frac{d_0[1+g]}{k_e - g}$$

(iv) Irredeemable (Undated) debt, paying annual after tax interest, $i\,(1\text{-}t)$, in perpetuity, where P_0 is the ex-interest value:

$$P_0 = \frac{i[1-t]}{k_{dnet}}$$

or, without tax:

$$P_0 = \frac{i}{k_d}$$

(v) Future value of S, of a sum X, invested for n periods, compounded at $r\%$ interest:

$$S = X[1+r]^n$$

(vi) Present value of £1 payable or receivable in n years, discounted at $r\%$ per annum:

$$PV = \frac{1}{[1+r]^n}$$

(vii) Present value of an annuity of £1 per annum, receivable or payable for n years, commencing in one year, discounted at $r\%$ per annum:

$$PV = \frac{1}{r}\left[1 - \frac{1}{[1+r]^n}\right]$$

(viii) Present value of £1 per annum, payable or receivable in perpetuity, commencing in one year, discounted at $r\%$ per annum:

$$PV = \frac{1}{r}$$

(ix)   Present value of £1 per annum, receivable or payable, commencing in one year, growing in perpetuity at a constant rate of $g\%$ per annum, discounted at $r\%$ per annum:

$$PV = \frac{1}{r - g}$$

Cost of Capital

(i)   Cost of irredeemable preference capital, paying an annual dividend, d, in perpetuity, and having a current ex-div price P_0:

$$k_{pref} = \frac{d}{P_0}$$

(ii)   Cost of irredeemable debt capital, paying annual net interest, $i(1 - t)$, and having a current ex-interest price P_0:

$$k_{dnet} = \frac{i[1 - t]}{P_0}$$

(iii)   Cost of ordinary (equity) share capital, paying an annual dividend, d, in perpetuity, and having a current ex-div price P_0:

$$k_e = \frac{d}{P_0}$$

(iv)   Cost of ordinary (equity) share capital, having a current ex-div price, P_0, having just paid a dividend, d_0, with the dividend growing in perpetuity by a constant $g\%$ per annum:

$$k_e = \frac{d_1}{P_0} + g \ \text{ or } k_e = \frac{d_0[1 + g]}{P_0} + g$$

(v)   Cost of ordinary (equity) share capital, using the CAPM:

$$k_e = R_f + [R_m - R_f]\beta$$

(vi)   Weighted average cost of capital, k_0:

$$k_0 = k_e \left[\frac{V_E}{V_E + V_D} \right] + k_d \left[\frac{V_D}{V_E + V_D} \right]$$

This page is blank

T4 – Test of Professional Competence - Part B Case Study Examination

September 2011

PUBLISHING

T4 – Part B Case Study Examination
Suggested solution
September 2011

Suggested Solution to Question 1a
This report, at around 4,600 words (excluding appendices), represents a comprehensive answer that would score highly. Tutor guidance has been provided for some sections to highlight key aspects that students should note. The highlighted sections show areas that differentiate an answer that would score highly from one that would just pass. When the highlighted sections are removed, the report would be around 3,000 words.

This is just one of many possible solutions.

REPORT TO THE BOARD OF DIRECTORS OF PAPY REGARDING THE MAIN ISSUES FACING THE COMPANY AND POTENTIAL STRATEGIES FOR THE FUTURE

CONTENTS

Prepared by: An.Accountant
Date: 31 August 2011.

1   Introduction

The supermarket retailing industry is intensely competitive meaning the big players must maintain a differentiating factor to attract, and ultimately keep customers. Having a reputation as a 'sustainable trader' has been used to differentiate by the likes of the Co-operative Group in the past. However, strong sustainable credentials are no longer a core competency; increasingly they are regarded as a threshold competency without which a company won't survive.

The Carbon Trust & McKinsey Company have estimated that companies that are well positioned and pro-active, that start tackling sustainability issues now, could create opportunities to increase their value by up to 80%. It is therefore clear that Papy needs to drive changes within its business, and communicate this well if it to maintain its competitive position.

> *Your introduction should look to score marks in 2 if not 3 of the marking criteria. As well as contributing to a report that is fit for purpose, scoring integration marks, it should also look to score a technical and diversity mark.*
>
> *Your introduction should ideally flow from the issues in the unseen and therefore you should have several ideas for the introduction as you walk into the real exam that you can flex to fit the issues raised on the day.*

2   Terms of reference

As a Management Accountant employed by Papy and drafted in to Arif's team, the author of this report is responsible for prioritising, analysing and evaluating the issues facing Papy and making appropriate recommendations.

> *Although a terms of reference adds some professionalism to your report, it adds very little it terms of actual marks (contributing to 1 integration mark at best). You are therefore advised to keep it as short as possible.*

3   Prioritisation of main issues facing Papy

The following issues have been prioritised from the SWOT analysis in Appendix A.

3.1   Management of change

The most important issue is to overcome any resistance to change within the company. Without the buy-in of all staff, from Board members down to checkout operators, Lucas and Arif are unlikely to achieve their goal of making Papy a more sustainable business.

Action is required to 'unfreeze' the existing culture of the business before establishing new patterns of behaviour that can be 'refreezed' into the organisation.

3.2   Carbon emissions targets

The second most important issue is to establish carbon emissions targets for the business that will challenge and motivate stakeholders towards driving change. This has been prioritised above the evaluation of the emission reduction proposals as without such targets the merits of the two proposals cannot be effectively assessed.

The new team led by Arif Karp must establish clear targets for the reduction in carbon emissions and must communicate these to stakeholders along with the co-ordinated strategy of how such reductions will be achieved.

3.3   Solar panels

Having established targets for the reduction of carbon emissions, the third most important issue facing Papy is to decide on whether to install solar panels in 200 of the Southern European stores.

This proposal has been prioritised above the new freezer cabinets due to the higher capital expenditure and the greater impact on carbon emissions.

This team must evaluate the potential benefits and weigh these against the likely costs.

3.4   Freezer cabinets

This proposal gives an opportunity to further reduce carbon emissions for a relatively low capital investment. However, unlike the solar panel installation, this proposal will change customers' buying habits and so the impact on the business as a whole will need to be carefully considered.

Again, this team will need to evaluate the costs and benefits being mindful of the impact on all stakeholders.

This is a definite exam of two halves. The management of change and the need to set challenging carbon emissions targets are without doubt the top two key issues in this exam. However, it is possible to justify that the carbon emissions targets should be ranked above the management of change (on the basis that the target can be used to help drive the change).

Similarly, whilst the two proposals are definitely priority 3 and 4, the order they appear in can be debated. The key is to not waste time worrying about this exact order as it is unlikely to make much difference to your overall mark.

This will have required you to work the calculations, at least in part, before finalising your order. Provided you have committed to an order before you start writing this is not a problem.

---

4   Management of change

4.1   Impact

Lucas Meyer has clearly identified a need for change within Papy. The need for an increased focus on sustainability has been triggered by external factors such as:

- Environmental factors (a PEST analysis reveals things such as increasing social awareness of CSR and political issues surrounding the need to meet emissions targets and the introduction of carbon taxes)

- Task factors including the intense competitive rivalry (as shown within Porter's Five Forces analysis) where many of Papy's competitors are using their sustainability credentials to gain advantages in the market.

These are in addition to internal triggers such as the departure of the previous CEO and the appointment of Arif Karp. The increased focus on sustainability is understandably changing the demands for information within the business.

Lewin's iceberg model breaks down the process of change into three stages: unfreezing, changing behaviours and attitudes, and refreezing. At present, Papy is stuck at the unfreezing stage as the resistance from staff at all levels means there is a lack of motivation to change. Without this, any plans are unlikely to succeed.

4.2   Alternative courses of action

Kotter & Schlesinger identified a number of approaches to deal with resistance. It is in the context of these approaches that the following options are suggested:

Improved communication

Arif believes that changing attitudes is an urgent task if Papy is to meet its revised carbon emissions targets. However, the change required can be described as transformational, requiring a fundamental reappraisal of the central assumptions and beliefs; this type of change can often meet with resistance, particularly if it is implemented in a quick, revolutionary type way as Arif is attempting to do.

By slowing down, and placing more emphasis on the education of and communication with employees, it may be possible to obtain a greater buy in from everyone and therefore unfreeze the current culture. Very few people would intentionally set out to damage the environment, and most people will generally agree with the intentions of the shift in focus. Communication, perhaps using a series of roadshows and internal messages in a company magazine or via the intranet will reduce any fears about the impact of the initiative on working conditions and will allow management to demonstrate the opportunities that make change desirable.

Use of a change agent

Many organisations seek to identify a change agent to help change attitudes and behaviours (the second stage of Lewin's model); this role is being filled by Lucas and Arif at present. However, for a change agent to be successful it is important that they are familiar and non-threatening to other people. Given that both Lucas and Arif are relatively new to the business and hold positions of seniority, they may not be the best people to take on this role.

A change agent is able to facilitate and support employees through the change process (as suggested by Kotter & Schlesinger). In this instance, changing the behaviour at store level might be best driven by the Operations and Finance departments, with the Corporate Affairs department having a more oversight role, as is the case at ASDA. From this head office level, the change process can be delegated throughout the senior management team and then down into change agents within each store. An alternative option would be to use Susanna Nec as the change agent given her experience within the company. This would have the added advantage of re-motivating her following the appointment of Arif.

Setting targets

The current focus on financial targets is not aligned with the new focus of leadership. By not only setting targets at a company-wide level (see section 5), but also driving these targets down to an individual store and even department level you can encourage a greater participation within the drive towards sustainability (another approach suggested by Kotter & Schlesinger). Such action will help to re-freeze the new culture within the organisation.

The key to success will be to ensure employees feel able to control the factors against which they are assessed. Staff could be encouraged to make suggestions on improvements rather than just gathering data.

A balanced scorecard approach could help to ensure store managers are focussed on a range of targets, not purely financial ones, although such a system will require a much greater variety of data to be collected.

> *A number of change management models have been used to drive this answer (and not all were required to score well). Lewin's ice-berg model is an effective foundation for explaining the impact of the problem. However, the specific requirement within the unseen of 'discuss actions required to bring about change in employees attitudes and to minimise employees' resistance to change' also provides scope to weave in other models. Although Kotter & Schlesinger was used above, Lewin's force field analysis would have been equally as useful.*
>
> *Finally, balanced scorecard principles are noted. To pick up the full technical and application marks it would be important to provide some specific KPIs for each perspective. This could be done here or as part of the recommendations.*

5   Carbon emissions targets

5.1   Impact

Setting achievable yet challenging targets can act as a real motivation for change. However, if set at an inappropriate level, either too high or too low, they can soon start to act as a de-motivator. Appendix B shows the impact of Lucas' revised targets of:

	2012	2013
Original forecast (kg / m2)	948	874
Revised forecast (kg / m2)	<u>821</u>	<u>697</u>
Additional reduction required	127	177

On the basis that the company is on track to deliver its 2011 forecast of 1,022 kg / m2, meeting these revised forecasts would mean reducing CO_2 emissions by nearly 200 kg/m2 between 2011 and 2012, and by 325 kg/m2 between 2011 and 2013. These compare with historic falls of between 30 and 70 kg/m2 per annum and so represent a challenging target.

The proposals evaluated in this report would be expected to produce the following reductions in carbon emissions (expressed in kg/m2 based on the forecast total sales area in each year)

	2012	2013
Solar panels	63	124
Freezer cabinets	<u>33</u>	<u>32</u>
Total reduction	96	156

These schemes alone would therefore only deliver approximately 50% of the required savings in both 2012 and 2013. Compared to the original forecasts, 75% (96 / 127) of the additional savings required would be achieved in 2012 and 88% (156/177) in 2013. It is therefore clear that these proposals alone would not be sufficient to deliver Lucas' ambitious plans.

5.2 Alternative courses of action

Reduce the targets

The first option would be to not set such challenging targets. The targets could be set at a level that could be achieved with just the proposals outlined below. However, the decision over whether to invest in these projects is being made centrally, meaning employees are unlikely to feel any need to contribute to the initiative.

By sticking with Lucas' revised forecasts the Board runs the risk of failing to meet them. Publishing targets that are not met would have a detrimental effect on the image of the company, and would most likely lead to a fall in the share price and investor dissatisfaction. Investors will already be concerned following the errors in the previous published data.

Implement Lucas' revised forecasts

Papy has fallen behind many of its competitors in the area of sustainability and so ambitious targets, if achieved, would go some way to making up this lost ground.

Additional reductions could be achieved by implementing suggestions from staff, who being closer to the 'coal-face' will no doubt have many innovative ideas. It may also be possible to increase the benefits from either or both of the proposals covered in this report. As solar panel technology improves, there is the possibility of installing these in more than just the Southern European stores. Equally, the proposal regarding the freezer cabinets currently only covers 500 of the over 1,100 stores. This could be extended, at relatively low capital cost.

5.3 Other factors to consider

The errors identified in the published carbon emissions figures in 2009 and 2010 show that flaws exist within the current system. It is important that these errors are corrected to ensure accurate data moving forward. Not only will greater emphasis be placed on such reporting in the future, but bonuses will be payable based on the results (see section 8 for more details).

> *When integrating your calculations into your report you should keep it simple and focus on the key results only. A tabular presentation, as shown above, can be a really effective way to present data.*
>
> *When deciding which numbers to include, ask yourself, "what would the reader be most interested in?"*

6 Solar panels

6.1 Impact

Appendix C shows that for a total spend of €600 million, the CO_2 emissions of the company would be reduced by 90 million kilograms in 2012 (approximately 63 kg / m2) and by 180 million kilograms in 2012 and subsequent years (approximately 124 kg / m2). Additionally the project delivers a positive net present value, based on a risk adjusted cost of capital of 9% of €91 million. These facts would imply that the project would be a great benefit of the company, however, a more detailed analysis is needed before a conclusion can be formed. This analysis can be performed using Johnson, Scholes & Whittington's model of suitability, feasibility, acceptability.

6.2 Analysis.

Suitability

Aside from the obvious advantage of reducing average carbon emissions and energy costs, the use of innovative solutions such as these will provide a very visual illustration of Papy's commitment to sustainable trading. No doubt much positive publicity can be gained from such projects.

Many of the leading supermarkets set targets on the amount of energy to be generated from renewable sources and this would enhance Papy's credentials in this area. For example, Sainsbury's have set a target of 20% of energy used to come directly from renewable sources by 2012.

Perhaps the greatest issue regarding suitability surrounds the timing of the investment and whether now is the best time to invest; given the expected improvements in the technology, an argument can be made to delay the project. However, the advances are not expected until 2017, by which time an investment made now would be substantially into its eight year payback period.

Already this technology is being more widely used within Northern Europe (as evidenced by the UK's Feed in Tariff system and the availability of grants for schools to install solar panels) although the payback period is generally much longer at around 10 – 12 years. It is possible that the advances expected over the next five years may enable Papy to roll out the initiative to more stores in other areas.

Feasibility

The €600 million investment cannot be funded out of existing cash reserves and will require additional capital to be raised; this therefore represents the main barrier to the feasibility of the project.

Appendix C shows the gearing ratio at 31 December 2010 to be 29%. If the €600 million capital was raised as debt finance this would increase to an estimated 41%. Although this is fractionally higher than the industry average, this calculation fails to reflect any repayments made on the existing loan in 2011 or the increase in equity that will result from the profits in the year. The position at 31 December 2011 would therefore likely be lower than 40%.

There is a good level of non-current assets suggesting that raising debt finance is unlikely to be difficult. However, the quality of these assets is unclear (property v fixtures & fittings) and so their ability to act as security is difficult to assess.

If debt finance could not be obtained, it may be possible to lease the solar panels instead of buy. This would reduce the financial return on the project but would still deliver the reduction in CO_2 and a fall in energy costs (albeit at a lower level).

Acceptability

The positive NPV of $91 million would suggest this project is acceptable on financial terms. With existing gearing levels being lower than industry average, further debt finance would be expected to reduce the cost of capital further, thereby resulting in a higher overall NPV and company value.

However, the payback period is quite long, which can create additional risk, particularly when technological advancement is so rapid. Overall, there appears to be a lack of consistency over the methods used to appraise investments (see comments under section 7). To ensure the correct decisions are taken based on the company's current goals, Papy may wish to carry out more sophisticated analysis, as is done at ASDA, by factoring in a shadow price of carbon into net present value calculations.

> *Additional technical and application marks are gained through the use of the SFA model to evaluate this proposal. Use the details given in the unseen to 'drive' your answer – it can often help to question why the examiner has provided you with each piece of information as this can help to reveal what you can use it for.*

7 Freezer cabinets

7.1 Impact

Tesco, the UK based chain of supermarkets, estimate that 16% of their total carbon footprint comes from the use of potentially damaging HFC gases in their refrigerators and Sainsbury's aim to have switched all refrigeration over by 2030, reducing their carbon footprint by more than a third when complete. This shows that Papy would not be alone in pursuing this strategy; in fact, they may be regarded as 'lagging behind' if they don't implement new technology such as that outlined.

Based on the calculations performed in appendix C, the proposal to change the freezer cabinets would payback after 4.28 years; less than the 5-year target set by the Finance Director (FD). The total capital cost would amount to €85 million, which is significantly less than the cash balance at the end of 2010 of just over €600 million.

7.2 Analysis of proposal

Advantages

As a result of the new cabinets, electricity costs will reduce by nearly €26 million per annum and the CO_2 emissions would fall by 47 million kilograms or approximately 33 kg / m^2.

Aside from these savings, the installation of new cabinets will also bring a greater uniformity, reducing the number of different models and sizes used. This may make it easier to maintain and service to equipment in the future.

It will also improve the appearance of these areas within the stores affected.

Disadvantages

Perhaps the biggest disadvantage is the reductions seen in the volumes of frozen foods purchased in the trial stores. Based on the information from the trial, this will be expected to reduce margins in the stores by an estimated €7.4 million per annum. However, this is just an expected value calculation meaning the actual outcome in each store could vary from nothing to €28,000 or more.

Furthermore, this calculation assumes there will be no impact on margins in the convenience stores. Since the trial was restricted to supermarkets only there is no evidence to support this. It is possible the impact could be more significant in these stores due to their 'convenience' nature.

Finally, the information from the trial is restricted to the volume of frozen food purchased. What this does not capture is whether customers are put off shopping with Papy altogether as a result of the new freezer cabinets.

One way of mitigating this risk is to clearly communicate with customers why these new cabinets are being used. For example, Tesco display stickers in the doors of the units telling customers how much CO_2 is being saved as a result of the units. By understanding the reasoning behind the decisions, customers may be more willing to maintain their existing buying habits.

Other factors to consider

The payback period is quite close to the criterion set by the FD. However, the FD has correctly questioned the validity of this method of investment appraisal. In a company where cash flow is not an area of concern, this technique is flawed if used in isolation.

A better approach would be to use a discounted cash-flow evaluation such as NPV; a technique which appears to have been used for evaluating the solar panels. Appendix C shows that assuming a 9% post-tax cost of capital, as used for the solar panels, and an estimated useful life of eight years (as used previously for freezer cabinets), the project delivers a positive NPV of €15.1 million. The project should therefore be accepted on pure financial grounds.

The new cabinets would also result in the old cabinets being scrapped. Not only would this result in a paper loss (and a reduction in reported profit for the year) of €25 million, it is not very environmentally friendly, scrapping resources that could be used effectively for much longer. This is particularly the case with refrigeration and freezer units where the disposal of these can be very damaging to the environment if not done properly.

> *Although this proposal could have also been evaluated using an SFA approach, we've opted for the more basic approach of advantages and disadvantages instead. This not only helps to vary the style of the answers given but also fits nicely with a thinking technique of 'plus, minus interesting' with the interesting points being noted under 'other factors to consider'.*

8   Ethical issues

It is important that a business should take a balanced view of the interests of its various stakeholders. Shareholder wealth is obviously a primary concern but a CSR focussed company considers and manages the impacts of its actions and commercial decisions on other stakeholders. Papy faces the following ethical dilemmas.

8.1   Cancellation of supplier contracts

Why this is an ethical issue

Cancelling the Fair Trade supplier contracts could be perceived as unethical behaviour since the justification for the action, based on an increased level of waste, results from Papy's actions and not the suppliers. Papy's senior management have failed to spot the decline in the amount being purchased and have therefore over-ordered, resulting in the additional waste.

This issue reflects a common ethical problem of conflict between profitability and the fair treatment of suppliers. In this case, it would appear that Papy is favouring profitability, at the expense ensuring a fair deal for other stakeholders.

Recommendation

Papy needs to perform more detailed analysis of the sales patterns for these products, and adjust its order quantities accordingly rather than completely cancelling the contracts. It may also be possible to run a promotion on these lines in order to stimulate further demand for the products. Papy's purchasing department should liaise with the supplier to find out whether other supermarkets have run such promotions and the impact that these had on sales.

8.2   Waste Management

Why this is an ethical issue

This issue presents two ethical dilemmas for the company, both of which stem from the significant differences in reductions in volumes versus the reductions in weight.

Appendix E shows that based on volume, waste is forecast to reduce by 4.4% and 4.9% in each of 2011 and 2012. However, the reduction in the weight of waste is much higher at 13.6% and 26.3% respectively.

If the company changes the basis on which it reports waste materials it could potentially mislead stakeholders regarding the reductions it has made. Secondly, Arif Karp is paid a performance related bonus based on the level of reductions achieved. This therefore presents a conflict of interest surrounding the decision on the basis of measurement to use.

Recommendation

To avoid misleading stakeholders it is recommended that both measures are published within the annual corporate and social responsibility report. This will ensure that all readers are equipped with the full facts.

To avoid any conflict of interest, the decision over which measurement to use as the basis of Arif's PRP should be taken by the other directors and communicated to Arif. It would be suggested that an average figure is taken to avoid undue emphasis on any one area.

Although it was possible to see either of these as business issues, the importance of them was much less than those covered in the main body of the report.

When writing about an ethical issue, it is important to ensure the nature of the ethical dilemma is clearly explained.

---

9   Recommendations

9.1   Management of change

Although Arif has attempted to involve senior management by asking for their opinions on sources of information, it would appear that they have little understanding of the purpose of the request. It is therefore recommended that a strategy of communication and education is employed, with all employees being informed about the goals and aspirations relating to sustainability.

This education process should be led by a change agent and it is recommended that Susanna Nec is asked to take on this role. Having steered the business through a number of changes during her 30 years service, she has a wealth of skills that are suited to this role. Most importantly, she is a familiar yet non-threatening figure so will be trusted by employees.

It is recommended that Susanna delivers a series of roadshows to senior management and then works with these people to roll the message out at store level. All employees should be encouraged to participate by suggesting ways in which Papy could improve its sustainability credentials; this could be facilitated via the intranet.

The targets set by the Board (see section 9.2) should be clearly communicated to the business, with each store being asked to set their own individual targets relating to carbon emissions. These targets should be reviewed and questioned by the Corporate Affairs team to ensure they are sufficiently challenging and that when combined, they will enable Papy to meet its overall target.

Work on the new IT system should be delayed for a short period until the staff have a greater awareness of the aim of such a system. Once this has been achieved, a task force should be assembled including representatives from different operational areas of the business in order to more formally scope the requirements of the system.

9.2 Carbon emissions targets

It is recommended that Lucas' revised targets are adopted and communicated throughout the organisation as part of strategy outlined in section 9.1. These forecasts represent an achievable yet challenging target that should help to further motivate all stakeholders. Most significantly, they increase the importance of contributions from staff meaning that employees will feel like they can make a difference.

Once up and running, the new IT system should be able to produce up to date, accurate data to allow progress towards the targets to be monitored on a regular basis.

Incentives should be put in place to encourage staff to make suggestions on other ways in which carbon emissions can be reduced. These could include individual awards such as additional holidays or financial bonuses as well as recognition for the best performing stores.

The proposals outlined in sections 9.3 and 9.4 should also be extended to more stores, following further financial evaluation (see below).

Arif Karp should work with Susanna Nec on a press announcement relating to the targets as well as the internal communication to all employees.

9.3 Solar panels

It is recommended that the solar panels are installed within the 200 stores in Southern Europe. Despite the expected advancements in technology, the investment still delivers a significant positive net present value over a 10-year period and will bring dramatic reductions in CO2 emissions.

As advancements are made, Arif and his team should continue to evaluate the viability of using solar panels within other stores in Northern Europe.

Arif should invite tenders from a number of solar panel suppliers. Each tender should be thoroughly reviewed and feedback sought from existing customers. Following the tender process, a single supplier should be engaged. This will help to ensure a smoother installation programme and will make resolving any issues much easier.

The finance department should look to raise the finance by issuing corporate debt. Advice should be sought on the issue from a merchant bank. Debt finance will have the benefit of lowering the overall cost of capital. The availability of grants to assist with such installations should also be investigated.

Finally, the finance department should perform work to quantify the financial impact of carbon emissions to enable a shadow price of carbon to be included in future investment appraisals. The appraisal process should be standardised using NPV techniques.

9.4 Freezer cabinets

It is recommended that Papy does invest in the new freezer cabinets. The positive investment appraisal (both payback and NPV), combined with the significant reduction in CO2 emissions means this is project makes sense from both a financial and a sustainability perspective.

To help mitigate the risk of shoppers changing their buying habits, or worse still, shopping elsewhere, it is recommended that stickers are placed on all freezer cabinet doors referring to the 47 million kgs of CO2 savings resulting from this project. Leaflets should also be distributed to customers shortly after the installation in each store providing further background on the technology and how the savings are generated. This will help to ensure customers understand the changes and will also promote Papy's sustainability credentials.

It will also be important to ensure the old units are disposed of properly, in order to minimise the environmental impact. Instead of scrapping the units, each store should advertise the units to the local community, perhaps giving them away to charitable causes or others who could make use of them.

The Operations and Logistics department should be instructed to place an order for the cabinets with the supplier and to agree an installation schedule that would see all proposed stores fitted with the units by 1 January 2012. The installations must be performed outside of store opening times in order to minimise the disruption to customers.

The Marketing department must design the door stickers and leaflets, in conjunction with the supplier to ensure customers are fully informed.

Each individual store manager should identify local causes who may benefit from the old units.

> *In this answer, each recommendation has been justified and supported by detailed action points, although not under specific headings. Whilst using headings works for some, other may find them constraining and difficult to work with.*
> *The answer illustrates that you don't need separate headings providing you still ensure all aspects are covered in your answer.*

10   Conclusion

Papy needs to establish and then communicate a clear and well defined strategy for reducing its carbon emissions in order to reassure stakeholders on the implications of its new stated objectives.

> *A conclusion is another section of your report which adds to the professionalism but doesn't actually score many direct marks. Only complete if you have time and keep it brief.*

Appendix A: SWOT ANALYSIS

Strengths

- Increasing EPS despite economic conditions.
- New CEO and Corporate Affairs Director keen to drive change within the business.
- Cash rich business providing scope for investment.

Weaknesses

- CSR strategy is disjointed and not strategically aligned or targeted meaning stakeholders are unsure of the impact of new objectives on them.
- **Resistance from employees to the cultural change necessary to reduce carbon emissions.**
- **Board room conflict due to a lack of support for the new focus on sustainability.**

Opportunities

- **Introduction on new technology relating to freezer cabinets will lower CO2 emissions.**
- **Using renewable energy solutions (solar panels) to lower the carbon footprint of stores in Southern Europe.**
- **Extending either of the above to cover more stores**
- **New IT system to help deliver carbon emissions data**

Threats

- **Failure to achieve targets could result in reputational damage.**
- *Changes to the presentation of waste management data could lead to claims of manipulation of data.*
- *Damage to long-term relationships with suppliers if Fair Trade contracts are cancelled.*

Appendix B: Overview of carbon emissions targets and reductions

	2009 Actual	2010 Actual	2011 Forecast	2012 Adj forecast	2013 Adj forecast	Notes
Published (kg million)	1,444	1,424				
5% understatement	72	71				
Revised carbon emissions (kg million)	1,516	1,495				
Actual sales area (m2)	1,340,800	1,366,700				
Revised carbon emissions (kg / m2)	**1,131**	**1,094**				
Original forecast			1,022	948	874	
Reduction achievable from freezer cabinets (kg / m2)				33	32	1
Reduction achievable from solar panels (kg / m2)				63	124	2
Carbon emissions after savings from new projects	1,131	1,094	1,022	852	718	
Updated forecast (based on Lucas' proposals)			**1,022**	**821**	**697**	
Shortfall				31	21	

Notes:

1. Based on savings of 47m kgs spread over the forecast sales area
2. Based on savings of 900,000 kg per converted store divided by the forecast sales area

> *The calculation of the 5% overstatement need not have been laid out in full as above. You could simply have taken the published figures in kg / m2 and multiplied by 1.05.*

Appendix C: Calculations relating to solar panels

Cost

Cost of solar panels = 200 store × €3 million = €600 million

Impact on CO2

900,000 kg / store × 100 stores = 90 million kg reduction in 2012
900,000 kg / store × 200 stores = 180 million kg reduction in 2013

Gearing

Gearing position (based on book values) at 31 Dec 2010

870 / (870 + 2,104.4) = 29%

Estimate of gearing with additional debt finance

(870 + 600) / (870 + 600 + 2,104.4) = 41%

The above assumes no repayment of existing debt or increase in equity and so if for illustration purposes only.

Appendix D: Calculations relating to the freezer cabinets

Cost of changing freezers (€'000)	85,000 (€200k × 400 + €50k × 100)
Total electricity costs saved p.a. (€'000)	25,800 (€60k × 400 + €18k × 100)
Total reductions in carbon emissions (kgs)	47,000,000 (110kg × 400 + 30kg × 100)
Expected impact on margin per store (€)	18,480 €560000 × 3% × 60% + €560,000 × 5% × 30%
Expected total margin impact in all stores (€'000)	7392

Non-discounted payback

	2011	2012	2013	2014	2015	2016
			Time period			
Investment in new freezers	(85,000)					
Tax relief on capital expenditure		21,250				
Savings in electricity costs		25,800	25,800	25,800	25,800	25,800
Expected loss of margin		(7,392)	(7,392)	(7,392)	(7,392)	(7,392)
Tax impact of loss of margin			1,848	1,848	1,848	1,848
Tax impact of electricity savings			(6,450)	(6,450)	(6,450)	(6,450)
Net cash flow p.a	(85,000)	39,658	13,806	13,806	13,806	13,806
Net cumulative cash flow	**(85,000)**	**(45,342)**	**(31,536)**	**(17,730)**	**(3,924)**	**9,882**

Payback occurs after 4.28 years (approx 4 years, 4 months)

NPV (based on 9% post tax cost of capital and assuming 8 year useful life)

	2011	2012	2013 - 2019
Net cash flow p.a	(85,000)	39,658	13,806
Discount factor @ 9% (W1)	1	0.917	4.615
Discounted cash flow	**(85,000)**	**36,366**	**63,715**

NPV = €15,081k

W1: 7 year delayed annuity factor (T2 - T8) = 5.033 × 0.917 = 4.615

> *The calculation of the non-discounted payback was essential as this was what was requested. The additional calculation showing the NPV was a 'nice to have' but relies upon several key assumptions regarding the cost of capital and estimated useful life.*

Appendix E: Calculations relating to waste materials

	2010 Actual	2011 Forecast	2012 Forecast
By volume (millions of cubic metres)	450	430	409
% reduction p.a.		*4.4%*	*4.9%*
By weight (kg million)	110	95	70
% reduction p.a.		*13.6%*	*26.3%*

Appendix F: Presentation to the Papy Board on the savings in carbon emissions

The aim of the summary is to identify and build on the key aspects from your earlier analysis, and present them in a succinct way that will assist in the presentation to the Board.
This is just one of many possible solutions.

Proposed strategies to reduce carbon emissions
- The solar panel project:
  - €600m capex
  - Reduction in CO_2: 63 kg/m2 in 2012 and 124 kg/m2 in 2013
- Freezer cabinet project:
  - €85m capex:
  - Reduction in CO_2: approx 33 kg/m2 in each year
- Further reductions of 31 kg/m2 in 2012 and 21 kg/m2 in 2013 needed to meet targets (see graph below)
- Could be achieved through staff involvement or by extending the reach of either project
- It is recommended that Lucas' revised targets are adopted and both projects are undertaken.

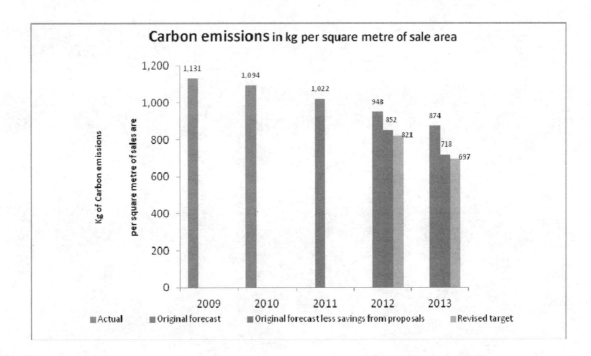

Appendix 3

Chartered Institute of
Management Accountants

T4 Part B Case Study Exam – September 2011 – Post Exam Guidance Report

General Overview

The main object of this report is to give help to candidates who were not successful in the September 2011 examination of the sustainable trading in the supermarket industry case (Papy). It is also intended to provide guidance to prospective candidates who plan to take future T4 Part B case study examinations. This report explains the basic rationale behind the case and the suggested approach to each of the assessment criteria. It also provides a brief marking guide, general comments on the candidates' scripts and a statement of common errors, including omissions, which were made by candidates.

The Papy supermarket chain generated total sales revenue of €12,911 million and produced gross profit of €2,608 million in the financial year ended 31 December 2010. Its operating profit was €658 million and earnings per share €4.544. There were 100 million shares in issue, the majority held by large investors, including institutional investors and 200 million authorised shares. The company operated an employee share scheme which rewarded all employees with free shares dependent on the achievement of individual store profitability targets as well as the achievement of a range of group financial targets.

It had 1,156 stores operational at 31 December 2010, 414 were large supermarkets and 742 were small convenience stores.

Papy split its Corporate Social Responsibilities into 5 sections being: sustainable trading, communities, responsible trading, nutrition and healthy eating and employees.

With regard particularly to sustainable trading, Papy had targets for its carbon emission measured as "carbon emission in kilograms (kg) per square metre of sales area." Papy was also reducing its waste materials and improving the volume and range of materials that it recycled. The availability of free disposable bags at checkouts was also discouraged. Papy had established a range of community and school projects and supported a range of charities. Initiatives were also introduced to treat suppliers and customers fairly and it had expanded its range of ethically sourced products. Employee training was viewed as very important especially in raising awareness of environmentally-friendly actions amongst staff. Papy was also keen to promote the right message to help customers make more healthy eating choices.

Due to its significant growth throughout Europe and the increase in the number of stores in operation, Papy had invested heavily in IT hardware and software to ensure that its IT capacity was able to cope with the forecast growth in the volume of goods procured and to control its inventory and retail transactions.

The Papy chain generated carbon emission by heating, cooling and lighting at stores and distribution depots, moving products to stores and in the construction of new stores. The company also recognised that carbon emissions were generated by its suppliers and customers. Papy's Board had set targets for reductions in carbon emission in an unstructured way but had not established an overall strategy to achieve these targets.

The thrust of the pre-seen material concerned the appointment of a new Chief Executive Officer and the establishment of a new board role, that of Corporate Affairs Director. Both the new CEO and the Corporate Affairs Director wished to make Papy a more sustainable retailer and to change the way in which the supermarket chain operated.

The unseen material required the candidate, as Management Accountant of Papy, to provide advice and recommendations to the Chief Executive on the issues facing the company. Specifically, the candidate was asked to prepare a report that prioritised, analysed and evaluated the issues facing Papy and make appropriate recommendations. In addition, the candidate was asked to prepare a presentation to the Papy Board on the savings in carbon emission that could be achieved by two proposals which were contained in the unseen material. The presentation had to contain no more than 5 bullet points, including a recommendation, and a graph which could be a column, bar or line chart. The graph was to show Papy's carbon emission expressed as "kilogram (kg) per square metre of sales area" for each of the 5 years 2009 to 2013 and had to include the savings in carbon emission that could be achieved if Papy were to implement both of the two proposals. The requirement for part (a) was worth 90 marks and part (b) was worth 10 marks.

The T4 assessment matrix has nine criteria, each of which carries between 5 and 30 marks. It should be noted that the Logic criterion has 30 marks associated with it, 20 marks for recommendations given in the answer to part (a) and 10 marks for the answer to part (b). It is important that the candidate earns high marks in the Judgement and Logic criteria as each of these carry 20 marks within part (a). It is also important that the candidate undertakes sufficient analysis to provide a sound base for discussion of the issues from which appropriate and logical recommendations can be made. The analysis should include appropriate financial and numerical calculations, particularly those which are discernable from the unseen examination material which is rewarded within the Application criterion.

It should also be noted by candidates that CIMA operates a policy of anonymous marking and therefore candidates MUST NOT identify themselves anywhere in their answers other than by their role or assumed job title, for example Management Accountant. Numerous candidates in this exam session provided their own actual name in the report for part A.

The main issues contained in the unseen material were:

1. Management of change. In order for Papy to become a more sustainable retailer and to meet the new targets for carbon emission it was necessary for the culture of the company to change.
2. Carbon emission targets. The Chief Executive wanted to make substantial reductions in carbon emission by investing in new technology and revised targets were proposed.
3. Solar panels. This was one of the initiatives to achieve a reduction in carbon emission. It involved large scale investment at 200 of Papy's supermarket stores and would reduce electricity usage by generating up to 30% of the stores' electricity needs.
4. Freezer cabinets. This initiative involved replacing the freezer cabinets at 500 stores to bring about energy savings and reductions in carbon emission. This would also have involved the write-off against profits of €25 million for the old freezer cabinets.

There were other areas which candidates could have discussed (and which were given credit within the marking) but it was critical that the issues relating to the management of change and carbon emission targets were fully addressed in the answer. This was because these two issues were fundamental to Papy achieving its objectives of becoming a more sustainable retailer and reducing its carbon emission. The attitude of staff needed to be that Papy, as a large listed European company, had to embrace sustainability and reduce its carbon emission for environmental welfare as a whole and also to avoid possible large fines in the future as the deadline of 2020, agreed in the Kyoto protocol, draws ever nearer. It was necessary to discuss carbon emission targets as a top priority because the two proposals to reduce carbon emission could not be adequately discussed unless the overall context and targets had been set.

Format of answers

The format of candidates' answers to part (a) was generally good. Candidates usually began with an introduction leading to very brief terms of reference, prioritisation of issues, followed by discussion of those issues. Ethical issues were discussed and advice given on how to resolve them and then recommendations were made on the issues which had been prioritised.

There was a noticeable improvement in the format of recommendations using the suggested format of recommendation, justification and actions to be taken. However, it should be made clear that candidates are not expected just to repeat in their recommendations what they have stated in their discussion earlier in the report. Essentially, in the discussion section, the candidate should consider alternative approaches to resolving any particular issue raised. In the recommendations section the candidate should select the approach which he or she wishes to recommend, justifying why this has been selected from the range of alternatives and then explain the follow-on action which is necessary to implement the recommendation. Only low marks will be awarded in the recommendations section for simply repeating what has already been said earlier in the discussion as these marks will have already been awarded in the earlier section. Additional marks will be awarded in the recommendations section if the points identified in the discussion are crystallised into a firm recommendation with justification and explained in much more detail, for example through actions which are required to implement the recommendation.

Finally, most candidates provided a brief conclusion. The appendices were usually contained in an Excel file or at the end of the report. Part (b) was often included as an appendix to the report, which is acceptable.

Once again, some candidates failed to address part (b) at all. Others failed to do the graph. These were dangerous omissions, given that part (b) is worth 10% of the marks. It is surprising that such omissions were made as this is now the seventh examination in which part (b) has been required and reference has been made to it in each of the previous Post Examination Guidance reports. Candidates are reminded that guidance exists on the CIMA website relating to the format of these reports which will be required. See:

http://www.cimaglobal.com/Documents/Student%20docs/2010%20syllabus%20docs/T4/Support%20Guide%20%20T4%20Part%20B.pdf

A final note in this section concerns the frivolous beautification of some reports which is really not necessary in the examination answer. Time spent on providing such things as over-elaborate colouring and imaginary house styles that the candidate thinks may be appropriate for the case company cut no ice at all with the marker. Time invested in these frivolous designs would be much better spent on analysing the case study material.

Discussion of general candidate performance under each assessment criteria

T4 Assessment Criteria

	Maximum marks available
Analysis of Issues (25 marks)	
Technical	5
Application	15
Diversity	5
Strategic Choices (35 marks)	
Focus	5
Prioritisation	5
Judgement	20
Ethics	5
Recommendations (40 marks)	
Logic	30
Integration	5
Ethics	5

<u>Analysis of issues</u>

PART (a):

Technical:

Rationale:

The purpose of this criterion is to assess the use of relevant theoretical techniques and frameworks to aid the analysis of the case material.

Suggested Approach:

It is recommended that candidates present their technical knowledge either in the form of appendices to the main report (in an Excel spread-sheet or at the end of the report itself in Word) or the relevant theories could be discussed within the report where appropriate.

Marking Guide:

Marks are awarded for technical models and theories which are relevant to the case. It is usually appropriate to limit the technical knowledge displayed to 5 separate items.

Commentary:

Most candidates were able to display sound technical knowledge principally comprising a SWOT analysis, the Johnson, Scholes and Whittington SAF framework, the Mendelow matrix, Lewin's three phase process of behaviour modification and a range of other strategic planning approaches. These were appropriate in this case study. As usual, most candidates performed well under this criterion. It was pleasing to note again that many candidates were more discerning over their use of strategic planning models, limiting their use to a few relevant models.

Common errors:

The guidance provided in previous Post Examination Guidance reports remains valid. It is important that candidates do proceed to apply the models they use to the unseen case material. Some candidates still produce models which they then do not use within their analysis of the issues. It is always appropriate to produce a SWOT analysis. It would be expected that the main issues to be discussed in part (a) of the answer will feature somewhere within the SWOT analysis which should not be too long but should contain the main issues affecting the case organisation.

Some candidates failed to recognise the key issue of staff resistance to change within their SWOT analysis. This could have been either a weakness or indeed a threat. However, it should have been a main feature within the SWOT analysis.

It is often better for candidates to use the technical knowledge as an illustration within the actual report itself, rather than as an appendix. For example, many candidates applied the Johnson, Scholes and Whittington SAF model or Mendelow's stakeholder analysis within their actual discussion of the issues contained in the case, rather than as an abstract appendix. In this case, it was very appropriate to apply Lewin's three phase process of behaviour modification to the need to change the culture of Papy.

Application:

Rationale:

The point of the Application criterion is to assess how well candidates use the techniques, frameworks and calculations to support their analysis of the issues in the unseen material and their subsequent recommended actions.

Suggested approach:

Candidates are advised to ensure that they apply relevant models, techniques and frameworks correctly, given the unseen case material. Thus it is important that rather than just stating the model or framework, it is presented in such a way that it provides information which is relevant to the case and enables candidates to use this information in their discussion of the issues. This also applies in respect of calculations, which should be relevant to the information given in the particular case.

Marking guide:

Marks are available for the relevant application of techniques, models, frameworks and supporting calculations but only if the candidate applies them to the specific case. Marks were awarded for the application of models to the case material and for relevant calculations, principally working out revised carbon emission targets, the savings in carbon emission from each of the two proposals in the unseen material, the financial evaluation of the new freezer cabinet proposal in the terms of the capital investment appraisal methods used by Papy, a summary of the savings in carbon emission and a comparison with the new targets. There were a lot of marks available for valid calculations and candidates who carried out sufficient numerical analysis were well rewarded. Candidates who did not adequately grasp the numerical and financial implications within the case lost the opportunity to gain marks and also demonstrated their general lack of understanding of the issues which would be expected from a competent management accountant.

Commentary:

Most candidates provided a SWOT analysis. It is essential that candidates take full account of the information contained within the unseen material and incorporate this into their SWOT analysis. Candidates are reminded, again, that it is the unseen material on which they should base their answers and should ensure that all the prioritised issues are included in the appropriate quadrant of the SWOT. Most candidates managed to provide some additional theoretical analysis by using appropriate models.

Common errors:

A surprising number of candidates failed to calculate the revised carbon emission targets accurately. Some failed to take account of the 5% increase which was necessary to be applied to the 2010 published level of emission. Others applied this to the total level of carbon emission in kg million rather than the published level of kg per square metre. This was a common error. It is expected that candidates will be able to demonstrate their understanding and grasp of the issues and display their competence as management accountants. There was a major clue given in the text of the unseen material which stated clearly that it was the kg per square metre which needed to be updated for the understatement. This was supported by part b. which required a graph which showed "kilogram (kg) per square metre of sales area". Candidates who adjusted the total level of carbon emission, despite being advised to change the published kg per square metre figure for 2010, showed lack of understanding. It was of course possible to work the revised targets out from the total level but this then needed to take account of the change in square metres of total sales area from 2010 in subsequent years. This unnecessarily complicated the calculations.

Many candidates failed to identify the impact on the carbon emission savings per square metre of sales area for each of the 2 proposals, again providing the total overall impact. This was given credit but was not as meaningful a measure because the published carbon emission per square metre of sales area was the one with which direct comparisons could be made year on year because the sales area changed every year. Additionally, some candidates calculated the carbon emission reductions per square metre of a typical supermarket or convenience store, rather than on Papy's overall carbon emission per square metre of sales area.

Having identified the impact of the 2 proposals, many candidates then failed to compare the forecast results with the targets and did not appreciate that, although very close, the proposals in themselves were insufficient to meet the proposed new targets.

The evaluation of the freezer cabinets should have been undertaken by reference to its undiscounted payback. This did not stop very many candidates applying their own discount rate (usually 9% which was the rate used for the appraisal of the solar panels) to work out an NPV of the freezer cabinets. This was not required and there was no suggestion in the unseen material that the same discount rate would be applied to both proposals. There was of course the opportunity for candidates to discuss the benefits and disadvantages of the capital investment appraisal methods used and this was hinted at in the unseen material with the Finance Director having reservations about the undiscounted payback method of appraisal.

Many candidates compared the undiscounted payback period for the freezer cabinets with the discounted payback period for the solar panels, which is clearly wrong in principle.

The financial evaluation of the freezer cabinets was at times woeful. Most candidates managed to work out the electricity savings, but very many failed to work out the forecast fall in gross margin for all the supermarket stores. Some managed to work the average figure out for each store but then failed to apply it to all 400 stores. Others ignored it altogether. Some managed to work out the tax relief on the capital cost, but then forgot there was a 1 year tax delay. Some ignored the 100% allowable relief and spread it over the five years. Many failed to account for the tax impact on the net cash flows each year and of those that did, many forgot there was a 1 year delay. An unforgiveable error made by many candidates was to show the write-off of the old freezer cabinets within the evaluation proposal for the new cabinets. Some candidates did the cash flow calculations for the freezer cabinets but then did not work out the payback.

One calculation which could have been made was a comparison of the capital cost per million kilograms of carbon emission saved for each of the 2 proposals. Very few candidates thought to do this comparison. Other calculations which should have been included was the effect that new debt, to finance the solar panels proposal, would have on Papy's gearing ratio.

Diversity:

Rationale:

This criterion seeks to assess knowledge and understanding of relevant real life situations in the same or similar context as that in which the case is set. It also assesses the recognition of commercial or organisational issues relevant to the case material whether or not they occur within the same industry.

Suggested approach:

Candidates should seek to introduce relevant examples at the point where they discuss the issue in their answer. Typically, this may occur in the introduction, the prioritisation section, discussion of the issues, ethics or within the recommendations. The main point is that a candidate should seek to bring in the relevant example at the point which enables him or her to elaborate or emphasise the issue which is being considered within the answer. Candidates are reminded that a long list of examples, all within the Introduction section, will earn limited marks as these examples are of a general nature rather than an illustration of a specific point. Similarly, a long list of examples which merely illustrate the same point being made, even if at different points in the script, will not earn any more than a single mark.

Marking guide:

Essentially, there is one mark available for each relevant example given, providing it is clearly stated why it is relevant. Additionally, general discussion of many real life companies in the introduction will not attract more than one mark, as they have not been related to the issues raised in the unseen material. The introduction should be relatively brief. The candidate needs to explain why the example is relevant to the point being made.

Commentary:

This was generally satisfactory with many good examples of supermarket companies from around the world being cited and especially those which have embraced the carbon emission agenda.

Common errors:

Some candidates gave few or no examples in their answers which is surprising for an industry which has an abundant supply of good examples.

Strategic choices

Focus:

Rationale:

This criterion requires candidates to select the issues that are regarded as the most important and which will be discussed further within the answer.

Suggested approach:

This is not a section of the report as such. Marks are awarded based on the issues which are contained and discussed within the report.

Marking guide:

There are five marks available for this criterion even if there are not 5 separate issues contained in the unseen material. It is for the candidate to determine the most relevant issues in the case that should be discussed. As it happened, there were four main issues, excluding the ethical issues, in the unseen material.

Commentary:

Most candidates were able to identify issues from the unseen case material and organise these into a priority order.

Common errors:

There were four main issues in this case, being management of change, carbon emission targets, the solar panel proposal and the freezer cabinets proposal. Candidates were awarded marks in Focus, as well as Judgment and Logic, based upon the comments made, irrespective of the specific heading within their report under which each of the issues had been discussed. Candidates should be aware that if an issue is prioritised (see next section) and then not actually discussed within the report, or simply provided with a heading but with no ensuing discussion, then the focus mark for that particular issue will not be awarded.

Prioritisation:

Rationale:

Under this criterion, the candidate is required to rank the issues and to state clearly and concisely the justification for that ranking. The ranking should reflect the impact of the issues on the particular organisation, which may include its urgency.

Suggested approach:

The priorities should be presented early in the answer under their own heading. The priorities should be set out with the issues ranked as either 1st, 2nd, 3rd etc. Each should be justified with a concise explanation of why the candidate has ranked it in such a position.

Marking guide:

High marks are awarded if the candidate presents the most important issues with a good rationale as to why they are ranked as main priorities. It should be noted that markers do give credit to candidates who make a case for prioritising issues differently from those contained in the suggested answer.

Commentary:

On the whole, candidates are accustomed to producing their rankings and generally manage to present their prioritised issues in an appropriate form. The SWOT analysis, if carefully carried out, should help to clarify which are the most important issues to be addressed. Many candidates felt that the freezer proposal or the solar panels proposal were the main issues. These were major issues for Papy, but the wider concern was really about the carbon emission targets as a principle. The two proposals were vehicles by which Papy might reduce its carbon emission and work towards achieving its target. They contributed to the achievement of the targets but the proposals themselves were not the specific reason why Papy needed to reduce its carbon emission. Hence the carbon emission target and the related need of the change in culture within Papy were the two main issues. The two proposals really followed on after these as specific proposals and the carbon emission relating to them could not sensibly be selected until Papy's carbon emission targets had been agreed.

Common errors:

Essentially, the main error was the failure of candidates to appreciate the need to recognise the principle or axiom of carbon emission targets. Others simply took this for granted and prioritised the two proposals without reference to targets at all. It was surprising how many candidates failed to recognise the need for Papy to manage cultural change within the company. A number of candidates only concentrated on IT issues under the heading of management of change when in fact there were much wider matters to consider than just IT. It seemed as though a number of candidates were scratching round seeking issues to prioritise and resorted to prioritising those which might more readily have lent themselves to being ethical issues. This was acceptable as all ethical issues also have a business aspect. However, unless the business aspect is clearly differentiated from the ethical point, marks will only be available in one place or the other. Candidates will not be awarded marks in both places unless both ethical and business issues are discussed. Some candidates only prioritised and discussed the IT aspect of the proposed new EMS system and did not consider the other more important issues concerning the management of change.

Judgement:

Rationale:

This criterion assesses the candidates' exercise of commercial and professional judgement in discussing the key issues which were prioritised.
Suggested approach:

It is important that the candidate discusses the impact the prioritised issues have on the organisation and what alternative actions, with reasons, could be taken to address them. This should include relevant supporting analysis drawn from the "Application" criterion. So for example, if a calculation is made within an appendix, for example relating to the financial analysis of the freezer cabinets proposal, then it should be used in support of the points made under that relevant heading within this section of the report. The purpose of undertaking the analysis by using appropriate planning models and relevant numerical and financial analysis is so that the findings can then be used to support discussion of the issues. It is appropriate for a candidate to make reference to his or her SWOT analysis when discussing each of the issues, highlighting their importance.

Marking guide:

Marks are awarded for discussing the different aspects of an issue and its impact on the company and also for providing appropriate alternative approaches to resolving it. Clearly, the alternative approaches will receive higher marks if they are accompanied by a valid rationale as to why they are being put forward and their advantages and disadvantages considered. This point cannot be emphasised enough. Candidates will receive reward for an in-depth analysis of the issues. This means that they need to carry out the analysis in the first place. They then must consider alternative approaches to resolving the issue. This may take various forms including the use of models such as Johnson, Scholes and Whittington's SAF framework or, in this particular case, Lewin's three phase process of behaviour modification.

Commentary:

The Judgement criterion is extremely important as it provides the facility for candidates to express their full analysis of the issues contained in the case. It is essential that sufficient time and effort is put into carrying out this fundamental analysis. It is not sufficient for a candidate to simply repeat the facts of the case and regard that solely as his or her analysis. Further, it is not enough for a candidate to simply mention possible alternatives to resolving the issue in passing. The alternatives need to be analysed in depth. The facts of the case should be used as evidence to support the commentary as part of candidates' analysis of the issues. It is essential that candidates state the impact and financial implications of a particular issue, citing evidence.

Once the impact has been stated then the candidate should consider the alternative actions which could be taken by the organisation in the case study and bring in relevant analysis in support of each alternative discussed. Candidates must consider each issue from the wider perspective of the impact it has or potentially will have on the case organisation, using the facts as evidence in support of the arguments being presented.

Common errors:

The standard main errors are listed (again) as follows:

- Simple repetition of the case material without any additional analysis. Candidates must be prepared to analyse the information given in the unseen material. The candidate is expected to provide sensible analysis to aid decision making.
- Failure to discuss all the issues prioritised. A surprising number of candidates prioritised an issue and then failed to discuss it.
- Serious lack of basic analysis of the issues including not discussing the financial implications.
- Brief discussion of alternative actions and little comparison of the overall advantages and disadvantages of each of the alternatives.
- Failure to distinguish between business and ethical considerations relating to an issue. Marks will be awarded irrespective of where the candidate discusses the point but candidates should be able to make this distinction.

In addition, the following errors were made in respect of this particular case:

- Failure to discuss change management techniques in detail.
- Reference to the balanced score card without explaining its meaning, principles and how it could be used effectively by Papy.
- Misunderstanding basic principles, including those not actually required in this case such as what the NPV actually means. An example of misunderstanding a basic principle was the candidate who wrote that since the P/E ratio was 5.9 and the write-off of the old freezer cabinets was €25 million this would cause the shareholders to lose "a whopping €148 million."
- Failure to calculate the correct total capital cost of the proposals and consequently discussing each one with flawed data.
- Inability to calculate the effect on gearing if either or both proposals were financed by debt.
- Using the debt to equity ratio rather than the gearing ratio (as referred to clearly in the unseen material) to establish the effect of financing one or both of the proposals with debt. A declaration then that the gearing level would rise dramatically from the level before the debt was increased, measured by the gearing ratio to that after the debt was increased, measured by the debt/ equity ratio demonstrated lack of appreciation that the two methods are different and are not directly comparable.

These are serious errors and lead to the conclusion that someone who is capable of stating such things would be a danger to the profession and is actually not displaying competence in management accounting.

It is essential that the candidate concentrates his or her mind on the issues contained in the actual case and on the unseen material and does not become confused with issues that have either occurred in a previous exam session or in a tuition provider's mock examination. If the issues in the unseen material are fully considered, with good numerical analysis where appropriate, then alternative approaches which might be adopted by the organisation in the case can be proposed and the benefits and disadvantages of each expressed. Analysing the issues in this way naturally leads the candidate to produce a rationale for his or her recommendations later in the report.

There is no single right answer to the issues and credit is given for the candidate's recommendations which are logically supported with a clear rationale, even if these do not correspond with the suggested answer. However, to do this effectively, the candidate must have first analysed the issues in depth. It is this lack of in-depth analysis which causes most candidates to fail the examination. This point must be stressed yet again.

Ethics – Strategic choices:

Rationale:

The candidate is required to use judgement to identify and analyse the ethical issues and state why these issues have ethical implications.

Suggested approach:

This section is normally coupled with the recommendations on how to resolve the ethical issues. It is perfectly acceptable to provide the answer in one section or it could be split over two as presented in the Assessment Criteria. The reason it is split in the Assessment Criteria is because the business issues often have an ethical dimension associated with them. This was the case with the cancellation of the 2 supplier contracts for example. It is therefore appropriate for the ethical issues to be discussed alongside the business dimension. It is for the candidate to choose the method with which he or she feels most comfortable.

Marking guide:

Marks are awarded for recognising each of the ethical issues and then it is crucial to explain why they are considered to be ethical issues.

Commentary:

On the whole, candidates were able to identify the ethical issues which were the cancellation of the two supplier contracts, the change in the reporting of the waste materials and Arif Karp's contract.

Common errors:

Generally, the ethical issues were reasonably well handled, although there were some candidates who did not discuss ethics at all. Candidates were mostly able to identify the ethical issues and provide a reasonable explanation of why the issue might be considered to be ethical although this was not always the case. A number of candidates categorised issues under the ethical heading when in fact they were more related to business. For example, the fact that Papy's staff were not embracing the carbon emission issue was not in itself unethical from Papy's point of view. It might have been personally unethical from the standpoint of the individual member of staff. Similarly, the process of the management of change was not an ethical issue per se, even if it involved some staff being dismissed if they did not make an effort to help Papy meet its targets. This was a business issue. Another example was that the disposal of the old freezer cabinets in itself was not an ethical issue as their replacement would reduce Papy's carbon emission overall. Further, there was no hint in the unseen material that the old freezer cabinets might not be disposed of properly.

A common error raised by candidates in Ethics concerned the 5% understatement of Papy's carbon emission. This was not considered to be an ethical issue as there was nothing to infer that Papy was trying to cover this up. Marks were awarded in Judgement and Logic for suitable comments and recommendations but not in Ethics.

Frequently candidates only discussed one ethical issue. This limits the marks which can be awarded. There are always at least two ethical issues in each unseen part of the case study.

Recommendations

Logic:

Rationale:

This criterion tests whether the candidate is able to make well-justified recommendations for each of the prioritised issues.

Suggested approach:

It is important that the candidate ensures that there are strong reasons for the recommended course of action. The recommendations should follow on from the weight of arguments and choices of possible actions in a logical manner. It is expected that candidates will present their recommendations, provide a justification of why these courses of action are being recommended and then state what should be the follow-on actions. It is appropriate to state that this approach seems to be have been adopted now by most candidates.

Marking guide:

Marks are awarded not just for the recommendations themselves but also, crucially, for the rationale and strength of argument supporting them, drawing from the earlier analysis of the issues and for explaining what the organisation should do next to make the recommendations happen. It must be stressed that marks will not be awarded to candidates for recommendations which merely repeat what has been said earlier in the discussion of the issues.

The recommendations section must be used to provide very clear recommendations drawn from the analysis and discussion earlier in the report. The candidate should have produced a range of alternative approaches to resolving an issue in the analysis and discussion. It is necessary then for him or her to select the recommended approach from the range of alternatives, providing justification for it and what the consequent follow-on actions should be. It is these candidates who score the high marks in the exam as they have analysed the issues, thought about alternative ways of tackling them and then selected the most appropriate approach and explained this within the recommendations section.

Commentary:

Recommendations will be given credit even if they are not consistent with those in the suggested answer. There is often no single right answer to the issues presented in the case. It is the rationale for the recommendation which is important. The follow-on actions must be consistent with the recommendations. Further, candidates must understand that recommendations must be consistent with each other and with recommendations on ethical issues where appropriate. Many candidates are now providing an explanation of the actions to be taken following a recommendation and its justification. The recommendation should explain why a particular course of action is recommended, rather than simply what should be done and how.

The recommendations should follow the analysis and discussion and therefore sufficient time should be allowed for the recommendations to be prepared.

Common errors:

Some candidates had problems with their time management and the recommendations provided were too brief.

Most of the common errors have been highlighted before in previous Post Examination Guidance reports and continue to feature.

- Time management issues with some recommendations being very short.
- Straight repetition of what had been said in the earlier discussion without sufficient amplification of why a course of action was being recommended. It is for the candidate to synthesise the benefits and disadvantages into a coherent explanation of why a particular course of action is being recommended.
- Some candidates produced weak rationales for their recommendations which did not really address the issue. The marker may not agree with the actual recommendation but will award marks if it is justified by the argument presented. The candidate must recognise that he or she is aiming to persuade the reader to a course of action, so it should not be left for the reader to work out for him or herself why a particular recommendation has been made.
- Failure to address the urgency of some issues.
- Failure to provide recommendations on all the prioritised issues. This may be due to time constraints but is therefore a feature of poor time management.
- Recommendations which did not follow on logically from the earlier discussion within the case.
- Sitting on the fence stating, for example, carry out more research on solar panels before agreeing the proposal.
- Carrying out part of the proposals without a clear justification, for example only do some of the freezer cabinets or some of the supermarkets for solar panels without saying why.
- Not being clear about what recommendations should be made relating to carbon emission targets for example agreeing the new target for 2013.
- Not being clear as to how the proposals for the solar panels and freezer cabinets would help Papy to achieve (or not) the proposed carbon emission targets.
- Poor rationale for rejecting a proposal. For example, rejecting the freezer proposal due to the fall in gross margin without recognising that the fall in gross margin was less than the savings from the reduced electricity costs.

In essence, the recommendations are a very important part of the answer and candidates should allow sufficient time to address them fully.

Integration:

Rationale:

The marks are all available for the overall functionality and quality of the report in part (a).

Suggested approach:

This is not a section of the report, but considers the report as a whole. As a guide therefore it is important that candidates present a report which is clear, sectionalised, addresses the main issues with good analysis and discussion and makes suitable recommendations based on the weight of evidence presented.

Marking guide:

Reports are deemed to be highly professional, sound, satisfactory, inadequate or poor. The whole 5 marks are available for a highly professional report and 0 or 1 mark for a poor report.

Commentary:

Good answers tend to divide the report into the following distinct parts:
- Table of contents
- Brief terms of reference
- A brief introduction
- Prioritisation of the key strategic issues
- A detailed analysis of the issues

- Ethical issues (which may be in one section or split across the detailed analysis and the recommendations)
- Recommendations
- Appendices including part (b).

It is important to effectively integrate the different parts of the report. So, for example, the recommendations should include the evidence base supporting them by reference to the earlier analysis which may be drawn from the main body of the report or the appendices.

A low mark will be awarded in Integration if the key issues were not properly addressed, or indeed were not discussed at all and the report was left incomplete. Further, a low mark is applied in Integration if analysis is not sufficiently carried out, for example, the discussion of the issues were vague and generally superficial in nature and did not specifically relate to the unseen case material, numerical analysis was weak or contained errors of principle or not undertaken at all.

Common errors:

Some reports simply did not address the main issue satisfactorily or provide sufficient depth of analysis or reasoning behind the recommendations to warrant a high mark. Sometimes the recommendations themselves were vague and the candidate did not commit to a particular course of action. This is not helpful to management. Candidates should be prepared to present their recommendations with confidence and support them with rational argument as to why they are being made.

Ethics - Recommendations:

Rationale:

This criterion judges candidates on their recommendations and reasoning for each of the ethical issues identified.

Suggested approach:

This section follows on from the identification and explanation of the ethical issues. It may either be contained in one complete section or split over two as presented in the Assessment Criteria.

Marking guide:

Marks are awarded for the quality and depth of advice on the ethical issues raised.

Commentary:

Candidates tended to give sensible advice on the issues raised in the report although this was often vague.

Common errors:

The main common error was that some candidates failed to provide any advice on the ethical issue raised. As made clear before, stating the ethical dilemma alone is not enough. The advice itself must be ethical and, usually, the ethical advice becomes clear when the ethical dilemma is understood. Candidates need to ensure that their advice is consistent with what they have recommended for the main issues they have discussed within Logic. The advice itself needs to be sound and logical. For example the ethical approach to Arif Karp's bonus package being linked to emission reduction was not to give the job of finding other initiatives to reduce emission to someone else other than Arif when that is his role in the company.

The advice given on the Fair Trade Suppliers issue was often poor or vague as to what could be done regarding the unsold produce. Many candidates concentrated their advice on the suppliers rather than in marketing methods to boost sales. The advice to reduce orders or to cancel the contracts earned low marks in Ethics as this was not an ethical stance for Papy to take.

Candidates could increase their marks under this criterion by explaining the rationale for their advice. Also, the advice provided by candidates is often too brief.

PART (b):

Rationale:

The purpose of part (b) is to test candidates' ability to communicate in a competent professional way their analysis, findings and the financial implications relating to a particular issue contained in the unseen material.

Suggested approach:

Candidates should consider carefully the purpose of the communication, for whom it is intended, and the salient points that he or she wishes to communicate. This means that the candidate needs to think carefully about the major points which need to be included in the communication. Thought also needs to go into the effectiveness of the communication which means that it should have clarity, be to the point and not be ambiguous or verbose. Candidates should follow the instructions or requirement for part (b). In this case the requirement asked for a presentation to the Papy Board on the savings in carbon emission that could be achieved by the replacement freezer cabinet proposal and the solar panels proposal. The presentation was to contain no more than 5 bullet points, including a recommendation and a graph as a column, bar or line chart.

Marking guide:

Marks are awarded on the strength of the communication provided. There are marks available for commentary on the strategic importance of an issue, the inclusion of relevant financial or numerical information, the benefits and disadvantages of a particular course of action and a recommendation where appropriate. In this case, a recommendation was specifically requested in the question.

Commentary:

As stated in previous Post Examination Guidance reports, candidates should recognise that if the guidance states "5 short sentences" that is what is required, not 10 or 2. It was disappointing that, again, some candidates chose not to attempt part (b) at all. It is dangerous not to attempt this part as it is worth 10% of the total marks available.

Common errors:

The common errors were:

- Failure to do part (b) at all.
- Failure to restrict the bullet points to 5.
- Failure to provide a graph at all, only the bullet points.
- Failure to label the axes on the graph.
- Failure to provide a heading for the graph; this was a presentation to the Board, so what was it all about?
- Failure to provide a graph showing five years, some showed data for one year only for each proposal.
- Failure to provide the capital cost of the two proposals; surely essential information to the Board?
- Failure to provide recommendations.
- Failure to include the actual carbon emission reductions in figures at the relevant points on the graph (as shown in the graphs in the pre-seen material).

To re-iterate what has been stated before in previous Post Examination Guidance reports, it should be understood that employers have made it clear to CIMA that they seek candidates who are not only competent in management accountancy but are also able to communicate effectively. This is the main reason why part (b) exists in the T4 case study examination.

Appendix 4

T4 – Part B Case Study Examination
Tuesday 28 February 2012

Instructions to candidates

You are allowed three hours to answer this question paper.
You are allowed 20 minutes reading time **before the examination begins** during which you should read the question paper and, if you wish, make annotations on the question paper. However, you will **not** be allowed, **under any circumstances**, to begin using your computer to produce your answer or to use your calculator during the reading time.
This booklet contains the examination question and both the pre-seen and unseen elements of the case material.
Answer the question on page 17, which is detachable for ease of reference. The Case Study Assessment Criteria, which your script will be marked against, is also included on page 17.
Maths Tables and Formulae are provided on pages 24 to 27.
Your computer will contain two blank files – a Word and an Excel file. Please ensure that you check that the file names for these two documents correspond with your candidate number.

Page

Contents of this booklet:

© The Chartered Institute of Management Accountants 2012

T4 Test of Professional Competence – Part B Case Study Examination

Jot – toy case

Industry background

There is a large number of companies of various sizes which design and sell toys to retailers globally. Most toy companies outsource the manufacture of their toys and currently 86% of the world's toys are manufactured in China. Most of the rest of the world's toys are manufactured in other Asian countries, with only low volumes of products manufactured in Europe and the USA.

The toy market is divided up into a variety of sectors, by children's age range and the type of toy. There are different sectors with toys aimed for babies under one year old, children aged 1 to 3 years and pre-school children of 3 to 5 years. There is a further sector for children of school age of 5 years and upwards. Additionally the toy market is broken down into categories of toys. Research has shown that children aged 2 to 4 years old receive the most toys in quantity but that the most money is spent on toys for the 6 to 8 year age group.

The current trend in toy sales is towards electronic toys and computer assisted learning. Many of these electronic toys are highly developed to be attractive to children. Sales of traditional toys and games have achieved relatively low growth in the European market over the last 10 years, whereas electronic toys and merchandise from popular films and TV programmes have seen reasonable growth. Merchandise from films and TV programmes are licensed to toy manufacturers or toy retailers which can achieve high short-term profits depending on the licensing arrangement and the volume of sales. However, fashion trends are difficult to predict and toy retailers can be left with large volumes of unsold inventories if the toys are unpopular or less in demand than originally anticipated.

The toy market is highly seasonal and is dominated by the pre-Christmas sales period. Typically, around 30% to 55% of toy sales occur in the fourth quarter of the calendar year (October to December).

China has established itself as a high quality, low-cost manufacturing base for a wide range of consumer products for global markets. It does not, as yet, principally design and create new products, but instead is capable of manufacturing products that have been created by Western companies. It is necessary for the companies which create the designs, whether the product is a toy, a range of clothing or a computer chip, to ensure that the design is protected by registering the design for intellectual property rights (IPR's). However, in many instances small changes can be made so that "copies" of the design do not breach the IPR. Legal protection of IPR's is becoming increasingly important in today's global markets, where resources are sourced in one area of the world, manufactured into finished products in another area (principally in China and other Asian countries) and then sold in other geographical markets.

Most toy retailers procure a range of products from many different toy companies. There is a wide range of companies, from small to very large multi-national companies, which operate as toy design and distributing companies. These companies design, patent or license the toys and then outsource the manufacture to specialist toy manufacturers. The toy companies then sell their products to toy retailers.

There are several global toy fairs each year which attract buyers from toy retailers across the world. One of the largest toy fairs is held in Hong Kong in January each year, where new toys are launched for the following Christmas market. Other global toy fairs are held in Europe, Russia and the USA, also early in the calendar year. At these toy fairs, buyers will assess and choose which of the new toys may achieve high sales. The toy fairs attract a wide range of exhibitors which are launching new toys, both large listed companies and small companies.

The level of sales achieved by many toy companies will often depend on orders generated from buyers attending these international toy fairs. Therefore, it is important that prototype toys and marketing literature is ready in order to meet the requirements of these global buyers at the start of each calendar year.

Jot

The Jot brand was established in 1998 by husband and wife team Jon and Tani Grun. The company initially designed a small range of toys which were manufactured in their home European country. These toys proved to be very popular in their home country and Jon Grun then expanded the range of products.

By 2003, within five years of starting Jot, the founders were encouraged to see Jot's products ordered by many large toy retailers across Europe. By this stage the company had grown considerably, and had annual sales of almost €2 million. Commencing in 2004, Jot started outsourcing all of its manufacturing to a range of manufacturing companies in China in order to reduce its cost base and to enable the company to price its products more competitively.

By the end of 2010 sales revenue exceeded €8 million and the company had achieved substantial sales revenue growth each year. Jot has seen its sales revenue grow by 16% in the year ended 31 December 2010 and by almost 18% in the year to 31 December 2011 (unaudited figures).

A summary of Jot's key personnel is shown in **Appendix 1** on page 11.

Jot's product range

Jot currently has a relatively small range of 34 products aimed at only 2 age groups. These are the pre-school age group of 3 to 5 year olds and the next age group of 5 to 8 year olds. It currently does not produce any toys aimed at babies aged less than one, toddlers aged less than 3 years old or children aged over 8 years old.

Jot's products include a range of toys designed by the company, for which it holds the IPR's, as well as some licensed toys, for which it pays a license fee to the companies which hold the IPR's. Jot's products mainly include electronic features and this is seen as one of the strengths of its products.

Jot currently launches around 5 totally new products each year. It also enhances certain aspects of some of its other products to refresh their appearance and features. It also has a range of toys that sell consistently well and have not changed materially for a few years.

Jot's products for the 3 to 5 year old age group include:

- Construction toys with sound effects and electronic actions.
- Learning products such as mini-computers which ask questions and the child responds by pressing different keys.
- Toy vehicles some of which have electronic features such as sounds and lights.
- Plastic toys which have "animatronics" to make the toys move, for example, toy dinosaurs.
- Toy cameras.
- Electronic learning products to aid learning the alphabet and basic maths skills.
- Licensed soft play toys based on film and TV programme characters.
- Licensed plastic figures, cars and machines based on film and TV programme characters, some of which include electronic features that generate movements and sounds, including theme tunes.

Jot's products for the 5 to 8 year old age group include:

- Toy cameras and video cameras.
- Dolls and action figures, some of which move and make sounds.
- Small hand-held games boxes for playing computer games and educational learning products to improve maths and readings skills.
- A range of games and educational learning products for the hand-held games boxes.

Jot's products are sold to toy retailers for between €7 and €38. These are Jot's selling prices to toy retailers. Most of the retailers will then sell these toys at a large mark-up, which can be as much as 50% to 100%, i.e. a toy procured from Jot at €10 could be retailed to the end customer at €20.

In the year ended 31 December 2011 Jot's actual sales volumes (unaudited) were over 706,000 units across Jot's entire range of products. The total sales revenue for the year ended 31 December 2011 (unaudited) was €9,866,000, which resulted in an average selling price of just under €14 per unit. Over 80% of Jot's product sales are sold to retailers for €20 or less.

Financials and shares

Jot has achieved a high annual growth in sales, with sales revenue reaching €9,866,000 in the year ended 31 December 2011 (unaudited), a growth of 17.9% from 2010 (€8,371,000 sales revenue for year ended 31 December 2010). Additionally, it has achieved an operating profit margin of 5.58% in the year to 31 December 2011, a rise from the previous year's profit margin of 5.41%.

An extract from Jot's accounts (unaudited) for the year ended 31 December 2011 is shown in **Appendix 2** on page 12.

Jot's Statement of Cash Flows for the year ended 31 December 2011 (unaudited) is shown in **Appendix 3** on page 13.

Jot is a young, growing company which is dependent on loan finance. Jot has three bank loans totalling €1,600,000, each at an interest rate of 10% per year, which are due for repayment as follows:

- Bank loan of €500,000 due in January 2014.
- Bank loan of €500,000 due in January 2015.
- Bank loan of €600,000 due in January 2020.

Jot's bank has been very responsive to the company's needs for cash in order to fund its growth but has indicated that at the present time it would not be able to provide any additional long-term finance.

Jot has an overdraft facility of €1,500,000, which the bank has stated is the maximum limit. The current cost of its overdraft is at an interest rate of 12% per year. At 31 December 2011, Jot's overdraft was €960,000.

Jot's business is highly seasonal with a significant proportion of sales occurring in quarters 3 and 4. As Jot builds up its inventory in preparation for higher levels of sales in quarters 3 and 4, cash flow is negative during the second half of the year. This is because outsourced manufacturing for the majority of all products occurs mainly from the end of quarter 2, during all of quarter 3 and the beginning of quarter 4.

Jot is a private limited company and not listed on any stock exchange. It has 40,000 shares in issue, each of €1 par value. The company has an authorised share capital of 200,000 shares. To date, the Board of Jot has not declared any dividends. The shares are held as follows:

	Number of shares held at 31 December 2011	Percentage shareholding
		%
Jon Grun	12,000	30
Tani Grun	12,000	30
Alana Lotz	8,000	20
Boris Hepp	4,000	10
Michael Werner	4,000	10
Total	40,000	100

Production of toys

Jot has its own in-house team of designers who are involved in designing toys that are unique, innovative and fun to play with. The production of new toys is split into two stages. Firstly, the design stage involves the design team developing a new toy and after it has been approved, the second stage is where the operations team is responsible for contracting an outsourced manufacturer for the mass production of each product.

The head of Jot's design team is Alana Lotz, Product Development Director. She is responsible for researching the market trends in toys globally and establishing the availability of new innovative technology which could be incorporated into new toy designs. This is what helps to make Jot's product range innovative and at the "cutting edge" of new technology, as the products incorporate new technology electronic chip components.

Research and development work on new product development usually occurs between May and December each year so that the new products have been fully tested ready for the annual launch of Jot's new range of toys each January. Jot currently launches 5 totally new products each year and the development costs are generally between €0.1 and €0.25 million for each new product. The total design and development costs are around €1.2 million each year. This is included in administration expenses in Jot's statement of comprehensive income.

Jot has just finalised its range of new products for 2012, so as to allow time to produce marketing literature and prepare prototypes ready for the global toy fairs being held in January to March 2012 in various locations around the world.

The design team develops all new products through the following stages:

- Brainstorming for new ideas.
- Designing a new product using Jot's CAD / CAM IT system.
- Production of first prototype.
- Market research and improvements through to production of second prototype.
- Sign off by design and management team.
- Application for intellectual property rights (IPR's) for each product design.

Jot uses a specialised company, based in Europe for the manufacture and testing of all prototype products and there are often two or three stages involved before the prototype product is produced to the satisfaction of the designers. Only when each product is signed off by the design and management team can Jot's legal team apply for the IPR's for the product design. Then the approved new product designs go into production by outsourced manufacturers.

The designs are then electronically transferred to Jot's operations team headed up by Michael Werner, Operations Director, for the selection and appointment of outsourced manufacturers. The stages in the production process are as follows:

- Designs are sent electronically to outsourced manufacturers for tender.
- Outsourced manufacturer(s) selected and appointed and volumes and delivery deadlines for production agreed.
- Packaging designs and artwork are prepared and approved.
- Production samples are reviewed by Jot's in-house Quality Assurance team located both in Europe and in Asia.
- Production is commenced to meet agreed volume and delivery deadlines.

Michael Werner is responsible for the selection, appointment and monitoring of Jot's outsourced manufacturers and all aspects of the management of the outsourced manufacturing process for Jot's products. Jot's products are all manufactured by a small number of specialised outsourced manufacturing companies which are all based in China. Jot is responsible for shipments of all products from its outsourced manufacturers to its warehouses or sometimes directly to customers.

Outsourced manufacturers

Currently Jot uses 20 off-shore outsourced manufacturing companies. Off-shore outsourced manufacturing is defined as shifting work to foreign, distant companies in order to reduce production costs. Some of the outsourced manufacturers are small companies each of which manufactures just one of Jot's products. Some of the larger outsourced manufacturing companies make several of Jot's products. All of these outsourced manufacturing companies do not work exclusively for Jot but manufacture toys, as well as other products, for a number of international companies. All of Jot's outsourced manufacturers are based in China.

When a product design has been approved and the IPR applied for, Michael Werner will send the product design with an indication of the number of products to be manufactured and the timescale for shipment, to a small range of outsourced manufacturers for them to tender for the manufacture of the product. Jot often asks the same outsourced manufacturing companies, which it has used previously, to tender for the manufacture of its new product designs each year. Therefore, there is a high level of "repeat business" and a good level of understanding and commitment established between Jot, based in Europe, and its outsourced manufacturers based in China.

When the tenders have been received, Michael Werner and his team review the outsourced manufacturing companies' submissions and then select the outsourced manufacturer to be appointed. Jot's designers and sales team will have already decided on an indicative selling price, so the unit price to be charged to Jot by the outsourced manufacturing company is often the determining factor when making the decision of which outsourced manufacturing company to use. Whilst other factors are considered, such as quality and ability to deliver the required volume of products to the required timescale, it is the unit price which is important in order to achieve the planned level of gross margin. Gross margin is defined as sales revenue less the outsourced manufacturing cost of units sold and excludes all other costs.

Jot's design team already knows the cost of making each product, based on the list of components required, so it is the cost of manufacturing that will vary between the different tenders. Generally, in most tenders, the unit prices quoted by different outsourced manufacturers are quite close to each other.

Most of Jot's products are manufactured using basic raw materials, such as plastic and electronic components for the toys and plastic and paper products for their packaging. The majority of Jot's products require a range of electronic components. These components are readily available from a variety of sources but are subject to price fluctuations. Each product design will specify which, and how many, of each component type is required. Some of the electronic components are specialised and contain "application-specific integrated circuits" (ASIC components) which are procured from specialist suppliers. Jot does not have any agreements with these specialised suppliers as all components, including ASIC components, are procured directly by the outsourced manufacturer appointed to manufacture each of Jot's products. Some of Jot's outsourced manufacturers, which manufacture a range of electronic products for Jot and other companies, have on-going supply contracts in place for several key components, which helps them to price their products competitively.

The timescales each year for the production of Jot's products is for tenders to be submitted and manufacturers appointed by the end of May. The major proportion of manufacturing occurs between June and early November each year. The last of the manufacturing occurs in early November to enable time for the products to be shipped to Jot's warehouses in Europe and the USA, or sometimes directly to Jot's customers, in time to meet the Christmas sales peak. All three of Jot's warehouses are leased.

Over the last 10 to 15 years many companies have outsourced their manufacturing to companies in China. However, with wage rates in China increasing, some companies have started to consider "near-shoring". Near-shoring is defined as the transfer of business processes to companies in a nearby country. Therefore, if Jot were to consider near-shoring, this would result in having some outsourced manufacturers based in Europe.

Sales

Jot's sales revenue for the year ended 31 December 2011 (unaudited) was €9,866,000. The geographical analysis of these sales is shown as follows:

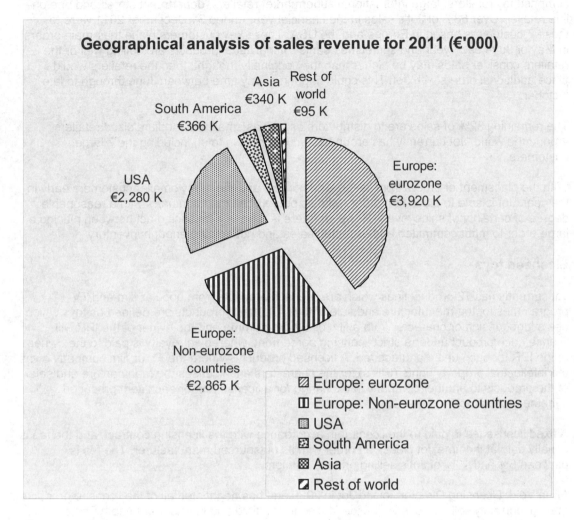

Geographical analysis of sales revenue for 2011 (€'000)

Asia €340 K
Rest of world €95 K
South America €366 K
USA €2,280 K
Europe: eurozone €3,920 K
Europe: Non-eurozone countries €2,865 K

Legend:
- Europe: eurozone
- Europe: Non-eurozone countries
- USA
- South America
- Asia
- Rest of world

Jot's customers are mainly:

- Retailers – these include large toy retailers as well as supermarket chains and other retailers

- Distributors – these distributors purchase Jot's products and sell them on to a wide range of smaller retailers.

Jot currently has three warehouses, two in Europe and one in the USA. Usually all products are shipped from each of Jot's outsourced manufacturers directly to one of Jot's three warehouses. In some instances, products are shipped directly to customers.

Jot's terms of sale are for payment within 30 days of invoice. Invoices are produced automatically, on a daily basis, based on information transferred to the sales ledger from the inventory control IT system. However, Jot is very dependent on sales to large retailers, which often do not pay until at least 60 days after the invoice date. Jot has little influence over these retailers and does not want to jeopardise future sales by chasing them too aggressively.

Sales of Jot's toys are highly seasonal as shown in the quarterly analysis of sales in **Appendix 4** on page 14.

In the year ended 31 December 2011, sales in quarter 3 (July to September) were 25% of annual sales and sales in quarter 4 (October to December) were 51% of annual sales.

Jot's sales are highly dependent on seven large retailers. These seven large companies comprise toy retailers, large international supermarket retailers, department stores and one on-line retailer. Over 68% of Jot's sales in the financial year ended 31 December 2011 were to these 7 customers based in Europe and the USA. These key customers place their main orders in May or June each year and sometimes earlier. If individual products are selling well or the retailers consider sales may be higher than they originally thought, then the retailers would place additional orders with Jot. This could happen at any time between June through to late October.

The remaining 32% of sales are to distributors as well as small and medium sized retailers around the world. Jot currently has around 350 customers in total, including the 7 large customers.

With the placement of orders from its large customers and the many smaller customers early in the year, Jot is able to place firm orders with its outsourced manufacturers with a reasonable degree of certainty of sales levels. However, there is always a balancing act between placing a large order to meet committed and expected sales and not holding enough inventory.

Licensed toys

Jot currently has 12 product lines which are licensed products from popular film and TV programmes for the manufacture and sale of toys. Licensed products are defined as toys which use a logo, design or character from a film or TV programme and the owner of the IPR will license each product under a strict licensing agreement, whereby a royalty is paid to the owner of the IPR for each unit manufactured. A licensed product is where the TV or film company owns the intellectual property rights (IPR's) for the characters and licenses the manufacture and sale of the products to another company in exchange for a license fee for each item produced (whether sold or not).

A fixed license fee is paid to the licensor in accordance with the licensing contract, and the fee is usually paid at the time Jot places an order with its outsourced manufacturer. The fee is between 5% and 10% of Jot's selling price to retailers.

Anna Veld, Licensing Director, joined Jot in 2009 and has negotiated all of the licensed products that Jot currently sells. She is very experienced in this field and in liaison with both Sonja Rosik and Boris Hepp, she has identified products for Jot to develop and sell. Licensed products now account for almost 10% of Jot's sales, in terms of the number of units sold.

Inventory control

Michael Werner is responsible for logistics and inventory control. There is always a difficult decision to be made when placing orders with outsourced manufacturers, between ordering too much inventory and not selling it and the opposite of losing sales because of lack of inventory. This is further exacerbated due to the seasonal nature of sales, which are predominantly made in quarters 3 and 4 of each calendar year.

At the start of each calendar year, any unsold inventory for products that Boris Hepp, Sales Director, considers to be out of date, are offered to Jot's customers at substantially reduced prices to clear them and the inventory value is written down. There are a few products which are sold on a regular basis throughout each year and their inventory value is not written down.

Inventory counts at the end of the financial year are reconciled with Jot's IT inventory control system and any discrepancies are written off. Jot's inventory is valued at the lower of cost or realisable market value, based on a first-in, first-out basis. Inventory value is based only on out-sourced manufacturing contracted charges, using the unit price from manufacturer's invoices, unless the realisable value is lower.

Inventory also includes a reserve for the write-down in value in respect of slow-moving and obsolete products. This valuation is based upon Jot's management team's review of inventories taking into account for each product the estimated future sales demand, anticipated product selling prices, expected product lifecycle and products planned for discontinuation. The valuation for inventory write down is reviewed quarterly. At 31 December 2011 the write-down reserve was €0.124 million. This is netted off against the value of the current inventory of products held in Jot's warehouses.

The Jot brand

The Jot brand name is synonymous with quality electronic toys. Jot's products are innovative and appealing to the targeted age groups. Sonja Rosik, Marketing Director, joined Jot three years ago when the role was separated from that of the Sales and Marketing Director, leaving Boris Hepp, Sales Director, free to concentrate on securing sales in wider geographical markets.

Marketing has become increasingly important in the promotion of new products. No longer can a company rely on a good product being identified by the key buyers for large retailers. It is of vital importance to market new products before, during and after the global toy fairs, which are held in several locations in the January to March period of each year. The toy fairs can often "make or break" the success of each new product and the need to gain a positive reaction from buyers, based on sample products, is very important.

The launch plans for new products and the marketing support Jot's customers receive can have an impact on the reaction of buyers at the global toy fairs. A significant volume of sales orders arise directly from these toy fairs and Sonja Rosik's team has made a very strong contribution to achieving positive press reports for new products and providing buyers with good quality and clear marketing literature. Boris Hepp is very pleased with Sonja Rosik and her team, which helps his sales team to secure firm sales orders for Jot's products.

Additionally, Sonja Rosik, has been working on the establishment of links and promotion of the Jot brand in new geographical markets as well as further market penetration in Europe and the competitive USA market.

IT systems

Tani Grun appointed an external IT consultancy company some years ago to provide the IT systems required for Jot's growing business. However, some of the systems are not ideal and do not provide Jot's management team with all of the data that it requires. There is also some replication of data between different IT systems.

The Finance Department operates a multi-currency nominal ledger and integrated sales and purchase ledgers. However, these IT systems do not accept data directly from any of Jot's other IT systems. The Finance Department also operates a fixed assets register.

Jot outsources the logistics of its products, both the movement of manufactured products and the sales to customers, to a global logistics company. This company operates a fast efficient service and with the increase in sales volumes over the last few years, a reduction on the unit costs has recently been negotiated. The outsourced logistics company provides Jot with access to all tracking and logistics data for products moving into Jot's three warehouses and prepares reports on products which have been shipped directly to customers.

The data concerning goods delivered to Jot's three warehouses is transferred electronically to Jot's inventory control system. This database system generates despatch notes for all orders that are fulfilled from each warehouse. The majority of customer deliveries are fulfilled from Jot's warehouses and not directly from the manufacturer. The despatch note data is transferred electronically to the Finance Department in order to raise invoices to customers for goods despatched. Information on customer orders which are delivered directly from the manufacturer is transferred by the outsourced logistics company to the Finance Department, in order to raise invoices.

All product designs and product drawings, which include a detailed listing of all parts and components, are prepared using a standard CAD / CAM IT system. This allows direct interface with Jot's outsourced manufacturers. This ensures that each new product design can be transferred to the appointed outsourced manufacturer's IT systems when the product is ready for manufacture, thereby eliminating any delays and confusion over the exact product specification and design.

Target markets for growth

Jot would like to expand its sales by specifically targeting other areas of the world, including the Russian and the Asian markets. These two specific markets have a growing demand for the types of product that Jot sells. Sonja Rosik has visited several countries in Jot's target markets and met with retailers and distributors of children's toys. She has been working with Michael Werner to establish distribution links for these markets and to arrange delivery of products direct to customers based in Asia, rather than have its products shipped to Jot's European warehouses for onward shipping back to Asia.

When Jot first entered the USA market in 2006, it was caught unawares by the higher than expected volume of demand and spent almost a year trying to meet the growth in demand for the products ordered. Jot has since discovered that it is necessary to manufacture larger numbers of each product, in order to ensure that its products are available if demand exceeds its expected supply levels, before launching into new geographical markets.

Extracts from Jot's 5-year plan is shown in **Appendix 5** on page 15.

The 5-year plan shows growth in sales revenue at 17% for 2012 and around 13% to 14% for the remaining 4 years of the plan period as well as a small growth in operating profit margins.

Corporate social responsibilities and product safety

Jot's management team is aware of the importance of its corporate social responsibilities (CSR) but so far it has not officially published what it does or how it will improve its CSR plans. This is an area which Michael Werner and Alana Lotz plan to develop in the next year, so that Jot can publish its CSR achievements and targets.

However, Jon Grun has always impressed on all of Jot's employees and managers the importance of its products exceeding, rather than simply conforming to, the required safety standards.

European Union (EU) law requires that all toys which are to be sold in any EU country must carry the "CE" marking. The "CE" marking confirms that "Certification Experts" have carried out all applicable testing to identify hazards and assess risks, in order to determine that the products meet the required product safety regulations of the EU. The "CE" marking may be on the toys themselves or on their packaging. In the EU a toy is defined as "any product or material designed or clearly intended for use in play by children of less than 14 years of age".

These EU safety regulations apply to all companies based in the EU which supply toys anywhere in the EU, and apply to all companies, whether they are manufacturers, importers, wholesalers, retailers or hirers. It is the responsibility of the toy company and the manufacturer to ensure that the product meets the safety regulations and that the "CE" marking is fixed on the product. Jot cannot delegate this responsibility.

Jot's key personnel

Jon Grun – Managing Director
Jon Grun, aged 48, is an engineer and has worked in a variety of large companies designing electrical products. He always wanted to establish his own company and was inspired to start the Jot toy company in 1998 when his children were young, as he felt there was a gap in the market for innovative, educational toys. Jon Grun owns 30% of the shares in issue.

Tani Grun – Finance and IT Director
Tani Grun, aged 44, is married to Jon Grun. She is a CIMA accountant and worked for some large companies in senior roles before taking on the Finance Director role for Jot when it was formed in 1998. Initially she worked part-time, but as the company has grown, she is finding the role more challenging. She is considering recruiting a new person to take responsibility for IT for Jot as she considers that outside experience is necessary to move the company forward. Currently, many of Jot's IT solutions are out-sourced. Tani Grun owns 30% of the shares in issue.

Alana Lotz – Product Development Director
Alana Lotz, aged 44, has been Tani Grun's friend for many years and trained as a design engineer and then worked for a global toy manufacturer for 12 years. Tani Grun recruited her when Jot was established in 1998 and she has been a leading force in the expansion of the range of new toys and in the recruitment and retention of Jot's design team. She holds 20% of the shares in issue.

Sonja Rosik, Marketing Director
Sonja Rosik, aged 35, was recruited in 2009 when the role of Marketing Director was separated from the previous role of Sales and Marketing Director. She has brought a wealth of new ideas and dynamism to Jot's marketing and has helped to expand Jot's products to new geographical markets. She does not own any shares.

Boris Hepp – Sales Director
Boris Hepp, aged 42, joined Jot in 2003 when sales in Europe were starting to grow rapidly. He held the joint role of Sales and Marketing Director until 2009, when the Board decided that he would be best employed in concentrating on capturing sales in new markets. Boris Hepp had known Jon Grun for many years before he joined Jot and was very impressed at how quickly the company had grown. Boris Hepp holds 10% of the shares in issue which he purchased when he joined Jot in 2003.

Michael Werner – Operations Director
Michael Werner, aged 50, is responsible for all operations, including management of outsourced manufacturing, logistics and inventory control. All stages from the handover of each product design through to delivery to Jot's customers are under Michael Werner's control. He joined Jot in 2008 from a large European based electrical company. He enjoys meeting the challenges faced by Jot's growth and also the freedom to manage operations without the large corporate culture that he found frustrating. He holds 10% of the shares in issue which he purchased when he joined Jot in 2008.

Anna Veld - Licensing Director
Anna Veld, aged 37, has extensive knowledge of licensing agreements from her previous roles working for a global film company which licensed its merchandising products and she has also worked for a large toy manufacturer. She has been instrumental in increasing the number of licensed products that Jot sells. She does not own any shares.

Viktor Mayer - HR manager
Viktor Mayer, aged 55, joined Jot in 2011 on a part-time basis to help with HR matters, which Jon Grun used to manage with the help of an outsourced HR agency.

Extract from Jot's Statement of Comprehensive Income, Statement of Financial Position and Statement of Changes in Equity

Statement of Comprehensive Income	Year ended 31 December 2011 (Unaudited)	Year ended 31 December 2010
	€'000	€'000
Revenue	9,866	8,371
Cost of sales	6,719	5,615
Gross profit	3,147	2,756
Distribution costs	552	478
Administrative expenses	2,044	1,825
Operating profit	551	453
Finance income	13	12
Finance expense	213	201
Profit before tax	351	264
Tax expense (effective tax rate is 30%)	105	79
Profit for the period	**246**	**185**

Statement of Financial Position	As at 31 December 2011 (Unaudited)		As at 31 December 2010	
	€'000	€'000	€'000	€'000
Non-current assets (net)		750		721
Current assets				
Inventory	542		470	
Trade receivables	4,065		3,173	
Cash and cash equivalents	21		29	
Total current assets		4,628		3,672
Total assets		5,378		4,393
Equity and liabilities				
Equity				
Issued share capital	40		40	
Share premium	90		90	
Retained earnings	802		556	
Total Equity		932		686
Non-current liabilities				
Long term loans		1,600		1,600
Current liabilities				
Bank overdraft	960		790	
Trade payables	1,781		1,238	
Tax payables	105		79	
Total current liabilities		2,846		2,107
Total equity and liabilities		5,378		4,393

Note: Paid in share capital represents 40,000 shares of €1.00 each at 31 December 2011

Statement of Changes in Equity For the year ended 31 December 2011 (Unaudited)	Share capital	Share premium	Retained earnings	Total
	€'000	€'000	€'000	€'000
Balance at 31 December 2010	40	90	556	686
Profit	-	-	246	246
Dividends paid	-	-	-	-
Balance at 31 December 2011	**40**	**90**	**802**	**932**

Statement of Cash Flows

	Year ended 31 December 2011 (Unaudited)	
	€'000	€'000
Cash flows from operating activities:		
Profit before taxation (after Finance costs (net))		351
Adjustments:		
Depreciation	240	
Finance costs (net)	200	
		440
(Increase) / decrease in inventories	(72)	
(Increase) / decrease in trade receivables	(892)	
Increase / (decrease) in trade payables (excluding taxation)	543	
		(421)
Finance costs (net) paid	(200)	
Tax paid	(79)	
		(279)
Cash generated from operating activities		91
Cash flows from investing activities:		
Purchase of non-current assets (net)	(269)	
Cash used in investing activities		(269)
Cash flows from financing activities:		
Increase in bank overdraft	170	
Dividends paid	0	
Cash flows from financing activities		170
Net (decrease) in cash and cash equivalents		(8)
Cash and cash equivalents at 31 December 2010		29
Cash and cash equivalents at 31 December 2011		21

Quarterly analysis of sales for 2009 to 2011

			Qtr 1 Jan - Mar	Qtr 2 Apr - June	Qtr 3 Jul – Sept	Qtr 4 Oct - Dec	Total
2011 Actual (unaudited)	Sales	€'000	988	1,380	2,490	5,008	9,866
		%	10%	14%	25%	51%	100%
2010 Actual	Sales	€'000	730	1,250	2,360	4,031	8,371
		%	9%	15%	28%	48%	100%
2009 Actual	Sales	€'000	548	1,010	2,025	3,622	7,205
		%	8%	14%	28%	50%	100%

Extracts from Jot's 5 year plan

	Actual (Unaudited) 2011	Plan 2012	Plan 2013	Plan 2014	Plan 2015	Plan 2016
Revenue €'000	9,866	11,568	13,124	14,791	16,840	19,260
Gross margin	31.9%	32.3%	32.6%	32.9%	33.2%	33.6%
Operating profit €'000	551	694	820	961	1,137	1,348
Operating profit	5.6%	6.0%	6.2%	6.5%	6.8%	7.0%
Number of unit sales '000	706.3	868.5	977.5	1,102.0	1,240.0	1,405.0
Number of countries products to be sold in	22	23	25	28	32	36
Number of new products to be launched each year	5	6	7	8	9	10

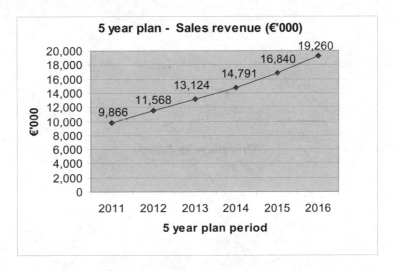

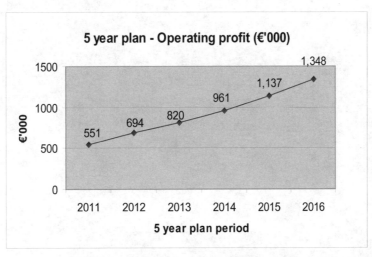

End of Pre-seen material

This page is blank

Additional (unseen) information relating to the case is given on pages 19 to 22.

Read all of the additional material before you answer the question.

ANSWER THE FOLLOWING QUESTION

You are the Management Accountant of Jot.

Jon Grun, Managing Director, has asked you to provide advice and recommendations on the issues facing Jot.

Question 1 part (a)
Prepare a report that prioritises, analyses and evaluates the issues facing Jot and makes appropriate recommendations.

(Total marks for Question 1 part (a) = 90 Marks)

Question 1 part (b)
In addition to your analysis in your report for part (a), Tani Grun, Finance and IT Director, has asked you to draft an email to Jot's management team. This email should set out the key criteria for the selection of outsourced manufacturers in general, together with your recommendation on which manufacturer(s) should be appointed for products YY and ZZ.

Your email should contain no more than 10 short sentences.

(Total marks for Question 1 part (b) = 10 Marks)

Your script will be marked against the T4 Part B Case Study Assessment Criteria shown below.

Assessment Criteria

Criterion	Maximum marks available
Analysis of issues (25 marks)	
Technical	5
Application	15
Diversity	5
Strategic choices (35 marks)	
Focus	5
Prioritisation	5
Judgement	20
Ethics	5
Recommendations (40 marks)	
Logic	30
Integration	5
Ethics	5
Total	**100**

This page is blank

Read this information before you answer the question

VP "own brand" proposal

A major toy retailer based in the USA, VP, has taken a keen interest in the growth of Jot and is impressed with its innovative products and their quality. VP is one of Jot's seven main customers and it sells most of Jot's product range. VP is Jot's main customer in the USA with over 90% of its sales in this geographical area. The remainder of sales in the USA are generated by many small retailers. Total sales to VP in 2011 were just over €2.0 million, out of Jot's total sales of €9.866 million in the year ended 31 December 2011.

VP wishes to increase its range of "own brand" labelled products. VP's Procurement Director has recently met with Jon Grun, Managing Director, and has proposed that Jot produces a range of toys using VP's "own brand" labelling. This proposal would be for a 5 year period starting 1 January 2013 (the start of Year 1). The proposal is summarised as follows:

- Jot would design, manage the outsourced manufacturing process and produce an agreed range of products which would be labelled and packaged using VP's "own brand" rather than the Jot brand.

- All VP "own brand" products would be sold only in the USA.

- VP would place firm orders for the "own brand" products in March each year and VP would bear the risk of any unsold inventory. Currently VP places several orders between March and September each year.

- Jot would design 1 product exclusively for VP each calendar year. VP would pay a fee for this exclusive product of €0.25 million each year which is forecast to just cover the design and pre-production costs.

- VP would pay a reduced price, compared to Jot's current selling prices, for each VP "own brand" product. VP has requested a price reduction of 20% across all products. Jot's current average selling price of products to VP is €14.00 per unit. This is forecast to stay the same for the next 5 years.

- VP forecasts that sales volumes of the "own brand" products would increase by 50% every year for the 5 year period, due to extensive marketing (paid for by VP), from its current level of 145,000 units for 2012.

- Shipping costs are currently €0.40 per unit, payable by Jot. This is forecast to stay the same for the next 5 years.

The average manufacturing cost of products sold to VP is currently €9.50 per unit. This is forecast to stay the same for the next 5 years. However, Michael Werner, Operations Director, considers that Jot will be able to secure a price reduction from its outsourced manufacturers of 5% due to the extra volumes for the proposed VP "own brand" products.

Alternatively, if Jot decides not to pursue the "own brand" proposal with VP, Jot forecasts that sales volumes to VP could grow at 12% each year from its current level of 145,000 units, at an average selling price of €14.00 per unit. This is forecast to stay the same for the next 5 years.

Tani Grun, Finance and IT Director, considers that an appropriate pre-tax cost of capital is 10%.

Quality problem

Anna Veld, Licensing Director, has secured the licensing arrangement for a range of action figures based on a new children's film which is due to be released in July 2012. Planned sales for 2012 are 80,000 units in total, although if the film is a box office success, sales could be higher. The license fee is €0.70 per unit and is payable on *all* units manufactured (irrespective of whether the manufactured units are scrapped, sold or held in inventory).

Following tenders and subsequent negotiations, Jot appointed outsourced manufacturer Q (Q), which is based in China, to produce 80,000 units of these licensed products. Jot has used Q once before with no problems. The manufacturing process uses the technology called "injection moulding" where master moulds for each of the action figure are made to reproduce all of the products. Michael Werner personally inspected and signed off the master moulds in January 2012 and production commenced.

The first shipment of 10,000 units arrived at one of Jot's warehouses in Europe in February 2012 and on inspection, it has been established that the products do not meet Jot's quality standards. Michael Werner contacted Q and insisted that all production be stopped immediately. In the meantime, a further 10,000 units have been manufactured. No payments have yet been made to Q.

Michael Werner has now visited Q's factory and he has established that the manufacturing process has been rushed and the plastic used was of poor quality. Jot's contract had not specified the details of the plastic to be used as Q had made acceptable quality products for Jot previously. Michael Werner has discussed these problems with the Managing Director of Q and was told "at the contracted manufacturing price of €6.00, this is the best that Jot will get". The Managing Director of Q reminded Michael Werner that it had originally tendered a price per unit of €7.00. However, Michael Werner put pressure on Q to reduce the price down to €6.00 through tough negotiations. The Managing Director of Q has confirmed that his company could produce better quality products but only if Jot agrees to the realistic price of €7.00 per unit.

An alternative outsourced manufacturer, P (P), has now tendered a cost per unit of €7.10. Jot has not used this outsourced manufacturer before but its quality of production is known to be very good. However, Michael Werner is concerned that new moulds would need to be made by P before manufacturing can commence. Jot requires delivery of all 80,000 units by the end of May 2012 to enable it to transport them to its customers.

Marketing material

Sonja Rosik, Marketing Director, is aware that the marketing promotional literature for one of Jot's newly launched electronic products, which is aimed at the 5-8 year old age range, gives the impression of having several features which the product does not actually have.

Sales orders have been placed by some of Jot's customers and the product is currently being manufactured. The packaging for the product also contains slightly misleading information and claims. Jon Grun, Managing Director, is very annoyed about the incorrect marketing literature and packaging. He recalls that when Jot was a smaller company he personally signed off all marketing literature. He has asked Michael Werner, Operations Director, to investigate what can be done about the packaging for this product, both for future production as well for the first consignment of products that have recently been delivered to one of Jot's European warehouses. Jot has not yet despatched any sales orders to its customers.

Jon Grun considers that Sonja Rosik has been negligent in allowing this exaggeration of features to be incorporated incorrectly into the marketing material and the packaging of this product. Sonja Rosik does not understand why Jon Grun is so annoyed about what she considers to be a minor error in the marketing material. She has stated that "no one will really notice that the toy does not do this". Jon Grun is considering asking Sonja Rosik to resign.

Manufacturing problems

All of Jot's products are currently produced by 20 outsourced manufacturing companies. Except for the production of prototype and trial products, all outsourced manufacturing is located in China. In the middle of February 2012, an earthquake hit the area in China where two of Jot's outsourced manufacturers' factories are located. The two factories and much of the surrounding area have sustained significant damage. It is envisaged that these two outsourced manufacturers will be unable to re-build their factories and supply any products to Jot, or to their other customers, until at least the start of 2013. The two outsourced manufacturers produced products YY and ZZ for Jot and had not manufactured any of these products in 2012 before the earthquake occurred. The planned data for these two products is as follows:

	Forecast volumes required for 2012	Selling price	Current contracted manufacturing charge to Jot
	Units	€ per unit	€ per unit
Product YY	120,000	9.00	7.05
Product ZZ	30,000	12.00	7.44

Over the last 2 weeks, Michael Werner, Operations Director, has invited tenders from outsourced manufacturers for products YY and ZZ for delivery of products to meet sales forecasts for 2012.

All of Jot's existing outsourced manufacturers *except one* (Manufacturer A), have confirmed that they do <u>not</u> have any spare capacity to manufacture any additional products for Jot in 2012.

Michael Werner has narrowed down the tenders received from outsourced manufacturers to three alternative outsourced manufacturers, which are summarised as follows:

		Manufacturer A	Manufacturer B	Manufacturer C
Current manufacturer for Jot		Yes	No	No
Tendered manufacturing charge per unit:				
Product YY	€ per unit	8.00	6.60	7.05
Product ZZ	€ per unit	7.60	6.60	7.75
Manufacturing set-up costs to be charged to Jot:				
Product YY	€	Zero (in unit cost)	€60,000	€12,000
Product ZZ	€	Zero (in unit cost)	€30,000	€12,000
Shipping & transportation cost	€ per unit	€0.40	€0.60	€0.02
Location		China (near to earthquake area)	A different Asian country	Eastern Europe
Quality of production (established from initial tests and references)		Reasonable	Reasonable	Very good
Jot's view of each company's corporate social responsibility (CSR) status		Some problems	Some problems	Acceptable
Maximum available capacity in 2012 (for both products YY and ZZ in total in any combination)		120,000 units	180,000 units	100,000 units

Inventory

The accounts for the year ended 31 December 2011 are currently being audited. The inventory valuation in the Statement of Financial Position is €542,000 which is net of a write-down reserve of €124,000 in respect of some slow moving products. However, the external auditors are concerned about the valuation of three specific slow-moving products, which have already been written-down in value. These are shown in the table below:

Products	Inventory volumes Units	Current written-down valuation € per unit
Product BB	4,900	6.30
Product CC	2,680	12.50
Product FF	1,200	7.00

At the start of each calendar year any unsold inventory for products which Boris Hepp, Sales Director, considers are out of date are offered to Jot's customers at substantially reduced prices to clear the inventory of them. This has not been done this year.

One of the external auditors has met with Boris Hepp about these three products. Boris Hepp stated that he considers that he could sell the remaining products BB and CC at the following revised values but that product FF was "worthless".

- Product BB – revised valuation €2.50 per unit
- Product CC – revised valuation €5.00 per unit

The auditor reported the outcome of his meeting with Boris Hepp to Tani Grun and the auditor has insisted that Tani Grun amends the accounts for the year ended 31 December 2011 to reflect these reduced inventory values.

Tani Grun is worried about the extent of these revised inventory valuations. She simply does not believe Boris Hepp's very pessimistic valuations. Tani Grun has told Boris Hepp that he must revise the valuations to a higher level and that he must inform the auditors that his comments and valuations were incorrect.

End of unseen material

This page is blank

APPLICABLE MATHS TABLES AND FORMULAE

Present value table

Present value of 1.00 unit of currency, that is $(1 + r)^{-n}$ where r = interest rate; n = number of periods until payment or receipt.

Periods	Interest rates (r)									
(n)	1%	2%	3%	4%	5%	6%	7%	8%	9%	10%
1	0.990	0.980	0.971	0.962	0.952	0.943	0.935	0.926	0.917	0.909
2	0.980	0.961	0.943	0.925	0.907	0.890	0.873	0.857	0.842	0.826
3	0.971	0.942	0.915	0.889	0.864	0.840	0.816	0.794	0.772	0.751
4	0.961	0.924	0.888	0.855	0.823	0.792	0.763	0.735	0.708	0.683
5	0.951	0.906	0.863	0.822	0.784	0.747	0.713	0.681	0.650	0.621
6	0.942	0.888	0.837	0.790	0.746	0705	0.666	0.630	0.596	0.564
7	0.933	0.871	0.813	0.760	0.711	0.665	0.623	0.583	0.547	0.513
8	0.923	0.853	0.789	0.731	0.677	0.627	0.582	0.540	0.502	0.467
9	0.914	0.837	0.766	0.703	0.645	0.592	0.544	0.500	0.460	0.424
10	0.905	0.820	0.744	0.676	0.614	0.558	0.508	0.463	0.422	0.386
11	0.896	0.804	0.722	0.650	0.585	0.527	0.475	0.429	0.388	0.350
12	0.887	0.788	0.701	0.625	0.557	0.497	0.444	0.397	0.356	0.319
13	0.879	0.773	0.681	0.601	0.530	0.469	0.415	0.368	0.326	0.290
14	0.870	0.758	0.661	0.577	0.505	0.442	0.388	0.340	0.299	0.263
15	0.861	0.743	0.642	0.555	0.481	0.417	0.362	0.315	0.275	0.239
16	0.853	0.728	0.623	0.534	0.458	0.394	0.339	0.292	0.252	0.218
17	0.844	0.714	0.605	0.513	0.436	0.371	0.317	0.270	0.231	0.198
18	0.836	0.700	0.587	0.494	0.416	0.350	0.296	0.250	0.212	0.180
19	0.828	0.686	0.570	0.475	0.396	0.331	0.277	0.232	0.194	0.164
20	0.820	0.673	0.554	0.456	0.377	0.312	0.258	0.215	0.178	0.149

Periods	Interest rates (r)									
(n)	11%	12%	13%	14%	15%	16%	17%	18%	19%	20%
1	0.901	0.893	0.885	0.877	0.870	0.862	0.855	0.847	0.840	0.833
2	0.812	0.797	0.783	0.769	0.756	0.743	0.731	0.718	0.706	0.694
3	0.731	0.712	0.693	0.675	0.658	0.641	0.624	0.609	0.593	0.579
4	0.659	0.636	0.613	0.592	0.572	0.552	0.534	0.516	0.499	0.482
5	0.593	0.567	0.543	0.519	0.497	0.476	0.456	0.437	0.419	0.402
6	0.535	0.507	0.480	0.456	0.432	0.410	0.390	0.370	0.352	0.335
7	0.482	0.452	0.425	0.400	0.376	0.354	0.333	0.314	0.296	0.279
8	0.434	0.404	0.376	0.351	0.327	0.305	0.285	0.266	0.249	0.233
9	0.391	0.361	0.333	0.308	0.284	0.263	0.243	0.225	0.209	0.194
10	0.352	0.322	0.295	0.270	0.247	0.227	0.208	0.191	0.176	0.162
11	0.317	0.287	0.261	0.237	0.215	0.195	0.178	0.162	0.148	0.135
12	0.286	0.257	0.231	0.208	0.187	0.168	0.152	0.137	0.124	0.112
13	0.258	0.229	0.204	0.182	0.163	0.145	0.130	0.116	0.104	0.093
14	0.232	0.205	0.181	0.160	0.141	0.125	0.111	0.099	0.088	0.078
15	0.209	0.183	0.160	0.140	0.123	0.108	0.095	0.084	0.079	0.065
16	0.188	0.163	0.141	0.123	0.107	0.093	0.081	0.071	0.062	0.054
17	0.170	0.146	0.125	0.108	0.093	0.080	0.069	0.060	0.052	0.045
18	0.153	0.130	0.111	0.095	0.081	0.069	0.059	0.051	0.044	0.038
19	0.138	0.116	0.098	0.083	0.070	0.060	0.051	0.043	0.037	0.031
20	0.124	0.104	0.087	0.073	0.061	0.051	0.043	0.037	0.031	0.026

Cumulative present value of 1.00 unit of currency per annum, Receivable or Payable at the end of each year for n years $\left[\dfrac{1-(1+r)^{-n}}{r}\right]$

Periods	Interest rates (r)									
(n)	1%	2%	3%	4%	5%	6%	7%	8%	9%	10%
1	0.990	0.980	0.971	0.962	0.952	0.943	0.935	0.926	0.917	0.909
2	1.970	1.942	1.913	1.886	1.859	1.833	1.808	1.783	1.759	1.736
3	2.941	2.884	2.829	2.775	2.723	2.673	2.624	2.577	2.531	2.487
4	3.902	3.808	3.717	3.630	3.546	3.465	3.387	3.312	3.240	3.170
5	4.853	4.713	4.580	4.452	4.329	4.212	4.100	3.993	3.890	3.791
6	5.795	5.601	5.417	5.242	5.076	4.917	4.767	4.623	4.486	4.355
7	6.728	6.472	6.230	6.002	5.786	5.582	5.389	5.206	5.033	4.868
8	7.652	7.325	7.020	6.733	6.463	6.210	5.971	5.747	5.535	5.335
9	8.566	8.162	7.786	7.435	7.108	6.802	6.515	6.247	5.995	5.759
10	9.471	8.983	8.530	8.111	7.722	7.360	7.024	6.710	6.418	6.145
11	10.368	9.787	9.253	8.760	8.306	7.887	7.499	7.139	6.805	6.495
12	11.255	10.575	9.954	9.385	8.863	8.384	7.943	7.536	7.161	6.814
13	12.134	11.348	10.635	9.986	9.394	8.853	8.358	7.904	7.487	7.103
14	13.004	12.106	11.296	10.563	9.899	9.295	8.745	8.244	7.786	7.367
15	13.865	12.849	11.938	11.118	10.380	9.712	9.108	8.559	8.061	7.606
16	14.718	13.578	12.561	11.652	10.838	10.106	9.447	8.851	8.313	7.824
17	15.562	14.292	13.166	12.166	11.274	10.477	9.763	9.122	8.544	8.022
18	16.398	14.992	13.754	12.659	11.690	10.828	10.059	9.372	8.756	8.201
19	17.226	15.679	14.324	13.134	12.085	11.158	10.336	9.604	8.950	8.365
20	18.046	16.351	14.878	13.590	12.462	11.470	10.594	9.818	9.129	8.514

Periods	Interest rates (r)									
(n)	11%	12%	13%	14%	15%	16%	17%	18%	19%	20%
1	0.901	0.893	0.885	0.877	0.870	0.862	0.855	0.847	0.840	0.833
2	1.713	1.690	1.668	1.647	1.626	1.605	1.585	1.566	1.547	1.528
3	2.444	2.402	2.361	2.322	2.283	2.246	2.210	2.174	2.140	2.106
4	3.102	3.037	2.974	2.914	2.855	2.798	2.743	2.690	2.639	2.589
5	3.696	3.605	3.517	3.433	3.352	3.274	3.199	3.127	3.058	2.991
6	4.231	4.111	3.998	3.889	3.784	3.685	3.589	3.498	3.410	3.326
7	4.712	4.564	4.423	4.288	4.160	4.039	3.922	3.812	3.706	3.605
8	5.146	4.968	4.799	4.639	4.487	4.344	4.207	4.078	3.954	3.837
9	5.537	5.328	5.132	4.946	4.772	4.607	4.451	4.303	4.163	4.031
10	5.889	5.650	5.426	5.216	5.019	4.833	4.659	4.494	4.339	4.192
11	6.207	5.938	5.687	5.453	5.234	5.029	4.836	4.656	4.486	4.327
12	6.492	6.194	5.918	5.660	5.421	5.197	4.988	7.793	4.611	4.439
13	6.750	6.424	6.122	5.842	5.583	5.342	5.118	4.910	4.715	4.533
14	6.982	6.628	6.302	6.002	5.724	5.468	5.229	5.008	4.802	4.611
15	7.191	6.811	6.462	6.142	5.847	5.575	5.324	5.092	4.876	4.675
16	7.379	6.974	6.604	6.265	5.954	5.668	5.405	5.162	4.938	4.730
17	7.549	7.120	6.729	6.373	6.047	5.749	5.475	5.222	4.990	4.775
18	7.702	7.250	6.840	6.467	6.128	5.818	5.534	5.273	5.033	4.812
19	7.839	7.366	6.938	6.550	6.198	5.877	5.584	5.316	5.070	4.843
20	7.963	7.469	7.025	6.623	6.259	5.929	5.628	5.353	5.101	4.870

FORMULAE

Valuation Models

(i) Irredeemable preference share, paying a constant annual dividend, d, in perpetuity, where P_0 is the ex-div value:

$$P_0 = \frac{d}{k_{pref}}$$

(ii) Ordinary (Equity) share, paying a constant annual dividend, d, in perpetuity, where P_0 is the ex-div value:

$$P_0 = \frac{d}{k_e}$$

(iii) Ordinary (Equity) share, paying an annual dividend, d, growing in perpetuity at a constant rate, g, where P_0 is the ex-div value:

$$P_0 = \frac{d_1}{k_e - g} \text{ or } P_0 = \frac{d_0[1 + g]}{k_e - g}$$

(iv) Irredeemable (Undated) debt, paying annual after tax interest, $i\,(1-t)$, in perpetuity, where P_0 is the ex-interest value:

$$P_0 = \frac{i[1 - t]}{k_{dnet}}$$

or, without tax:

$$P_0 = \frac{i}{k_d}$$

(v) Future value of S, of a sum X, invested for n periods, compounded at $r\%$ interest:

$$S = X[1 + r]^n$$

(vi) Present value of £1 payable or receivable in n years, discounted at $r\%$ per annum:

$$PV = \frac{1}{[1 + r]^n}$$

(vii) Present value of an annuity of £1 per annum, receivable or payable for n years, commencing in one year, discounted at $r\%$ per annum:

$$PV = \frac{1}{r}\left[1 - \frac{1}{[1 + r]^n}\right]$$

(viii) Present value of £1 per annum, payable or receivable in perpetuity, commencing in one year, discounted at $r\%$ per annum:

$$PV = \frac{1}{r}$$

(ix)   Present value of £1 per annum, receivable or payable, commencing in one year, growing in perpetuity at a constant rate of $g\%$ per annum, discounted at $r\%$ per annum:

$$PV = \frac{1}{r - g}$$

Cost of Capital

(i)   Cost of irredeemable preference capital, paying an annual dividend, d, in perpetuity, and having a current ex-div price P_0:

$$k_{pref} = \frac{d}{P_0}$$

(ii)   Cost of irredeemable debt capital, paying annual net interest, $i\,(1 - t)$, and having a current ex-interest price P_0:

$$k_{dnet} = \frac{i[1 - t]}{P_0}$$

(iii)   Cost of ordinary (equity) share capital, paying an annual dividend, d, in perpetuity, and having a current ex-div price P_0:

$$k_e = \frac{d}{P_0}$$

(iv)   Cost of ordinary (equity) share capital, having a current ex-div price, P_0, having just paid a dividend, d_0, with the dividend growing in perpetuity by a constant $g\%$ per annum:

$$k_e = \frac{d_1}{P_0} + g \;\; \text{or} \;\; k_e = \frac{d_0[1 + g]}{P_0} + g$$

(v)   Cost of ordinary (equity) share capital, using the CAPM:

$$k_e = R_f + [R_m - R_f]ß$$

(vi)   Weighted average cost of capital, k_0:

$$k_0 = k_e \left[\frac{V_E}{V_E + V_D} \right] + k_d \left[\frac{V_D}{V_E + V_D} \right]$$

T4 – Test of Professional Competence - Part B Case Study Examination

March 2012

T4 – Part B Case Study Examination
Suggested solution
March 2012

Suggested Solution to Question 1a
This report, at just over 4,700 (excluding appendices), represents a comprehensive answer that would score highly. Tutor guidance has been provided for some sections to highlight key aspects that students should note. The highlighted sections show areas that differentiate an answer that would score highly from one that would just pass. When the highlighted sections are removed, the report would be just over 3,200 words.

This is just one of many possible solutions.

REPORT TO JON GRUN, MANAGING DIRECTOR OF JOT REGARDING THE MAIN ISSUES FACING THE COMPANY AND POTENTIAL STRATEGIES FOR THE FUTURE

CONTENTS

Prepared by: An.Accountant
Date: Today.

1 Introduction

Jot has an aggressive 5 year growth plan that if achieved would almost double sales revenue and see operating profit rise by over 150%. Key to achieving its forecast will be maintaining its differentiating factor of quality electronic toys and attracting orders from key retailers and wholesalers through effective marketing strategies.

However, it will also be necessary to exercise good cost control in order to protect profitability. The KPMG/Ipos Retail Think Tank reported in January 2012 that 'the UK's retail health is now considered to be worse than it was during the 2008 credit crunch'. With a similar economic outlook across Europe, Jot's margins will be threatened by increased pressure from the powerful retailers (as per Porter's Five Forces) as they seek to reduce costs and attract customers.

> *A generic introduction is unlikely to score any specific marks in the marking criteria.*
>
> *However by tailoring the introduction to the unseen information and bringing in a technical model and a diversity example this could now score up to 1 technical, 1 application and 1 diversity mark.*

2 Terms of reference

As a Management Accountant employed by Jot, the author of this report is responsible for prioritising, analysing and evaluating the issues facing Jot and making appropriate recommendations.

> *Although a terms of reference adds some professionalism to your report, it adds very little it terms of actual marks (1 integration mark at best). You are therefore advised to keep it as short as possible.*

3 Prioritisation of main issues facing JOT

The following issues have been prioritised from the SWOT analysis in Appendix A:

3.1 Manufacturing problems

The most important issue is the potential disruption to supply brought about by the recent earthquake in China. The affected outsourced manufacturers were scheduled to produce just over 17% of Jot's 2012 forecast sales units and so it is important to secure availability in alternative manufacturers to avoid a loss of sales and possible reputational damage. That so few manufacturers have spare capacity makes this an urgent decision to make.

It is vital for management to decide on a course of action to restore the supply whilst being mindful of the impact on profit and reputation, whether related to the quality of the product or CSR issues.

3.2 Quality problem

The second most important issue is to decide what action should be taken regarding the quality problems identified on the action based figures. It is necessary to balance the potential longer-term reputational damage against the financial impact of reproducing the sub-standard units.

Whilst this issue could be regarded as having a similar level of urgency as the manufacturing problems, a lesser number of units are affected meaning a lower impact overall. For this reason the issue has been prioritised second.

3.3 VP "own brand" proposal

The third most important issue facing Jot is to evaluate the proposal made by VP for Jot to manufacture their own-brand products. VP currently account for 20% of all sales made and a stronger relationship with them could be instrumental in Jot achieving its ambitious five-year plan.

Although this issue is of significant impact to the business, the quality problem must be resolved as if Jot's reputation were to be damaged, VP may no longer be willing to strike a deal.

Management need to assess the impact of the proposal on both profitability and cash flow before deciding whether to proceed.

3.4 Marketing material

The fourth most important issue is the misleading marketing material. Not only does this have the potential to create customer dissatisfaction, leading to reputational damage, it is also creating conflict within the Board and raising concerns about the culture within the business.

Management must decide how to resolve the external issue in the short-term as well as addressing the internal cultural problems to ensure such an issue does not reoccur.

Although the external issue is the more serious, this only affects one product line at present. It is equally a fairly commonplace practice within the industry and so is unlikely to cause as much reputational damage as the quality problems.

3.5 Other issues

The issue relating to inventory valuation reported by the auditor is a historic, internal issue that is not viewed as a key business issue. However, the financial impact will need to be assessed. The ethical implication associated with the information supplied to the auditor is discussed in section 8 of this report.

The prioritisation of issues in this paper is difficult as many of the issues can be justified as having high impact and urgency. As usual, thinking through the long-term impact rather than just focusing on the short-term is important (as we see with the quality problem and considering the potential for longer-term reputational damage). You may have decided to prioritise the inventory problem as a business issue, and relegate the marketing material to an ethical issue. This would be perfectly acceptable.

Having said this, the thing that will have the greatest impact on your overall score is taking too much time worrying about your prioritisation. Remember, this is only worth five marks in total.

---

4 Manufacturing problems

4.1 Impact

Uncontrollable factors such as natural disasters have the potential to significantly disrupt the supply chain as was seen by many Japanese manufacturers such as Toyota and Sony immediately after the Japanese earthquake and tsunami in 2011. This is particularly true when production is concentrated in one specific country or area.

The direct impact on Jot will be less due to the seasonal trend in toy sales, with over 50% of sales taking place in the final quarter. However, as existing products within Jot's range, there will be a demand for these products prior to Q4 and it will be necessary to re-establish production as soon as possible.

4.2 Analysis of alternative options

When considering the three alternative manufacturers short-listed by Michael, there are a number of factors to consider.

Financial considerations

Assuming that the original suppliers were not charging any set-up costs, and that the shipping and transportation costs were the same as for manufacturer A, these two products were expected to deliver a profit of €310,800 (see appendix B).

Given the respective tendered manufacturing charges, transportation costs and set-up costs, appendix B shows that this profitability could be fractionally improved to €313,000 if production was scheduled as:

Manufacturer C – 100,000 units of Product YY

Manufacturer A – 20,000 units of Product YY

Manufacturer A – 30,000 units of Product ZZ

From a purely financial perspective, this is the optimum production plan. However, this fails to consider a number of other non-financial factors.

Quality and CSR reputation

Jot has differentiated itself on the basis of high quality electronic toys. Therefore, manufacturer C would fit best with this strategy as well as with the stated intention to improve the company's performance in the area of CSR.

However, manufacturer A is an existing supplier, suggesting that a rating of 'reasonable' quality and 'some problems' for CSR status, would not be out of step with Jot's existing set up. Where issues may arise is with product YY where the manufacturing will be split between a supplier assessed as being of 'very good' quality and one assessed as 'reasonable'. This could lead to inconsistencies in the items hitting the shelves and could lead to complaints.

Location

In addition to their 'acceptable' CSR assessment, C's location in Eastern Europe will also help to reduce Jot's carbon footprint as the goods will not have to travel so far. Additionally, a 'near-shoring' option could help to pave the way for new business model in the future. Analysts BCG are predicting that wage rates in China could grow by as much as 13% per annum over the next five years meaning that the company will be forced to identify other manufacturing locations in order to protect margins and achieve the five-year plan. Manufacturer A's proximity to the earthquake zone does bring risks of further disruption.

Set-up costs

The profitability of the production schedule suggested is affected by the high set-up costs being charged by manufacturer B. If it was possible to reduce these set-up costs, or to convert them into a per unit charge, then it may be possible to improve the profitability still further.

Complexity of supply chain

The production schedule that would maximise financial return would be a more complex solution than the original arrangements. Scheduling production of one product across two different suppliers will require more careful co-ordination and planning. However, there is no suggestion that this would be beyond the capabilities of Jot's current systems. It would also give the advantage of reducing the risk associated with single sourcing.

Prior experience

The assessment of manufacturers B & C in terms of quality and CSR status is based on tests and references. However, Jot has no prior experience with these suppliers and so it is possible they may take some time to bed in.

4.3   Recommendations

Recommendation

It is recommended that Michael Werner immediately contact manufacturers A & C and schedule production of products YY & ZZ as suggested in the earlier table.

Justification

By placing a large amount of the production (the maximum possible at 100,000 units) with manufacturer C, Jot will help to improve the quality of their products, as well as enhance their CSR credentials and pilot a new 'near-shoring' business model that could be crucial to maintaining future profitability.

The only risks with this recommendation are:

-   The potential inconsistency in the quality of product YY between those manufactured by A and those manufactured by C. This could be overcome by ensuring each sends products to different customers in different countries rather than one customer receiving goods manufactured by two different suppliers.

-   The close proximity of manufacturer A to the earthquake zone. However, the supplier has not been affected by the recent quake and just because it is nearby doesn't necessarily place it at any more risk than any other place now that the risk of after-shocks will have subsided.

Actions to be taken

To help reduce the risk of inconsistencies, Michael Werner should provide very clear specifications of product YY to manufacturer A in an attempt to increase the quality of the product they deliver. He should also insist on inspecting and signing off an initial unit before the product goes into full manufacture. This is all the more important given the recent quality problems seen on the action figures.

More frequent quality checks should be performed on these units as they arrive into Jot's warehouses.

A member of the finance team should investigate the cost of insurance to cover acts of God. Jot has been fortunate on this occasion as it has been possible to re-schedule production. If such a disaster occurred later in the year, the financial cost to the company could be a lot more.

> _This is an example of a 'multiple proposal': where a problem is presented alongside some alternative solutions. With such an issue your role is to analyse the alternatives presented. Discussing each in turn can sometimes be inefficient, especially if it leads to repetition of points, as would have been the case here. An alternative approach is to identify key factors that might influence a decision and base your analysis around these instead._

5   Quality problem

5.1   Impact

Michael Porter identified two main strategies a company could follow to achieve competitive advantage: cost leadership or differentiation. Jot pursues a strategy of differentiation based on its high quality toys. Using this strategy it has been able to win orders from large multinational retailers as well as secure license agreements for popular films and TV programmes.

Procurement is one of the key secondary activities within the value chain. By pushing manufacturer Q into supplying at the lowest possible price, Jot was acting more as a cost leader, and was not being consistent with its differentiation strategy. In addition, this action presents an ethical issue, as undue pressure was placed on the supplier to reduce their prices.

If a Jot toy failed to deliver on the expected quality, this would undermine Jot's differentiation strategy. Customers and consumers alike may be left disappointed and Jot's ability to charge a premium price in the future will reduce, leaving them 'stuck in the middle'.

5.2 Analysis of alternative courses of action

Continue with the existing products

The easiest and cheapest option would be to allow manufacturer Q to continue with the production of the action figure as planned. However this could damage Jot's reputation, both with its customers and with licensing agents meaning they could find it harder to obtain orders and win licenses in the future.

Transfer production to P

Jot could decide to sever all links with Q and transfer production to P. The cost per unit will be €1.10 higher than had been forecast, thereby reducing profit by €88,000. Furthermore, the license fee will need to be paid on the 20,000 manufactured by Q. This amounts to €14,000.

This would result in a better quality toy hitting the shelves but would be financially quite damaging. Equally, the new moulds will take time (and money) to produce, which may push the delivery beyond the dates scheduled. Given the need to have the products in the shops in time for the film's launch, this could be disastrous and may mean that not all 80,000 units are sold.

Finally, manufacturer Q is unlikely to be happy with this approach and could raise a legal claim against Jot for the money owed. Their actions were as a direct result of the pressure placed on them by Jot to reduce prices so walking away from the contract could be perceived as unethical or even illegal.

Re-negotiate with Q

Jot could agree to Q's amended offer of €7 per unit. Although this will reduce the expected profit per unit, it will ensure a suitable quality product that will uphold Jot's reputation. It will also ensure the final products are delivered on time.

Consideration must also be given to the 20,000 units already manufactured. Jot could refuse to pay for any of these units although this would not fit with an intention to continue a business relationship with Q. Alternatively, Jot could negotiate with Q to pay a lesser amount (perhaps even down to cost price). This could be part of the conditions around Q maintaining the contract and would spread the financial impact between the two companies.

It may also be possible to sell on these lower quality items (subject to the quality being sufficient to meet legal requirements) through wholesalers once the initial buzz surrounding the film has subsided. This would prevent cannibalisation of the main sales but would allow some revenue to be earned from these units. However, this runs the risk of causing long-term damage to the Jot brand.

Longer-term prevention

Once the short-term situation is resolved, it will be necessary to amend the procedures to ensure this situation doesn't arise again.

5.3 Recommendations

Recommendation

It is recommended that Jot retains manufacturer Q as the supplier of these licensed action figure toys, at a higher price of €7 per unit. A further 80,000 units should be manufactured and a settlement for the initial 20,000 units negotiated.

The initial 20,000 units should be scrapped in order to protect Jot's reputation.

Tighter control procedures regarding 'signing off' on products should be implemented.

Justification

Meeting the deadline of delivery in time for the film is of paramount importance and so the option of transferring to manufacturer P has been ruled out on this basis.

In order to protect Jot's reputation, the most important thing is to improve the quality of the product, and increasing the per unit price to €7 would appear to be the only option; this is supported by the amount quoted by manufacturer P.

Jot cannot risk its reputation by selling these sub-standard units; the short term revenue raised would be more than offset by reduced sales in the long-term if the Jot brand is devalued.

Errors such as these can cost significant amounts of money, and reduce net cash flow, something that Jot can ill afford. Tightened control procedures that involve an initial sign off of a product (not just the mould) and prevent further units being manufactured until after this sign off has occurred will minimise the future risk.

Actions to be taken

Michael Werner should immediately contact manufacturer Q to discuss the situation. The offer of an amended contract for a further 80,000 units at €7.00 per unit subject to the cancellation of the existing contract and the negotiation of the original 20,000 units being sold at cost should be made.

If agreeable, an initial unit (or batch) should be made, and approved by Michael before any further production takes place. If Q fails to agree to these terms, the contract should be terminated and production transferred to P.

In the longer-term, when suppliers are found for any new products, all contracts should be made conditional on the approval of an initial unit or small batch of items prior to full manufacturing commencing.

> *It would have been acceptable to argue that Jot should transfer production to P on the basis that Q has let them down on the key differentiating issue of quality. There are often alternative answers that would score equally as well provided they are well justified.*

6 VP "own brand" proposal

6.1 Impact

Jot currently has 7 major customers based in Europe and the US that accounted for 68% of its sales in 2011. VP alone accounts for 20% of sales worldwide and over 90% of its sales in the US. Hence VP represents a very major part of Jot's existing business and jeopardising this (by turning down this offer) could see significant reductions in turnover and margin.

Michael Porter identified five key forces that could threaten a company's profit margin, one of which was power of buyers. VP would be viewed as having a high power over Jot, and as such it is able to make demands of Jot that may threaten its ability to earn good margins. This proposal is an excellent example of this, as although it would lead to a significant increase in sales volumes, the increase in profitability is far more modest.

6.2 Analysis of proposal

This proposal can be analysed using Johnson, Scholes and Whittington's framework of suitability, feasibility and acceptability.

Suitability

Jot's five-year plan is targeting sales of 1,405,000 units by 2016. Appendix C shows that if this proposal was accepted, unit sales to VP alone would rise to 734,000 by 2016 (year 4 of the proposed agreement). Assuming sales volumes to existing customers were maintained, the contract would ensure this target was met, and would have VP accounting for nearly 40% of all units sold by this time (734k ÷ (1,405k − 238k + 734k)).

However, as these products would be under the VP own-brand label, this increase in sales wouldn't help to build the Jot brand or enhance the company's image. It would also make Jot extremely reliant on VP in the future.

This sort of relationship is not uncommon in the industry, and often ultimately leads to the retailer acquiring the toy company (for example Chad Valley with Woolworths and later Home Retail Group). It needs to be questioned whether this is a future strategy the Board may want to consider.

Acceptability

Appendix C shows that the proposal has a positive incremental NPV over a five-year period of just over €447,000. Based on a project with no initial outlay, this is a very impressive outcome and would suggest the proposal is acceptable on purely financial grounds.

However, this would represent a significant risk for Jot as so much of its business would be focussed on VP. Much of the positive value in the contract is focused on the later years, with the present value of cash flows in years one and two being negative. The assumption that sales levels will increase by 50% per annum every year throughout the five-year period is a very aggressive assumption. If the actual level turned out to be similar to the 12% growth expected under the existing arrangements, Jot will have given away significant margin for no benefit.

There is also a risk that the Jot brand could become diluted or that other customers might also insist on own brand versions of toys at lower margins.

One mitigating factor is VPs commitment to placing firm orders in March each year and to bearing the risk of any unsold inventory. With the current inventory write off reserve at €124,000 and the auditors proposal to increase this by a further €47,000 (see appendix D), this is a significant transfer of risk.

Feasibility

Perhaps the biggest concern regarding feasibility centres around cash flow. The negative net cash flows in the early years of the projects shows that Jot will actually have less cash coming in as a result of this proposal. Given the critical nature of the company's cash balances, particularly in Q3 and Q4 of a year, this may result in Jot breaching its overdraft limits in 2013 and 2014. There may also be concerns about Jot's ability to handle the additional sales volume. However, as all manufacturing is outsourced, as are the logistics provision, this is unlikely to be a significant concern.

6.3   Recommendations

Recommendation

It is recommended that Jot accept in principle the offer of producing VP's own brand products. However, Jot should attempt to negotiate on key elements of the agreement.

Justification

If the assumptions are to believed, this proposal will yield a significant amount of value for Jot and will more than realise the Board's ambitions for growth. However, there is significant risk if the per annum forecast growth isn't achieved. Inserting additional clauses into the contract relating to the amount that will be spent by VP on marketing these products, and how they will be marketed may help to reduce this risk. A further step would be to introduce the proposed 20% discount on all products in stages when various growth targets are met. As an incentive to accept these revised terms, Jot could offer a greater discount (perhaps 25%) towards the end of the contract if the volumes are as expected.

Actions to be taken

Jon Grun should meet with VP's Procurement Director again, with the revised proposal. It will be important to appear enthusiastic about the venture whilst also presenting the concerns regarding the additional risks for Jot and how Jot feels the revised terms will be of benefit to both parties.

Assuming the revised terms are acceptable, and a contract is signed, the design team will need to commence work on the new product for 2013 as soon as possible. Equally, VP will need to place their 2013 order and Jot's suppliers notified of the increased volumes. Michael Werner should use the increase to secure the anticipated 5% discount, with a view to increasing this further in future years.

> *The use of SFA for this analysis is very effective, in particular at highlighting the risks that Jot would be exposed to. To score higher marks, consider ways in which Jot could mitigate those risks and be prepared to suggest amendments to the deal. Don't forget to view the negotiations from both sides and state what Jot should be prepared to offer in return.*

7 Marketing material

7.1 Impact

As a business grows and moves from an entrepreneurial structure to a functional structure, issues can arise if adequate controls are not introduced and if the culture of the organisation is not well enough established. In particular, decisions may be made that are not congruent with the overall company strategy, as is being seen here. As a result, boardroom conflict could result.

Of key importance here is that customers are being misled and this results in a significant ethical issue. Selling products on the basis of certain features that are not true to life amounts to dubious practice and will not reflect well on Jot and its management.

7.2 Analysis of alternative courses of action

There are short and long term factors (both internal and external) to be considered.

Short-term / External

In the short term it is necessary to decide what to do about the misleading marketing material and packaging. Michael Werner is already investigating the options regarding the packaging and although additional costs may be incurred, changing the packaging would appear to be the best way to safeguard Jot's reputation with the end consumer.

However, this won't address the situation with any customers who have placed orders for this product based on the marketing promotional literature. One option would be to ignore the situation and hope that none of the customers notice. As this product is just one of a large number of products stocked by these companies, it is more than likely that the issue will pass without any significant fallout. It is fairly commonplace within the industry for toy companies to produce adverts that 'exaggerate' the appearance of their toys; however, just because others do it does not mean it is the 'right thing to do'. Very infrequently do advertising standards authorities rule against such promotions, with their focus tending to be on those mis-stating the extent of promotional offers (as was the case when a Sainsbury's commercial was withdrawn after it claimed ALL toys were half-price when in fact it was only toys bought online).

An alternative, and more ethical option, would be to contact all of the customers who have placed orders, explain the mistake that has been made and give them the opportunity to amend their order. Whilst this may result in some orders being lost, it will demonstrate that Jot is a fair and transparent organisation and may enhance relationships in the longer term.

Longer term / Internal

Although Jon could ask for Sonja's resignation, this would be knee-jerk reaction and could lead to motivation problems amongst remaining members of staff. One of the lower levels of Maslow's hierarchy of needs relates to security; if staff perceive that their job might not be secure, and could be lost due to just one mistake, they are unlikely to feel motivated.

This option could also be viewed as unethical and unfair; Sonja's mistake seems comparable with the mistakes made by Michael and his team regarding the quality problems, yet it is not being proposed to ask Michael to resign.

Sonja and her team have made a very positive contribution to Jot since she joined the business. Losing her expertise could be very damaging to Jot's future success.

An alternative option would be to discipline Sonja, by issuing her with a verbal warning. Jot's zero-tolerance policy on misleading advertisements could be explained and a general communication issued to all members of the marketing department laying down specific guidelines for how Jot's toys must be marketed. Sonja could also be provided with training on the importance of business ethics.

7.3 Recommendations

Recommendation

All customers placing orders for this toy should be contacted and given an opportunity to amend their order. This is the ethically preferred approach and is the 'right thing to do'.

Sonja should not be asked to resign. Instead she should receive a verbal warning.

Formal guidelines for the marketing of Jot's products should be written and circulated to all within the marketing department.

Justification

By contacting all customers and explaining the mistake, Jot is showing that it is a good company to do business with.

The loss of Sonja's expertise would be detrimental to Jot's future and could lead to motivational problems within the company. By clearly communicating expectations to both Sonja and the rest of the marketing team, Jot will prevent such an issue arising again, or if it does, there will be a more solid base on which to take action.

Actions to be taken

Boris Hepp should immediately contact all customers to apologise for the mistake and give them a two week window in which they can amend their order.

Jon Grun should meet with Sonja within the next week to explain the culture of Jot, why this mis-selling is not something Jot wants to be associated with, and to issue a formal verbal warning.

Boris and Sonja should work together to write a set of guidelines for the marketing of Jot's products. This should be ready for the next Board meeting so it can be approved before being issued to the relevant staff.

> As a fourth issue it is likely that you may be under time pressure at this point in the exam. To secure marks across the marking criteria it is important to try and fully cover 4 main issues in your report. This will not only impact your judgement and logic marks but also maximise your integration marks by producing a complete report that is fit for purpose.

8 Ethical issues

It is important that a business should take a balanced view of the interests of its various stakeholders. Whilst it is acceptable to pursue shareholder wealth as a primary objective, this should be tempered by due consideration being given to the effect of commercial decisions on other stakeholders. In addition to the undue pressure placed on suppliers (see section 5) and the ethical issues surrounding the mis-leading marketing information (see section 7), the following ethical issue exists:

8.1   Inventory write-down

Tani appears to be placing undue pressure on Boris Hepp to amend his statement to the auditors in order to reduce their proposed write down of inventory. The proposed write-down will reduce operating profit by €47,120 or about 8.6% (see appendix D).

The exertion of pressure in this way represents unethical behaviour as it is forcing Boris to go against his beliefs.

Recommendation

To ensure the integrity of the accounting process Tani should not order Boris to amend his statement but should instead meet with Boris to understand the basis of his assessment and to find out why these products have not been offered to Jot's customers as would normally be done.

If no evidence can be found to support a higher valuation, the proposed adjustment should be made in the accounts.

Finally, from a business perspective, every effort should be made by the sales team to realise some revenue from these items as soon as possible. This will provide the best possible evidence of a higher valuation.

> *With only 10 marks available in total for ethical considerations it is important to cover all of the areas that will score marks as succinctly as possible. You must clearly define and analyse the ethical issue and make a clear recommendation with action points where possible.*
>
> *It is advisable, but not essential, to briefly offer an alternative solution before making your recommendation.*
>
> *In this situation, two ethical issues had been covered within the main body of the report, you could perhaps drop this section altogether. However, there is the opportunity to cover the fifth and final issue here, picking up ethics marks as well as potentially some further judgement and logic marks.*

9   Conclusion

Jot is a successful toy designer but it has an aggressive 5 year growth plan. However, this will not happen if Jot does not protect its reputation by implementing suitable internal control systems to monitor and manage its growth.

> *A conclusion is another section of your report which adds to the professionalism but doesn't actually score many direct marks. Only complete if you have time and keep it brief.*

Appendix A: SWOT ANALYSIS

Strengths

- Strong relationships with Chinese manufacturers providing low cost, high quality production.
- Reputation for quality designs popular with children and parents.
- Strong sales growth of 37% in last two years.

Weaknesses

- *Undue pressure on suppliers to reduce prices has led to quality issues.*
- **Lack of controls to detect quality problems earlier in the production process.**
- ***Lack of appropriate guidance and effective internal controls over the approval of marketing material.***
- Failure to offer unsold inventory to customers at reduced prices.

Opportunities

- **Growth in sales volumes and profit through VP "own brand" proposal.**
- **Potential to increase profit and reduce risk by transferring production of YY & ZZ to other suppliers.**

Threats

- **Potential logistical disruption caused by earthquake in China.**
- ***Additional inventory write-down will reduce profitability and may make securing additional finance harder.***
- Reliance on seven major customers for core business (68% in FY2011).

Appendix B: Manufacturing problems
Current expected profitability:

Product YY: €9 - €7.05 - €0.40 = €1.55 × 120,000   €186,000

Product ZZ: €12 - €7.44 - €0.40 = €4.16 × 30,000   €124,800

Total   €310,800

Note: Assumes no set-up costs and transport costs consistent with manufacturer A.

Updated position:

	Product YY (120,000 units)			Product ZZ (30,000 units)		
	A	B	C	A	B	C
Contribution per unit (€) (selling price – manufacturing charge)	1.00	2.40	1.95	4.40	5.40	4.25
Shipping cost (€)	0.40	0.60	0.02	0.40	0.60	0.02
Profit per unit before set-up costs (€)	0.60	1.80	1.93	4.00	4.80	4.23
Number of units[1]	120,000	120,000	100,000	30,000	30,000	30,000
Total profit before set up costs	72,000	216,000	193,000	120,000	144,000	126,900
Set up costs (€)	-	60,000	12,000	-	30,000	12,000
Profit after set-up costs (€)	72,000	156,000	181,000	120,000	114,000	114,900
Ranking	3	2	1	1	3	2

[1] Based on maximum available capacity for each manufacturer and quantity of goods demanded, excluding combinations of goods (see next step).

Optimum selection to maximise profitability

Product ZZ

30,000 units at Manufacturer A =   €120,000

Product YY

100,000 units at Manufacturer C =   €181,000

20,000 units remaining:

@ A – profit = 20,000 units ×€0.60   €12,000

OR

@ B – revised profit after set up costs =
(€1.80 × 20,000 units) - €60,000 = €24,000 loss. So A is preferred

Total profit   €313,000

Note: Alternative for Product YY

120,000 units at Manufacturer B   €156,000

Since €156,000 < (€181,000 + €12,000), initial option is preferable from a financial perspective.

Appendix C: VP "own brand" proposal calculations

Cost cards:

	Original	**VP own brand**	**Workings**
Selling price	€14.00	€11.20	€14 × 0.8
Cost	€9.50	€9.025	€9.5 × 0.95
Shipping	€0.40	€0.40	
Product margin	€4.10	€1.775	

Note: Product margin in this instance is being used to denote selling price – per unit cost and shipping cost.

Net present value:

	T1	**T2**	**T3**	**T4**	**T5**
Sales levels (units):					
Current (12% p.a. increase)	162,400	181,888	203,715	228,160	255,540
VP (50% p.a. increase)	217,500	326,250	489,375	734,063	1,101,094
	€	€	€	€	€
Current profit (sales level × product margin)	665,840	745,741	835,232	935,456	1,047,714
VP brand profit (sales level × product margin)	386,063	579,094	868,641	1,302,962	1,954,442
Difference	(279,777)	(166,647)	33,409	367,506	906,728
10% discount factor	0.909	0.826	0.751	0.683	0.621
Present value	(254,317)	(137,650)	25,090	251,007	563,078

Net present value = €447,208.

Since NPV is positive the project is financially acceptable.

Note: the cost of new product development has been assumed to equal the €0.25 million fee payable by VP so both have been excluded from the calculation.

Alternative solution

The above solution merges the two options together, taking an opportunity cost approach. It would have been just as acceptable to have calculated two separate NPVs and compared them to reach a decision. This would look as follows:

NPV of maintaining the current contract

	T1	*T2*	*T3*	*T4*	*T5*
Sales levels (units):					
Current (12% p.a. increase)	*162,400*	*181,888*	*203,715*	*228,160*	*255,540*
	€	*€*	*€*	*€*	*€*
Current profit (sales level × product margin)	*665,840*	*745,741*	*835,232*	*935,456*	*1,047,714*
10% discount factor	*0.909*	*0.826*	*0.751*	*0.683*	*0.621*
Present value	*605,249*	*615,982*	*627,259*	*638,916*	*650,630*

NPV = €3,138,036

NPV of manufacturing VP own-brand

	T1	T2	T3	T4	T5
Sales levels (units):					
VP (50% p.a. increase)	217,500	326,250	489,375	734,063	1,101,094
	€	€	€	€	€
VP brand profit (sales level × product margin)	386,063	579,094	868,641	1,302,962	1,954,442
10% discount factor	0.909	0.826	0.751	0.683	0.621
Present value	350,931	478,332	652,349	889,923	1,213,708

NPV = €3,585,243

Net positive NPV of VP own-brand over existing contract = €3,585,243 - €3,138,036 = €447,207

Appendix D: Inventory calculations

Additional write down required of inventory:

Product	Workings	Write down (€)
BB	4,900 × (€6.30 - €2.50)	18,620
CC	2,680 × (€12.50 - €5.00)	20,100
FF	1,200 × €7.00	8,400
Total		47,120

Write down as % of unaudited operating profit result = 8.6%

Suggested Solution to Requirement 1(b)

The aim of this document is to identify the key aspects from your earlier analysis, and present them in a succinct way that outlines the case for a course of action.

This is just one of many possible solutions.

E-mail

To: Jot Management team

From: Accountant

Date: Today

Re: Key criteria for the selection of outsourced manufacturers

Following the recent manufacturing problems after the earthquake in China, and the quality problems experienced on the action figure toy produced by manufacturer Q, I thought it would be useful to summarise the key criteria we should be focusing on when selecting outsourced manufacturers.

Jot's reputation for quality toys is critical to the company's success; quality of product should therefore be the number one criteria.

Price is obviously important. Jot exists to make a profit and with increasing wage pressure in China, this will be more of an issue in the future.

Alongside price are other direct costs such as transportation costs or set-up costs. It is important to factor these into the decision to ensure all factors are considered.

CSR will undoubtedly increase in importance as Jot's major supermarket customers insist on a strong CSR stance within their supply chain. To ensure we achieve our ambitious growth targets we must ensure our supply chain is equally as robust in this area.

For these reasons, it has been decided that the full capacity of manufacturer C will be used to make 100,000 units of product YY, with the remaining 20,000 units being given to manufacturer A, along with the 30,000 units of product ZZ. This will result in profit of €313,000, fractionally more than was originally forecast.

Kind regards

An Accountant.

Appendix 6

Chartered Institute of
Management Accountants

T4 Part B Case Study Exam – March 2012 – Post Exam Guidance Report

General Overview

The main object of this report is to give help to candidates who were not successful in the March 2012 examination relating to the Jot toy case. It is also intended to provide guidance to prospective candidates who plan to take future T4 Part B case study examinations. This report explains the basic rationale behind the case and the suggested approach to each of the assessment criteria. It also provides a brief marking guide, general comments on the candidates' scripts and a statement of common errors, including omissions, which were made by candidates.

This case related to the Jot toy company which was unlisted and whose brand was established in 1998 by husband and wife team Jon and Tani Grun. Jon was the Managing Director and Tani the Finance and IT Director. The toys proved to be very popular and in 2004, Jot began outsourcing all of its manufacturing to a range of companies in China in order to reduce its cost base and to price the toys more competitively. It sold a small product range of 34 toys aimed at two age groups being three to five year olds and five to eight year olds. Jot's products included a range of toys designed by the company for which it held intellectual property rights (IPR's) and also sold some licensed toys for which it paid a license fee to the companies which held the IPR's. It normally launched 5 totally new toys each year. In the year ended 31 December 2011, Jot sold 706,300 toys across the entire product range.

Jot's sales revenue grew by 16% in the year ended 31 December 2010 and by almost 18% in the year ended 31 December 2011. Its toys were sold to toy retailers for between €7 and €38 which were then sold on at a mark-up normally of 50% to 100%.

Jot's revenue in the year ended 31 December 2011 (unaudited) was €9,866,000 and produced an operating profit of €551,000. At 31 December 2011 there were 40,000 shares in issue of €1.00 each nominal value and authorised share capital of 200,000 shares. Jon and Tani Grun each held 30% of the issued shares, the remaining 40% were held by three of the other directors. Jot had three bank loans falling due in January 2014, 2015 and 2020 and had an overdraft limit of €1.5 million which cost the company 12% per year. At 31 December 2011, Jot's overdraft was €960,000.

The ambitious five year plan aimed to increase revenue by 95% and operating profit by 145% over the revenue and operating profit achieved in 2011. Jot also intended to steadily increase the number of new products launched in each of the five years from five in 2011 to 10 by the end of the plan period in 2016. It also proposed to increase the number of countries in which it sold products from 22 in 2011 to 36 in 2016.

The unseen material required the candidate, as Management Accountant of Jot, to provide advice and recommendations to the Managing Director on the issues facing the company. Specifically, the candidate was asked to prepare a report that prioritised, analysed and evaluated the issues facing Jot and make appropriate recommendations. In addition, the candidate was asked to draft an email to Jot's management team which set out the key criteria for the selection of outsourced manufacturers in general, together with a recommendation on which manufacturer (s) should be appointed for two specific products after their manufacture had been disrupted due to an earthquake. The requirement for part (a) was worth 90 marks and part (b) was worth 10 marks.

The T4 assessment matrix has nine criteria, each of which carries between 5 and 30 marks. It should be noted that the Logic criterion has 30 marks associated with it, 20 marks for recommendations given in the answer to part (a) and 10 marks for the answer to part (b). It is important that the candidate earns high marks in the Judgement and Logic criteria as each of these carry 20 marks within part (a). It is also important that the candidate undertakes sufficient analysis to provide a sound base for discussion of the issues from which appropriate and logical recommendations can be made. The analysis should include appropriate financial and numerical calculations, particularly those which are discernable from the unseen examination material which is rewarded within the Application criterion.

The main issues contained in the unseen material were:

1. The loss of two outsourced manufacturers following a recent earthquake. They were unable to manufacture any products for Jot for the remainder of 2012. Therefore new outsourced manufacturers needed to be identified and appointed urgently in order to manufacture two key products (YY and ZZ), which between them were scheduled to total 150,000 units in 2012 representing over 17% of Jot's planned sales in 2012.
2. There was a problem with the quality of a range of licenced action figures produced by one outsourced manufacturer (Q). The current quality was not acceptable and the order of 80,000 needed to be started again. However, it needed to be considered whether the order should have been retained by outsourced manufacturer Q at a higher price than the original contract or whether Jot should have appointed a different outsourced manufacturer (P).
3. A large 5 year contract for the design and production of "own brand" toys for one of Jot's seven main customers, VP was also an important issue. Jot had never produced branded products for any retailer before, only its own "Jot" brand, so this would have been a new venture for the company.
4. A realistic inventory valuation for three slow moving products needed to be established to ensure that the accounts for the year ended 31 December 2011 were accurate and reflected realistic valuations. The valuations proposed by the Sales Director would have resulted in a significant write-down.

There were other issues which candidates could have discussed (and which were given credit within the marking), for example some inaccurate marketing material. However, it was critical that the issues relating to the manufacturing problems and quality problem were fully addressed in the answer. This was because these issues had an immediate impact on Jot and would have seriously affected its reputation, its potential sales and consequently would have impacted adversely on its cash flow.

Format of answers

The format of candidates' answers to part (a) was generally good. Candidates usually began with an introduction leading to very brief terms of reference, prioritisation of issues, followed by discussion of those issues. Ethical issues were discussed and advice given on how to resolve them and then recommendations were made on the issues which had been prioritised. This is the standard way of approaching the examination and generally leads to a logical way of presenting the report.

While the suggested format of recommendation, justification and actions to be taken was again applied when candidates prepared their recommendations, it needs to be made clear again that candidates are not expected just to repeat in their recommendations what they have stated in their discussion earlier in the report. In the discussion section, the candidate should consider alternative approaches to resolving any particular issue raised. In the recommendations section the candidate should select the approach which he or she wishes to recommend, justifying why this has been selected from the range of alternatives and then explain the follow-on action which is necessary to implement the recommendation. Low marks will be awarded in the recommendations section for simply repeating what has already been said earlier in the discussion as these marks will have already been awarded under the Judgement criterion.

Finally, most candidates provided a brief conclusion. The appendices were usually contained in an Excel file at the end of the report itself. Part (b) was often included as an appendix to the report, which is acceptable.

Once again, some candidates failed to address part (b) at all. Others missed the main point of it by concentrating only on the two products YY and ZZ. Part (b) is worth 10% of the marks. This is not a new requirement and reference has been made to it in each of the previous Post Examination Guidance reports since it was introduced. Candidates are reminded that guidance exists on the CIMA website relating to the format of the part (b) assessment which will be required. See:
http://www.cimaglobal.com/Documents/Student%20docs/2010%20syllabus%20docs/T4/Supp ort%20Guide%20%20T4%20Part%20B.pdf

Discussion of general candidate performance under each assessment criteria

It is appropriate to make at this point two general comments. The first is that this examination demonstrated many candidates' unwillingness to demonstrate competence in management accounting by not addressing or refusing to think around the specific issues contained in the unseen material. For such candidates, it is as if they arrived at the examination with a pre-conceived notion of what the examination would contain and were not prepared to think about what the implications for the Jot were when the actual issues in the unseen material differed from their pre-conceptions.

The second comment is that many candidates provided recommendations which were commercially unsound and did not consider the wider view for Jot. For example, the opportunity existed for Jot to engage more than one outsourced manufacturer so that all 150,000 units of YY and ZZ, as required by Jot, were produced. However, many candidates restricted their answers to the strict limits applied by each manufacturer, recommended the appointment of either manufacturers A or C (but not both) and consequently reduced overall contribution and profit to Jot. Others recommended appointing manufacturers to produce volumes which were beyond their capacity. Such recommendations were not well rewarded in the marking as they demonstrated a lack of understanding and competence and disregard for data provided in the unseen material.

T4 Assessment Criteria

	Maximum marks available
Analysis of Issues (25 marks)	
Technical	5
Application	15
Diversity	5
Strategic Choices (35 marks)	
Focus	5
Prioritisation	5
Judgement	20
Ethics	5
Recommendations (40 marks)	
Logic	30
Integration	5
Ethics	5

Analysis of issues

PART (a):

Technical:

Rationale:

The purpose of this criterion is to assess the use of relevant theoretical techniques and frameworks to aid the analysis of the case material.

Suggested Approach:

It is recommended that candidates present their technical knowledge either in the form of appendices to the main report, (in an Excel spread-sheet) or the relevant theories could be discussed within the report where appropriate. It is usually better to present the technical knowledge within the report where possible as it is then applied to the subject matter of the case material.

Marking Guide:

Marks are awarded for technical models and theories which are relevant to the case. It is usually appropriate to limit the technical knowledge displayed to 5 separate items.

Commentary:

Most candidates were able to display sound technical knowledge principally comprising a SWOT analysis, Johnson, Scholes and Whittington's Suitability Acceptability Feasibility (SAF) framework, the Mendelow matrix and a range of other strategic planning models. As usual, most candidates performed well under this criterion. It was pleasing to note again that many candidates were more discerning over their use of strategic planning models, limiting their use to a few relevant models.

Common errors:

Once again, some candidates think simply stating a model is enough. It isn't; it must be applied to the content of the case material. One noticeable example was the production of the template for the PEST or PESTEL model but then not stating how the headings apply to Jot in particular. There are still occasionally candidates who do not produce a SWOT analysis. It is always appropriate to produce a SWOT analysis. It would be expected that the main issues to be discussed in part (a) of the answer will feature somewhere within the SWOT analysis which should not be too long but should contain the main issues affecting the case organisation.

It is often better for candidates to use the technical knowledge as an illustration within the actual report itself, rather than as an appendix. For example, many candidates applied the Johnson, Scholes and Whittington SAF model or Mendelow's stakeholder analysis within their actual discussion of the issues contained in the case, rather than as an abstract appendix. This approach is welcomed.

Application:

Rationale:

The point of the Application criterion is to assess how well candidates use the techniques, frameworks and calculations to support their analysis of the issues in the unseen material and to form a sound basis for their subsequent recommendations.

Suggested approach:

Candidates are advised to ensure that they apply relevant models, techniques and frameworks correctly, given the unseen case material. Thus it is important that rather than just stating the model or framework, it is presented in such a way that it provides information which is relevant to the case, enabling candidates to use the information in their discussion of the issues. This also applies in respect of calculations, which should be relevant to the information given in the particular case. There was a lot of scope for relevant calculations to be made in this case examination.

Marking guide:

Marks are available for the relevant application of techniques, models, frameworks and supporting calculations but only if the candidate applies them to the specific case. Marks were awarded for the application of models to the case material and for relevant calculations, principally a comparison of the minimum cost or maximum profit, which could be achieved by appointing a mix of the outsourced manufacturers for products YY and ZZ and a comparison of the net present values which could be achieved by either accepting the VP "own brand" proposal or not accepting it.

There were a lot of marks available for valid calculations and candidates who carried out sufficient accurate numerical analysis were well rewarded. Candidates who did not adequately grasp the numerical and financial implications within the case demonstrated their general lack of understanding of the issues. Those who presented inaccurate calculations showed they lacked the competence which would be expected from a management accountant and therefore lost the opportunity to gain marks as did those who failed to make any attempt at some or all of the calculations. Furthermore, flawed calculations affected candidates' ability to accurately discuss the alternative courses of action and to prepare financially sound recommendations.

Commentary:

Most candidates provided a SWOT analysis. It is essential that candidates take full account of the information contained within the unseen material and incorporate this into their SWOT analysis. Candidates are reminded, again, that it is the unseen material on which they should base their answers and should ensure that all the prioritised issues are included in the appropriate quadrant of the SWOT. Pre-learned SWOT's derived from the pre-seen material are of little value in the examination itself. SWOT analyses should not be too long but should concentrate on the essential issues which affect the case company. Most candidates managed to provide some additional theoretical analysis by using appropriate models.

Common errors:

There were very few errors relating to the non-financial area, the only one worthy of note is the failure to recognise the quality problem as a weakness or a threat or the manufacturing problems as a threat to Jot within the SWOT analysis.

There were many errors in the calculations. This never fails to surprise the markers given that detailed and soundly prepared technical calculations are usually required in order to pass earlier papers in the syllabus. How is it that candidates can progress to T4 and yet fail to undertake straight forward management accounting and financial management calculations? Failure to make a satisfactory attempt at such calculations will seriously jeopardise a candidate's likelihood of passing the T4 examination.

The following errors relate to the numerical and financial calculations.

Net Present Values relating to "own brand" proposal from VP:

- Timing of cash flows
- Not taking account of shipping costs

- Incorrect calculation of forecast sales units
- Failure to show the difference between the two NPV calculations
- Non-completion of the NPV calculations
- Only completing one and not the other NPV calculation
- Completing one NPV calculation by taking the differences in volumes but then not accounting for the differences in selling prices or unit costs
- Belief that the €250k design fee was income to Jot, without recognising that it would cover cash costs incurred and therefore was not relevant to the NPV calculation
- Adding the units of manufacture in to the financial values in the calculations, (which is just careless)

Manufacturing problems calculations:

- Confusion regarding the distribution of the volumes for products YY and ZZ, that is some candidates got them the wrong way round
- Failure to recognise the capacity constraints
- Ignoring the set-up costs
- Calculating the set-up costs as a per unit cost and then changing the number of units to be manufactured by, say, Manufacturer B to only 20,000 units and ignoring that the set-up costs had been calculated on a larger number of units
- Failure to recognise that production could have been split across different manufacturers
- Making different assumptions about the distribution of products YY and ZZ contrary to what was contained in the unseen case material, for example halving the capacity available from each manufacturer
- Failure to complete the calculation altogether
- Simply repeating the parameters for the calculations to be made without actually doing it

Other calculations:

- Not calculating the financial effect accurately of the various options for resolving the Quality problem by using either outsourced manufacturer Q or P
- Not calculating the effect of the inventory write-downs accurately
- Some candidates did not include the complete write-down of product FF in the inventory write-down calculations.

Many of these errors are careless and some relate to specific management accounting principles. Such inaccuracies are unacceptable. **Candidates must realise that to demonstrate their competence they must provide accurate calculations (numerical and financial) in any report they produce. Any report which provides inaccuracy in its numerical or financial content will always lose the confidence of the reader.** It is critical that candidates produce accurate calculations in their answers as these will inform later discussion of the issues and form part of the basis of their recommendations. Remember, calculations are not just about gaining marks in Application, as weak or flawed calculations will affect the credibility of the entire report.

Diversity:

Rationale:

This criterion seeks to assess knowledge and understanding of relevant real life situations in the same or similar context as that in which the case is set. It also assesses the recognition of commercial or organisational issues relevant to the case material whether or not they occur within the same industry.

Suggested approach:

Candidates should seek to introduce relevant examples at the point where they discuss the issue in their answer. Typically, this may occur in the introduction, the prioritisation section, discussion of the issues, ethics or within the recommendations. The main point is that a candidate should seek to bring in the relevant example at the point which enables him or her to elaborate or emphasise the issue which is being considered within the answer. A long list of examples, which merely illustrate the same point being made, even if in different places in the script, including the introduction, will not earn any more than a single mark.

Marking guide:

Essentially, there is one mark available for each relevant example given, providing it is clearly stated why it is relevant. Additionally, general discussion of many real life companies in the introduction will not attract more than one mark, as they have not been related to the issues raised in the unseen material. The candidate needs to explain why the example is relevant to the point being made.

Commentary:

This was generally satisfactory with many good examples of toy companies and manufacturers of "own brands" from around the world being cited.

Common errors:

Some candidates gave few or no examples in their answers which is surprising for an industry which has a large supply of good examples.

Strategic choices

Focus:

Rationale:

This criterion requires candidates to select the business issues that are regarded as the most important and which will be discussed further within the answer.

Suggested approach:

This is not a section of the report as such. Marks are awarded based on the issues which are contained and discussed within the report.

Marking guide:

There are five marks available for this criterion even if there are not five separate issues contained in the unseen material. It is for the candidate to determine the most relevant issues in the case that should be discussed. As it happened, there were four main issues, excluding the ethical issues, in the unseen material.

Commentary:

Most candidates were able to identify appropriate issues in the case and therefore gain marks under this criterion.

Common errors:

There were four main business issues in this case, being the manufacturing problems, the quality problem, the VP proposal and the realistic inventory value. The marketing material was not considered to be a major issue but marks were awarded under Focus (and Judgment and Logic) if this issue was discussed in the report. Candidates were awarded marks in

Focus, as well as Judgment and Logic, based upon the comments made, irrespective of the specific heading within their report under which each of the issues had been discussed. Candidates should be aware that if an issue is prioritised (see next section) and then not actually discussed within the report, or simply provided with a heading but with no ensuing discussion, then the focus mark for that particular issue will not be awarded.

Prioritisation:

Rationale:

Under this criterion, the candidate is required to rank the issues and to state clearly and concisely the justification for that ranking. The ranking should reflect the impact of the issues on the particular organisation, which may include its urgency.

Suggested approach:

The priorities should be presented early in the answer under their own heading. The priorities should be set out with the issues ranked as either 1st, 2nd, 3rd etc. Each should be justified with a concise explanation of why the candidate has ranked it in such a position.

Marking guide:

High marks are awarded if the candidate presents the most important issues with a good rationale as to why they are ranked as main priorities. It should be noted that markers do give credit to candidates who make a case for prioritising issues differently from those contained in the suggested answer.

Commentary:

On the whole, candidates are accustomed to producing their rankings and generally present their prioritised issues in an appropriate form. The SWOT analysis, if carefully carried out, should help to clarify which are the most important issues to be addressed. Some candidates presented the marketing material as one of the main issues. This was accepted, even though it was not shown as a main issue within the Suggested Answer.

Common errors:

Most candidates recognised that the manufacturing problems and the quality problems at least featured within the top three issues and were duly given credit. Some however ranked them below the top two without sufficient justification and earned only low marks under this criterion. The "own brand" proposal from VP was important but lacked the urgency of these two other issues.

Judgement:

Rationale:

This criterion assesses the candidates' exercise of commercial and professional judgement in discussing the key issues which were prioritised.

Suggested approach:

It is important that the candidate discusses the impact the prioritised issues have on the organisation and what alternative actions, with reasons, could be taken to address them. This should include a discussion of the relevant supporting analysis drawn from the "Application" criterion. So for example, if a calculation is made within an appendix, for example the NPV of the "own brand" proposal, then it should be used in support of the points made under that relevant heading within this section of the report. The purpose of undertaking the analysis by using appropriate planning models and relevant numerical and financial analysis is so that the findings can then be used to support discussion of the issues. It is appropriate for a candidate to make reference to his or her SWOT analysis when discussing each of the issues, highlighting their importance.

Marking guide:

Marks are awarded for discussing the different aspects of an issue and its impact on the company and also for providing appropriate alternative approaches to resolving it. Clearly, the alternative approaches will receive higher marks if they are accompanied by a valid rationale as to why they are being put forward and their advantages and disadvantages considered. Candidates will receive reward for an in-depth analysis of the issues raised, including incorporating the results of accurate numerical and financial analysis. This means that candidates need to carry out the analysis in the first place. They then must consider alternative approaches to resolving the issue. This may take various forms including the use of models such as Johnson, Scholes and Whittington's SAF framework.

Commentary:

The Judgement criterion is extremely important as it provides the facility for candidates to express their full analysis of the issues contained in the case. It is essential that sufficient time and effort is put into carrying out this fundamental analysis. It is not sufficient for a candidate to simply repeat the facts of the case and regard that solely as his or her analysis. Further, it is not enough for a candidate to simply suggest possible alternatives to resolving the issue without carrying out a proper evaluation of the suggestions being made. The alternatives need to be analysed in depth. The facts of the case should be used as evidence to support the commentary as part of candidates' analysis of the issues. It is essential that candidates state the impact and financial implications of a particular issue, providing *accurate* evidence where appropriate.

Once the impact has been stated then the candidate should consider the alternative actions which could be taken by the organisation and bring in relevant analysis in support of each alternative discussed. Candidates must consider each issue from the wider perspective of the impact it has, or potentially will have, on the case organisation, using the facts as evidence in support of the arguments being presented.

Common errors:

The "usual" errors, as presented before in previous PEGs, are listed as follows:

- Simple repetition of the case material without any additional analysis. Candidates must be prepared to analyse the information given in the unseen material. The candidate is expected to provide sensible analysis to aid decision making.
- Failure to discuss all the issues prioritised. Once again, some candidates prioritised an issue and then failed to discuss it. This often contributes to a candidate failing the examination. It is essential that candidates manage their time effectively.
- Serious lack of basic analysis of the issues including not discussing the numerical or financial implications which may have been reasonably accurately calculated. This implies that the candidate may actually be able to undertake a reasonably accurate calculation but is unable to interpret what it means. That is of limited use to an employer and indicates the inability of the candidate to think about what he or she is doing.
- Brief discussion of alternative actions and little comparison of the overall advantages and disadvantages of each of the alternatives, i.e. with no support analysis to back-up the suggestion being made.
- Failure to distinguish between business and ethical considerations relating to an issue. Marks will be awarded irrespective of where the candidate discusses the point but candidates should be able to make this distinction.

In addition, the following main errors were made relating to this particular case:

- Failure to recognise the capacity constraints in discussing the manufacturing problem.
- Misunderstanding that the set-up costs in the manufacturing problem applied to each of products YY and ZZ for each manufacturer.
- Failure to appreciate that two, or indeed all three, of the manufacturers could be used to make products YY and ZZ. Some candidates ruled out Manufacturers A and C as they did not have sufficient capacity to manufacture all 150,000 units of both products and therefore simply defaulted to select Manufacturer B.
- Lack of discussion on the impact on costs or profitability of the three alternative manufacturers.
- Not recognising that it was VP which held the entire risk of unsold inventory in the "own brand" proposal.
- Failure to recognise that if the "own brand" proposal was rejected by Jot there was a serious risk that VP would cease trading with Jot altogether.
- Over concentration on Jot's own brand development when it had the opportunity to achieve high income, based on high sales growth with limited risk for five years with very limited risk for five years.
- Over emphasis of the acceptance by Jot of the VP proposal could cause Jot to lose other US customers, when VP accounted for 90% of Jot's US sales.
- Failure to recognise that Jot was partly responsible for the quality problem in their negotiation of a low price with outsourced manufacturer Q and in not specifying the quality of the plastic to be used in its contract with Q.
- Believing that the inventory write-down had cash implications for Jot which is a serious error in the understanding of this accounting principle.

It is very important that candidates concentrate their minds on the issues contained in the actual case and on the unseen material and do not become confused with issues that have either occurred in a previous examination session or in a tuition provider's mock examination. If the issues in the unseen material are fully considered, with good numerical and financial analysis where appropriate, then alternative approaches which might be adopted by the organisation in the case can be proposed and the benefits and disadvantages of each set out. Time must be allowed to carry out this analysis effectively. Analysing the issues in this way will lead to the candidate producing a rationale for his or her recommendations later in the report.

There is no single right answer to the issues posed in the examination and credit is given for candidates' recommendations which are logically supported with a clear rationale, even if these do not correspond with the suggested answer. It is the lack of in-depth analysis which causes most candidates to fail the examination.

Ethics – Strategic choices:

Rationale:

Candidates are required to use judgement to identify and analyse the ethical issues and state why these issues have ethical implications.

Suggested approach:

This section is normally coupled with the recommendations on how to resolve the ethical issues. It is acceptable to provide the answer in one section or it could be split over two as presented in the Assessment Criteria. The reason it is split in the Assessment Criteria is because the business issues often have an ethical dimension associated with them. This was the case with the marketing material issue, the inventory valuation and the quality problem relating to outsourced manufacturer Q.

Marking guide:

Marks are awarded for recognising each of the ethical issues and then it is crucial to explain why the candidate considers them to be weak ethical values.

Commentary:

On the whole, candidates were able to identify the main ethical issues which were: the pressure being placed on the Sales Director to re-value the inventory, the incorrect marketing material and the pressure placed on outsourced manufacturer Q to reduce its original tender price.

Common errors:

Generally, the ethical issues were reasonably well handled, although there were some candidates who did not discuss ethics at all. This is a very dangerous strategy as the Ethics criterion is worth 10% of the marks for the examination. Candidates were mostly able to identify the ethical issues and provide a reasonable explanation of why the issue might be considered to be ethical. For example, there was no ethical obligation on Jot to assist or provide a contract to its outsourced manufacturers affected by the earthquake. It may be argued that Jot could provide some support as a social gesture, but Jot was not a major company and had an ethical obligation to satisfy the demands of its other stakeholders, principally the shareholders and employees, by ensuring that its products were available for customers to buy.

A main common error was that many candidates did not recognise that it is the Financial Director (Tani Grun) who was herself acting unethically in seeking to pressurise the Sales Director to re-value the inventory. Similarly some candidates did not recognise that it was unethical for the Managing Director to consider asking for an employee's resignation as a result of her displaying weak values.

Once again, many candidates only discussed one ethical issue. This limits the marks which can be awarded. There are always at least two ethical issues in each unseen part of the case study.

Recommendations

Logic:

Rationale:

This criterion tests whether the candidate is able to make well-justified recommendations for each of the prioritised issues.

Suggested approach:

It is important that the candidate ensures that there are strong reasons for the recommended course of action. The recommendations should follow on from the weight of arguments and choices of possible actions in a logical manner. It is expected that candidates will present their recommendations, provide a justification of why these courses of action are being recommended and then state what should be the follow-on actions. This approach seems to be have been adopted now by most candidates. In order to gain good marks, it is essential that each recommendation is commercially sensible and realistic. For example, a candidate who recommended that Manufacturer C was used for all production would be rewarded with very low marks as the capacity constraint given in the unseen material had been ignored.

Marking guide:

Marks are awarded not just for the recommendations themselves but also, crucially, for the rationale and strength of argument supporting them, drawing from the earlier analysis of the issues and for explaining what the organisation should do next to make the recommendations happen. It must be stressed that marks will not be awarded to candidates for recommendations which merely repeat what has been said earlier in their discussion of the issues.

The recommendations section must be used to provide very clear recommendations drawn from the analysis and discussion earlier in the report. The candidate should have produced a range of alternative approaches to resolving an issue in the analysis and discussion. It is necessary then for him or her to select the recommended approach from the range of alternatives, providing justification for it and what the consequent follow-on actions should be. Recommendations which are clear, concise, are justified and then lead to relevant follow-on actions are given good marks. Often <u>candidates are vague in their advice which is no help whatsoever to the report reader.</u>

Recommendations such as 'should do something about', 'more controls are needed', 'the Board should meet to discuss', 'the Board should review', 'appoint a consultant to review', lack clarity, are evasive and therefore are not acceptable. In order to earn good marks candidates must prepare clear, justified, well-argued recommendations. It is very important that the report makes appropriate recommendations and does not leave any of the issues undecided. It is for candidates to present all the arguments for and against a course of action and to weigh them up to reach well considered recommendations. It is the depth of discussion and the strength of arguments and the justification behind the recommendations that earn marks. Ill-thought through analysis and poor recommendations are not rewarded.

Commentary:

Recommendations will be given credit even if they are not consistent with those in the suggested answer. There is often no single right answer to the issues presented in the case. It is the rationale for the recommendation which is important. The follow-on actions must be consistent with the recommendations. Further, candidates must understand that recommendations must be consistent with each other and with advice on ethical issues where appropriate. Any recommendation provided should explain why a particular course of action is recommended, rather than simply what should be done and how.

The recommendations should follow the analysis and discussion and therefore sufficient time should be allowed for the recommendations to be prepared. It is apparent that some candidates rush their recommendations because they have not left time to present them fully or in some cases do not present any recommendations at all for one or more issues. Marks cannot be awarded if there is nothing presented.

Common errors:

Many of the common errors have been highlighted before:

- Time management issues with some recommendations being very short.
- Straight repetition of what had been said in the earlier discussion without sufficient amplification of why a course of action was being recommended.
- Some candidates produced weak rationales for their recommendations which did not really address the issue. The marker may not agree with the actual recommendation but will award marks if it is justified by the argument presented.
- Failure to provide recommendations on all the prioritised issues. This may be due to time constraints but is therefore a feature of poor time management.
- Recommendations which did not follow on logically from the earlier discussion within the report.
- Recommending unfeasible solutions to the manufacturing issue, such as that all units of products YY and ZZ should be produced by outsourced manufacturer A or alternatively, all should be produced by outsourced manufacturer C. Sometimes this was "justified" on the basis of dealing with just one manufacturer or in the case of C because of its alleged good CSR credentials. The fact was that such a recommendation was unrealistic as candidates had not recognised the capacity

constraints and that this would result in lost contribution if the entire production order of 150,000 units could not be manufactured.

- Making recommendations without undertaking any numerical or financial analysis at all where it was clear that such analysis was essential. This is not only incompetent but arrogant especially when the recommendations themselves are simply not feasible.

- Making recommendations which are commercially unsound, such as rejecting the VP "own brand" proposal on the grounds that it will potentially damage Jot's relationship with other US retailers and the Jot brand. In one sense, Jot had little option but to accept the proposal given its sheer scale and the volume of Jot's sales made to VP. Could Jot afford the potential cash flow implications of rejecting VP, especially as there was a huge risk that VP would respond to a negative attitude by seeking another supplier to replace Jot altogether?

- Failure to recognise that Jot was liable to pay the licence fee on the already spoilt production from outsourced manufacturer Q.

The recommendations are an essential part of the answer and candidates should allow sufficient time to address them fully. Candidates should also think about what they are actually writing and ask themselves the simple question, "Does this actually make sense given my earlier analysis?"

Integration:

Rationale:

The marks are all available for the overall functionality and quality of the report in part (a).

Suggested approach:

This is not a section of the report, but considers the report as a whole. As a guide therefore it is important that candidates present a report which is clear, sectionalised, addresses the main issues with good analysis and discussion and makes suitable recommendations based on the weight of evidence presented.

Marking guide:

Reports are deemed to be highly professional, sound, satisfactory, inadequate or poor. The whole 5 marks are available for a highly professional report and 0 or 1 mark for a poor report.

Commentary:

Good answers tend to divide the report into the following distinct parts:
- Table of contents
- Brief terms of reference
- A brief introduction
- Prioritisation of the key strategic issues
- A detailed analysis of the issues
- Ethical issues (which may be in one section or split across the detailed analysis and the recommendations)
- Recommendations
- Appendices including part (b).

It is important to effectively integrate the different parts of the report. So, for example, the recommendations should include the evidence base supporting them by reference to the earlier analysis which may be drawn from the main body of the report and the appendices.

A low mark will be awarded in Integration if the key issues were not properly addressed, or indeed were not discussed at all and the report was left incomplete. Further, a low mark is applied in Integration if analysis is not sufficiently carried out, for example, the discussion of the issues were vague and generally superficial in nature and did not specifically relate to the unseen case material, numerical analysis was weak or contained errors of principle or not undertaken at all.

Common errors:

The common errors which have been highlighted before seem to remain. Reports which do not address the main issue satisfactorily or provide sufficient depth of analysis or reasoning behind the recommendations will not be rewarded with a high mark under this criterion. Vague recommendations or the candidate not committing to a particular course of action will not be rewarded because this is not helpful to the reader. Candidates should be prepared to present their recommendations with confidence and support them with rational argument as to why they are being made.

Ethics - Recommendations:

Rationale:

This criterion judges candidates on their recommendations and reasoning for each of the ethical issues identified.

Suggested approach:

This section follows on from the identification and explanation of the ethical issues. It may either be contained in one complete section or split over two as presented in the Assessment Criteria.

Marking guide:

Marks are awarded for the quality and depth of the advice given and the rationale for the advice offered for each of the ethical issues discussed.

Commentary:

Candidates tended to give sensible advice on the issues raised in the report although this sometimes lacked depth.

Common errors:

The main common error was that some candidates failed to provide any advice on the ethical issue raised or that the advice offered was vague and as such unhelpful or was itself unethical advice. As made clear before, stating the ethical dilemma alone is not enough. The advice itself must be ethical and, usually, the advice becomes clear when the ethical dilemma is understood. Candidates need to ensure that their advice is consistent with their recommendations for the main business issues that they have provided within Logic. The advice itself needs to be sound and logical.

Candidates could increase their marks under this criterion by explaining the rationale for their advice.

PART (b):

Rationale:

The purpose of part (b) is to test candidates' ability to communicate in a competent professional way their analysis, findings and the financial implications relating to a particular issue contained in the unseen material.

Suggested approach:

Candidates should consider carefully the actual requirement, the purpose of the communication, for whom it is intended and the salient points that he or she wishes to communicate. This means that the candidate needs to think carefully about the major points which need to be included in the communication. Thought also needs to go into the effectiveness of the communication which means that it should have clarity, be to the point and not be ambiguous or verbose. Candidates should follow the instructions or requirement for part (b). In this case the requirement asked for a draft of an email to Jot's management team which set out the key criteria for the selection of outsourced manufacturers in general together with a recommendation on which manufacturer(s) should be appointed for products YY and ZZ. The email had to contain no more than 10 short sentences.

Marking guide:

Marks are awarded on the strength of the communication provided. There are marks available for commentary on the strategic importance of an issue, the inclusion of relevant financial or numerical information, the benefits and disadvantages of a particular course of action and a recommendation where appropriate. In this case, a recommendation was specifically requested in the question.

Commentary:

Once again some candidates chose not to attempt part (b) at all. It is dangerous not to attempt this part as it is worth 10% of the total marks available and time should be set aside to complete it.

Common errors:

The common errors were:

- Failure to do part (b) at all.
- Failure to restrict the sentences to 10.
- Failure to provide short sentences.
- Failure to address the criteria for selection of outsourced manufacturers in "general" as required and just concentrating on those to provide products YY and ZZ.
- Over use of bullet points rather than 10 short sentences, containing a subject, an object and a verb.
- Failure to consider that quality of output was a key criterion for selection of an outsourced manufacturer.
- Failure to provide any financial justification for the recommendation made in respect of products YY and ZZ.
- The usual grumble whenever an email is required in part (b). "Hi" or "Hi guys" is not appropriate for an email of this nature. Why do some candidates persist in antagonising markers with this over familiar term in respect of an email of such importance, particularly bearing in mind that it was written on behalf of the Finance and IT Director, i.e. the candidate's senior manager?

To re-iterate what has been stated before in previous Post Examination Guidance reports, it should be understood that employers have made it clear to CIMA that they seek candidates who are not only competent in management accountancy but are also able to communicate effectively. This is the main reason why part (b) exists in the T4 case study examination.

Index

Index